# Social Work in Rural Communities

## *Third Edition*

Edited by

Leon H. Ginsberg

Council on Social Work Education
Alexandria, VA

Second printing, 2000.


Library of Congress Cataloging-in-Publication Data

Social work in rural communities / edited by Leon H. Ginsberg. – 3rd ed.
     p.  cm.
  Includes bibliographical references and index.
  ISBN 0-87293-061-0
  1. Social service, Rural–United States.  2. Social work education–United States.
I. Ginsberg, Leon H.

HV91.S625 1998
361.973'09173'4–dc21                                  98-11310
                                                      CIP

Manufactured in the United States of America.

# Table of Contents

# *Preface to the Third Edition*

The rural and small town population of the United States has historically been disadvantaged compared to its suburban and metropolitan counterparts. Whatever the subject or indicator—per capita income, health care, education, employment opportunity, or transportation—the nonmetropolitan people of the nation have less. Over the more than 200 years of American history, there has been a steady erosion in the population and the quality of life of America's rural people. As this book makes clear in many ways, rural people are more likely to be very young or very old; to be members of disadvantaged minorities; to lack the kinds of opportunities that are available to their metropolitan counterparts; and to need the help of human service agencies and professionals, especially social workers.

Despite the needs of rural people (this book uses the terms "rural" and "nonmetropolitan" interchangeably—the definitions are discussed in several chapters), they have remained a population that is largely neglected by major social programs and by social workers. It is difficult to believe that the human services industry, which exists to help those who are disadvantaged, and the social work profession, which regularly reaffirms its concerns for those with the greatest needs, have traditionally paid so little attention to the needs of the rural population.

Although the rural population constitutes less than a fourth of the total U.S. population, the numbers of people in smaller communities are still enormous—larger in many cases than the total population of other nations. Some have referred to the regular neglect of rural life as a product of deliberate national policy. Although it is difficult to assert that the United States has purposely ignored the problems of rural people, national policies that provide special help to metropolitan areas or promote services that make larger community life more attractive than small-town life have the obvious effect of reducing small-town populations and increasing the populations of cities. Better educational and health programs attract in-migrants. Better services attract industry. Declines and stagnations in services discourage the location of industry. The attractions of large cities encourage the most promising rural residents to relocate and, similarly, discourage urban people from relocating to nonmetropolitan areas. The decline in rural population and the increase in metropolitan population are not, in themselves, problems—although depopulation exacerbates rural difficulties—but instead are symptoms of the effects of policies that make some areas more (and others less) desirable. (Here it should be noted that, in addition to the Department of Agriculture, many other federal agencies have programs designed to improve rural American life. For example, the National Institute of Mental Health and the Public Health Service provide some programs and some grants to support programs in rural areas.)

The first edition of this book was published in 1976 at a time when the federal government had begun to acknowledge and work to redress some of the problems of rural areas. In fact, it was a time when the nonmetropolitan population was actually growing more rapidly than the metropolitan—the first time this had happened since the earliest days of American history.

At the time of publication of this third edition, there is evidence once again of a growing pattern of relocation to rural areas. The distinct and perceived advantages of small towns, such as lower crime rates, opportunities for professional advancement, and larger labor pools with lower wage expectations than urban workers, lead some families and corporations to move to rural areas. Although the natural increase of the much larger metropolitan population will likely keep that group larger than their rural counterparts, the relative sizes of both may not change very much in the future. It is possible that the proportion of rural people will grow in comparison to the total population, but probably no very much. Parenthetically, it is also worth noting that a sizable minority of rural people are far from disadvantaged. Many who have significant wealth live in rural communities. They are often property owners, professionals, and business people. Many are sophisticated travelers and regional or national leaders in their churches, businesses, and professions. Although they are not the usual focus of social work efforts, they may also have problems that require the help of social workers. Family conflicts, mental illness, developmental disabilities, and many other problems that are central to social work practice are not always related to economic disadvantage.

Since 1976, there has been a steady growth in social work interest in rural areas. Shortly after the first edition was published, social workers and social work educators with a special interest in rural issues began sponsoring annual institutes on the subject. Those institutes, which have not been privileged by the receipt of consistent federal or foundation funds, have continued year after year as a special interest and special effort of those who care about small town life and its relationship to social work programs and services.

The rural social work movement—which has more than 20 uninterrupted years of history behind its most recent incarnation—has also raised the consciousness of those who operate service and educational programs. Although many social work practitioners view their assignments to small town offices as unfortunate way-stations on their progress to work in important cities, many also now understand the special challenges and rewards of rural problems and rural practice. The large number of social work education programs that are located or primarily engaged in nonmetropolitan areas now understand that they have special contributions to make to the people and communities they serve—that they can perhaps educate more versatile social workers than their metropolitan counterparts because of the special needs and challenges of rural areas. In many ways, the concepts underpinning rural social work led to the now pervasive idea of generalist social work practice, an idea that is central to accredited baccalaureate social work education and required in graduate education, as well.

Rural America helps all of us better understand how public policy affects human well-being. Rural America and its degrees of prosperity, services, and even population grows and declines in relation to government decisions about the value of money, transportation rules and regulations, as well as agricultural and environmental matters. Some policies encourage people to move to and others to move from rural areas. When there are good salaries to be earned and investment opportunities that can grow in rural areas, those areas prosper. When poverty prevails and when industries are encouraged to relocate to metropolitan areas, rural areas decline. We have seen both growth and decline in rural areas in the second half of the 20th century, and these shifts may be readily traced to public policy decisions.

There have also been opportunities to trace rural developments with the various U.S. presidents who have served in recent years. Three of the presidents elected since 1960 have had strong rural experiences and ties. Lyndon Johnson of Johnson City, Texas, Jimmy Carter of Plains, Georgia, and Bill Clinton of Hope, Arkansas, are not strangers to rural life. Vice President Al Gore, from Tennessee, is also one who has had largely rural constituencies. However, the origins of U.S. presidents have not always influenced public policy. Although the issues of rural America were "rediscovered" under the presidency of Lyndon Johnson, some of the policies of the Carter administration, especially transportation deregulation, did not serve rural America well.

Some things have not changed very much. Although rural dwellers probably have access to a better distribution of services now than in 1976, there is still a serious lack of professionals in rural areas. Many government projects, seminars, and research efforts focus on recruiting human services professionals for rural areas and on retaining professionals who are already there. The attractions of metropolitan America—professional stimulation, salaries, cultural and social activity—still make it difficult for rural areas to compete with the metropolitan.

This third edition of *Social Work in Rural Communities* has been developed for some encouraging and practical reasons. First, all of the copies of the first and second edition have been sold. The Council on Social Work Education, however, continues to receive orders for the book for use in classrooms and research. Second, many things have changed about rural America and rural social work practice, as this preface and the introduction to this volume make clear.

Several content changes have been made for the third edition. Some of the subjects that seemed critical in the past are no longer as important now. That is true, in part, because additional texts and books of readings on these subjects have been published. In addition, a journal dedicated to content on small-community work, *Human Services in the Rural Environment,* is published at Eastern Washington University's school of social work.

For this edition, we have added reprints of several important articles on rural matters. The documentation styles used in the various chapters are those of the original versions. Therefore, not all the chapters use the same citation system. Most of these additions are from *Human Services in the Rural Environment,* and we are grateful to Dr. Lynn Clemmons Morris, the editor, for helping in our selections and for permission to reprint the articles. We have also omitted some articles that are no longer as relevant as they were in the first or second edition. For example, my own chapter in the second edition on the implications of the Family Support Act of 1988 for rural social services is no longer important because of the passage, in 1996, of the Personal Responsibility and Work Opportunity Reconciliation Act. All of us who have contributed to this volume hope that it is helpful to its readers. We are intrigued by the issues of human services in rural America. Most of us live in areas that would not be defined as metropolitan, but we who live in metropolitan areas maintain our interest in and commitment to rural life. I moved from West Virginia to Columbia, South Carolina, a metropolitan area, since the publication of the first edition. However, because the South Carolina population is only a bit more than half metropolitan, it is not difficult to maintain contact with rural people and communities. Of course, every state has a large nonmetropolitan component, so it is entirely possible for people from large cities to retain and develop their rural interests and commitments.

I was saddened to learn that two of our authors, Janet Fitchen and Carel Germain, died since the second edition was published. They were both able scholars who made major contributions to the rural social work literature. Both have works that are included in this edition.

The authors of these chapters are pleased to continue their interests in small-community social work. We hope this edition will improve our readers' understanding of these critical issues and raise their consciousness about rural issues—a subject that is one of our academic passions.

*Leon H. Ginsberg*

# *Acknowledgments*

Rural social work in the United States has been a steady, although appropriately small, area of special interest for social work practitioners and educators for some 25 years. That interest rekindled earlier attention to small-town work that appeared to have declined about the time of World War II, when American population shifts and social problems were focused on cities. Still, there have always been large numbers of rural, small-community social workers and social agencies. The United States has always had a significant small-town population and, in many states, rural people constitute a numerical majority.

The Council on Social Work Education has played a consistent role in the development of educational concepts for rural social work. It invited me to speak on education for rural social work at its 1968 Annual Program Meeting in Cleveland. It secured funds for the Advisory Committee on Rural Social Work, which operated in the 1970s and sponsored workshops on the subject throughout the United States. It also published the first two editions of this book in 1976 and 1993, which were used as texts in many courses and which have been one of the largest sellers of all the Council's publications.

I am grateful for the help of the late Richard Lodge, the CSWE executive director who inspired and shepherded this project, along with many other staff members who have assisted with the development of rural social work ideas over the intervening years.

Don Beless, the CSWE executive director, and Michael Frumkin, who was the president when the second edition was developed, saw the virtue of updating the book. Both have been supporters of and advocates for rural social work practice. President Moses Newsome, Jr., and the CSWE Publications and Media Commission, chaired by Ann Weick, made this new edition possible.

I am also grateful to CSWE director of publications and media Michael Monti for initiating the project and bringing it to fruition.

More than any of us who were involved in writing this book, I am grateful to the thousands of social workers in the United States and other nations who have maintained their interest in and concern for rural populations. As this book makes clear, rural social work has the elements of a social movement—a movement which insists that the majority metropolitan population keep small towns and rural people in mind in social work education, social work practice, and social welfare policy. I hope this book will aid that movement in all its endeavors.

*Leon H. Ginsberg*

# Part 1

## Small Community Social Work: Concepts and Definitions

Part 1 provides some basic definitions and explanations of social work in smaller communities, covering rural (or nonmetropolitan) and metropolitan areas in terms of both size and social definitions.

The introductory article, which was written by the editor, traces the history of scholarly and practice developments in the field of social work in rural communities. Some of the fundamental ideas about the ways in which rural communities operate, as distinguished from more complex, metropolitan communities, are covered in the Introduction and Chapter 3, which describes natural helping processes in rural communities.

A series of educational assumptions for rural social work prepared under the auspices of the Southern Regional Education Board early in the evolution of social theory are reprinted in Chapter 2. The assumptions are so fundamental that they continue to lay part of the groundwork for writings, workshops, and courses that are taught about working in small communities.

Joseph and Judith Davenport then provide some new scholarship on rural communities in transition, describing the ways in which rural communities go through various processes of change.

According to the 1990 U.S. Census, 22.5% of the population lived in nonmetropolitan communities—those with fewer than 50,000 people—and the following states had the largest nonmetropolitan populations: Idaho, Vermont, South Dakota, Wyoming, Maine, West Virginia, North Dakota, Arkansas, Alaska, and Iowa. The smallest population per square mile was in Wyoming, with 479 people per square mile. Alaska had 524 people per square mile in 1988. Vermont had 557 per square mile and North Dakota 667. Although Idaho had 80% of its population living in nonmetropolitan areas, it had 1,003 people per square mile.

A key issue in rural practice ethics is dual relationships, and Pam Miller discusses this dilemma and the rural culture in her article in Chapter 5. Joanne Mermelstein and Paul Sundet, frequent writers on rural issues, provide a 20-year perspective on their efforts, as well.

Part 1 provides a backdrop for the other three sections of the book, which offer more specific information on the practice of social work in rural communities, the people of rural America, and the impact of social programs in rural communities.

# 1

# Introduction: An Overview of Rural Social Work

by Leon H. Ginsberg

Rural issues have captured the interest of social work for all of its history. Although much of the literature focuses on urban and metropolitan issues, concerns about the rural population and the serious social problems it faces have preoccupied policymakers and scholars. That is because, as this introductory chapter and others make clear, the problems faced by rural people are as great and often greater than those of city dwellers.

For most of the 20th century, the major social phenomenon has been the depopulation of rural areas and migration to the cities. That is true of the United States, where the movement of rural southern African Americans to northern cities and to the urban areas of the south was the largest and most dramatic population shift in national history. But it is also true of the rest of the world–Africa, the Middle East, Asia, Latin America–where rural residents have tried to escape poverty and deprivation by moving to large cities, whether Bangkok, Cairo, Mexico City, or Nairobi. Some of the world's largest cities are now in "Third World" nations.

Social work's interests in rural areas are multiple. In one way, the profession and the policymakers who finance its programs are concerned about human need wherever they find it. Yet many problems, such as housing, transportation, and inaccessibility to human services, are more severe in rural areas than in their urban counterparts. There is also public interest in retaining the rural population. A nation in which almost no one lives on most of the land faces some special problems.

There are many reasons for the rural-to-urban shift, as this chapter makes clear. Economic opportunity is the primary motivation for younger people who have seen agriculture, the largest rural industry, employing fewer people. Mining and other kinds of mineral extraction also employ smaller numbers of people. Despite the fact that agriculture and mineral extraction continue as viable economic factors in the United States, modern techniques and equipment require many fewer people to grow food, mine coal, and extract chemicals.

Some changes in U.S. public policies dealing with trade and international relations have also been problems for rural areas. The North American Free Trade Agreement (NAFTA), which created a kind of common market for Canada, Mexico, and the United States, has been harmful for rural Americans, some evidence indicates. Agricultural products from the other two nations can often be produced less expensively and sold in the United States for lower prices than similar products produced in the United States. That has led to unemployment in many rural farming areas. Similarly, the further opening of trade with the rest of the world, including Asia, has reduced production and employment in some other rural areas. The textile industry, which has been at least partly located in rural areas, has to compete with Asian textile producers in addition to those in Canada and Mexico. That, too, has led to rural unemployment.

For many rural residents, there is simply no economic alternative to relocating to a city. However, those who relocate to metropolitan areas to seek economic opportunity are usually young and healthy with prospects for effective employment. People with severe disabilities and older people have not been most likely to relocate. Therefore, the remaining rural populations are often those with severe health, personal, and social problems, which makes rural concerns even more significant for social workers.

Of course, as other sections of this chapter note, economics are only part of the reason for the rural–urban migration. The excitement, opportunity, and potential for growth in big cities attract many rural residents. In the late 1960s and early 1970s, a time of great social ferment in this country, there was a growing social work interest in rural areas. That interest developed at about the same time as the movements to secure social work attention for minority group members and others who often face discrimination and socioeconomic deprivation. The attention given African Americans, Asian Americans, Hispanics, Native Americans, and women and those with minority sexual orientations is well known and continues. But at that time efforts were also made to provide help to white ethnic groups, such as people of Italian and Polish descent and from a minority religious background, such as Jews. Concern for people in rural areas was similar. There was also a growing rural social work consciousness. Social workers who served rural clients, faculty members in the large number of rural colleges and universities with social work education programs, and others, including people who had moved to rural areas as part of a "back to the land" movement, called for rural social work emphases.

There was also population growth in some rural areas because industries relocated there. Several major manufacturers and other companies (including those in textiles in the south), as well as government services, moved from cities to towns and, in turn, helped retain the rural populations in some areas and attracted newcomers to others. The seemingly inexorable movement from rural to metropolitan areas could perhaps be reversed or at least arrested.

Since that time, as other sections of this chapter discuss, many efforts developed to improve rural life and to extend social services to rural areas. Rural social work issues have been a major interest of a relatively small but dedicated group of social work practitioners and educators. Rural caucuses developed in many of the professional social work organizations, including the National Association of Social Workers (NASW) and the Council on Social Work Education (CSWE). Specialized groups were developed and continue to operate in fields such as rural health and rural mental health. Each year, professional meetings on rural social welfare issues attract social workers from smaller communities. Sessions on rural issues are part of most national meetings. And, for almost 25 years, those interested in rural issues have sponsored an annual Institute on Social Work in Rural Areas, which rotates around the United States.

A professional journal, *Human Services in the Rural Environment*, is now published regularly at the Inland Empire School of Social Work and Human Services at Eastern Washington University. Several chapters in this new edition were originally published there. Of course, scholarly contributions on rural issues are also included in the rest of the professional journals, including *Social Work* and the *Journal of Social Work Education*. Presentations on rural issues are also a part of major professional meetings, such as CSWE's Annual Program Meeting.

In the 1980s and 1990s, several texts were published that dealt, at least in part, with rural issues. Two of the most important were Farley et al.'s (1982) *Rural Social Work Practice* and Johnson's (1980) *Rural Human Services: A Book of Readings*. Martinez-Brawley, who also contributes to this volume, wrote *Perspectives on the Small Community: Humanistic Views for Practitioners* (1990) in addition to her body of work on the history of social work in rural communities. Johnson and Schwartz (1994) also deal with rural matter.

Several federal and state government agencies have also established special programs to deal with rural areas and concerns. Grant programs to provide funds for dealing with rural problems have been sponsored by such agencies as the National Institute of Mental Health, the Public Health Service, and the Department of Housing and Urban Development. Most states have special organizations that deal with rural concerns, rural development, and rural services.

The remainder of this introductory chapter provides an overview of some of the basic issues and concepts that inform much of the work that has been done on rural social work.

## Basic Concepts of Rural Social Work

The United States, like the rest of the world, is increasingly urban and metropolitan. According to the 1990 Census, 77.5% of the U.S. population live in metropolitan areas, which are cities or urbanized areas with populations of 50,000 or more (Ginsberg, 1995).

The trend toward metropolitanization of the U.S. population has been a relatively consistent pattern throughout U.S. history. In the first census, taken in 1790, only 5% of the population lived in nonrural settings. In 1840, the U.S. population was 10% urban, and in 1890 it had become one third urban. By 1950, 56% of the U.S. population lived in metropolitan areas. The urban population has increased by over 20% in the intervening years.

Although the proportionate size of rural America may not change very much in the future, there continues to be a nonmetropolitan renaissance. According to Pooley (1997), 2 million more Americans moved from metropolitan to nonmetropolitan areas as moved in the other direction in the 1990s so far. A special cover article on the movement to small towns was the focus of *Time* magazine in late 1997, with Pooley's article providing the lead information.

Perhaps because of the growing trend toward urban living in the United States, social work as a profession has tended to focus on metropolitan issues and problems. In fact, the growth of the social work profession has coincided with the growing proportion of the U.S. population that lives in urban or metropolitan areas. (For ease of definition and communication, the terms urban and metropolitan are used interchangeably in this chapter, as are the terms rural and nonmetropolitan. However, the official U.S. Bureau of the Census definitions mark rural areas as those with 2,500 people or fewer; urban areas as those with populations of more than 2,500 but less than 50,000; and metropolitan areas as those with populations of 50,000 or more.)

Raymond T. Coward (1992) of the University of Florida suggests that scholarship on rural areas is sometimes impeded by efforts to create dichotomies as a way of understanding the differences between rural and nonrural areas. Instead, he proposes that residence be conceptualized as a continuum with very large cities at one end and very small communities at the other. The important concepts in such a conceptualization are, therefore, matters such as the total population of a geographic area, its distance from metropolitan service areas, and its population density. Thus, one may discuss the implications of being at one point on the continuum or another, rather than a community's arbitrary classification as rural or nonrural.

Generally, observers of social issues and social problems suggest that the complexity of life, the incidence of social problems, and the intensity of those problems increase in proportion to the degree of urbanization or metropolitanization. Therefore, it is not surprising that social work services are more likely to be provided and to grow in metropolitan areas than in rural communities.

However, the reality of American life is that, although their proportion has declined, the number of people in nonmetropolitan areas is very large. If 77.5% of the population is metropolitan, then 22.5% of the population is nonmetropolitan. Percentages may mask the magnitude of the rural population. The nonmetropolitan population of the United States is over 55 million people; it is larger than the populations of all but a few of the world's nations and nearly equals the population of France or England. Furthermore, as shown in several chapters of this book, the social and economic problems faced by the people of nonmetropolitan America are often as severe or even more serious than those faced by their metropolitan fellow citizens. Therefore, the interest of social work in the smaller community populations of the United States is justified and critical for the well-being of this large segment of the nation.

## Problems in Rural Areas

Several chapters in this text make it clear that nonmetropolitan areas in the United States have all of the problems of metropolitan areas, plus some that are either unique to or more severe within smaller communities. For example, although many people assume that problems such as inadequate housing are primarily encountered in metropolitan areas, housing difficulties are even more severe in nonmetropolitan communities. For examples, see Leonard, Dolbeare, and Lazere's (1989) *A Place to Call Home: The Crisis in Housing for the Poor* on rural housing needs. Such basic economic problems as unemployment are typically more severe in nonmetropolitan than in metropolitan communities. Even when unemployment is very low in major cities of states such as South Carolina, their large number of rural areas experience rather high unemployment. Chronic and high unemployment are more likely to be experienced in rural, nonmetropolitan areas than in major cities.

A number of services and other resources are more likely to be deficient in rural communities than in metropolitan areas. As this book is being written, access to health care is an increasing problem in the United States, especially for those not covered by private health insurance or other third-party programs. In nonmetropolitan areas, however, the problem is even more severe because of a lack of health services. There are simply not as many physicians, nurses, pharmacies, or hospital beds in rural areas per capita than there are in metropolitan communities. Health care providers and other professionals frequently want to practice where they can work with peers, where they are likely to have enough patients or clients to support a specialized practice, and where they are likely to have better services and schools for their families. Thus, professionals often prefer to locate in metropolitan rather than rural communities.

One of the basic problems of rural communities is the lack of transportation, especially public transportation. Large-city residents have the advantage of access to buses, trolleys, and subways, which, for a relatively low cost, take residents to work, church, and recreation. Rural areas have few public transportation systems. Residents who have to rely on taxis find they are expensive and therefore travel has to be foregone or strictly limited. Many are able to contract with neighbors or friends for transportation, but even that may be expensive. The only consistent and practical transportation in most rural areas is the privately owned automobile, which is the most expensive kind of transportation, once one considers the purchase price of the vehicle, fuel, maintenance, depreciation, and insurance.

### Social and Recreational Limits

Other limits on small-town life have been reported in the literature and are discussed in other chapters of this book. These limits include the relative lack of recreational facilities and programs and of stimulating social contacts. People in smaller communities often find life less than tolerable because their social contacts are with people they have always known, such as relatives, in places and situations too familiar to be exciting.

### Advantages of Technology

In some ways, however, modern technology and resources have democratized entertainment so that people in smaller communities can, through cable television, see the same films as people in larger communities, at the same time and at the same cost. The video cassette recorder now also makes the same movies available to all Americans, and to people all over the world, often within a short time after theater release.

The widespread use of the World Wide Web and e-mail have also connected rural areas with the rest of the world in effective ways. Without the costs of telephone or travel, rural residents can know about and react to information, ideas, and products all over the world. Providing service to clients through such technologies has become a reality throughout most of the United States. Medical and health diagnosis and treatment are often conducted over television. In some states, mental health professionals who know American Sign Language are able to help deaf clients by communicating through television, an extension of communication through devices that use the written word.

In small-town America, however, much of social life continues to revolve extensively around high school athletic teams, bands, church social activities, and comparable institutions and events. Concerts by major groups, professional athletic events, and even nationally recognized amateur sports are, in large measure, phenomena of the larger cities.

## Social Work and Rural America

The social work profession's interest in and specialized training for service in rural America has both grown and declined over the decades. The first edition of this book grew out of a resurgence of social work interest in nonmetropolitan areas that developed in the late 1960s, a time of great awareness of discriminatory practices and the deprivation of services to various populations. Social work's concern for the generally unrecognized and often neglected rural populations developed as the nation and the profession began to express greater concerns about ethnic minority groups, the poor, the aged, and women. Part of this interest was stimulated by the publication of a federal government study, *The People Left Behind* (President's National Advisory Committee on Rural Poverty, 1967), which documented the relative disadvantage of rural people. Organizations such as Rural America, the American Rural Health Association, and the Congressional Rural Caucus were founded at this time to address special problems, gaps in services, and the need for federal funding.

### Social Work Practice in Rural Areas

The essential and unique quality of social work in rural areas is the way the profession is *practiced.* During the development of theories about social work practice in small communities, it became clear that, to be effective, practice had to be specifically adapted to small communities. Those of us who developed these theories reasoned that small communities were likely to have fewer resources than larger communities, especially professional resources such as other social workers. Thus, it appeared to us that the social worker in the rural community would have to know how to do a bit of everything, or at least know how to make a bit of everything available to clients in smaller communities. No matter the setting, the rural social worker would have to provide direct counseling or casework services, community development skills, administrative ability, and research competence. The rural social worker would also have to analyze, develop, and implement social policy of all kinds.

### The Generalist Model

For those reasons, the builders of rural and small community social work theory concluded that the social worker in less-populous areas would have to be a generalist. That is, the worker would have to understand and demonstrate skill in the whole range of services—to individuals, to families, to small groups, and to communities—and to show mastery of the social work processes described in the preceding paragraphs. The first edition of this book propounded the notion that social workers in small communities would have to be generalists, if they were to be effective.

The book's first edition was published before models were developed for baccalaureate-level social work education and before the term *case management* was widely used. Although the term *generalist* was developed and has been used most commonly in connection with small-community social work, the term has now been adopted by the entire social work educational enterprise.

All baccalaureate-level social work education programs are now designed to prepare students for work as generalists. The CSWE accreditation standards and policies require that all BSW graduates be equipped to carry out any of the professional roles expected of social workers. No distinction is made in the standards for baccalaureate social work education between metropolitan and nonmetropolitan areas. The educational philosophy for undergraduate programs is that all who complete them should be prepared as generalists who can work in large or small communities and who can fit, with proper education and orientation, into any reasonably defined BSW-level social work position (CSWE, 1992a).

As social work education curriculum policies and philosophies have developed, MSW programs also have been required to build their curricula upon the generalist model required for BSW programs. Therefore, MSW programs must define and operate foundation programs, which are typically coterminous with the first year of social work education, and advanced or specialization programs, which are coterminous with the second year of the MSW (CSWE, 1992b).

In their first or foundation year, two-year MSW students are required to learn about the range of social work roles and to develop the kinds of skills that the generalist BSW graduate would have developed in an undergraduate social work education program. Therefore, the concept of generalist preparation, which rural theorists began explicating in the 1960s and 1970s as the appropriate preparation for small-community work, has become the standard for all professional social work education. That is, all baccalaureate programs are required to have generalist orientations, and all MSW programs are required to have foundation programs, which are essentially comparable to the BSW generalist preparation (CSWE, 1992a, 1992b).

Those who developed small-community social work theories had suggested in their scholarship that all effective social work practice may be generalist practice, which is ultimately adapted to the specific community and setting (Ginsberg, 1969). Therefore, they agreed with those who expanded the idea of the utility of generalist preparation to all social work education and professional social work preparation.

## Rural Practice

### Fitting into the Community

One of the paradoxes of social work in smaller communities is that, although there are often shortages of and difficulties in attracting professionals, the professionals in social work, psychology, medicine, nursing, and other fields who locate in rural areas find that they do not necessarily gain immediate acceptance just because their services are needed or desirable.

Smaller communities operate on a highly personalized basis. They rely upon primary institutions, such as the church, the family, and the peer group, for their decisions and values. People in rural communities often want to know and to work with others in the community—especially those who provide services—on a personal basis. Therefore, effective rural professionals in all disciplines find that they first must spend time learning the community and its people and allowing the community to come to know them before they can be effective in carrying out their responsibilities.

Effective professionals in all disciplines spend some of their early weeks in a small community visiting related agencies and becoming acquainted with professional peers. These visits are part of their effort to learn how to work in the community and to gain community acceptance of themselves as persons who can do their work. An excellent videotape, *Coming to the Country,* which was produced in Nebraska, tells the story of a clinical psychologist and his efforts to become a part of his new rural community and, thereby, to become capable of providing services within that community (Great Plains Training Project, 1989).

George Timms (1992), a home health services specialist with the Department of South Carolina Health and Environmental Control in Winnsboro, notes that, in a rural social services office, one does not call for the food stamp worker. One calls for *Cookie* because that is her name. There is little confidentiality in rural areas, according to Timms. It is just not possible. Contacts are made in supermarkets as often as in social agency offices. There may be no formal services so one has to find a way to create them. Police departments may provide emergency services. "Breakfast clubs" may provide many services in rural communities, Timms says. These are groups of people—usually men—who meet in a local coffee shop for breakfast. They are often willing to raise a few dollars for an individual or family or for some services. These groups are not formal but are frequently very effective in obtaining services for clients.

In smaller communities, becoming integrated into the community's life may mean several things, such as:

- avoiding offending the leadership of social agencies and the community's influential members, in general;
- being somewhat tentative and cautious about expressing one's social and political ideas;
- participating in community activities such as religious services, popular festivals, and social functions; and
- being generally conventional in terms of one's personal life, dress, alcohol consumption, and associations.

People from small communities resent others from distant places (which may mean cities as close as 100 miles) who come to their towns and try to foster changes to make the community resemble the newcomer's former residence. Some professionals who come to rural communities think that they must bring to their new locations the organizational structures, services, and ideologies that they knew and respected in their former, often metropolitan, residences. Rural communities are generally unable to sustain such structures and systems. Also, small communities often reject the trappings of larger cities. Many rural residents continue to live in small communities because they resist and, at times, actively dislike metropolitan attitudes and behaviors.

The newly arrived professional may think it essential to have, for example, a coordinating council for the community social agencies. The community may already be carrying out that function effectively with informal contacts among the agencies and the professionals in the community. Attempting to impose one's ideas before understanding what the community's ideas and wishes are is generally a mistake. It is equally a mistake in metropolitan and nonmetropolitan areas. However, it can be a fatal mistake in a nonmetropolitan community. The community may reject and never subsequently trust the newly arrived professional, who may be always perceived as making plans to impose an idea, system, or structure that the local community simply does not want.

Perhaps the essential requirement for the social worker in the small community is to take the time to adapt to the community properly before attempting to make an impact on and integrate within that community. Some writers think that time in rural communities has different connotations than time in metropolitan areas. One may be considered a newcomer for many years in a town that has few newcomers or departures of longtime residents. People in small communities are often not in the kind of hurry that metropolitan people often seem to be, as well. They have time to converse, reflect, and give thought to the ways problems may best be defined and resolved. Often, the community has been without the services that a social worker or other professional might provide. In some cases, the community may never have had the services on a formal basis and, therefore, may not know exactly what those services may mean or how they may best be delivered.

Although new social services or social work programs in small communities may appear to be free from competition or conflict, the reality is that many of the services of social welfare agencies have always been provided by someone or some agency within the rural community, even though they may not have been formally defined as services. For example, when a new mental health service is instituted in a small town, it is unlikely that there had been no mental health services in that town before. A local clergyman, physician, teacher, or school guidance counselor may have been the community's mental health social worker for years.

### Rural Adaptations

Social workers in rural areas often find they must adapt their usual approaches to social work practice to the different circumstances. Some also find that they must modify what they learned in social work education to effectively fit into the rural community.

For example, confidentiality is a special problem in rural areas. It is difficult to avoid public knowledge of clients receiving services when there are few social services offices with little traffic. Who comes for help can quickly become a matter of public knowledge in such circumstances. Similarly, home visits are difficult to keep confidential when neighborhoods are small and when neighbors recognize autos parked in driveways. Besides, many in the community may know a client is experiencing marital problems or is coping with substance abuse well before that client seeks services. In some ways, confidentiality for the rural worker often means not inappropriately revealing information about clients. That is often the extent to which the social worker can protect the client's privacy and the confidentiality of the case.

Similarly, the NASW Code of Ethics cautions social workers about maintaining "dual relationships," such as doing business with those who are or whose family members are also clients. Rural social work observers agree with that principle and believe it is reasonable for metropolitan areas. However, for rural workers, many relationships are multiple. One's friends, fellow church members, grocers, auto dealers, and organizational colleagues may also be clients or may be related to clients. So the rural worker may have to be especially careful to avoid problematic dual relationships, although avoiding them entirely may be nearly impossible.

Rural workers also often find it difficult to separate their work from their everyday lives. It is not unusual for a worker to be approached about a social work matter at a party, in the grocery store, or on the street. One's job is not a 40-hour, five day per week matter. It is one's whole identity, and the community expects the social worker to be on the job or at least able to talk about the job at all times.

Rural workers may also find that they are expected to participate in such activities as church membership and attendance, which they might not choose in metropolitan communities. Religious involvement is an expectation of many people in rural communities. Of course, members of religious minorities, such as Buddhists, Jews, and Muslims, may simply note that they go to religious services in a nearby city or town and, of course, do not affiliate with Christian worship.

### Rural Ethnic Groups

Some observers of rural social welfare practice think of rural communities as largely enclaves of white and Protestant people. Of course, observers of rural life and rural social work issues know that is not the case. Rural America is as diverse or perhaps more diverse than metropolitan America, as other sections of this book make clear.

Unexpectedly, Eastern and Central European ethnic groups often dominate rural community life in parts of the United States. It was certainly my experience in rural Texas that many of the farmers, ranchers, and business people had close ties to languages, such as Czechoslovakian, and to Germanic and other European cultures. In the south-central Texas towns where my mother was raised and where I have a large number of relatives, *Bohemian* does not refer to a lifestyle but to a living culture and language.

In small-town West Virginia, where I worked as an educator and public official for 18 years, I noted early in my work there that many of the coal-mining and steel-making communities had originally been settled by people from Italy and other parts of Europe. Those cultures were still dominant in many areas of a state that had somehow been defined as largely or even totally Protestant. That was probably a consequence of the 1960 Democratic presidential primary when John Kennedy, the only Roman Catholic ever to serve as President of the United States, proved he could win election in a Protestant state by carrying the West Virginia primary. The irony was that West Virginia was by no means a Protestant state. In fact, the influence of the Roman Catholic Church in many populous parts of the state was then, and continues to be, great.

The minorities of color are also significant in rural America, a topic that is covered in other chapters of this volume. Although the greatest migration and demographic change in the history of the United States was the movement of southern, rural African Americans to northern states, there are still large numbers of African Americans in the rural South. Many in that community suffer from financial and other forms of deprivation. Some of the comments above regarding unemployment in rural South Carolina refer to areas with large African American populations. Interestingly, South Carolina's history is unique: It is the only state ever to have had a majority population of African Americans. Of course, that was during slave-holding times when the labor force was largely African American and plantation owners and operators were exclusively white. However, the slave system obviously required fewer slave holders, overseers, and managers than laborers, which explains the population differential. Even today, in South Carolina and in many other southern states, the labor force is largely African American. Mississippi and South Carolina have the largest proportions of African-American citizens among their total populations.

African Americans are the largest rural minority, but they live almost totally in the rural South. States with large African American populations, such as Pennsylvania, New York, Michigan, and Illinois, have few rural African Americans. Migration from the rural South to the rural North by African Americans has been very small. There is even a reverse migration of African Americans who are coming back to southern states after leaving them for the metropolitan areas of the North. The predominant pattern of African American migration in recent years, however, has been from the rural South to the metropolitan South.

Other minorities of color can often be found in many parts of rural America, as well. For example, although large numbers of Native Americans have moved to metropolitan areas in recent years, they are still a largely rural population. Many live on reservations and in small, nonreservation communities throughout the United States. Oklahoma, which has a very large population of Native Americans, does not have reservations. However, it is dotted with small towns that are exclusively or largely populated by Native Americans. In addition, the Hispanic populations of many rural communities in the Southwest are very large, particularly in Texas, which is home to many Mexican Americans.

Many new immigrant groups have settled in rural areas, some because they came from rural areas in their native homes and were engaged in agriculture, or simply because they felt more comfortable in rural areas. Others came because of the opportunities in rural areas, especially for skilled professionals, which characterizes many of the new immigrants to the United States. A number of ethnic groups from Southeast Asia came to this country after the Vietnam War. The many Asian Americans in rural areas from nations such as Cambodia, Korea, and Vietnam have created important rural Asian-American communities. Ethnic Asian restaurants, especially Chinese, which were once found almost exclusively in cities, can now be found in small towns and rural areas.

It is clear that rural America is culturally diverse—perhaps as culturally diverse as metropolitan America. The ethnic mixes are different but still significant. For this reason, rural community social workers must be especially sensitive to, and competent to work in, ethnically diverse circumstances.

### Social Welfare as an Economic Factor

Although it is not often discussed in the human services literature, social welfare has strong economic implications in various kinds of communities. In rural areas, social welfare programs are often the most important economic factor in the community. Services and transfer programs, such as Social Security, Supplemental Security Income, and Temporary Assistance for Needy Families, may provide the largest single block of income in the community. These transfer payments, along with the in-kind economic impact of the Food Stamp program, may drive the retail industry in the community, provide much of the tax revenue, and serve as factors in real estate and other aspects of the community's economy. In metropolitan communities, transfer payments are also a large economic component, but for most citizens and for the metropolitan economy as a whole, they are relatively minor when compared with private industry, government, education, and other economic elements.

Social welfare in rural communities is also a critical economic factor in other ways. Social service agencies rent or purchase office space in buildings from real estate agents and property owners. Social service clients who come to county seats to make applications or receive services become a major element in retail trade when they purchase items in local stores, pay for parking, and eat in local restaurants.

This writer, who once served as a state chief executive officer for a human services agency, was forced, due to budget constrictions, to close several local welfare offices because there were no longer sufficient funds to pay rents. The building owners in many communities, however, donated their space to the state so that the offices could stay open. Community retailers and public officials invested their personal and community funds to keep the offices open because they were such significant economic allies in the community.

## Employment

Many small communities are one- or two-industry towns ("company towns"). Of course, the primary rural employment has been in agriculture and in mining. However, there are many other kinds of rural community industries, such as tourism, services to retirees, and, to some extent, warehousing and manufacturing. Most smaller communities do not provide a diversity of employment, though, and young people often find that they must either find a job within the limited number of local industries or move elsewhere for work. Rural employment for well-educated people is often available only in public schools, churches, small colleges, or social service agencies. Much employment in rural areas also requires extensive commuting. Trains and buses are not generally available in smaller towns, particularly in the South and West. Therefore, commuting is by private automobile, which is expensive and often unreliable.

A trend that began in the 1970s and has continued into the 1990s has been the location of various kinds of industries in relatively small rural communities. Mack Truck, for example, has established a major manufacturing center in rural South Carolina. The German auto manufacturer BMW is also establishing a manufacturing plant there. Mercedes Benz has located a plant in Alabama that employs some rural people. Many of these moves from small northern communities to small southern communities have occurred because of lower labor costs and less aggressive or less powerful labor unions in the South.

Farming has, of course, been reduced significantly, although agriculture remains the driving force in many rural communities. Only 1.9% of the U.S. population live on farms now, compared with 15.3% in 1950 (Wright, 1991).

As indicated at the beginning of this chapter, rural, nonmetropolitan unemployment is generally at a significantly higher rate than unemployment in the cities, even though an assumption is made that unemployment problems predominate in metropolitan areas.

## Some Positive Aspects of Social Work in Small Communities

Readers of this book should not be disturbed by the commentaries on problems or challenges in rural communities. In fact, it is the nature of social work to be problem-focused and challenging, wherever it is practiced. Those who serve metropolitan populations may encounter difficulties that match or exceed those encountered by rural or small community workers. Almost all social workers find that they must work across cultural lines of some kind. Those who hold baccalaureate or master's degrees, for example, most frequently work with clients who have much more limited education and educational aspirations.

Social work has significant rewards for those who serve in smaller communities. The following are some of the rewards:

- *Independence.* Social workers in metropolitan areas frequently are responsible to a fairly complex administrative and supervisory structure. They may find their work closely monitored. They may have extensive reporting requirements in the organization. Social workers in rural communities are more likely to be relatively autonomous and to work with little or no supervision because there are simply fewer social workers in the agency. A metropolitan social services agency, for example, might have hundreds of social work employees. The rural office of the same agency might have only a handful of workers. Therefore, those who are ambitious to work independently or prefer setting their own courses and critiquing their own performances may find it much more satisfying to work in a smaller community.

- *Rapid advancement.* Social workers in smaller communities can often expect relatively rapid advancement. Workers may move from direct worker to supervisor and to administrator or manager in a relatively short time because other workers find smaller communities to be unattractive locations for their work. The competition for promotion or other opportunities is often not nearly as great in smaller communities as it is in metropolitan areas.

  Most American social workers, like most other Americans, come from metropolitan areas. Their family and social ties are in such communities, and, therefore, many are reluctant to relocate in rural communities. Such attitudes and behaviors only enhance the opportunities for workers who enjoy life in smaller communities.

- *Tangible results.* Social workers in smaller communities often find that they can see tangible results from their efforts. That is, they can see the impact of their efforts on the lives of the people in the community. Seeing the difference that one makes is one of social work's rewards in all settings and in communities of all sizes. In a rural community, one can make a difference at micro and macro levels. One can see changes made in individuals and families, as well as changes made in the larger community and in the social system.

- *Personal rewards.* Great personal rewards are possible for human services professionals in many small communities. Because they are independent and can make a difference in the lives of many people, rural workers may find themselves being thanked for the work they do. A small-community physician, Dr. Michael Watson (1992), reported that some of his clients tell him that they "love" him for what he has done to help them. A nurse practitioner, who serves with him and who performs some of the primary health care tasks that might be done by physicians in larger communities, receives similar kinds of comments from her patients. Another nurse, who is also a midwife in Dr. Watson's community, has delivered many of the children in that small community. This nurse-midwife is a good example of what can happen to the rural professional. She is relatively autonomous and works under the direction of only one physician, who provides her with consultation more than supervision. She practices a skill that is not as frequently used by nurses in metropolitan communities. She has special relationships with her clients and has won their respect and affection.

- *Recognition.* While many people prefer anonymity, there is a special joy for many in being well known and recognized in the community. The social worker who is known to everyone, who is spoken to by everyone on the street, in the grocery store, and in the post office, has the special satisfaction of being an important person in the rural community. Rarely are social workers in metropolitan areas accorded the same kinds of respect that social workers are often given in nonmetropolitan communities. The social worker may be a frequent speaker at major civic clubs or a consultant to local government who is quoted regularly in the local newspaper. In many ways, rural social workers establish stronger and broader relationships than their metropolitan counterparts might have.

### Professional Contacts

One of the difficulties faced by practitioners of any profession in smaller, more isolated communities is the lack of stimulation from fellow professionals. Social workers in rural communities must make special efforts to attend professional meetings, such as those of the National Association of Social Workers or other specialized human services or social welfare groups. Practitioners in larger cities may have professional contacts and relationships on a daily basis in the course of their work. Workers in smaller communities, who may have contacts with no more than a few colleagues at any time, often find it beneficial to attend professional meetings regularly, to keep up with the professional literature, and to seek opportunities for exchange with friends, fellow graduates from social work programs, and persons who are practicing related professions in their community or region.

The lack of anonymity in a small community sometimes means that the social worker must find ways to be alone from time to time and ways to pursue personal activities without being on guard among community leaders, clients, and peers. Therefore, many social workers in smaller communities spend weekends and holidays in cities or other small towns with friends, family, or even former colleagues. Being alone or being in a different environment often helps the worker have the kind of autonomy needed to return to work refreshed.

### Social Welfare Policy and Services Considerations

Much of this chapter has been about educating for the practice of social work in rural communities. A variety of social welfare policy and services issues ought to be addressed because they are unique to rural areas. For example, it is useful for social work education programs to help students understand the importance of ensuring that services be provided on a statewide basis. When the focus of service delivery is on metropolitan communities, people in smaller communities frequently do not have access to those programs.

In addition, programs should always have a transportation component or an outreach component if they are to be effective with small community populations. Finding ways to bring services to the people, or to bring people to the services, is critical in service planning and delivery in nonmetropolitan areas.

Several larger social welfare and non–social welfare policies have great impact on the well-being of rural citizens. For example, the deregulation of transportation in the 1970s, which made sense in a growing society dominated by metropolitan perspectives, held severe disadvantages for rural people. The deregulation of the airline industry has meant that many small communities once served by large airlines are now served, if at all, by commuter companies and small commuter-sized planes. Similarly, the deregulation of trucking has meant that many rural products cannot reach markets as readily as they could when there were strict controls on tariffs for the transport of goods. Transportation policies have had a significant impact on the economic well-being and, therefore, the social well-being of many rural communities. Not the least of the problems has been the isolation of elderly and disabled people who cannot afford transportation to cities from their nonmetropolitan communities.

Major social welfare changes, such as 1996's Personal Responsibility and Work Opportunity Reconciliation Act, which eliminated Aid to Families with Dependent Children and established Temporary Assistance for Needy Families, required several provisions for work requirements that may be more difficult to implement in rural areas than in major cities. Those jobs that are available may require extensive travel, which is more difficult and expensive in rural areas because of the lack of public transportation. There were special considerations in the act for rural areas, which the Congressional Rural Caucus ensured were included as part of its general advocacy and monitoring functions.

Other policies not normally discussed in social work curricula are critical to the preparation of workers who can understand and function effectively in rural communities. Farm price support policies, for example, have an impact on rural community life, as do agricultural extension programs, which should be treated as social welfare programs because of their emphasis on developing the community, improving family functioning skills, and advocating for small-community populations in many states.

Any social welfare policy issue has a rural twist, and, therefore, courses on social work in rural communities must pay special attention to social welfare policy and services for small communities.

## Field Instruction in Rural Communities

To prepare students effectively for this work, field instruction placements should be made in smaller communities. Such placements have a number of advantages. They communicate directly and soundly that effective social work is possible in small communities. They help retain professional social workers in rural communities because one of the goals of many ambitious professionals is to provide field instruction as part of the educational process. Such placements also help communities understand and appreciate the contributions social workers can make in dealing with social problems in the community.

Sometimes "preceptors" can be used to carry out social work field instruction programs effectively in rural communities. These may be non-social workers who have extensive experience and strong interest in helping students work within their community agencies, such as cooperative extension, health care, and social services. Consultation and professional supervision are often provided under such circumstances by social workers with a BSW or MSW, who help students identify and learn the professional social work elements of the work they are doing.

### Delivery of Rural Content in the Curriculum

Although a few schools have emphasized social work in small communities as their major curriculum orientation, this is not true for most BSW and MSW programs. Despite being located in smaller communities, many schools want to provide opportunities for their students to understand and obtain employment in large city agencies, which are more attractive to people from small communities than are positions in their own communities.

Nevertheless, some social work education programs—including some that are located in large, metropolitan areas—have a special interest in educating students for smaller community work. In those cases, a combination of field instruction placements in rural communities and special courses on social work in smaller communities has special merit. The "rural elective," which is the popular term used for such course offerings in many programs, is often an elective provided to students with an interest in working in small communities. An effective course includes some content from all four curriculum areas—social welfare policy and services, social work practice, human behavior and the social environment, and research. These courses help students adapt their knowledge of the social work curriculum to the specialized context of the smaller community.

For example, students may learn about human behavior and the social environment in the foundation program. However, a specialized course should provide them with material on the unique human behavior and the social environment issues in smaller communities—the face-to-face nature of relations, the smaller scale of life, the varied communication patterns, and the frequent differences in decision-making processes from metropolitan areas. (See chapters by Emilia Martinez-Brawley and Janet Fitchen in this volume.)

Specialized courses to help students integrate their general knowledge with a specialized field, such as rural or nonmetropolitan social work, appeal to many of the theorists of rural social work because of their belief that generalist practice is the most useful preparation for small community service.

### Rural Research

There are many issues that could effectively lend themselves to research on rural communities or issues of social work practice in such communities. Many of the theories suggested here are based upon observation, practice wisdom, and years of discussion with rural practitioners. However, most of these findings have not been confirmed, in any broad or convincing sense, by research findings.

There are many questions about the true nature of the rural social work specialist's practice. Is the advocate of small-community social work different in outlook and orientation from a metropolitan counterpart? No one knows with certainty and, therefore, research on the subject would be worthwhile.

Standard research efforts taught in social work education programs, such as program evaluation and evaluation of one's own practice—including single-subject design—would have special value, merit, and validity in rural communities. Social workers in small communities can just as easily evaluate their practice, using single-subject designs and comparable methods, as can their urban or metropolitan counterparts.

Simple tasks such as maintaining journals are beneficial for small community workers, who might be able to share their experiences and observations through the publication of articles based on their journals.

## Conclusion

This introductory chapter has outlined some of the key issues involved in studying social work in rural communities. Others chapters in this volume expand on some of the ideas and make them more specific. Emilia Martinez-Brawley writes on community-oriented social work, which, she demonstrates, has its roots in rural social work theory. The late Janet Fitchen, a leading expert whose research on rural poverty was financed by the Ford Foundation, contributes a chapter on rural social work and rural poverty. Joseph and Judith Davenport have updated their important work on rural boom towns. H. Wayne Johnson, editor of an important text on rural social work, provides some special insights into rural crime, delinquency, and corrections. Joanne Mermelstein and Paul Sundet, who wrote about social work education for rural program development in the first edition of this book, provide a new, updated article in this third edition. In addition to these and other original articles, the book includes reprints of important articles from the professional literature on subjects such as the differences between rural and urban practice, rural health issues, and rural minority matters.

The authors hope this new edition will be a help to educators, students, and practitioners in their efforts to better understand and be part of social work in rural communities.

## References

Council on Social Work Education. (1992a). *Curriculum policy statement for baccalaureate degree programs in social work education.* Alexandria, VA: Author.

Council on Social Work Education. (1992b). *Curriculum policy statement for master's degree programs in social work education.* Alexandria, VA: Author.

Coward, R. T., McLaughlin, D. K., Duncan, R. P., & Bull, C. N. (1992, September). *An overview of health and aging in rural America.* Presentation at national symposium on same topic, San Diego, CA.

Farley, O. W., Griffiths, K. A., Skidmore, R. A., & Thackeray, M. G. (1982). *Rural social work practice.* New York: Free Press.

Ginsberg, L. H. (1969). Education for social work practice in rural areas. *Social Work Education Reporter, 15*(1).

Ginsberg, L. H. (1995). *Social work almanac* (2nd ed.). Washington, DC: NASW Press.

Great Plains Training Project. (1989). Coming to the country [video tape]. Lincoln, NE: Author. (Available from Department of Psychology, University of Nebraska, 304 Burnett, 68588-0375)

Johnson, L. C., & Schwartz, C. L. (1994). *Social welfare: A response to human need.* Needham Heights, MA: Allyn and Bacon.

Johnson, H. W. (Ed.). (1980). *Rural human services: A book of readings.* Itasca, IL: Peacock.

Lazere, E. B., Leonard, P. A., & Kravitz, L. L. (1989). *A place to call home: The crisis in housing for the poor.* Washington, DC: Center on Budget and Policy Priorities and Low Income Housing Information Service.

Martinez-Brawley, E. (1990). *Perspectives on the small community. Humanistic views for practitioners.* Washington, DC: NASW Press.

Pooley, E. (1997, December 8). The great escape. *Time,* 53-63.

President's National Advisory Commission on Rural Poverty. (1967). *The people left behind.* Washington, DC: U.S. Government Printing Office.

Timms, G. (1992). Comments made to interdisciplinary course on rural health care. University of South Carolina, Columbia, SC, Summer semester.

Watson, M. (1992). Comments made to interdisciplinary course on rural health care, University of South Carolina, Columbia, SC, Summer semester.

Wright, J. W. (Ed.). (1991). *The universal almanac, 1992.* Kansas City, MO: Andrews and McMeel.

# 2

# Educational Assumptions for Rural Social Work

by the Southern Regional Education Board Manpower
Education and Training Project's Rural Task Force

The following are assumptions developed by the Southern Regional
Board about social work in rural communities.

1.  There is no clear, universally accepted definition of "rural areas," and in fact such a definition is unimportant. What is important is the fact that many baccalaureate-level social workers will be working with people and with communities that are geographically outside the urban–suburban area.

2.  There is a great variance among rural communities, for example, rural–industrial, rural farming, rural nonfarming, and so on. They are very different in style, customs, economic situation, population density, geographic location, and topography.

3.  Rural areas, like urban and suburban areas, change in response to population mobility, technology, and other factors.

4.  People in rural areas are more like people in nonrural areas than they are different from them. We need to look at the economic, political, and social institutions and conditions that have shaped the lives of people in rural areas, because such institutions will be different in rural areas.

---

Several years ago, the Southern Regional Education Board, with financing from the United States government, created a project to promote the development of baccalaureate social work programs in the South, which, at the time, had few such programs.

As part of its efforts, the Board wrote and promulgated a series of assumptions about social work in rural communities. These assumptions have been part of the basis for the evolution of theory about social work in rural communities. The principles appear to be, in large measure, applicable to social work in rural communities today. The assumptions are reprinted in this volume for their value to social work educators, students, and theorists.

---

Reprinted with permission of the Southern Regional Education Board.

5. There are unique problems in rural areas, particularly in the lack of basic public services. Problems of rural areas tend to be more like problems of underdeveloped countries; that is, basic public services and necessities are lacking. Services related to *sustaining life* (i.e., food, shelter, health, transportation, etc.) will have priority over services focused on the *quality of life*.

6. Rural communities have problems which are common to all communities everywhere. For example, such problems as mental retardation, physical and emotional disabilities, alcoholism, drug abuse, and delinquency are not unique to rural areas.

7. Many of the problems of people living in rural areas must be viewed within the context of unique social, economic, and political systems which have been dysfunctional, exploitive, unjust, and inadequate to many persons in rural areas, most particularly in Appalachia and the South.

8. Poverty in rural areas tends to be long standing and generational, due to the plantation system and other forms of economic organization.

9. Poverty tends to be scattered in rural areas; for example, very poor families may live within a stone's throw of middle-income families. The exception to this may be in areas where segregation of minority groups has developed.

10. Social welfare delivery systems of rural areas have unique features. They may be less formal, with informal networks and resources which are not commonly viewed as part of the traditional welfare system. These systems need to be studied so that the positives are recognized and strengthened. Programs based on urban experience may be dysfunctional in rural areas.

11. Some people in rural areas, due to the long-standing nature of their problems and generational poverty, may tend to be more resistant to or suspicious of change.

12. Unusual and unique barriers exist to participation in community decision making. The scattered nature of much of the population, lack of transportation, population diversity, and lack of access to, or knowledge of, technical assistance and resources are among these barriers.

13. Rural communities tend toward greater conformity with conventional norms and remain as the last stronghold for some conventional virtues and prejudices. The strengths which are an inherent part of such conformity must be recognized and valued by the social worker.

14. Rural people have more limited experience with professional persons and professional roles. The social worker tends to be viewed as the "welfare worker" who provides financial help and has not been a prime resource in helping the community to deal with problems.

15. Certain ethnic and cultural differences characterize many rural communities. Such differences must be recognized and respected. Social workers must be sensitive to the desires of such communities in terms of the kind of helping person the community feels it can effectively work with and relate to if there is to be an intimate involvement with the community and its problems.
16. Because of the fewer formal social welfare agencies which deal with specific problems, rural communities have a special need for workers who can help them define problems and develop solutions.
17. Because of the nonavailability of many of the formal, more specialized welfare services, the rural social worker must often react to problems as a generalist.
18. There are many myths, stereotypes, and generalizations about rural life and rural communities which the social work practitioner must examine carefully and critically.
19. There is a common core of generic content to all of social work practice. Such a core includes knowledge of human behavior and skill in analysis, problem solving, and basic practice. There is, however, substantive knowledge which is unique to rural communities and which social workers must know if they are to be helpful to people in rural areas.

Some of the characteristics of effective rural social workers are:

1. They are especially skillful in working with a variety of helping persons who are not social workers or who may not be related to the profession of social work, as well as with peers and colleagues.
2. They are able to carry out careful study, analysis, and other methods of inquiry in order to understand the community in which they find themselves.
3. They utilize their knowledge of the customs, traditions, heritage, and contemporary culture of the rural people with whom they are working to provide services with special awareness and sensitivity.
4. They are able to identify and mobilize a broad range of resources which are applicable to problem resolution in rural areas. These include existing and potential resources on the local, state, regional, and federal levels.
5. They are able to assist communities in developing new resources or ways to more fully use existing resources to benefit the rural community.
6. They are able to identify with and practice in accordance with the values of the profession and grow in their ability and effectiveness as professional social workers in situations and settings where they may be the only professional social worker.

7. They are able to identify and analyze the strengths and/or gaps and shortcomings in governmental and nongovernmental social policies as they affect the needs of people in rural areas.

8 . They accept their professional responsibility to develop appropriate measures to encourage more responsiveness to the needs of people in rural areas from governmental and nongovernmental organizations.

9. They are able to help identify and create new and different helping roles in order to respond to the needs and problems of rural communities.

10. They initiate and provide technical assistance to rural governing bodies and other organized groups in rural communities.

11. They are able to practice as generalists, carrying out a wide range of roles, to solve a wide range of problems of individuals and groups as well as of the larger community.

12. They are able to communicate and interact appropriately with people in the rural community, and adapt their personal lifestyle to the professional tasks to be done.

13. They are able to evaluate their own professional performance.

14. They are able to work within an agency or organization and plan for and initiate change in agency policy and practice when such change is indicated.

15. On the basis of continuous careful observation, they contribute knowledge about effective practice in rural areas.

# 3

# Old Wine in New Bottles: Utilizing Gender-Specific Natural Helping Capacities in Rural Social Work

by Shirley L. Patterson, Jay L. Memmott, and Carel B. Germain

*Investigated were gender differences in the helping process of 200 rural natural helpers (119 females; 81 males) representing all adult age groups. In-person interviews were conducted with respondents identified by a modified snowball sampling method. The interview guide was constructed to obtain data on helper-recipient characteristics; relationship (i.e., relative, friend, neighbor), helper style; problem type; motivation for helping; perceived aim and outcome of help and closeness to help recipient. Significant gender differences emerged on all major variables examined. In order to support natural helping processes, restore broken relationships, or create opportunities for these relationships to develop systematically, the findings suggest that rural social workers must be attentive to the different ways female and male natural helpers assist relatives, friends, and neighbors with their daily problems-in-living.*

For years, anthropologists and sociobiologists struggled to explain altruism, which was viewed as an evolutionary enigma. Altruistic behaviors, sometimes referred to as informal helping, were thought to be nonadaptive, even detrimental to one's own survival. However, kin selection was offered as one solution to this puzzle. It was noted that an altruist's self-sacrificing behaviors were often directed toward kin. The altruist may lose his or her life, but those who carry copies of the altruist's genes survive (Bilsborough, 1992). A complementary solution was entailed by the concept of reciprocal altruism: "Insofar as reciprocated behaviors create coalitions of reciprocators, who may by virtue of their coalitions prevail over those who do not reciprocate, then reciprocity should be selected" (Brown, 1991, p. 107). Few would dispute the suggestion that

Reprinted from *Human Services in the Rural Environment* (Spring/Summer 1995), with permission of the Eastern Washington School of Social Work and Human Services.

reciprocity and its exchange-obligation dynamic creates a kind of social glue which binds people into friendships, marriages, families, and communities (Harris, 1989). Certainly, the origins of altruism, empathy, and everyday helping are lost in the millennia of time. Along with kinship, toolmaking, and language, these properties are what make us distinctly human (Leakey, 1994; Leakey & Lewin, 1992). Perhaps our knowledge of these socially valuable acts is limited because we take them for granted; after all, they are so ordinary, ubiquitous, and invisible

Since 1980, we have been engaged in a study of the perceptions, motives, and actions of natural helpers in the rural Midwest and New England. Based on earlier conceptualizations (Patterson, Holzhuter, Struble & Quadagno, 1972), a natural helper can be distinguished from an informal helper by a relatively high level of independent helping activity over time, demonstrated effectiveness, and socially embedded helper-recipient relationship marked by equality and mutuality. Given these distinctions, natural helping may take the form of informal neighboring, but it occurs apart from organized neighborhood care as postulated by Abrams (see Bulmer, 1986). Many of the helpers described by Wuthnow (1991) in his remarkable book *Acts of Compassion* are natural helpers, but some helping activities are structured and directed by volunteer agencies. In this sense, the helpers have engaged in informal helping, not natural helping.

A review of the professional literature reveals an increase in natural helping theory, research, and practice applications over the past ten years. Investigators have described the patterns and characteristics of natural helpers (Patterson, Memmott, Brennan & Germain, 1992) and provided evidence of their effectiveness (Patterson, Germain, Brennan & Memmott, 1988). There has been a tendency however, to overlook or minimize the impact of variables such as age, gender, and geographic location on the helper, the recipient, the relationship, the outcome, and the like (D'Augelli & Ehrlich, 1982; Israel, 1985; Kendall & Kenkel, 1989; Kenkel, 1986; Vallance & D'Augelli, 1982; Warren, 1981; Young, Giles & Plantz, 1982). Notable exceptions include a study of helping strategies and orientations of rural natural helpers and professional social workers serving rural clients (Memmott, 1993; Brennan, 1988) and helping patterns of older natural helpers (Patterson, 1987).

In this paper, we will report on the gender differences observed in our samples. Findings related to age and geographic location will be addressed in another, forthcoming article. Our study design rests on the ecological perspective in social work with its dynamic veiw of person-to-environment relationships and the life model of social work, especially its conception of life space comprised of three interdependent domains: the temporal (i.e., transitions of life), the interpersonal, and the environmental (Germain, 1979; Germain & Gitterman, 1980). Accordingly, a painful stressor may appear in any or all of the life space domains. If efforts to cope with it are not successful, the resultant stress may culminate, leading in a recursive fashion to an almost limitless variety of problems-in-living. One's response to stress may be physiological, cognitive, emotional, and/or behavioral. The concept of stress, whether it is tied to major life events or daily hassles, is important because studies have established the significance of natural helpers in the prevention and management of such sequelae. Our data show that natural helpers do not simply serve as buffers between stressors and the people they help. Natural helpers function as informal case managers, actively intervening in the help recipient's environment (i.e., management of resources external to the recipient). In the context of personal relationships, they help recipients develop and enhance coping abilities, gain insight, work through emotional turmoil, and alter frames-of-reference, thereby opening up new pathways for problem solving (i.e., management of internal resources–those within the recipient).

## Study Sites

The study was conducted in a farming township in Kansas, relatively comfortable financially, and in an impoverished rural town in northeast Connecticut. Each had a population of approximately 1,800 persons, all of white European stock (only one person reported himself as an American Indian - in Kansas), so this study provided no data on variations due to race and ethnicity.

One hundred natural helpers in each community were located through a modified snowball sampling method. A semi-structured interview with some open-ended questions was conducted with each respondent. The interviews lasted anywhere from 35 minutes to two hours.

To test Litwak and Szelenyi's (1969) hypothesis that type of help varied according to the helper-recipient relationship (i.e., relative, friend, neighbor), we asked our subjects to describe examples of their help-giving in each relationship category. Segments of each interview were audio taped. A fourth segment was included to examine the other side of mutuality: the helper's experience receiving help from a relative, friend, or neighbor. For each helping account, we gathered data regarding the demographic characteristics of the helper and the recipient; the nature of the helper-recipient relationship; the kind of life stress experienced by the recipient and associated problems-in-living; the helping aim, styles, and techniques employed by the helper; the perceived outcomes; and evaluations of the helper's effectiveness.

## Sample Characteristics

The subjects ranged in age from 16 to 82, but the average age was 52 years. In fact, 164 of the subjects were middle-aged or older, and 36 were age 35 and under. One hundred and nineteen helpers were women while 81 were men. They were long-term residents of their communities, averaging 32 years (with a range of 1 to 82 years). A little over half lived in town and the rest in the countryside. Ninety-one percent of the men were married and living with their spouses; none was divorced or widowed. Eighty-two percent of the women were married and living with their spouses, but four women were divorced and 11 were widowed. Two women and seven men had never been married. Ninety percent or all but 12 of the 119 women, and 83 percent or all but 14 of the 81 men had living children.

A majority of the women and men considered themselves to be religious, with two thirds belonging to Protestant churches, and the rest to Catholic churches. A small sprinkling were members of other sects. The women were slightly better educated than the men. Eighty-eight percent were high school graduates or had additional vocational or college education, in contrast to 75 percent of the men. Of the 126 employed full or part time outside the home, 50 percent of the women and 62 percent of the men were in professional or managerial positions, with the balance in skilled work.

## Findings

Statistical tests appropriate for the type of data to be analyzed were performed (e.g., Chi square analyses for nominal data; one-way analyses of variance for interval data). Dependent variables associated with significant gender differences included mutuality, helping style, type of problem, aim of helping and perceived helping outcome.

Mutuality refers to the nature of the relationship between helper and recipient. Two categorical dimensions were considered: the reason or motivation for helping, and the circumstances of involvement (Patterson et al., 1972). With motivation as the dependent variable, it was found that significantly more women than men helped others simply because they cared while more men than women gave help because it was the moral or right thing to do: $X^2(3, N=200)=24.3$, $p<.001$ (see Table 1).

When involvement became the dependent variable, it was found that significantly more women than men offered help before it was requested, while significantly more men than women became involved in helping after being asked by the recipient: $X^2(3,N=200)=19.2$, $p<.001$ (see Table 2).

*Helping Style.* Helping style was operationalized as facilitating (attempting to promote a growth process by working with and through the people), doing (actively attempting to eliminate or relieve a stressful situation), and

### Table 1. Motivation for Helping Others by Helper Gender

| Motivation | Helper Gender | |
|---|---|---|
| | Female (n=119) | Male (n=81) |
| Caring | 92* | 41 |
| Reciprocity | 2 | 3 |
| Morality | 13 | 32* |
| Other | 12 | 5 |

*$p<.001$

facilitating-doing (using both styles differentially according to the situation) (Patterson, et al., 1972). Significantly more women than men showed a preference for the facilitating-doing style of help when helping relatives: $X^2(2, N=200)=6.9$, $p<.05$. Significantly more women than men tended to utilize both the facilitating and facilitating-doing styles of help with friends [$X^2(2, N=200)=14.5$, $p<.001$] and with neighbors [$X^2(2,N=200)=19.4$, $p<.001$]. Less than half of all helpers employed the doing style with friends.

## Type of Stressor

While no significant gender differences were found with regard to problem type for help involving relatives or friends, significantly more women than men helped neighbors with environmental problems: $X^2(2, N=200)=6.9$, $p<05$. This was true even though the majority of the helpers tended to describe helping situations having an environmental component across all three categories of relationships.

## Aim of Helping

For helping episodes involving relatives, significantly more women than men attempted to temporarily ease the stressor and improve the coping capacity of recipients; while more males than females attempted to get rid of the problem (i.e., eliminate the stressor): $X^2(4, N=200)=36.2$, $p<.001$. A similar pattern emerged regarding females helping friends: they attempted to alleviate the stressor and strengthen coping capacity: $X^2(3, N=200)=16.4$, $p<.001$. The analysis of data regarding help given to neighbors indicated that significantly more women than men sought to improve coping capacity while more men than women tried to eliminate the stressor: $X^2(3, N=200)=27.3$, $p<.001$.

## Perceived Helping Outcome

The general pattern noted for helping aim held for this dependent variable, too. First, significantly more women than men said they helped relatives temporarily reduce the stressor and find better ways to cope with it, while more men than women stated they helped relatives eliminate

**Table 2.** Method of Involvement in the Helping Process by Helper Gender

| | Helper Gender | |
| --- | --- | --- |
| Motivation | Female (n=119) | Male (n=81) |
| At recipient's request | 2 | 15* |
| Helper offered help | 101* | 53 |
| Other's suggestion | 2 | 3 |
| Other | 14 | 10 |

*$p<.001$

stressors completely $X^2(4, N=200)=21.8$, $p<.001$. When help was directed toward friends, significantly more females than males reported temporarily alleviating the stressor: $X^2(4, N=200)=12.1$, $p<.05$. The helpers' assessment of helping outcome for neighbors mirrored their assessment for relatives. Significantly more women than men noted that they temporarily reduced the stressor and helped recipients find better ways to cope. Further, more men than women said they had eliminated stressors associated with neighbors' problems: $X^2(4, N=200)=18.7$, $p<.001$.

## Perceived Closeness

To discern whether or not there were any significant sex differences with regard to perceived closeness before and after the helping episodes, a 2x2x(3 x 2) higher order repeated measures analysis of variance was performed. Helper location (Kansas, Connecticut) and helper gender (female, male) served as between-subjects factors. Helping relationship (relative, friend, neighbor) and time of relationship assessment (before, after) served as within-subjects factors. Results indicated that there were two significant main effects for helper gender and time of relationship assessment. First, female helpers tended to rate themselves as feeling significantly closer to recipients than male helpers did: $F(1,168) = 11.31$, $p<.001$; means for female and male helpers respectively were 5.55 and 5.15 (see Table 3). Second, helpers overall tended to rate themselves as feeling closer to recipients at the conclusion of the helping effort than at the beginning: $F(1,168) = 69.38$ $p<.001$; means were 5.11 and 5.59 for before and after ratings respectively.

To summarize our findings on significant gender differences:

1. Women's motivation to help tends to arise more out of a sense of caring, while men help out of a sense of moral duty.

*Table 3.* **Analysis of Variance for Perceived Closeness between Helpers and Recipients**

| Source | df | MS | F |
|---|---|---|---|
| Between Subjects | | | |
| Location (L) | 1 | 12.83 | 3.54 |
| Helper Gender (HG) | 1 | 41.05 | 11.31* |
| LxHG | 1 | .85 | .23 |
| Error | 168 | 3.63 | – |
| Within Subjects | | | |
| Time (T) | 1 | 65.00 | 69.38* |
| LxT | 1 | .12 | .13 |
| HGxT | 1 | .53 | .57 |
| LxHGxT | 1 | .11 | .12 |
| Error | 168 | .94 | – |

*$p<.001$

2. Women typically reach out and offer help before it is requested, men after it is requested.

3. Women tend to use facilitating and facilitating-doing styles of help more often than do men.

4. No significant gender differences were found with regard to problem type for helping episodes involving relatives or friends, but women helped neighbors with environmental problems more than men did.

5. Women focus more on temporarily easing the impact of the stressor and strengthening coping capacities, while men focus more on eliminating the stressor.

6. Both men and women reflected the same pattern in their perceptions of helping outcomes, with men indicating that they had eliminated stressors and women stating that they had temporarily reduced the impact of stressors and strengthened the coping capacities of the people they helped.

7. Women tended to feel closer to the people they helped than did their male counterparts. All helpers, however, felt closer to recipients at the conclusion of helping effort than they did at the beginning.

### Examples of Gender Differences

Typical examples of gender differences illustrate some but not all of the significant findings. For example, a 68-year-old man reported:

> My neighbor just started out in the chicken business. And he dug several wells, and he had trouble locating a good one. He spent a lot of money drilling wells. So he got short of water because it was dry that year. And he had to have water for his chickens; there was no two ways about it. We had a tank truck that we used for spraying corn to kill weeds. So I filled the truck up with water at home because we got plenty of water; then I'd take it up there and drop a hose in his well; and we'd fill it up. He'd bring the empty truck back and I'd take it back to him the next morning. And, of course, he had to have the water for the chickens. The fellow had just started it and was in debt over his eyebrows, I imagine; so he needed the help. So we give it to him. We helped him clean his coop. It needed cleaning, so we cleaned it for him. We helped him out. And in helping him we helped ourselves because we use the chicken manure for our corn. So I don't know if you could say I helped him or not.

In one interview, an 81-year-old woman told the interviewer:

> What I give my friend is moral support. When something is bothering her, she calls me on the phone, and vice versa. In my case, she gives me a sense of a deeply religious faith which unfortunately I don't possess. And what I give her, that I really wouldn't know,

except an ability to talk things over when a problem arises with some of the family. I give her a bit of advice which I know she accepts. Why I don't know, but she definitely considers my advice important. Perhaps it's due to the fact that we have spent practically our whole life in the same vicinity, growing up together from the time we were little. She was two, I was four, and her older sister was six, and our parents had the same ideals. And they go back to that.

Reflecting on his activities as a helper, a 56-year-old male postal employee said:

My friend was a clerk carrier at another post office and was having an awful lot of problems with the postmaster there. He reduced my friend's hours to 10 or 12 a week. He had to get a second job to support the family, which I felt was not right. The hours were there. It was getting to the point where he was pretty well disgusted and was wondering what he should do. I kind of talked him into more or less staying because of the time he already had in. I said I didn't want him to lose it. I thought he would be foolish. I told him more or less to use his head and I'd make a few phone calls for him. And we did get the information we needed, which in turn did help him because since then he's been transferred from this job. I talked to him like a father, I guess, and gave him a little gumption to pursue the thing a little bit further.

A 77-year-old woman gave this account:

My friend had a disastrous marriage. It had broken up once before and they had made up, and then the second round was it. He was abusive and very, very, very abusive of their son. When the divorce was finally completed, it made her very sad because it all started because of alcohol. She really still liked the guy but she was determined this was it. As a result, she was badly in need of friends. And that's where I thought I helped... more by listening than anything else because I couldn't do anything else.... Just talking and listening to what she had to say. When you're with somebody a lot, you just communicate. It's communication, that's what it is. I like that word.

## Discussion

The findings on gender differences in natural helping present notable parallels to the findings of Gilligan (1982) in her exploratory studies of differences in female and male world views and moral judgments. Gilligan observed that most women strive to maintain relationships, display sensitivity to the needs of others, and attempt to avoid hurt in the resolution of moral dilemmas. Most men, in contrast, apply logic, take an objective position, and follow formal rules of conduct. Women resolve moral conflict in a context of caring and responsibility for others and men in a context of impartial justice.

Hence, the male voice speaks of separateness and rights, and the female of connectedness and responsibilities. Our Kansas and Connecticut subjects, rural men and women who help their relatives, friends, and neighbors, did speak in different voices.

It can be argued that at least in the past, forces of socialization have prepared females for submissiveness and nurturance in expressive, care-giving roles, and males for dominance, authority, and achievement in instrumental roles. Hence, with contemporary shifts in the socialization of children which will affect later age cohorts of adults, it can be expected that definitions of gender roles will change. How much this will affect the different developmental experiences of females and males remains to be seen, insofar as Gilligan asserts they arise from differences between the mother-daughter and the mother-son relationships in early life. Despite these unknowns, adults of all ages and both genders are already transcending traditional age and sex roles in large numbers, although our own samples did not reflect this trend. If the numbers of younger people in our sample had been larger, we could have tested for a shift among them in the possible direction of more androgynous forms of helping; that is, more caring orientations among the men and more instrumental forms of helping among the women. If this had proved to be the case, one might assume that such differences were already products of changing patterns in the socialization of children and younger adults since the 1960s.

As it stands with our sample of 200 individuals, we can say with confidence that the women tended to be motivated by caring and operated in a context of relatedness. Further, they believed they were effective in temporarily relieving discomfort and strengthening the coping abilities of those they helped. On the other hand, the men tended to be motivated by moral obligation and offered help in the context of what is "only right to do." They believed they were effective in removing stressors, which were seen as the source or cause recipient problems. Typically, men relied on the doing (i.e., instrumental) style of helping and women on the facilitating (i.e., emotive) or doing-facilitating (i.e., combination) style. These differences characterized helpers in both rural Kansas and rural Connecticut.

Some differences between formal and informal systems that may account for the prevalence and easy acceptance of natural helping among our rural Kansas and Connecticut subjects, and studies of urban natural helping bear this out. Formal systems of care tend to be characterized by impersonality, social distance, power differentials between helper and recipient, and degrees of rigidity in hours, office location, and rules of eligibility for help. In contrast, informal systems of help tend to be characterized by personal caring and mutuality, social closeness, markedly reduced power differentials between helper and recipient, and almost total availability (in the dwellings of helpers or recipients, outdoors, by telephone, and at any time, day or night, except for constraints imposed on helpers who were employed or who had other commitments). Indeed, many of our subjects expressed surprise that we wished to interview them, "because this is just the way it is here."

If the medically and disease-oriented health care system were to assume responsibility for the care of all those who receive help from informal helpers, it would be overwhelmed (Kohn, 1990; Wuthnow, 1991). The same is probably true of our mental health and child welfare systems. As social workers, it behooves us to draw upon these rich environmental resources which restore connectedness, support health, promote growth and adaptive functioning, and prevent adverse outcomes associated with stress.

## Conclusions and Implications

Because life stress is experienced by all people across the life span to varying degrees, depending on their resources and circumstance, we believe that knowledge specific to both rural and urban informal helping systems is important whether the social worker is involved with individuals, families, groups, or communities in direct or indirect practice.

People who are referred to social workers are usually experiencing or are anticipating stressful demands. We can enhance our services by enlisting natural helpers and working collaboratively with them in behalf of those we serve. Of course, our clients may hesitate or express reluctance to accept these terms. Perhaps we need to develop strategies and tactics which enable clients to accept help while saving face and feeling secure that their confidentiality will be respected and preserved. By the same token, we subscribe to the position that natural helper spontaneity and self-efficacy must be preserved. The supportive social work role should be free of attempts to professionalize the natural helper through supervision or training.

Beyond this, we suggest that gender differences found among rural natural helpers need to be respected and utilized. For example, in the case of stress arising from loss or from relationship issues, including conflict and social or emotional isolation, the worker might encourage the client to talk with a female helper. In the case of an environmental problem, the worker might encourage the client to talk and work with a male relative, neighbor, or friend.

Second, social workers and agencies can give attention to strengthening informal support systems already in existence by helping restore broken connections and by creating opportunities for such systems to develop where they are missing in a community, a workplace, or the lives of vulnerable populations such as deinstitutionalized, persistently mentally ill people; the elderly; the chronically physically ill and disabled; one-parent families; and families and children at risk for neglect and abuse. Such attention can extend the informal system of help in rural and urban communities where formal services and resources are limited or at a distance. In turn, community residents are empowered by their increased capacities for relatedness, competence, self-direction, and self worth.

New stressors are coming to the fore in city and country life. The deficit and, paradoxically, our efforts to reduce it fuel poverty, which is growing at the same time social and human services are being cut back. Large and small employers are downsizing. Economic and environmental disasters stretch and strain local and regional resources. The working poor are being joined by people dispossessed of their homes and their land: farmers and ranchers; merchants and shopkeepers; engineers and science technicians; craftsmen and kindred workers. Consequently, women in particular confront overwhelming financial problems. Many end up for the first time assuming major responsibilities for the survival of their families, accepting with little choice unskilled, low-status, minimum wage jobs. Added to this are the additional burdens of homemaking and child-rearing. As caregivers, they are expected to cope silently, nurture and support their children selflessly, and effectively deal with the anxiety and depression of their spouses, many of whom resort to alcohol, drugs, and other forms of self or other human abuse. Natural helping on a woman-to-woman basis, given the caring, nurturant approach of female natural helpers, can be encouraged and supported.

Given the instrumental, morally objective orientation of men, social workers can refer clients struggling with environmental problems to male helpers who can provide tangible services (e.g., general labor, house or mechanical repairs); facilitate direct linkages with employment, legal, and health care resources; and initiate or sustain the development local self-help and mutual aid groups and organizations (Israel, 1985). Perhaps even more important is the need for social workers and informal helpers to work together for social change and social justice, for it is clear that stressors such as poverty, financial loss, and unemployment are created and perpetuated by society. Only through collective resolve and action can these social ills be resolved. By taking a proactive stance and adopting a truly ecological orientation toward communities and society, we as social workers, operating individually and within social agencies, can reclaim our heritage and renew our professional commitment to creating and sustaining a more just and caring society.

## *References*

Bilsborough, A. (1992). *Human evolution.* New York, NY: Blackie Academic & Professional.

Brown, D. E. (1991). *Human universals.* Philadelphia, PA: Temple University Press.

Bulmer, M. (Ed.) (1986). *Neighbours: The work of Philip Abrams.* New York, NY: Cambridge University Press.

D'Augelli, A. R. & Ehrlich, R. P. (1982). Evaluation of a community-based system for training natural helpers: Effects on informal helping activities. *American Journal of Community Psychology, 10,* 447-456.

Germain, C. B. (Ed.) (1979). *Social work practice: People and environments.* New York, NY: Columbia University Press.

Germain, C. B. & Gitterman, A. (1980). *The life model of social work practice.* New York, NY: Columbia University Press.

Gilligan, C. (1982). *In a different voice.* Cambridge, MA: Harvard University Press.

Harris, M. (1989). *Our kind.* New York, NY: Harper & Row.

Israel, B. A. (1985). Social networks and social support: Implications for natural helper and community level interventions. *Health Education Quarterly, 12,* 65-80.

Kendall, K. S. & Kenkel, M. B. (1989). Social exchange in the natural helping interaction. *Journal of Rural Community Psychology, 10*(2), 25-45.

Kenkel, M. B. (1986). Stress-coping support in rural communities: A model for primary prevention. *American Journal of Community Psychology, 14,* 457-478.

Kohn, A. (1990). *The brighter side of human nature.* New York, NY: Basic Books.

Leakey, R. (1994). *The origin of humankind.* New York, NY: Basic Books.

Leakey, R. & Lewin, R. (1992). *Origins reconsidered.* New York, NY: Doubleday.

Litwak, E. & Szelenyi, I. (1969). Primary group structures and their functions: Kin, neighbors, and friends. *American Sociological Review, 34,* 465-481.

Memmott, J. L. (1993). Models of helping and coping: A field experiment with natural and professional helpers. *Social Work Research & Abstracts, 29*(3), 11-21.

Memmott, J. L. & Brennan, E. M. (1988). Helping orientations and strategies of natural helpers and social workers in rural settings. *Social Work Research & Abstracts, 24*(2), 15-20.

Patterson, S. L. (1987). Older rural natural helpers: Gender and site differences in the helping process. *The Gerontologist, 27,* 639-644.

Patterson, S. L., Memmott, J. L., Brennan, E. M. & Germain, C. B. (1992). Patterns of natural helping in rural areas: Implications for social work research. *Social Work Research & Abstracts, 28* (3), 22-28.

Patterson, S. L., Germain, C. B., Brennan, E. M. & Memmott, J. L. (1988). Effectiveness of rural natural helpers. *Social Casework, 69* (5), 272-279.

Patterson, S. L., Holzhuter, J. L., Struble, V. E. & Quadagno, J. S. (1972). *Final Report: Utilization of human resources for mental health* (Grant No MH 16618). Lawrence, KS: National Institute of Mental Health, University of Kansas.

Vallance, T. R. & D'Augelli, A. R. (1982). The helping community: Characteristics of natural helpers. *American Journal of Community Psychology, 10,* 197-205.

Warren, D. I. (1981). *Helping networks: How people cope with problems in the urban community.* South Bend, IN: University of Notre Dame Press.

Young, C. E., Giles, D. E., Jr. & Plantz, M. C. (1982). Natural networks: Help-giving and help-seeking in two rural communities. *American Journal of Community Psychology, 10,* 457-469.

Wuthnow, R. (1991). *Acts of compassion: Caring for others and helping ourselves.* Princeton, NJ: Princeton University Press.

# 4

# Rural Communities in Transition

by Joseph Davenport III and Judith A. Davenport

This chapter on rural communities in transition was prompted by the authors' experiences in working with energy "boom towns" in the late 1970s and early 1980s and farming "bust towns" in the 1980s and 1990s. Personal experiences also contributed to the authors' interest in this topic. One grew up in a rural locale where the family had resided since 1775, and the other grew up as a newcomer in a succession of small Southern towns. Each dealt with sudden social, economic, political, and demographic changes.

The senior author's deep roots in Claiborne County, Mississippi, probably resulted in his picturing the county as a kind of pastoral Eden before the Fall; bedrock American democracy in action and Jeffersonian agrarianism at its finest. Norman Rockwell would have loved the quiet streets of Port Gibson, Mississippi: a town Ulysses S. Grant called "too beautiful to burn" and Alistair Cooke called one of his "five favorite places in North America." A history of the county is even titled *The Promised Land*!

Indeed, Port Gibson in the 1950s and early 1960s could literally have been thought idyllic. Main Street bustled with banks, drug stores, furniture stores, hardware and department stores, barber shops, grocery stores, cafes, medical and law offices, and almost anything else required for everyday living. Citizens bought most products and services in town, supplemented by mail orders from J.C. Penney and Sears Roebuck, or an occasional shopping trip to Vicksburg, 28 miles up U.S. Highway 61.

Family life was traditional; extended families were the norm. The father worked outside the home while the mother was a housewife or helped in a small family business. Individuals were surrounded by grandparents, aunts, uncles, cousins, and friends whose ever-present eyes helped the community to maintain norms, regulate social behavior, and instill a sense of heritage, tradition, and continuity. Streets were safe, doors were kept unlocked, and children roamed the streets and lanes without fear. Huck Finn and Tom Sawyer would have felt at home along the Bayou Pierre at the edge of town, and was that Opie heading for the fishing hole around the bend? Social roles and statuses were secure. A sense of order and stability pervaded. The future was not in doubt.

Hit the fast-forward button on the VCR of history, and you'll wonder what in the hell happened over the last 20 years. Did someone change the tape, or was it edited by revisionists, deconstructionists, or other mean-spirited social gremlins?

Main Street is not deserted, but it certainly doesn't bustle. One block stands as an oasis with the familiar bank, newspaper office, insurance agency, clothing store, and jewelry store maintaining some semblance of order. Some businesses have closed forever with family owners leaving town. Several stores have relocated to the edge of town for more space and easier parking. Following a fire, half of one block has become an empty lot. Another lot stands where a building simply fell down. Some new businesses have opened, but they appear seedy and unprosperous. Other businesses, such as service stations, are now owned by outside interests. More shoppers go to Vicksburg, especially to the malls, for greater variety and lower prices.

Family life, including the extended family, is still important, but the foundation appears to be weakening. Many young people drift away to Vicksburg, Jackson, Atlanta (the capital of the New South), all three coasts, and even international locales. Older family members die or leave town to join "expatriate" children. Christmas, Easter, and class reunions still lure the family members home; nevertheless, the social bonds are not as strong. Social networks diminish slowly, natural helping systems lose importance, and the community's informal means of control and regulation give way to more formal measures, such as a much larger police force and a mental health center. Doors are now locked, the streets are not as safe, and more residents openly question the future.

At first glance, Port Gibson could be any one of thousands of small towns experiencing change from a loss of population, function, and importance. However, it is a better example than most due to the complex currents of its transitional shoals. The relative stability of the 1950s and early 1960s was shattered by a civil rights revolution in the late 1960s, which saw the 80% African American majority gain control of public institutions (e.g., government and schools) while minority whites retained control of many private entities (e.g., banks, businesses, country club, and private school).

While the races coexisted in an uneasy peace, the so-called "rural renaissance" flowered in the 1970s. Agricultural and timber businesses were prospering and exporting to national and world markets. All-out boom growth occurred in the mid-1980s when a nuclear power plant was built. Employment opportunities were plentiful, most businesses had golden years, and tax dollars poured in for public expenditures. While the town wasn't quite as wild and woolly as many Western boom towns, Port Gibson had not seen so much excitement since U. S. Grant and his rowdies came through in 1863.

Then, the pendulum swung again in the late 1980s. The whole idea of a rural renaissance was called into question as the "rural crisis" devastated farmers, agribusiness, and rural communities (Davenport & Davenport, 1988). Completion of the nuclear power plant meant the loss of thousands of construction jobs, while many of the good administrative and operator positions were held by commuters from Vicksburg. Additionally, the race issue remained. Some whites have left because of their minority status, and many businesses, unofficially of course, will not locate where African Americans constitute 30% or more of the population.

Thus, Port Gibson's last quarter century has included relative stability, rapid social change as African Americans achieved political power, all-out growth from agriculture and energy, and major decline as the rural renaissance faltered and the nuclear power plant was completed. Current efforts focus on a continued reliance on agricultural and lumber activities, while retaining and attracting small industry, establishing a Mississippi River port, developing river boat gambling, promoting tourism in the historical area between Natchez and Vicksburg, and exploring the possibility of a toxic waste storage facility that would provide an estimated 500 jobs.

Several caveats or observations are in order. Rural advocates and supporters, including these authors, tend to describe the past as the "best of times" and the present as "the worst of times." The senior author, especially, views the changes from the perspective of a white male descendant of aristocratic pioneers who possessed vast plantations and many slaves. The African-American majority of Claiborne County probably has gained from many of the social structural changes. Females have acquired more opportunities from changing roles and status, even though their movement out of the home has changed the nature and strength of neighborhood life. Many residents who left for urban America undoubtedly found opportunities not available in a small town. Gay people and others with alternative lifestyles have probably always found more support in urban subcultures.

Another tendency is to view the past as primarily a great continuity of stability and the present as a period fraught with change and upheaval. The history of this region and many others calls this assumption into question. The Natchez, a Native American tribe of Aztec origin or influence, came from the West to displace and war with the Choctaws, who also fought with the Chickasaws to the north. Tribal life was anything but secure, as territory and village sites often changed hands or disappeared.

The arrival of European explorers and settlers resulted in great change for Native Americans, as English, French, and Spanish colonists dueled over control of the land. A resident could have been a citizen of three or four different nations in a single decade, with changes in language, religion, laws, and customs. Community life was frequently disturbed as some groups were forced to leave or to adapt to change. Native populations were displaced until only a small reservation community remained in central Mississippi.

While the United States gained control of the area, technological innovations had a profound effect upon the nature of community life. The invention of the cotton gin led to the plantation culture and widespread use of slave labor. The steamboat destroyed the tavern communities and transportation system along the Natchez Trace and enabled river communities to flourish. The railroad weakened the river communities, while natural changes, such as cave-ins and river course changes, doomed some of the most important communities in the state. Grand Gulf, the second largest town in Mississippi, experienced a cave-in, a tornado, and a yellow fever epidemic, as well as shelling from Union forces, before the Mississippi River changed course and consigned the community to the pages of history.

The War Between the States, the abolition of slavery, and the reconstruction resulted in waves of change and transition. Mechanization of agriculture displaced thousands of farm families, and modern roads and automobiles meant the end of many crossroads communities. Indeed, the great forces of industrialization and urbanization led to major population shifts and social problems that required a new profession—social work—to deal with them. Unfortunately, the fledgling profession too often focused primarily upon urban problems, while neglecting the hinterlands.

In summary, Port Gibson may serve as an example of how rural communities experienced change and transition over years, decades, and even centuries. No two communities are exactly alike, but the commonality of transitional change must be understood by social workers and others who deal with rural individuals and communities.

## Communities in Decline

Communities may decline for myriad reasons: A military base closes as the Cold War ends, a state institution falls victim to budget cuts or the development of community-based services, a college closes its doors, a lumber mill shuts down because of environmental concerns, an energy or mineral company exhausts its resources or cannot compete with international prices, an interstate highway bypasses a town, a railroad ends service, recreational interests change, structural changes continue in agriculture, and plants or factories close or relocate. And, of course, a number of communities face these problems simultaneously. Agricultural changes and plant closures probably constitute two of the greatest threats.

Perrucci, Perrucci, Targ, and Targ (1988) cite the importance of understanding the broad context of socioeconomic changes transforming the world economy. The manufacturing base of the United States is declining as capital flows to areas of cheap labor and little regulation. Major declines have been experienced in such industries as automobile, steel, electronics, rubber, and textiles. New jobs are often in service industries with smaller salaries and fewer benefits.

Urban areas, such as St. Louis and Kansas City, have been hit hard by reduced defense and manufacturing jobs, but their economies are more diversified, thereby causing less pain. For example, the loss of 950 jobs at McDonnell-Douglas in St. Louis is hardly pleasant, but imagine the effects of taking 950 RCA jobs from Monticello, Indiana, a town of 5,000 in a county of 23,000. The Office of Technology Assessment (OTA) (1986) concluded:

> Displacement can be devastating for communities and regions as
> well as individuals....Large losses of employment have ripple effects
> in the community. A large layoff in one industry also affects workers
> in supplier industries and workers in local service establishments
> when laid-off workers reduce spending. (p. 10)

Affected communities lose payroll taxes, property taxes, and even chari-
table contributions as demands increase sharply for assistance and social
services.

Research findings by Brenner (1973), Marshall and Funch (1979),
Catalano and Dooley (1977, 1979), and Dooley et al. (1981) suggest that
there is a relationship between unemployment rates for some unit (e.g., a
county) and the psychological well-being of the general population (e.g.,
admissions to state mental hospitals, reported rates of depression in samples
of unhospitalized persons).

This relationship was demonstrated in Monticello, Indiana, where
increases in demand for Aid to Families with Dependent Children, food
stamps, and child welfare services were accompanied by adverse effects on
community mental health, reflected in increased rates of depression, anxiety, alcoholism, and emotional disability. Health personnel also reported more
headaches, smoking, and stomach problems. Social integration was weakened, and residents appeared alienated, detached, and distrustful of social
institutions. Many left family, friends, and neighbors to seek employment elsewhere. Others found work locally, but suffered major salary reductions, reduced benefits, lowered living standards, and decreased social status.

Plant closures and similar sudden changes, which are expected to
continue, are dramatic events which attract considerable media and political attention. Local, state, and federal governmental units may join with
private forces to forestall or delay a closure, reopen a plant or attract new
industry, counsel displaced workers and families, provide unemployment
insurance and other benefits such as food stamps and commodities, and
provide education, training, and relocation assistance. Social workers may
do many things, including crisis intervention, program administration, or
development of policy initiatives.

The farm crisis, an important component of the overall rural crisis, has
an impact upon individuals, families, and communities, but with significant, qualitative differences deserving attention. Thomas Jefferson saw
national strength as based on agrarian life, with extended families and
stable communities in close relationship with the soil. And, in fact, most
Americans resided in rural areas and farmed for many decades. This
relationship with the land evolved into a heritage and culture that was
more a way of life than an occupation.

Many farm families had acquired land from the English Crown, through
a Spanish land grant, as a reward for military service or even by home-
steading in the West. Generations poured their blood, sweat, and tears into
cultivating, nurturing, and being sustained by the earth. Women gave birth

at home and the dead were buried in the family cemetery. Farm families faced many enemies, including Native Americans, English, French, Spanish, and Yankees, as well as depressions, floods, droughts, locusts, and boll weevils. Many viewed the family farm as a generational bond–a sacred trust to be defended and maintained at all costs.

Losing the farm–and breaking that trust–became a common phenomenon in the 1980s. The causes and deleterious effects of the farm crisis received considerable attention and documentation from social workers and related professionals. Herrick (1986) identified contributing factors such as lower agricultural prices from overproduction, reduced international demand due to a world recession, plunging land values, high interest rates, high costs of farm equipment and supplies, declining numbers of farm workers, and lack of safety net programs such as unemployment compensation. Many farmers who had borrowed heavily on their inflated land values found that this debt exceeded the now-deflated value of the land. Hundreds of thousands of American farmers had debt loads of more than 70% of their assets– the threshold at which the U.S. government estimates that bankruptcy is inevitable.

The economic bloodletting of widespread farm failures had profound human consequences. Mermelstein and Sundet (1986) surveyed 50 mental health centers in 12 Midwestern states and found that 64% experienced a moderate to very large increase in dysfunctioning in their communities, while only 15% indicated no increase and 20% saw a slight increase. Presenting problems included: depression, withdrawal/denial, crisis behaviors, substance abuse, spouse abuse, psychosomatic responses, suicide, and psychosis. Clinicians indicated that up to one half of their clients suffered problems related to the agricultural crisis.

These findings were confirmed by social workers at local, state, regional, and national conferences, especially the National Institutes on Social Work in Rural Areas, sponsored by the Rural Social Work Caucus. The National Association of Social Workers surveyed the national scene and in a feature article in *NASW News* ("Social workers aid," 1985) concluded that:

> Emotionally, financially, sociologically, farm families are in crisis.
> The stress has become so great on rural communities that it is having an effect on all categories of psychological indices. Rural areas have seen rises in child abuse and neglect cases, divorce rates, suicides, and the demand for mental health counseling. (p. 3)

Social workers were involved in a wide variety of roles and activities: educating the country through such national media as the *New York Times, NBC Nightly News,* and the *Phil Donahue Show;* starting support groups for farm wives, husbands, and children; planning community forums; leading task forces; training clergy and others; developing farm crisis hot lines and directories of service; retraining and relocating displaced farmers; lobbying for needed services; advocating for desperately needed action; and organizing and/or participating in coalitions and networking.

In short, many "tried and true" social work methods and skills have been employed in addressing the farm crisis. Good social work is good social work anywhere, and good social workers consider culture, constituencies, contexts, and locality-relevant practice. For example, most clinical social workers understand stress and use stress inventories. But a rural social worker uses a "farm stress inventory," which measures the stress from such events as insect infestation, loss of a prize bull, or crop loss from hail, and so is in a better position to understand and help the rural client.

Most clinical social workers know that change and loss may require grief work. However, social workers such as Zeller (1986), who know that losing a way of life is more traumatic than simply losing a job, usually do a better job of establishing rapport and assisting the farmer through a crisis. Finally, good social workers are used to organizing and working in coalitions to effect change. The social worker in a rural locale may join forces with agricultural organizations and farm groups unfamiliar to most urban social workers, even though some of these groups may have opposed other human service initiatives favored by most social workers. Social workers recognize that their common goal must be to help this particular client group and not to "even the score" with these groups for previous sins, whether real or imaginary.

While the authors and many other rural social workers wish otherwise, the reduction in the numbers of family farms and farmers will continue, according to most authorities. Indeed, the litany of factors contributing to rural community decline is long and could get longer. Coping with such transitions should be a primary goal of social work.

## Boom Towns and Rapidly Growing Communities

While the preceding section focused upon transitional communities in decline, rural America has many other communities experiencing social problems from rapid growth. The world's energy crisis of the 1970s and early 1980s resulted in thousands of boom towns as corporations exploited coal, oil, uranium, and hydroelectric resources, while they experimented with oil shale, tar sands, geothermal plants, and solar farms. The attention devoted to and knowledge gained from energy boom towns increased awareness of other forces contributing to growth.

Military expenditures on new facilities, such as the MX system in Cheyenne, Wyoming, and the Trident submarine base at King's Bay, Georgia, required thousands of construction workers, followed by defense personnel. Rural areas also attracted nuclear waste disposal sites, toxic waste sites, and general waste disposal operations as urban America sought to dispose of its garbage. Poor areas, especially Native American reservations, had the lure of jobs and dollars waved in front of them.

Dozens of small towns, such as Boaz, Alabama, have been revitalized by developing outlet malls featuring name brands at discount prices. Major manufacturers insist that these outlets be placed in rural areas in order to avoid competition with urban retailers.

Other towns have benefited from emphasis on their entertainment, recreational, and historic resources. Branson, Missouri, an erstwhile sleepy crossroads, now challenges Nashville for country music supremacy. The Colorado Rockies are full of old mining communities that are now bustling ski resorts. And while Colonial Williamsburg, Virginia, may be an extreme example, many historic communities attract tourists to their sites, hotels, bed-and-breakfasts, restaurants, tours, and gift shops.

Numerous hamlets and villages near urban areas have become "bedroom communities" for people who are employed in cities but wish to escape urban problems such as crime, congestion, pollution, and high taxes. This trend should continue, and probably accelerate, as inner cities lose population, edge cities develop, and more people are able to live even further out in the country. Another increasingly important development is the location of retirement communities in rural environments. Retirees who once thought of Miami or other urban centers now take their pensions and savings to mountain meccas in the Ozarks, north Georgia, and the Carolinas. Their general affluence and need for services make them increasingly appealing to economic developers and small-town planners.

Location of public and private institutions, such as correctional, rehabilitation, educational, and psychiatric facilities, may also pump energy and life into a dormant locale. And while plant closures generate attention, many small towns are managing to attract and/or develop new industries. Attracting BMW to South Carolina, Toyota to Kentucky, and Saturn to Tennessee provides thousands of automobile jobs, plus thousands of jobs in support services. Areas which are dependent on agricultural and lumber resources may prosper if they develop finished products such as canned goods and furniture. Changing market conditions and mechanization of farm jobs may cost jobs, but creative alternatives, such as the burgeoning labor-intensive catfish industry in the Mississippi Delta, may also provide new opportunities for growth. Catfish must be raised, fed, harvested, dressed, packaged, and transported. All of these elements provide jobs, as does the need for accountants, attorneys, public relations specialists, market experts, and a host of others.

These examples are illustrative, rather than comprehensive, but they do counter the common belief that all of rural America is in decline. They also should provide a degree of hope and some ideas for economic revitalization. Considering the severe socioeconomic consequences of decline, one might legitimately wonder if growth should not be viewed as a panacea. However, social work's experiences with rapidly growing communities in the 1970s and 1980s provided evidence that boom-town conditions could be just as damaging to the social fabric as decline.

The Denver Research Institute (1974) concluded that a small town could accommodate a 5% increase in growth. But they also concluded that an annual growth rate of 10% strains local service capabilities, while a 15% growth rate seems to cause breakdowns in local and regional institutions. Cortese and Jones (1977) defined the boom town as "the rapid and extreme growth of population in communities adjacent to mines and construction sites" (p. 76), while Weisz (1979) described "a community which is undergoing rapid growth and rapid change" (p. 2). Davenport and Davenport (1981) posited that a boom town is:

1. a community experiencing above average economic and population growth,
2. which results in benefits for the community (e.g., expanded tax base, increased employment opportunities, social and cultural diversity),
3. but which also places or results in strain on existing community and societal institutions (e.g., familial, educational, political, economic). (p. 144)

These problems were documented by a plethora of authors from social work and related disciplines. Bates (1977), in looking at the "people problems" of Western boom towns, found that "frontier expansions" were consistent in their crass, unplanned development, and that boom town results

> seem always to leave in their wake the grim statistics of spiritual depression, family disorganization, emotional damage and alcoholism, impaired social development of children, delinquency, suicide, dissipation and death. (p. 55)

Hanks, Miller, and Uhlman (1977) described the sociophysical problems resulting from impact as:

> superinflation by which the already critical national inflation is exacerbated with the special added inflation of boom towns arising from high labor costs, shortages (such as in housing and shopping facilities and services), and quick-buck exploitation by "get-rich" entrepreneurs: the inundation of demands from the markedly increased population on government and related facilities and services, such as law enforcement, courts, streets, sewers, schools, hospitals, retailers and supportive business services and all social services, such as mental health, welfare, senior citizen programs, vocational rehabilitation, employment services and Social Security District services. (p. 3)

E. V. Kohrs (1974), a social scientist and clinical director of the Central Wyoming Counseling Center in Casper, Wyoming, provided a graphic description of life in a boom town and the resulting sociobehavioral consequences. Kohrs's coining of the phrase "Gillette Syndrome" was derived from the problems he observed in Gillette, Wyoming-a town which experienced an oil boom followed by massive development of coal. The phrase became a fixture in the lexicon of boom town researchers, as did "trailer trash," a term for residents of trailer parks, "aluminum ghetto," a description of the trailer park itself, and "boom town bifurcation," a term describing the tensions and differences between old-timers and newcomers (Davenport and Davenport, 1981).

Weisz (1979) clarified the nature of these problems by applying to Gillette a community stress profile, based on the Holmes Rahe Social Readjustment Rating Scale (SRRS). He discovered an extremely high percentage of people experiencing major stressors from life changes affecting finances, places of residence, living conditions, and work hours or conditions. Major community stressors included cost of living, traffic and congestion, medical services, and overworked city services. As expected, these high stress rates were correlated with high rates of health and mental health problems.

Ayers, Farley, and Griffiths (1987) compared rapid growth in energy boom towns with recreational development boom towns. They discovered similar problems. Seventy-nine percent of their respondents believed that rapid growth had diminished the quality of life in their community, and 44% believed that the stress had been detrimental. The most prevalent problems were alcohol and drug abuse, family problems, and depression.

As might be expected, social workers assumed many roles and performed diverse functions in addressing rapid-growth problems. Social workers in public welfare departments, community mental health centers, and schools met the problems head-on and provided graphic descriptions of the human toll in the boom town maelstrom. Overwhelmed workers performed advocacy and linkage activities, delivered individual and group therapy, established support groups and new programs, and tried desperately to plan and coordinate, using newly formed planning mechanisms that replaced the informal structures of an earlier, quieter time. Social work assistance also came from state and federal agencies, energy company impact programs, and universities.

The Wyoming Human Services Project (WHSP) (Davenport & Davenport, 1979a, 1979b, 1980), funded by the National Institute of Mental Health and operated by the University of Wyoming Department of Social Work, became a model for the United States, Canada, and many other countries. The WHSP used multidisciplinary faculty to train multidisciplinary teams from 23 disciplines. Impacted communities used tax revenues, energy company money, and other resources to fund time-limited teams to relieve overburdened service personnel and, most importantly, to spend 50% of their time on community organization and development functions. As the WHSP gained experience with boom towns, it became a center with formal and informal functions, including: training, research, planning, coordination, publication, consultation and education, advocacy, and policy. It also served as a library and clearinghouse, especially for the American and Canadian Rocky Mountain West.

## Other Types of Transitional Communities

While many rural communities experience transitions caused by rapid population growth or decline, other areas may face different kinds of change. For example, until the civil rights movement of the 1960s and 1970s, many southern communities maintained a strict system of segregation with whites holding complete economic, political, and social control. Civil rights legislation, especially the Voting Rights Act, resulted in profound changes in such places as Fayette and Port Gibson, Mississippi, which had African-American majorities of better than 80%.

White politicians, who sometimes possessed political legacies of generations, and county or municipal employees were often replaced with newly enfranchised African Americans. Social roles and statuses changed overnight. The educational system experienced integration with conflict and eventual accommodation, although resegregation often appeared as whites left public schools and flocked to private academies. While African Americans have benefited economically from integration of public institutions, whites still control most businesses, property, and wealth. Social relationships between the groups appear strongest in business and employment environments and weakest in individual and family socializing.

Such changes in basic social institutions and the upheaval in individual, family, and community life should provide a fertile field for social work intervention. Anecdotal evidence suggests that social workers have assumed roles in school desegregation programs, conflict-resolution measures, community forums and educational campaigns, interagency planning, and counseling on individual concerns. However, race relations remains curiously under-researched in rural social work and deserves further analysis.

Some declining or stagnating rural locales may become rejuvenated with the infusion of relatively affluent older people with pensions, savings, and health insurance. The population may stabilize or grow gradually, but the composition and nature of the population may necessitate change. Production and extraction jobs in agriculture, forestry, and mining often give way to service jobs in health and gerontology. These jobs provide opportunities, although they often require education and training. Community planning is essential if locales are to maximize their chances for growth. Existing service personnel, such as social workers in community mental health centers, must prepare for the needs of a different population; and the overall health requirements of the older group will call for the recruitment of additional health personnel with gerontological backgrounds. Some cultural change and even conflict should be anticipated, especially if the retirees have urban backgrounds and different ethnic or religious affiliations. However, well-educated retirees are valuable assets, especially in community projects needing able volunteers. Many small communities view such transitions as highly desirable and promote them as important parts of their economic development plan. Of course, not all rural communities have this option since older people frequently look for pleasant areas such as the Ozarks or the mountains of north Georgia.

Other rural communities attempt to diversify their economic bas through development of recreational and resort attractions. Matsuak and Shera (1991) investigated the impact of such development on the island of Lana'i in Hawaii and found that residents, while expressing some ambivalence, were generally supportive of change. Concerns focused on loss of culture and heritage; increased crime, living costs, an alcohol and drug problems; and fear of "top-down" direction by outside management interests.

Residents placed strong emphasis on "controlled growth on their terms." Specific actions recommended by Matsuaka and Shera included community-based economic development, enhancement of sociocultural cohesion, monitoring of social impacts over time, comprehensive social planning, and independent community decision making. Such decision making could be through a community development corporation or similar entity which could also negotiate for needed resources with corporations, county and state agencies, and legislatures.

## Strategies for Coping with Transitions

The previous sections have described the experiences and consequences of sudden change on small towns and rural locales and the roles and functions of social workers in assisting communities to cope with these transitions. This section will focus on management strategies for mitigating the impact of such change.

While many professions (e.g., planning, psychology, economics, sociology) are involved with transitional communities, social work seems uniquely qualified for this task. Most disciplines have a somewhat narrow orientation, which makes it difficult for them to see "the big picture." Social work's generalist framework and ecosystems perspective allows for analysis of all levels and systems affected by change. Since change usually affects all aspects of community life, social work's problem solving approach enables it to enhance social functioning and prevent social dysfunctioning among individual, family, group, and community units.

Social work's integrated approach encompasses especially useful theoretical material from sociology and psychology. The impact of sudden change on social structures, roles, and relationships is best understood through the research of such sociologists as Cortese and Jones (1977), Little (1977), and Freudenburg (1984). Psychologists such as Weisz (1979, 1980) delineate how stress theory can be applied to the disruptions of communities in upheaval. Social work intervention that is based on such theoretical frameworks is more likely to succeed.

One of the more useful tools for social workers is the *Social Service Field Guide: Management Strategies for Mitigating Population Impact* by Farley et al. (1985). This document provides an extensive bibliography, which should be reviewed by those interested in transitional communities. The authors of the study reviewed this literature and distilled eight management categories. Then, they conducted research involving 38 social service professionals and 106 community leaders from five counties. One county was experiencing rapid growth, two were enjoying stable environments, and two were struggling with decline. This group examined 15 to 60 specific management strategies for each management category and selected the top 5 strategies, according to importance and usefulness. These categories and strategies are listed in Figure 1.

Social workers interested in additional strategies and program ideas should refer to the Utah study. Each management category lists another five strategies of lower priority, which, since communities differ, might be of higher priority in other areas of the country. Although these strategies are illustrative

### *Figure 1.* Effective Management Strategies for Transitional Communities

I. Data Collection and Utilization
  - Collect data on individuals, groups, classes, and seminars according to types of services provided and number of clients served.
  - Report all service data to the public through an association of governments.
  - Compare growth in service demands to population shifts.
  - Obtain and use data from industry in making service projections.
  - Monitor growth in service demands as any new industry begins its start-up process.

II. Planning
  - Consider community values in planning.
  - Communicate agency needs to county government.
  - Communicate agency needs to state government.
  - Work with county commissioners to coordinate and plan for human services.
  - Utilize prevention planning, especially for high-risk populations.

III. Funding
  - Write special grant proposals for private and government agency support.
  - Use statistical information to support funding needs.
  - Have regular planned meetings with state and local government officials to present needs and request funding.
  - Monitor ongoing funding needs in the agency.
  - Utilize needs assessment and program evaluation data to support funding requests.

IV. Staff Support
  - Use in-house staff support through regular case staffings.
  - Communicate appreciation to staff and acknowledge work done well.
  - Utilize in-house staff support through group training sessions.
  - Emphasize the hiring of experienced staff.
  - Provide flexible or individual staff scheduling

V. Service Coordination
  - Utilize the co-location of agencies to facilitate service coordination between agencies.
  - Utilize a voluntary human service council for information sharing.
  - Utilize an interagency directors'council to coordinate services between agencies.
  - Utilize child protection teams to coordinate services between agencies.
  - Utilize an association of governments to sponsor human service committees to make recommendations for coordinating resource allocation.

VI. Client Access to Services
  - Use on-call duty rotation for after-hours client contact.

(continued next page)

and suggestive, rather than comprehensive and directive, their primary value stems from their source: they come from professionals and community leaders actually in rural communities, as opposed to "outside experts." This detailed list of management strategies has proven effective in transitional communities. Since rural communities are dynamic, with periods of relative stability, social work should expect transitions and prepare for them accordingly.

## References

Ayers, M., Farley, O. W., & Griffiths, K. A. (1987). Stress in a rural rapid-growth recreational-development community. *Human Services in the Rural Environment, 10*(3), 24-28.

Bates, V. E. (1977). The rural impact of energy development: Implications for social work practice. In R. K. Green & S. A. Webster (Eds.), *Social work in rural areas: Preparation and practice* (pp. 54-72). Knoxville, TN: University of Tennessee School of Social Work.

Brenner, M. H. (1973). *Mental illness and the economy.* Cambridge, MA: Harvard University Press.

Catalano, R., & Dooley, D. (1977). Economic predictors of depressed mood and stressful events in a metropolitan community. *Journal of Health and Social Behavior, 18*, 292-307.

Catalano, R., & Dooley, D. (1979). Does economic change provoke or uncover behavioral disorder? A preliminary test. In L. A. Ferman & J. P. Gordus (Eds.), *Mental health and the economy* (pp. 341-346). Kalamazoo, MI: Upjohn Institute for Employment Research.

*Figure 1.* **Effective Management Strategies for Transitional Communities   (continued)**

---

- Co-locate with other human service agencies.
- Provide marriage and family counseling.
- Make home visits.
- Create an information and referral system within the community.

VII. Special Agency Services
- Provide individual therapy.
- Implement a crisis line.
- Initiate preschool programs for the developmentally disabled.
- Provide outpatient therapy to victims and perpetrators of domestic violence.
- Provide family therapy for spouse abuse.

VIII. Community Consultation and Education
- Utilize advisory boards of citizens, politicians, and human services providers.
- Develop educational programs in parenting skills.
- Develop educational programs in communication skills.
- Encourage multipurpose use of social service and recreational facilities.
- Develop educational programs in stress management.

---

Source: *Social Service Field Guide: Management Strategies for Mitigating Population Impact* (1985).

Cortese, C. F., & Jones, B. (1977). The sociological analysis of boom towns. *Western Sociological Review*, *8*(1), 76-90.

Craypo, C. (1 984). The deindustrialization of a factory town: Plant closings and phasedowns in South Bend, Indiana, 1954–1983. In D. Kennedy (Ed.), *Labor and reindustrialization: Workers and corporate change* (pp. 27-67). University Park, PA: Pennsylvania State University.

Davenport, J. A., & Davenport, J., III (Eds.). (1979a). *Boom towns and human services*. Laramie: University of Wyoming Press.

Davenport, J. A., & Davenport, J., III. (1979b). The Wyoming Human Services Project: A model for overcoming the hugger-mugger of boom towns. In U.S. Commission on Civil Rights (Ed.), *Energy resource development* (pp. 32-41). Washington, D.C.: U.S. Government Printing Office.

Davenport, J., III, & Davenport, J. A. (1980). *The boom town: Problems and promises in the energy vortex*. Laramie: University of Wyoming Press.

Davenport, J. A., & Davenport, J., III (Eds.). (1981). *The human side of energy*. Laramie: University of Wyoming Press.

Davenport, J. A., & Davenport, J., III (Eds.). (1988). Special issue on the rural renaissance. *Human Services in the Rural Environment*, *11* (4), 1-48.

Denver Research Institute. (1974). *A growth management case study: Sweetwater County, Wyoming*. Denver, CO: Denver Research Institute.

Dooley, D., Catalano, R., Jackson, R., & Brownwill, A. (1981). Economic, life, and symptom changes in a nonmetropolitan community. *Journal of Health and Social Behavior*, 22, 144-154.

Farley, O. W., Jorgensen, L. B., Griffiths, K. A., & Chidester, F. M. (1985). *Social service field guide: Management strategies for mitigating population impact*. Salt Lake City, UT: University of Utah Graduate School of Social Work.

Freudenburg, W. R. (1984). Differential impacts of rapid community growth. *American Sociological Review*, *49*(5), 697-705.

Hanks, J. W., Miller, K. A., & Uhlmann, J. M. (1977). *Boom town inter-disciplinary human services project*. Paper presented to the Fifth Biennial Professional Symposium of the National Association of Social Workers, San Diego, CA.

Herrick, J. M. (1986). Farmers revolt! Contemporary farmers' protests in historical perspec tive: Implications for social work practice. *Human Services in the Rural Environment*, *10*(1), 6-11.

Hogarth, J. M., & McGonigal, J. W. (1989). The New York farm net experience: A program model for rural areas. *Human Services in the Rural Environment*, *12*(3), 22-27.

Kohrs, E. V. (1974). *Social consequences of boom growth in Wyoming*. Paper presented at the meeting of the Rocky Mountain American Association of the Advancement of Science, Laramie, WY.

Little, R. L. (1977). Some social consequences of boom towns. *North Dakota Law Review*, *52*(3), 410-425.

Marshall, J. R., & Funch, D. P. (1979). Mental illness and the economy: A critique and partia replication. *Journal of Health and Social Behavior*, *20*, 282-289.

Matsuoka, J. K., & Shera, W. J. (1991). The impact of resort development on an Hawaiian island: Implications for community preservation. *Human Services in the Rural Environment,* *15*(1), 5-9.

Mermelstein, J., & Sundet, P. (1986). Rural community mental health centers'responses to the farm crisis. *Human Services in the Rural Environment,* *10*(1), 21-26.

Office of Technology Assessment. (1986). *Technology and structural unemployment: Reemploying displaced adults.* Washington, D.C.: Congress of the United States.

Perrucci, C. C., Perrucci, R., Targ, D. B., & Targ, H. R. (1988). *Plant closings: International context and social cost.* New York: Aldine DeGruyter.

Social workers aid harried farm families. (1985). *NASW News, 30*(5), 3-5.

Weisz, R. (1979). Stress and mental health in a boom town. In J. A. Davenport & J. Davenport, III (Eds.), *Boom towns and human services* (pp. 31-48). Laramie: University of Wyoming Press.

Weisz, R. (1980). Coping with the stress of a boom: Mental health alternatives for impacted communities. In J. Davenport, III & J. A. Davenport (Eds.), *The boom town: Problems and promises in the energy vortex* (pp. 43-54). Laramie: University of Wyoming Press.

Zeller, S. N. (1986). Grieving for the family farm. *Human Services in the Rural Environment, 10*(1), 27-29.

# 5

# Dual Relationships in Rural Practice: A Dilemma of Ethics and Culture

by Pamela J. Miller

*The National Association of Social Workers (NASW) added language about nonsexual dual relationships to its code of ethics effective July 1, 1994. This change sparked controversy for rural practitioners, advocates, and academics. This article describes the history of the changes in the code and addresses the inconsistencies between state licensing standards and the NASW code of ethics. There is little research on dual relationships from a rural perspective. The uniqueness of rural and culturally sensitive practice is discussed through context and theoretical orientation. The implications for social work education are delineated and a case example is provided.*

Through the 1993 Delegate Assembly of the National Association of Social Workers, several changes were made in the Code of Ethics. Some of the changes addressed professional conduct and ethical responsibility to colleagues. New language about dual relationships was added to Section II of the Code which states that "The social worker should not condone or engage in any dual or multiple relationships with clients or former clients in which there is a risk of exploitation of or potential harm to the client. The social worker is responsible for setting clear, appropriate, and culturally sensitive boundaries" (p. 5, II.F.4, NASW Code of Ethics, 1994).

The new language poses some dilemmas for social workers who practice in rural areas. Dual relationships in rural settings are hard to avoid since options for all services are limited and often professional social workers are very involved in their communities. This article describes how language about dual relationships entered the social work code of ethics and how individual state licensing standards may differ from the national code. The article focuses on the potential impacts of the new language in the code on nonsexual dual relationships, and does not include a discussion of sexual dual relationships. Culturally sensitive practice in the rural

Reprinted from *Human Services in the Rural Environment* (Fall 1994), with permission of the Eastern Washington School of Social Work and Human Services.

context is discussed through theoretical orientation. The implications of dual relationships in rural practice for social work education are delineated and a case example is provided.

Little research exists on dual relationships in general and there is even less information on rural practice issues in particular. Most of what is available casts a negative light on dual relationships and discourages their development. However, this perspective on dual relationshps has been developed in an urban context. In rural practice, dual relationships are unavoidable and sometimes beneficial. This ethical dilemma poses cultural and contextual overtones which are not easily dismissed.

## Brief History

NASW decided that the profession of social work needed to address nonsexual dual relationships because many questions and possible violations of ethical conduct appeared to stem from this concept. The California Chapter took the lead in the desire for language and action about ethical standards and dual relationships. In 1992, the Board of Directors of NASW appointed an ad hoc Code of Ethics Review Task Force to analyze the code of ethics and formulate new language about dual relationships. The code of ethics at that time did not provide either practice guidelines or a basis for legal action when a dual relationship complaint was brought against a practitioner. This committee was composed of three scholars on social work ethics and the Chair of the National Committee on Inquiry. Their recommendations were forwarded to the 1993 Delegate Assembly.

The changes in the code were adopted by the 1993 Delegate Assembly, although there was much debate about whether dual relationships should be prohibited or discouraged. Dual relationships, as defined in the code, occur when a social worker has a second role or relationship with a client. This would also prohibit bartering or the exchange of goods as payment for services. Since the National Rural Social Work Caucus advocated for language which was less restrictive to those who practiced in rural communities, the wording of the code discourages dual relationships but does not prohibit them (NASW News, p. 7, October 1993).

## State Licensure

Individual states have laws and ethical codes which guide their licensed professionals. Social work currently has legal regulation in all 50 states and 32 states have vendorship (Evans, 1995). Licensure rules, regulations and/ or vendorship may at times differ or even conflict with the NASW Code of Ethics. Some state licensing rules may be more restrictive about nonsexual dual relationships and this disparity may also affect rural social work practice and provide more ethical dilemmas for both worker and client(s).

As an example, the Oregon LCSW rules state that a Licensed Clinical Social Worker (LCSW) cannot enter into any other relationship with a client until one year after the professional services were rendered. The rationale for this length of time is explained by the issues of power and transference. This rule is much more explicit than the National Code of Ethics on dual relationships. This is only one example of the difference between the broader National Code and the more specific Oregon guidelines for LCSW regulation. This contrast deepens the concern for how to handle the inevitable question of dual relationships in rural practice.

Since the professional social worker may operate under both national and state guidelines, it is imperative to know and understand both sets of ethical standards and conduct. This would include the need to incorporate not only how the national and state guidelines compliment each other, but also how they differ and to what extent. Practice decisions in a rural setting are influenced by many factors and both agency based and private practice social workers need to be aware of and balance ethical standards, risks, and professional judgment.

## Research Review

There is little research to guide social workers in relation to dual relationships in rural practice. Borys and Pope (1989) are probably most cited in the research on dual relationships. Their study involved psychologists, psychiatrists and social workers from around the nation. In general, male respondents tended to rate social or financial dual relationships as more ethical and engaged in this type of behavior more than the female subjects. The other finding was that men tended to enter into nonsexual dual relationships more with female clients than with male clients. Fifteen percent of the subjects believed it would never be ethical to become friends with a former client. An overall finding was that social workers and psychologists rated nonsexual dual relationships as more ethical than did psychiatrists.

Ramsdell & Ramsdell (1993) conducted a study about client and counselor behaviors and their impact on therapy. This was an urban based study which surveyed clients rather than professionals and asked questions about contact across a range of behaviors and the effect this behavior could have on therapy outcomes. The subjects were asked to give their opinion, not reveal what specifically happened to them in counseling. Three behaviors were thought to be potentially helpful: using the counselor's first name, visiting the client while hospitalized, and the professional's willingness to share personal information. The behaviors found to be possibly harmful to the professional relationship were dating, visiting in the professional's home, employing the client, and going out for recreation. The authors list their methodology problems with the research design although their efforts to study the effects of dual relationships from the client's perspective is admirable.

Kagle & Giebelhausen (1994) offer an overview of dual relationships in their recent *Social Work* article. Although the article contains a good literature review and offers some practice issues and recommendations for training in this area, the overall tone of the article is that dual relationships are harmful and must always be avoided. This would appear to ignore not only theoretical and cultural issues but also sensitive, contextual rural practice. An across the board rejection of dual relationships will not make this ethical dilemma go away. In light of current theoretical bases and the unique context of rural social work, dual relationships will exist.

## The Realities of Rural Practice

When we think about rural generalist practice, the concepts of high visibility, multiple community roles within multiple systems and access to individuals and organizations become tools for entry and change. Josephine C. Brown in her 1933 book *The Rural Community and Social Case Work* states that the social worker's "contact with people in a rural community is much closer than it is in a city. The people among whom she (sic) works will seek first to know her (sic) as a person... willing to drop all formality...able to become a part of the community in which she (sic) lives" (p. 69). These points are well-taken even in today's thinking about rural practice.

Theoretical foundations have also changed over the years away from psychodynamic models to those of systems, strengths, advocacy and empowerment. Feminist theory has also had an impact on rural social work (Mermelstein, 1991). This shift has decreased the power and social distance between social worker and client. It has become more educationally acceptable to teach and discuss self-disclosure and integration into community. These theoretical concepts have been a part of rural social work practice for some time (urban models took some time to catch up). The point is that dual relationships may be a part of the complexity involved when working with people rather than professional indiscretion (Bograd, 1992). The problem may not be dual relationships but inadequate and unskilled social workers.

The distinction between social, individual, and professional boundaries quickly becomes blurry to those who practice in rural communities. What the social work professional does at work, buys at the grocery, and even where he or she lives becomes general knowledge to former, current and future clients. The analogy of rural practice in a fish bowl rings true.

Urban rules for practice may not apply in rural settings. For assistance with problems, many rural people turn to clergy, family or friends (Waltman, 1986). Professional helpers or agencies are often contacted as a last resort. Since many families may have lived in an area for three or four generations, informal help seems more acceptable.

There are many dilemmas the rural practitioner must face. How does one keep social and professional relationships separate or distinct? What is the risk involved in working with someone about whom the practitioner knows through community involvement? How will confidentiality hold up? Are there issues of informed consent or conflict of interest (Kutchins, 1991)? What does the worker do when a client(s) is seen at the store? What are the risks of a dual relationship? What if the client cannot afford to pay for a service but very much wants to donate a service or product to either the social worker or the community?

The dilemma of bartering for goods or services is very tricky and unique. Since overall poverty rates tend to be higher in rural communities, it is sometimes possible that a client cannot pay for a service and receiving a service for free may not be acceptable. However, one culturally acceptable alternative is the exchange of goods or services in lieu of payment. Bartering has been a part of rural culture for a very long time. So it seems natural to utilize this method of payment for professional services as well. The exchange could involve farm products, a service that benefits the professional, or the provision of a community service. This is a very individualized process and definitely involves boundaries for both the client and the social worker (Dean & Rhodes, 1992). The issues of exploitation and fairness must be addressed. At a recent conference on ethics, one rural practitioner described his experiences with bartering as generally positive. Another stated that she participated in bartering but would not discuss it. A third rural practitioner said she never does it. So, the prevalence of this type of payment is unknown. However, culturally it is sometimes appropriate and ethically there are risks. One unfortunate side effect of the new code is that some social workers who previously participated in bartering may now decide it is too precarious. This may have some long term effects on rural needs.

## Teaching and Training

Many would agree that more time must be spent on the ethical issue of dual relationships, both in the classroom and the field. Students and practitioners need time to explore this idea and reflect on the implications for professional judgment (Holland & Kilpatrick, 1991). Students, professionals and supervisors need a safe place to share their ideas and feelings about dual relationships and make decisions for future action. It seems that a blanket avoidance of dual relationships in rural practice is impossible. The question then becomes how to recognize and then deal with a dual relationship. Each situation will most likely need fresh thought and action. There is not one answer and there are no easy answers. In rural practice, this will be a perpetual balancing act.

Borys & Pope (1989) offer an excellent conclusion to their study that lists seven ethical principles.

- Above all, do no harm.
- Practice only with competence.
- Do not exploit.
- Treat people with respect for their dignity as human beings.
- Protect confidentiality.
- Act, except in the more extreme instances, only after obtaining informed consent.

- Practice, insofar as possible, within the framework of social equity and justice.

The authors stress the need for equal consent between client and professional. The vulnerability of the client as well as practitioner influence can make the client(s) susceptible to the power and authority of the social worker. These issues must be taken into consideration during client involvement when a dual relationship unfolds.

The unique context of rural social work practice furnishes a difficult practice setting. Could it be that rural social workers have to be even more diligent and skilled in order to be effective? The following case example is a real practice situation. It reveals many of the points described in this paper. The case and the questions that follow could be a good starting point for discussion about dual relationships in rural practice.

## Case Example

Mrs. X came into contact with a home health agency after a short hospital stay for congestive heart failure. Upon discharge from the hospital, home health services were ordered by Mrs. X's physician and social work consultation was part of the discharge plan.

Mrs. X, 81 years old, lived alone in a large, somewhat dilapidated, old two-story home. The home was in a very isolated area of the county and access by car was sometimes difficult. The house sat far back from the road on top of a large hill which overlooked the valley below. Mrs. X lived on the first floor of the house since the steps had posed some difficulties for at least two years. The first floor consisted of a large kitchen and the living room also served as a bedroom and bathroom.

The house had electricity, but there was only one light in the kitchen which hung from the ceiling and had to be pulled with some effort in order to be turned on. There was cold water only in the kitchen sink and a hot plate was used for cooking and heating food. The two rooms were heated with a small coal stove and Mrs. X used a bucket for toileting which she would then carry out to the outhouse, which stood about 50 feet behind the house.

Mrs. X was alert and oriented but quite hesitant to let anyone from the agency into her home. The first nursing visit was done through a crack in the door and Mrs. X allowed the nurse to examine her on the second visit—on the front porch! For the first social work visit, Mrs. X peered out of the door and eyed the worker and her vehicle for quite some time. When she discovered that all the social worker would do was "talk," she allowed her to enter her home and her life.

Mrs. X had done just fine in her home and felt very proud of her independence. She loved the view from the hilltop and often pretended that she owned all the land she could see from her vantage point. A neighbor looked in on her occasionally and brought her groceries. She rarely needed anything else. When the heart pains and swelling started,

Mrs. X found it increasingly difficult to take care of the coal stove and bathroom needs. Her neighbor took her to the hospital when she found Mrs. X sitting outside between the house and the outhouse.

Mrs. X and the social worker met over a period of weeks. Mrs. X described her life and history. She did not have any family in the area. As winter approached, she began to understand the dangers of staying alone in her own home. The coal stove was inadequate and hard to maintain. Heating water and cooking were becoming difficult. These chores made Mrs. X short of breath and also produced chest pains.

Mrs. X slowly warmed to the idea of temporarily moving into a boarding home until the worst of winter passed. She realized, however, that her income was inadequate to pay for two or three months of care. Mrs. X came up with the idea that she had some antiques in her upstairs rooms which she could sell and then use the money to pay for the boarding home. She could not however, tolerate selling them to "strangers" and asked the social worker, whom she now trusted, to buy them so that "I can know who has them and rest easier. They are very special things." The items were a dresser, a mirror (looking glass) and a clock.

This posed a dilemma for the social worker. Mrs. X adamantly refused to sell the items to anyone else. However, the payment for the three pieces could be enough to keep Mrs. X in the boarding home for three months of winter.

Questions:

- What might the social worker do?
- What are the cultural aspects of this case?
- If the social worker says no, what are some of the consequences?
- If the social worker says yes, what are some of the consequences?
- What is/are the dual relationship(s) in this case?
- How do you feel about this situation?

The social worker in this case faces a serious and complicated predicament. If she says yes and barters with Mrs. X., she could be found in violation of both national and/or state ethical codes for engagement in a dual relationship and possible exploitation. If she says no, the client might decide to remain in an unsafe situation and there would not be enough community resources to assure continued independent living. Since the home health agency would soon have to discharge the client, the social worker's refusal to bargain could be interpreted as abandonment. There are consequences to both the worker and client for either a yes or no on the decision to buy the client's furniture.

The social worker could get the items appraised to assure the payment to Mrs. X of fair market value. The social worker would certainly want to discuss this case with her supervisor and receive consultation and guidance about how to proceed. Community people, neighbors or other agency staff could hear about this situation and misunderstand its merits. Confidentiality and professional judgment could potentially come under serious question by some not directly involved.

This case points out that the social worker did an excellent job in establishing rapport and building trust with a client who had not let a stranger into her home for years. The result was the potential for a culturally sensitive intervention that might assure safety and also preserve self-determination and independence. However, the complexities of this case created an ethical dilemma within a cultural context. Practice which is culturally sensitive and empowers people should drive our assessments and interventions despite the risks involved.

Dual relationships may at times be a natural part of social work practice in rural communities. Practitioners may need to learn how to examine and sometimes even embrace the second relationship, particularly if it arises out of the essentials of culture. The dilemmas that may arise are real and precarious yet necessary to assure effective social work practice.

## References

Bograd, M. (1992). The duel over dual relationships. *Networker, 16*(6), November/December, 32-37.

Borys, D. S., & Pope, K. S. (1989). Dual relationships between therapist and client: A national study of psychologists, psychiatrists, and social workers. *Professional Psychology: Research and Practice, 20*(5), 283-293.

Brown, J. C. (1933). *The rural community and social case work.* New York: Family Welfare Association of America.

Dean, R. G., & Rhodes, M. L. (1992). Ethical-clinical tensions in clinical practice. *Social Work, 37*(2), 128-132.

Evans, M. (1995). Executive Director's Report. *NASW Newsletter, Oregon Chapter, 18*(1), 4-5.

Holland, T. P., & Kilpatrick, A. C. (1991). Ethical issues in social work: Toward a grounded theory of professional ethics. *Social Work, 36*(2), 138-144.

Kagle, J. D., & Giebelhausen, P. N. (1994). Dual relationships and professional boundaries. *Social Work, 39*(2), 213-220.

Kutchins, H. (1991). The fiduciary relationship: The legal basis for social workers' responsibilities to clients. *Social Work, 36*(2), 106-113.

Mermelstein, J. (1991). Feminist practice in rural communities. In M. Bricker-Jones, N. R. Hooyman, & N. Gottlieb (Eds.), *Feminist social practice in clinical settings* (pp. 147-171). New York: Sage.

Ramsdell, P. S., & Ramsdell, E. (1993). Dual relationships: Client perceptions of the effect of client-counselor relationship on the therapeutic process. *Clinical Social Work Journal, 21*(2), 195-212.

Waltman, G. H. (1986). Main street revisited: Social work practice in rural areas. *Social Casework,* October, 466-474.

# 6

# Rural Social Work Is an Anachronism: The Perspective of Twenty Years of Experience and Debate

by Joanne Mermelstein and Paul A. Sundet

Nineteen years ago a small band gathered in Knoxville to proclaim to the professional social work community the uniqueness of practice in the rural environment. There was an almost messianic zeal in that pioneer group who accepted a rural-urban dichotomy as an article of faith and whose mission, in light of it, was to empirically chart the rural landscape. The thesis was simple: A social profession is shaped by and must be responsive to the social needs of time and place in which it operates. Context matters. If the social structures and processes of rurality were, in fact, different than urban, then the practice of social work must be modified to fit that context.

Toward that end, the academics in the group began building a transmissible knowledge base for social work. Campbell and Webster (1977) refuted the myth of a rurality devoid of services; Ginsberg (1976) and Wayne Johnson (1980) edited textbooks focused on service delivery and practice differences; Martinez-Brawley published the history of rural social welfare (1981); and Buxton and Bast (1976) began printing the first rural human services journal.

The subsequent annual Social Work and Human Services in the Rural Environment conferences continued to stimulate research and analysis of programs and practice with "rural" defined, for the most part, by each individual analyst. The tenth anniversary, in Missouri, was a time to take stock of progress. Two entwined themes predominated.

On the one hand, the scholarship and sophistication of the rural social work movement had clearly advanced. But a disturbing note was sounded. Jacobsen, who had studied the history of rural social work (1987), pointed out that what had been initiated in Knoxville was not new. There had been an earlier incarnation of such a movement in the 1920s and 1930s which disappeared with the Great Depression as rural advocates lost faith

---

Reprinted from *Human Services in the Rural Environment* (Spring/Summer 1995), with permission of the Eastern Washington School of Social Work and Human Services.

in the premise of fundamental rural-urban differences. To explain this phenomena he quoted from Swanson's (1972) earlier analysis:

> In short, the belief in a fundamental rural-urban dichotomy, the belief upon which the whole idea of rural social work rested, disappeared among social workers. Rural social work lost its distinctiveness, quietly dropped its claim as a significant social work variation, and became social work in rural areas rather than rural social work.

Jacobsen (1987) concluded that with acceptance by non-rural social work leaders, the rural advocates began to address concerns other than the critical rural-urban differences and that the decline in debates and controversies also began the death of the specialization.

Five years later in Fredonia, New York, Martinez-Brawley's (1990) keynote address picked up on a variant of this theme to ask "Have we arrived?" She concluded we had not and of particular concern was the apparent failure of rural workers to truly honor a "community orientation" in their work.

Now, yet another five years have passed and it is again time to take stock, to chart the future and, even more critically, examine once again whether a unique niche remains for a specialty entitled "rural social work."

The current debate vis a vis the differences between rural and urban communities, to the extent that one is being carried on at all, seems to focus primarily upon issues of helping methodology, service delivery or, at most, social policy (Rank & Hirschl, 1987; Steblay, 1987; Whitaker, 1986; York, Denton & Moran, 1989). However, the more fundamental question which Jacobsen posed ten years ago remains, i.e., are there things so basically different about the urban and rural contexts that we can justify a specialty, a title, a journal, a special alcove in the halls of social work? Increasingly the evidence suggests "NO."

Much of the defense for this specialization is rooted in the concept of the rural-urban continuum contained in the classic sociological studies and governmental panel reports on rural communities and/or traditional societies such as Sanders (1958), Gans (1962), Copp (1964), Sanderson and Polson (1939), the President's Task Force (1970), the Advisory Commission on Rural Poverty (1967), Hicks (1947), Landis (1948), Vidich and Bensman (1958) and on and on. Those studies and reports have historical significance and, perhaps, are useful guides to some third-world countries but they have little relevance to the reality of 21st century America.

One can add to that venerable general list the locality-specific literature of the same era dealing with Appalachia, the "Old South," Plainville—even revisited—and Main Street. It, too, has little applicability in 1995.

## Definitions and Framework for Analysis

An unsentimental view of rural reality today begins with the definitional issue. Urban and rural are terms no longer used by social planners and policy makers. They have metamorphosed into metropolitan and non-metropolitan. But this is no semantic change.

Non-metro is now officially considered a residue, that is, whatever is left over after the census takers define metropolitan. Looking for the bright spot in such a far-reaching definition, Gilford and his colleagues (1981) note that the concept of rurality once had significant economic, social and political associations, but the non-metropolitan concept that has replaced it is primarily, though perhaps not totally, geographic: one of the still distinctive features of rural areas is the distances that separate the homes of rural people! Not so tongue-in-cheek, rural sociology professor Daryl Hobbs (1992, p. 25) suggests that "...rural is the 22% of the population that is less tightly squeezed together than the 78% that is termed metro."

Using the metro/non-metro concept, is there any unity to the latter beyond spaciousness? Well, Hilton Head, Aspen and Palm Springs are as rural as are Yellow Knife, Butcher Hollow and Dry Gulch using the definition of non-metro.

But what about lifestyle and community? Are there not still metro/non-metro distinctions? The straightforward paradigm of Roland Warren (1963, p.9) provides an appropriate framework for such analysis. He defines community as "...that combination of social units and systems which perform the major functions having locality relevance." There are five such functions: (1) production-distribution-consumption; (2) socialization; (3) social control; (4) social participation; and (5) mutual support.

## Rural-Urban Comparisons

### Production-Distribution-Consumption

When non-metro counties are classified according to the principle source of their economy, the concept of diversity is reinforced. In 1960, over 70% of all rural counties had agriculture as the primary industry. Now 36% of rural income derives from manufacturing in contrast to only 12% from farming and the majority of this is in the corporate, not the "family farm" sector (Henry, Drabenstott & Gibson, 1987). Eleven percent of the non-metro population lives in a county in which farming is the primary activity, less than those areas primarily dependent upon regional trade/service centers (16%) or government institutions (12%) and the same as those where the retirement industry is paramount (U.S. Census, 1992). Economic diversity affects lifestyle, social organization, social class structure, demographic composition and institutional stability.

For instance, there has been much talk about "reverse migration" into rural communities. However, even where that can be documented, it is not to farming-dependent rural counties, and "rural" is again misleading. Most farming-dependent communities across the nation are continuing to lose population as they have for years while retirement, trade, and commuting communities are growing (Falk & Lyson, 1988). The latter, although still technically and descriptively termed non-metro, have much more in common with coastal or sunbelt suburbia than they do with the once thriving, Great Plains county seats.

Twenty years ago, the locus of production and consumption in rural communities was largely in the immediate environment (town/township, county or adjacent community). A commonly accepted urban-rural difference was the degree of autonomy and independence enjoyed by the family farmer and small business person. Much effort in the rural social work movement in the past two decades has been devoted to maintaining that independence. Today, the locus has shifted almost entirely to the national and international levels, even in traditional agriculture. Translocal control of product, distribution, selection and pricing is evident in the industrial centralization process typified by Tyson and Archer-Daniels-Midland in agriculture and Walmart in retailing.

Consumer behavior in the non-metro world has been transformed by the great strides in communications and transportation, first into the mass society and more recently, into the global economy (Hobbs, 1992). More and more frequently, rural consumers make their purchases at the same shopping mall as their urban cousins, even if it is 75 or 100 miles from the old homestead.

Other commonalities between rural and urban in the economic sphere include the percentage of income derived from salary vs. self-employment, the percentage of women in the work force, the percentage of women with minor children in the work force, the average length of daily commute (measured in minutes) and percent of total income from transfer payments (Lichter & Costanzo, 1987).

In all these categories, the urban-rural differences were significant thirty-five years ago and at the least measurable at the time of our Knoxville gathering. Now they are all but indistinguishable from one another, and differences within non-metropolitan areas are greater than between these areas and metropolitan counties.

## Socialization

Socialization is concerned with the inculcation of values, attitudes and behavior patterns of individuals throughout the life cycle. The family is the traditional socialization agent of a society and it is augmented by other core community institutions, particularly the church and school.

Mass media, as part of the educational subsystem of a community, are influential culture carriers as well. As mentioned in consumer behavior, there are empirical data that demonstrate that non-metro people watch the same television shows, read the same newspapers, play the same movies on their home VCRs and attend the same cultural events in the nearest urban playhouse and art museum as their metro cousins (Hobbs, 1992; Reid, 1990). But twenty years ago, mass media and the information age were mediated by local community processes and institutions which reinforced local values (Flora, Flora, Spears, Swanson, Lapping & Weinberg,

1992; Lingeman, 1980). Does that happen today? The data suggest otherwise because of the changes in all the core rural institutions: family, church and school.

## Rural Family Changes

Beset by relentless economic pressures, the structure of the rural family first signals the major change. Many more rural women have joined the labor force, often in multiple part-time jobs (Gassen, 1988; Lichter, 1989). Non-metro unemployment rates now exceed metro (Lichter & Eggebeen, 1992) so many former wage earners, primarily male, are out of the work force. Marital quality has suffered from the cumulative effect of this stress while family efforts to adapt have often fallen short of the mark (D'Argemir, 1987; Johnson & Booth, 1990).

Fuguitt, Beale and Reibel (1991) report both rural and urban fertility rates have fallen since the 1960s and much of the difference between them has been eliminated. The remaining differences are attributable to a lower than average age of marriage in non-metro areas (Heaton, Lichter & Amoateng, 1989), and a marked difference in abortion rates.

Non-metro household composition changed between 1960-1990 with the absence of more fathers from the home. The percentage of non-metro children living with both parents declined from 90.9 to 79.9. In 1987, 30% of non-metro residents lived in female headed households while 45% of urban dwellers did (Bonnen, 1994; Lichter & Eggebeen, 1992) but the trend line is clear.

The changing family structure in the direction of urban trends has given substantial demographic impetus to the rise of child poverty in non-metro areas (Bedics, 1987; McLaughlin & Perman, 1991). Between 1980 and 1990, the poverty rate among non-metro children increased from 18.3 to 21.2% (Lichter & Eggebeen, 1992). O'Hare (1988) reported that rural poverty overall is increasing faster than central city poverty and there is a slightly higher incidence of poverty in non-metro areas than in the central cities of the United States (Lerman & Mikesell, 1989).

One striking indicator of the "residual community" (White, 1980) and the impact of outmigration on rural families is their ability to help their elderly members (Scheidt & Norris-Baker, 1989). Powers and Kivett (1992) reported that the amount of assistance received by older rural adults from all levels of kin was most strongly and frequently related to geographic proximity. Weekly help was provided by no more than 1/3 of adult children and much less by other kin. The moderate levels of support provided by these rural families is compatible with results from urban studies (Cicirelli, 1981; Seelbach, 1978; Seelbach & Sauer, 1977).

Like its urban counterpart, the rural family struggles to stabilize. It faces stressors that detract from its ability to socialize its members to traditional values and norms.

## The Rural School

Next in importance to the family as community socialization agent is the rural school which is also converging with urban models. Often the symbol of community identity in rurality, the school was central in the transmission of community values. Lowe and Pinhey (1980) found no attitudinal differences between rural and urban people on the value placed on formal education.

Down from 128,000 in 1930, there are approximately 15,600 school districts in the U.S. today. Rural districts account for about 3/4 of the total but serve only about 1/4 of the elementary and secondary students (Elder & Hobbs, 1990; Jess, 1985). Driven by the changing rural economy and federal and state laws mandating that schools treat all students fairly, both rural and urban schools have adopted an array of innovations that bridge earlier differences between them.

Cognizant of the need to prepare youth for social and employment mobility (Gimlin, 1990), rural curricular emphases, content and standards have changed substantially over the last two decades, and not without controversy (Smith, 1984). The introduction of computer technology has facilitated sophisticated individualized learning for students while satellite importation of some urban-originating coursework further expands school boundaries and resources (Barker & Garrett, 1987-88). The chronic finance shortfall in rural schools has motivated administrators to seek external grant funding with universal program requirements that further reduce rural-urban differences (Ward, 1988).

While the same social problems among youth have always existed in rural and urban areas, the degree of acknowledgment of those problems and their solutions often varied. Today, McGruff the dog (mascot and symbol for drug education), red ribbons (drug-free schools symbols) and school-provided baby nurseries are found in non-metro schools, often with the same fanfare and controversy as in their metro counterparts.

And the demographic characteristics of rural students have changed as well (Davidson, 1991; Fitchen, 1992; Knop & Jobes, 1988). With the influx of the metropolitan poor into Midwestern, non-metro, commuting counties and magnet counties housing prisons and drug rehabilitation facilities, rural schools are experiencing more racial and ethnic diversity in their student populations and many more disadvantaged and disturbed children (Robinson, 1990). Declining revenues from a diminishing tax base in rural districts and repeated school bond failures due both to the economy and the antipathy and alienation among community subgroups, have led to metropolitan-type solutions.

## The Rural Church

The rural church has not escaped massive social change either. Rathege and Goreham (1989) underscore that the church is challenged to respond to the changing rural environment as a requirement for survival. The in-migration into retirement communities and energy boomtowns has both enlarged and further stratified the membership, resulting in greater heterogeneity of values and alienation of some indigenous groups (Jobes, 1987; Koeberneck, 1986). Outmigration of residents in economically declining communities has robbed the church of the fiscal and human resources necessary to function as a socialization mechanism (Knop & Jobes, 1988). The middle-aged women who sustained church operations are in the work force and trying to hold the family together (Lichter, 1989). Elderly women who looked forward to enjoying the fruits of their earlier labors as they transferred responsibilities to their younger sisters, have been marginalized by the diminishing social supports the church can offer and its eroding gemeinschaft character (Krout, 1988; Scheidt & Norris-Baker, 1989). With smaller congregations to support a full-time pastor in these residual communities, imported, circuit-riding clergy are proliferating (Fitchen, 1991; White, 1980; Wilkerson, 1990). Such stress has lowered the average length of stay of a pastor in rural churches, frequently to less than two years. Without the pastor's physical presence in the community, its visibility and ultimately its authority as a socializing force is reduced. Thus, another rural institution edges toward the impersonality and narrowing of focus typically associated with metropolitan areas.

## Social Control

A third essential dynamic of community functioning, social control, was first conceptualized by Edward Ross, George Mead and August Hollingshead to explain the internal and external constraints that society needed to enforce as urban life became increasingly more impersonal. They, and subsequent theorists, pointed to an ever growing shift from self-imposed behavioral restraints to those provided by social agents, in particular officials of some sort, as characteristic of the industrialized urban population concentrations. They assumed that in the traditional rural environment, the shared values and primary group interaction were suffficient to produce norm enforcement and that the unity of the social group was such that meaningful sanction to ensure conformity could be applied. While one can argue with that proposition by pointing out that there was always social deviance in the rural community, it is harder to minimize the importance that family, kin and neighborhood groups, school and church have had on maintaining rural community equilibrium. Law enforcement and public regulatory bodies have always played a secondary and often, minor, role. Why the difference? The answer was found in the core element of social control, system stability.

Rural social institutions at all systemic levels were characterized by permanence, continuity, a respect for and reliance upon tradition, and a shared sense of identity (Hummon, 1986). But the 1991 U.S. Census data clearly put the lie to any notion of a distinguishing rural stability. Using standard social indicators such as marriage, remarriage and divorce rates, single parent households, housing permanence, and employment longev-

ity, urban and rural communities not only have moved toward convergence during the past twenty years, they are now, on most stability scales,
virtually identical. The likelihood of being victimized by crime in rural
America is still lower than both the inner city or other metro areas.
Bachman (1992) points out however, that with respect to crimes of violence, the incidence is not much lower than in metro areas and one
particularly large rural population—the elderly—is as likely to be the victim
of some crimes as its metro counterpart.

The rise in the importance of formal social control systems is evident
in the increasing prominence of police, zoning commissions and the courts
in both defining and enforcing rural social controls.

## Mutual Support

The locality relevant function of mutual support refers to the type of
help sought or offered in instances where individual and family crises
present needs which are not otherwise satisfied in the usual pattern of
organized social behavior (Warren, 1963). The critical urban-rural difference was always the extent to which residents relied on family, kin and
neighborhoods, i.e., natural helping systems versus formally organized, special services. Rural social workers have written extensively about the nature
and complexity of the tri-part rural human service delivery system and the
rural community's suspiciousness of the role of professionals within it (Brown,
1933; Buxton, 1976; Ginsberg, 1977; Johnson, 1980; Kirkland & Irey, 1978; Locke
& Lohmann, 1978; Mermelstein & Sundet, 1976; Murty, 1984; Patterson, 1977;
Webster, 1984; Webster & Campbell, 1977).

In 1995, the vast majority of non-metro natural helping systems have
disappeared. The formal service systems are regionalizing, retrenching
and almost constantly reorganizing (Bergland, 1988; Celenza, 1988; Fitchen,
1991; Pollack, 1984). These realities yielded very different findings than the
rural experiences of twenty years ago (Hessler & Sundet, 1995). Four
hundred family units were asked where they would turn for assistance if
one of their children got into serious trouble (drugs, school discipline,
pregnancy, delinquency, arrest). The first choice of 38% of the respondents
was a social agency, followed in order by friends (21%), school counselor
(17%), minister (9%), extended family (7%), neighbor (4%), and all others
including law enforcement and youths, the remaining 4%. But the optimis-
tic fact that nearly 2/5 of the families said they would voluntarily seek the
help of a social agency in time of trouble was shattered by a subsequent
question on the survey which asked them to identify specific social agencies they would use. Only a very small minority could name a local facility
and even fewer could describe the services offered.

In the health sector of the mutual support arena, health care reform
measures, particularly the formation of health maintenance organizations
covering large geographic areas, have irreversibly altered the relationship
between all consumers and health professionals. Community-based services do not mean consistent, locally-known providers. Like the circuit-riding

clergy of the new rural church and governmental managers (Seroka, 1990), medical specialists and home health providers enter and exit the service base from the central office without regard to competing or even complementary support services. In both metro and non-metro areas, these service providers may have little understanding of the immediate context and no incentive for trying to learn about it. The uninsured poor, more often the working poor in non-metro than in metro areas, are left out of this health delivery system—left out in a marketplace devoid of alternative help (Rowland & Lyons, 1989). HIV and AIDS victims are increasing, posing another challenge to the metro and weakened rural health system (HSITRE-Special Issue, 1989; Rounds, 1988).

Despite the higher non-metro poverty rates noted above, the rural poor are less likely to be eligible to receive welfare assistance because they are more likely to be employed and have some assets that make them ineligible for benefits (Lerman & Mikesell, 1989; McLaughlin & Perman, 1991; Mermelstein & Sundet, 1987; Rank & Hirschl, 1987; Tolbert & Lyson, 1992).

Homelessness is becoming as significant a social problem in rural areas as it is in urban (Lazare, Leonard & Kravitz, 1989; Patton, 1988), due again to the collapse of the familial (natural) support networks. The non-metro homeless are slightly younger than their urban counterparts and the previous pattern of "doubling or tripling up" with kin is often not possible (Fitchen, 1991, 1992). Homeless shelters are rare in non-metro areas as is aid to address the unique complex of needs of homeless people.

In a context of accelerating social problems that threatens the health, safety and basic security of non-metro and metro people alike, the rural community's capacity to provide adequate mutual support appears to be as precarious as the city's.

## Social Participation

The final locality-relevant function in Warren's conception is social participation which entails the provision of opportunities for the social interaction of residents on the basis of mutual interest as well as physical proximity (neighbors).

In the United States today, an ever more transient and cosmopolitan population has elected to participate almost exclusively in groups and activities that transcend any local community, metro or non-metro. Alternative interpretations of "community lost" and "community liberated" refer, in part, to this phenomenon (Hunter, 1978). To the extent that voluntary citizen participation in community-serving groups is diminished by extralocal participation in largely self-serving groups, the "sense of community" and attachment to place suffer (Etzioni, 1993).

Oldenburg (1989) wrote of the need for "the 3rd place" in community life, locations beyond home or workplace where informal public life could be experienced. He stressed the importance of typical small town gathering places, coffee shops, post offices, bars, and general stores, to instill a sense of community and offer access to social participation. Such places are rarely found in suburbia with the possible exception of the more impersonal shopping mall, and they are withering with the decline of Main Street in rural America.

Arendt (1993), in a similar vein, believed that the sense of community is best fostered in the "traditional town" design, a spatial layout of businesses and dwellings in pedestrian-friendly patterns. Rural communities featured an accessible downtown with stores that met residents' daily needs, fronting on tree-lined sidewalks and with houses abutting commercial property. Frequent downtown visits to the grocery, drugstore or post office stimulated informal social participation. Today's boarded-up, deserted streets in many Midwestern rural towns have the same effect on the residents' social participation as the violent, drug-infested streets in some metro areas. They offer mute testimony to the increasing isolation and loneliness of rural people.

## Conclusions and Suggestions

If, as the foregoing evidence indicates, there is very little to distinguish rural from metro environments using the core elements of locality relevant functions, and if the very definitions of urban and rural (metro/non-metro) in official use only obfuscate the matter, is there anything left for an organization such as the Rural Caucus to do, or have the forecasts of Swanson and Jacobsen come true? The answer may be "yes" to both questions. First, there is a role and mission for those who define themselves as rural social workers but the focus of the specialty needs far greater specificity than it now has. And second, the predictions of Jacobsen ten years ago have, or at the very least are well on their way to coming true because scholarship has lagged behind the elemental changes in the rural arena. Susan Murty (1990) framed the issue in her article "Your rural and my rural: are they the same?" Her answer was "no" and that answer has even greater verity today.

### Role and Mission

First, some brief suggestions on what needs to be done about role and mission. By every index of social articulation, material, attitudinal or social network, those characteristics which have long been posited as central and unique to rural communities are no longer predominant. But unlike the urban setting where impersonalization and social disintegration have been recognized as facts and at least some systematic efforts have been made to develop ersatz and compensatory structures to deal with community disintegration, responses in rural areas have been sporadic, idiosyncratic or, in their worst form, based on a succession of federally directed economic development initiatives that have only exacerbated the problems of community deterioration.

In the Midwestern areas the current initiatives fall into two categories: industrial development, and preservationist.

In the first alternative, substantial expenditure of scarce resources is spent in competition to attract low-tech manufacturing to the area. If successful, this strategy results in overburdening the local infrastructure, attracting a commuter work force with little if any attachment to the immediate locality and duplicating the urban model salaried line workers, except at a lower wage scale. It also is a very temporary answer. As soon as market, political, or technological conditions change, the plant relocates, for it is increasingly more economically feasible to resettle than to retool. Left behind is a publicly owned vacant building, industrial development bonds to be paid off and a widespread anomie that Durkheim would surely recognize.

The second strategy borrows from the ecology movement and attempts to turn back the economic and social clock to what proponents view as a preferable time and mode of living best typified in the "save the family farm" movement. The economic tide runs strongly against this strategy as the numbers indicate and those numbers are only a portion of the story. Many statistically counted "family farmers" who remain have already given up that most highly prized property, independence, and are, in fact, contract workers for Green Giant or Hormel or Central Dairy.

The critical deficit in both approaches is that they ignore precisely what they aim to save, the rural community. And that is where social work should have its unique niche for by heritage it has been the profession that addressed the issues of community building. At the very first conference, Webster and Campbell (1977) suggested that this loose knit confederation of professionals should begin examining the specialty of "rural social developer." That call has gone largely unheeded. The traditional expertise in community building that was the hallmark of this profession has been, by default, passed on to others. More and more special interest groups such as rural economic developers, health care planners, youth service advocates, ecologists, elementary and secondary education reformers, and political activists are promoting broad-based citizen coalitions as a primary tool. Terms such as empowerment, leveraging, indigenous resources, asset assessment and systemic analysis are suddenly being discovered and popularized in these disciplines. While we should rejoice that community building is having such a renaissance, are social workers in the forefront? Not in many areas. Rural schools prepare practitioners for clinical work within traditional social welfare agencies. Rarely are graduates equipped to take leadership roles in regional planning structures, small business development consortia, cooperative extension nor not-for-profit institutes and foundations that now are spearheading rural community building. The core methodology and principles are well known in social work. However, as rural has changed so must the techniques employed in that context. For instance, there is much to learn from the pioneer work in distance learning that is taking place at St. John's in

Newfoundland and at the Universities of South Carolina, North Dakota, and Tennessee. Just as group work in the urban settlement houses and conjoint therapy in mental health originated with the social workers, creative use of fiber optic technology to knit rural people and communities together should be our expertise.

## Research and Scholarship

In the scholarship area much remains to be accomplished, not the least of which is to arrive at a far greater degree of precision in terminology. Social work is not alone in this concern. Fourteen years ago a panel report of the National Academy of Sciences addressed the policy significance and implications of the definition of rural. In *Rural America in Passage: Statistics for Policy* (1981) the panel concluded that our knowledge of rural people and their environment is not only imperfect and incomplete but that rural areas are much more heterogeneous than are urban areas. And then the report hastens to add that it has no way of objectively measuring that conclusion!

The concern about specificity and precision is not simply from some arcane academic interest nor a desire to compete with colleagues in the social and behavioral sciences. Rather it arises from what Christenson and Carpenter (1994) refer to as "responsiveness," the need to articulate the condition of uncounted Americans living in low density population areas whose requirements are increasingly ignored in national and even state policymaking. The major national data sets (National Longitudinal Surveys, Panel Study of Income Dynamics, Survey of Income and Program Participation and the Census of Population) are aggregations that are limited in their applicability to diverse rural environments and in their ability to provide geographic specificity. Twenty years ago Leon Ginsberg referred to this situation, in the opening address of the First National Institute as the "audibility gap," i.e., people who have problems in rural areas are not always well heard and because they are not always well heard, they are not always well served. Today, it is even harder for them to be heard. Through the Caucus, its annual conference and the journal, there is access to rich repositories of data cutting across all the "rurals:" retirement, tourism, extraction, farming and trade center communities. The opportunities for cooperative and coordinated research into policy, program, and practice are almost boundless. The expertise is already here present. Funding, particularly for support of multi-institution and agency consortia, can be obtained. What is needed is the commitment, the renewed sense of mission of two decades ago and a willingness of this leadership to assign their talents to a common research agenda. The idea certainly is not new but the urgency is.

We can refocus practice and research to again articulate the unique rural social work movement and mission, or we can expend all our limited resources on justifying why we do things a little differently in the hinterland. History shows us where the latter approach leads.

# References

Arendt, R. (1993). *Rural by design.* Chicago, IL: American Planning Association, Planners Press.

Bachman, R. (1992). Crime in non-metropolitan America: A national accounting of trends, incidence rates, and idiosyncratic vulnerabilities. *Rural Sociology, 57*(4), 546-560.

Barker, B. & Garrett, S. (1987-88). German by satellite: Alternatives for small schools. *The Rural Educator, 9*(2), 5-8.

Bast, D. (1976, June). *Human Services in the Rural Environment Newsletter, 1*(1). Madison, WI: University of Wisconsin-Extension.

Bedics, B. (1987). The history and context of rural poverty. *Human Services in the Rural Environment, 10*(4) & *11*(1): 12-14.

Bergland, B. (1988). Rural mental health: Report of the National Action Commission on the Mental Health of Rural Americans. *Journal of Rural Community Psychology, 9*(2) 29-39.

Bonnen, J. T. (1994). Rural data needs in rapidly changing times. In J. A. Christenson, R. C. Maurer and N. L. Strang (Eds.), *Rural data: People & policy.* Boulder, CO: Westview.

Bosak, J. & Pearlman, B. (1982). A review of the definition of rural. *Journal of Rural Community Psychology, 3*(1), 3-34.

Brown, J. (1933). *The rural community and social case work.* New York: Family Welfare Association of America.

Buxton, E. (1976). Delivering social services in rural areas. In L. Ginsberg (Ed.), *Social work in rural communities* (pp. 29-40). New York: Council on Social Work Education.

Celenza, C. M. (1988). Survival strategies for rural mental health centers. *Journal of Rural Community Psychology, 9*(2), 77-84.

Christenson, J. A., & Carpenter, E. H. (1994). Rural data needs: The comparative advantage of university research. In J. Christenson, R. Maurer and N. Strang (Eds.), *Rural data: People & policy.* Boulder, CO: Westview.

Copp, James. (1964). *Our changing rural society: Perspectives and trends.* Ames, IA: Iowa State University Press.

Critchfield, R. (1994). *The villagers. Chained values, altered lives: The closing of the urban-rural gap.* New York: Anchor.

Daniels, T. L., & Lapping, M.B. (1987). Small town triage: A rural settlement policy for the American Midwest. *Journal of Rural Studies, 2*, 31-40.

D'Argemir, D. C. (1987). The rural crisis and the reproduction of family systems. *Sociological Ruralis, 27*(4), 263-277.

Davenport, J. A., & Davenport, J., III. (Eds.). (1979). *Boom towns and human services.* Laramie: University of Wyoming Department of Social Work.

Davenport, J., Davenport, J., & Wiebler, J. (Eds.). (1980). *Social work in rural areas: Issues and opportunities.* Laramie: University of Wyoming Department of Social Work.

Davidson, O. G. (1991). *Broken heartland: The rise of America's rural ghetto.* New York: Doubleday.

Deavers, K., Hoppe, R., & Ross, P. (1986). Public policy and rural poverty: A view from the 1980s. *Policy Studies Journal, 15*(2), 291-309.

Denton, R. T., York, R. O., & Moran, J. R. (1988). The social worker's view of the rural community: An empirical examination. *Human Services in the Rural Environment, 11*(3), 14-21.

Elder, W., & Hobbs, D. (1990). From reform to restructuring: New opportunities for rural schools. *The Rural Sociologist, 10*(3), 10-13.

Etzioni, A. (1993). *The spirit of community.* New York: Crown Publishers.

Falk, W. W., & Lyson, T. (1988). *High tech, low tech, not tech: Recent industrial and occupational change in the South.* Albany, NY: University of New York Press.

Fitchen, J. M. (1991). *Endangered spaces. endangered places.* Boulder, CO: Westview.

Fitchen, J. M. (1992). On the edge of homelessness: Rural poverty and housing insecurity. *Rural Sociology, 57*(2), 173-193.

Flora, C. B., Flora, J. L., Spears, J. D., Swanson, L. E., with Lapping, M. B., & Weinberg, M. L. (1992). *Rural communities: Legacy & change.* Boulder, CO: Westview.

Fuguitt, G. V., Beale, C. L., & Reibel, M. (1991). Recent trends in metropolitan/nonmetropolitan fertility. *Rural Sociology, 56*(3), 475-486.

Gas, H. (1962). *The urban villagers: Group and class in the life of Italian Americans.* New York: Free Press.

Gasson, R. (1988). Changing gender roles. *Sociology Ruralis, 28*(4), 300-305.

Gilford, D., Nelson, G., & Ingram, L. (Eds.). *Rural America in passage: Statistics in policy.* Washington, DC: National Academy Press.

Gimlin, H. (1990, July 20). The continuing decline of rural America. *Editorial Research Reports, 11*(27), 414.

Ginsberg, L. (1976). *Social work in rural communities.* New York: Council on Social Work Education.

Ginsberg, Leon. (1977). "Rural social work." In *Encyclopedia of Social Work.* Washington, DC.: National Association of Social Workers.

Heaton, T. B., Lichter, D. T., & Amoateng, A. (1989). The timing of family formation: Rural urban differentials in first intercourse, childbirth, and marriage. *Rural Sociology,* 54, 1-16.

Henry, M., Drabenstott, M. & Gibson, L. (1987). Rural growth slows down. *Rural Development Perspectives, 3*(3).

Hessler, R., & Sundet, P. (1995). Perception of kinship resources for youth at risk. Unpublished paper, University of Missouri-Columbia.

Hicks, G. (1947). *Small town.* New York: Macmillan.

Hobbs, D. (1992). The rural context for education: Adjusting the images. In M. Galbraith (Ed.), *Education in the rural community.* Malabar, FL: Krieger Publishing Co.

Honour, R. (1979). The impact of federal policies on rural social service programs. *Human Services in the Rural Environment, 1*(1), 12-19.

Hummon, D. (1986). City mouse, country mouse: The persistence of community identity. *Qualitative Sociology,* 9, 3-25.

Hunter, A. (1978). Persistence of local sentiments in mass society. In D. Street and Associates (Eds.), *Handbook of contemporary urban life* (pp. 134-156). San Francisco: Jossey-Bass.

Jacobson, M. (1987). Scholarship and the rural social work movement. In A. Summers, J. Schriver, P. Sundet, & R. Meinert (Eds.), *Proceedings of the 10th national institute on social work in rural areas.* Batesville, AR: Arkansas College.

Jess, J. D. (1985, Winter). The needs of rural schools. *Illinois School Research and Development, 21*(2), 6-14.

Jobes, P. C. (1987). The disintegration of gemeinschaft social structure from energy development: Observations from ranch communities in the western U.S. *Journal of Rural Studies, 3*, 219-229.

Johnson, D. R., & Booth, A. (1990). Rural economic decline and marital quality: A panel study of farm marriages. *Family Relations, 39*(2), 159-166.

Johnson, L. (1977). Social development in nonmetropolitan areas. In R. Green & S. Webster (Eds.), *Social work in rural areas: Practice and preparation.* Knoxville: University of Tennessee-Knoxville School of Social Work.

Johnson, L. (1980). Human service delivery patterns in nonmetropolitan communities. In W. Johnson (Ed.), *Rural human services.* Itasca, IL: Peacock.

Kirkland, J., & Irey, K. (1978). Confidentiality: Issues and dilemmas in rural practice. In E. Buxton (Ed.), *2nd national institute on social work in rural areas reader* (pp.142-150). Madison: University of Wisconsin-Extension, Center for Social Service.

Kivett, V. R. (1985). Consanguinity and kin level: Their relative importance to the helping network of older adults. *Journal of Gerontology, 40*, 228-234.

Knop, E., & Jobes, P. (1988). *The myth of non-metropolitan community stability: Patterns and implications of turnover migration in Montana and Colorado cases.* Paper presented at the Rural Sociological Society, Athens, GA.

Koeberneck, T. (1986). Lifestyle opportunities and non-metropolitan migration. In *The small city and regional community,* Vol. 7 (53-62). Stevens Point, WI: Center for the Small City and Regional Community.

Krout, J. (1988). The elderly in rural environments. *Journal of Rural Studies,* 104-14.

Landis, P. (1948). *Rural life in process.* New York: McGraw-Hill.

Lazere, E. B., Leonard, P. A., & Kravik, L. L. (1989). *The other housing crisis: Sheltering the poor in rural America.* Washington, DC: Center on Budget and Policy Priorities.

Lerman, D. L., & Mikesell, J. J. (1989). Rural and urban poverty: An income/net worth approach. In H. R. Rodgers, Jr. & G. Weiher (Eds.), *Rural poverty* (1-24). New York: Greenwood.

Lichter, D. T. (1989). The underemployment of American rural women: Prevalence, trends and spatial inequality. *Journal of Rural Studies, 5*, 199-208.

Lichter, D. T., & Costanzo, J. A. (1987). Nonmetropolitan underemployment and labor force composition. *Rural Sociology, 52*(3).

Lichter, D. T., & Eggebeen, D. J. (1992). Child poverty and the changing rural family. *Rural Sociology, 57*(2), 151-172.

Lingeman, R. (1980). *Small town America*. New York: Putnam.

Locke, B., & Lohmann, R. A. (1978). Effective models for the delivery of services in rural areas: Implications for practice and social work education, *Proceedings from the Third Annual National Institute on Social Work in Rural Areas*. Morgantown: West Virginia University School of Social Work.

Lowe, G. D., & Pinhey, T. K. (1980). Do rural people place a lower value on formal education? New evidence from national surveys. *Rural Sociology, 45*(2),325-331.

Martinez-Brawley, E. E. (Ed.). (1981). *Pioneer efforts in rural social welfare: First hand views since 1908*. University Park, PA: Pennsylvania State University Press.

Martinez-Brawley, E. E. (1990). Have we arrived? Rural practice tenets, myths and realities. In J. Borner, H. Doueck, & M. Jacobsen (Eds.), *Emerging from the shadows: Papers from the 15th national institute on social work and human services in rural areas* (pp. 3-15). Buffalo: State University of New York at Buffalo.

McLaughlin, D. K., & Perman, L. (1991). Returns vs. endowments in the earnings attainment process for metropolitan and non-metropolitan men and women. *Rural Sociology, 56*(3), 339-365.

Mermelstein, J., & Sundet, P. (1973). Community control and the determination of professional role in rural mental health. *Journal of Operational Psychiatry*.

Mermelstein, J., & Sundet, P. (1978). Education for social work practice in the rural context. In L. Hulen (Ed.), *Educating for social work practice in rural areas*. Fresno: California State University, Fresno, School of Social Work.

Murty, S. (1984). Developing the trust of a rural community. *Human Services in the Rural Environment, 9*(2), 15-20.

Murty, S. (1990). Your rural and my rural: Are they the same? In J. Borner, H. Doueck & M. Jacobsen (Eds.), *Emerging from the shadows: Papers from the 15th national institute on social work and human services in rural areas*. Buffalo: State University of New York at Buffalo.

Oldenburg, R. (1989). *The great good place*. New York: Paragon House.

Patterson, S. (1977). Toward a conceptualization of natural helping, *Arete, 4*(2).

Patton, L. T. (1988). *The rural homeless*. Rockville, MD: National Center for Health Services.

Pollack, R. (1984). Bitter years: A special report on more than thirty key Federal programs (Book review). *The Progressive, 48*, 47.

Powers, E. A., & Kivett, V. R. (1992). Kin expectations and kin support among rural older adults. *Rural Sociology, 57*(2), 194-215.

President's National Advisory Commission on Rural Poverty. (1967). *The people left behind*. Washington, DC: U.S. Government Printing Office.

President's Task Force on Rural Development. (1970). *A new life for the country*. Washington, DC: U.S. Government Printing Office.

Rank, M. R., & Hirschl, T. A. (1987). A rural-urban comparison of welfare exists: The importance of population density. *Rural Sociology, 53*(2), 190-206.

Rathge, R. W., & Goreham, G. (1989). The influence of economic and demographic factors on rural church viability. *Journal for the Scientific Study of Religion, 28*(1), 59-61.

Reid, J. N. (1990, April). *Education and rural development: A review of recent evidence.* Paper presented at the American Educational Research Association Annual Conference, Boston.

Revicki, D. A., & Mitchell, J. P. (1990). Strain, social support and mental health in rural elderly individuals. *Journal of Gerontology, 45*(6), 267-268.

Robinson, G. M. (1990). *Conflict and change in the countryside.* New York: Belhaven Press.

Rounds, K. A. (1988). Responding to AIDS: Rural community strategies. *Social Casework: The Journal of Contemporary Social Work, 69*(6): 360-365.

Rowland, D., & Lyons, B. (1989). Triple jeopardy: Rural, poor and uninsured. *Health Services Research, 23*(6), 975-1004.

Sanders, I. (1958). *The community: An introduction to a social system.* New York: Roland Press.

Sanderson, D., & Polson, R. (1939). *Rural community organization.* New York: Wiley.

Scheidt, R. J., & Norris-Baker, C. (1989). *Small town to ghost town: Rural elderly at risk?* Paper presented at the American Psychological Association, New Orleans, LA.

Seelbach, W. C. (1978). Correlates of aged parent's filial responsibility expectations and realizations. *The Family Coordinator, 27,* 341-350.

Seroka, J. (1990, March/April). Inter-rural administrative cooperation: Issues and opportunities. *National Civic Review, 79,* 138-151.

Smith, H. B. (1984). School and community: Are they on a collision course? *The Rural Educator, 6*(1), 23-24.

Specht, H., & Courtney, M. (1994). *Unfaithful angels.* New York: Free Press.

Special Issue: AIDS in Rural America. (1989). *Human Services in the Rural Environment, 13*(1).

Steblay, N. M. (1987). Helping behaviors in rural and urban environments: A meta-analysis. *Psychological Bulletin, 102*(3), 346-356.

Sundet, P. (1987). A summary and a report card: Closing remarks. In A. Summers, J. Schriver, P. Sundet, & R. Meinert (Eds.), *Proceedings of the 10th national institute on social work in rural areas.* Batesville, AR: Arkansas College.

Sundet, P., & Mermelstein, J. (1983). The meaning of community in rural mental health. *International Journal of Mental Health, 12*(1-2), 25-44.

Sundet, P., & Mermelstein, J. (1987). Helping the new rural poor. *Public Welfare, 45*(3), 14-20.

Swanson, M. (1972). Professional rural social work in America. *Agricultural History, 46.*

Tolbert, C. M., & Lyson, T. A. (1992). Earnings inequality in the non-metropolitan United States: 1967-1990. *Rural Sociology, 57*(4), 494-511.

U.S. Bureau of the Census. (1992). *Statistical abstract of the United States: 1991.* Washington, DC: U.S. Government Printing Office.

Vidich, A., & Bensman, J. (1958). *Small town in mass society: Class, power and religion in a rural community.* Princeton, NJ: Princeton University Press.

Ward, J. (1988). *City schools, rural schools.* Normal, IL: Center for the Study of Educational Finance.

Warren, R. (1963). *The community in America.* Chicago: Rand McNally.

Webster, S. (1984). Rural helping systems. *Human Services in the Rural Environment,* 9(1), 17-23.

Webster, S., & Campbell, P. (1977). Contextual difference in the rural social work environment. In D. Bast & J. Schmidt (Eds.), *2nd annual northern Wisconsin symposium on human services in the rural environment reader* (pp. 2-9). Madison, WI: University of Wisconsin-Extension.

White, P. E. (1980). Migration loss and the residual community: A study in rural France, 1962-1975. In P. E. White & R. I. Woods (Eds.), *The geographical impact of migration.* London: Longman.

Whitaker, W. A survey of perceptions of social work practice in rural and urban areas. *Human Services in the Rural Environment, 9*(3), 12-19.

Wilkerson, I. (1990, Jan. 3). With rural towns vanishing, states choose which to save. *New York Times.*

York, R. O., Denton, R. T., & Moran, J. R. (1989). Rural and urban social work practice: Is there a difference? *Social Casework, 70*(4), 201-209.

# Part 2

## Social Work Practice
## In Rural Communities

Part 2 covers the practice of social work in rural communities. York, Denton, and Moran provide fundamental information on the similarities and differences between urban and rural social work practice. The late Janet Fitchen writes about the deterioration of life for many in rural communities.

Many social workers have come to believe there are no significant differences between social work practice in rural communities and practice in metropolitan areas, after all. They believe that good social work practice is good social work practice, regardless of where it takes place. However, in many cases, social workers in rural communities adapt to the special nature of their jobs, which require more diverse functions than those in metropolitan areas.

Two articles describe issues of religion and spirituality, which are important matters throughout the United States and may be of special importance in rural areas, where church affiliation and participation is often an expectation and a community norm. Part 2 also includes chapters on specific social work practice examples designed to help the reader understand the ways social work is carried out in some specific settings in rural communities.

# 7

# Rural and Urban Social Work Practice: Is There a Difference?

by Reginald O. York, Roy T. Denton, and James R. Moran

T he theory and practice of social work in rural areas, after a hiatus during the 1940s and 1950s, have reemerged as relevant concerns for the profession. Part of the stimulus for this renewed concern is the perception that social work practice principles derived from urban settings may not be relevant to rural problems.[1] If the rural context is different in terms of its needs, culture, and value systems, then the logical assumption would be that social work must be practiced differently if it is to be appropriate to its context.

The literature on rural social work specifies that rural social workers emphasize different professional roles, are generalists rather than specialists, and rely more upon the use of informal networks than do their urban counterparts.[2] However, little empirical evidence suggests that social workers in rural areas actually differ from their urban counterparts in relation to these practice issues. In fact, the little empirical work completed thus far seems to suggest that rural and urban social work practice are not different.[3]

The purpose of this chapter is to report on an empirical study designed to explore the differences between urban and rural social work practice. Reports of social workers regarding their practice are analyzed within the context of a rural–urban continuum.

---

[1] Emilia E. Martinez-Brawley, ed., *Pioneer Efforts in Rural Social Work: Firsthand Views Since 1908* (University Park, PA: Pennsylvania State University Press, 1980).

[2] Joanne Mermelstein and Paul Sundet, "Worker Acceptance and Credibility in the Rural Environment," in *Rural Human Services: A Book of Readings*, ed. H. Wayne Johnson (Itasca, IL: F. E. Peacock, 1980), pp. 174-178; Leon H. Ginsberg, ed., *Social Work in Rural Communities: A Book of Readings* (New York: Council on Social Work Education, 1976); Louise C. Johnson, "Networking: A Means of Maximizing Resources," *Human Services in the Rural Environment* 8 (2, 1983): 27-31.

[3] William H. Whitaker, "A Survey of Perceptions of Social Work Practice in Rural and Urban Areas," *Human Services in the Rural Environment* 9 (3, 1986): 12-19; Carol Austin, Kevin Mahoney, and Frederick Seidl, "Exploring the Base for Rural Social Work Practice," *Human Services in the Rural Environment* 3 (6, 1978): 7-21.

---

Reprinted from *Social Casework: The Journal of Contemporary Social Work* (April 1989), with permission from Family Service America.

## Defining Rurality

A principal difficulty in describing rural social work practice is the persistent problem of defining rurality. This difficulty has been discussed by numerous authors.[4] The analysis of definitional problems with the concept of rurality led the Southern Regional Education Board's Rural Task Force to conclude that no clear, universally accepted definitions of rurality exist.[5]

Several approaches have been used to define rurality. In rural sociology, most definitions fall into three categories: occupational, ecological, or sociocultural. The vast majority of the literature has relied upon an ecological definition, that is, reference to the distribution of people in space. Therefore, many professionals measure rurality in terms of population size and population density, although some authors have cautioned against overemphasis of these variables.[6]

Although some definitions of rural tend to propose a dichotomy between rural and urban, many researchers and theoreticians have long recognized that rural–urban differences are best represented along a continuum. Robert Redfield and Ferdinard Toennies recognized the interpenetration of rural and urban settings.[7] Richard Duford hypothesized a rural–urban continuum ranging from isolated farms to metropolitan areas based upon population and proximity to urban areas.[8] One of the more elaborate efforts to conceptualize rural–urban differences by population is illustrated by the work of William Whitaker.[9] Using both a ten-category classification of counties developed by the United States Department of Agriculture and a rural–urban typology employed by the Maine State Planning Office, he developed a complex rating typology by which respondents could classify both their work and home communities. This typology essentially represented a continuum.

In an overview of research on rural–urban differences in attitudes and behavior, Norvail Glenn and Lester Hill examined support for the idea of

---

[4] Robert C. Bealer, Fern K. Willits, and William P. Kuvlesky, "The Meaning of Rurality in American Society: Some Implications of Alternative Definitions," *Rural Sociology* 30 (September 1965): 255-66; O. William Farley et al., *Rural Social Work Practice* (New York: Free Press, 1982).

[5] Ginsberg, ed., *Social Work in Rural Communities: A Book of Readings.*

[6] Bealer, Willits, and Kuvlesky, "The Meaning of Rurality in American Society: Some Implications of Alternative Definitions."

[7] Robert Redfield, *The Primitive World and Its Transformation* (New York: Cornell University Press, 1953); Ferdinand Toennies, *Community and Society* (New York: Harper and Row, 1963).

[8] Cited in Farley et al., *Rural Social Work Practice,* p. 6.

[9] Whitaker, "Survey of Perceptions of Social Work Practice in Rural and Urban Areas."

a continuum. [10] They pointed out that the largest communities usually differ from the medium-sized communities about as much as the medium-sized communities differ from the smallest communities, and that the direction of these differences is consistent from one size to the next. This pattern of variation suggests that it is useful to conceive of rurality as a continuum.

Farming is another variable that characterizes the rural community. Glenn and Hill, for example, referred to the differences in attitudes and behavior between farm and nonfarm communities. They contended that farming is one of the best ways to characterize the rural community. [11] Their argument is based on the fact that farmers are the only major segment of the population for which both place of work and place of residence are in the open countryside. Further support for the focus upon farming was offered by Olaf Larson, who reported on a wide array of differences in values and beliefs between rural and urban inhabitants. [12]

In summary, the literature stresses the use of a continuum rather than a dichotomy in the conceptualization of rurality. Furthermore, although a clear consensus does not exist, key variables to be used on the continuum appear to be population, population density, and extent of farming.

## Rural Social Work Practice

The literature on rural social work practice focuses less upon defining rurality than upon delineating the sociocultural features of rural areas that affect practice. Three central themes have dominated this discussion. The first theme concerns the effect of geography on both services and the types of problems experienced. It is argued that greater distances between people pose special problems for service delivery. Rural persons have also been characterized as having a greater tendency toward certain social problems than do urban populations. [13] In general, rural areas and people have been characterized as possessing more social problems proportionally and having fewer social services than do urban dwellers.

---

[10] Norvail Glenn and Lester Hill, "Rural–Urban Differences in Attitudes and Behaviors in the United States," *Annals of the American Academy of Political Science* 123 (January 1977): 36-50.

[11] Ibid.

[12] Olaf Larson, "Values and Beliefs of Rural People," in *Rural U.S.A.: Persistence and Change*, ed. Thomas Ford (Ames, IA: Iowa State University Press, 1978), pp. 91-112.

[13] Richard S. Edwards, Gail Durtz, and Nancy S. Dickinson, "Identifying Training Needs and Developing a Training Response to Rural Social Workers in Title XX Provider Agencies," in *Social Work in Rural Areas: Issues and Opportunities*, ed. Joseph Davenport, Judith A. Davenport, and James Wiebler (Laramie, WY: University of Wyoming, 1980), pp. 122-131.

A second theme in the literature focuses on the characteristics of the people in rural areas, with emphasis on values and lifestyles. Overall, rural inhabitants are seen as more conservative in their values and more traditional in their lifestyles. [14]

The third theme deals with the characteristics of the service providers and the environment in which they practice. [15] The rural community has been viewed as relying more on informal helping networks and decision makers than does the urban community. These considerations have led various authors to conclude that rural social workers must be generalists in their functioning in order to meet the tasks that are required. [16]

Since Leon Ginsberg first suggested that rural social workers should be generalists in their work activities, this idea has become axiomatic in rural social work literature. [17] This assumption has had its critics, however. Several authors have addressed either the vagueness of the concept or have argued for fundamental revisions in the generalist formulation. [18] A major theme among these authors has been the definition of social work practice in relation to practice roles. Those persons who argue for the generalist model have suggested that social workers in rural areas engage in activities that subsume a wider range of roles than is the case with the urban social worker.

With the adoption of the generalist model as the *sine qua non* of rural social work, a debate has ensued as to which roles should be preeminent. The majority of articles emphasize some version of the model developed by the Southern Regional Education Board. [19] [See chapter 2.] In an effort to define social work practice, the Southern Regional Education Board pub-

---

[14] Mermelstein and Sundet," Worker Acceptance and Credibility in the Rural Environment"; Barbara Whittington, "The Challenge of Family Work in a Rural Community," *Social Worker* 53 (Fall 1985): 104-107.

[15] Southern Regional Education Board, Rural Task Force, "Educational Assumptions for Rural Social Work," in *Social Work in Rural Communities: A Book of Readings*, pp. 41-44.

[16] Richard E. Doelker, Jr., and Bonnie C. Bedics, "An Approach to Curriculum Design for Rural Practice," *Journal of Education for Social Work* 19 (Winter 1983): 39-46.

[17] Leon Ginsberg, "Social Work Education for Rural Areas," in *Social Work in Rural Communities: A Book of Readings.*

[18] Steven A. Webster and Paul M. Campbell, 'The 1970s and Changing Dimensions in Rural Life—Is a New Practice Model Needed?" in *Social Work in Rural Areas: Preparation and Practice*, ed. Ronald K. Green and Steven A. Webster (Knoxville: University of Tennessee School of Social Work, 1977), pp. 75-92; Farley et al., *Rural Social Work Practice*; Beverly Couch et al., "A Specialist–Generalist Model of Social Work Practice for Contemporary Rural America," in *Social Work in Rural Areas*, pp. 95-105.

[19] Southern Regional Education Board, Rural Task Force, "Educational Assumptions for Rural Social Work."

lished a list of the activities necessary to meet client needs. These activities were organized into 12 categories or roles. This typology included the roles of outreach worker, broker, advocate, evaluator, teacher, behavior changer, mobilizer, consultant, community planner, care giver, data manager, and administrator. Of these, the first seven roles were the focus of the clinically oriented worker, whereas the second seven were in the province of the community-oriented worker. The roles of behavior changer and mobilizer overlapped the clinical and community categories.

Others, however, have raised questions about the applicability of these roles to rural areas. Steven Webster and Paul Campbell, for example, have advocated for a rural social worker who is oriented toward program development and have questioned the appropriateness of certain roles such as mediator, therapist, and advocate. [20] Joanne Mermelstein and Paul Sundet have indicated that rural social workers should be prepared to perform five roles—broker, technical expert, consultant, manager, and advocate. [21]

William Farley and co-workers attempted to redefine the roles of the generalist social worker.[22] Their model consists of 13 roles, including teacher, friend, organizer, and coordinator. Although they used a different terminology than that used in the model of the Southern Regional Education Board, closer examination suggests that the new model is not very different from the old one. [23]

For the purposes of the present study, the notion of practice role is conceived as a meaningful way to identify how social work practice differs in communities that vary along the rural–urban continuum. According to this reasoning, one would expect social workers in rural communities to differ from social workers in urban communities with regard to emphasis upon various practice roles.

Whitaker, however, found few differences between rural and urban social workers with regard to practice roles. In a survey of social workers in the state of Maine, Whitaker employed 4 measures of rurality and 87 dependent variables related to worker activities, worker values, practice problems, and so forth. In light of the finding that none of the dependent variables was significantly associated with more than two of the independent variables related to rurality, Whitaker concluded that his survey did not support the contention that many important differences can be found

---

[20] Webster and Campbell, "The 1970s and Changing Dimensions in Rural Life—Is a New Practice Model Needed?"

[21] Mermelstein and Sundet, "Worker Acceptance and Credibility in the Rural Environment."

[22] Farley et al., *Rural Social Work Practice.*

[23] Robert J. Teare and Harold L. McPheeters, *Manpower Utilization in Social Welfare* (Atlanta: Southern Regional Education Board, 1970).

between rural and urban social work practice. [24] Although Whitaker's study conceived of rurality as a continuum, it treated this independent variable as nominal and employed chi-square for statistical analysis. Therefore, the utility of rurality as a continuum was not fully taken into consideration. Another limitation of the study was that no respondents worked in a city with a population greater than 61,000. Consequently, the effects of the rural–urban continuum upon practice in large urban areas could not be assessed.

Discussion of the use of resources in rural communities has led researchers to focus on the use of informal networks. [25] It is assumed that rural workers utilize and help develop these networks in the absence of formal service systems. However, a study of services for the aged in Wisconsin revealed that informal support systems were not more prevalent in rural communities. [26] This study also revealed that few important differences existed between the needs and desires of rural and urban aged and between the ways social services were delivered in rural and urban communities.

The disparate definitions of the problems encountered by rural workers have complicated efforts to arrive at a clear delineation of rural social work's task. Different authors have tended to emphasize various combinations of problems; consequently, they have arrived at varying conclusions. To be consistent with the generalist premise, a rural worker must encounter client problems ranging from those of an intrapsychic nature to those of a broad community nature. Similarly, urban workers must be more specialized and encounter a narrower range of problems.

In summary, the literature indicates that social workers in rural areas function in an environment that is characterized by traditional lifestyles and values, by special service delivery issues, and by a wide range of problems. This environment calls for a social worker who practices as a generalist and makes use of various informal helping networks.

## Research Focus

The following basic research question was posed in this study. Does the practice of rural social workers differ from the practice of urban social workers? Factors that were considered in the comparison included the degree of emphasis upon various practice roles, the degree to which specialization among those roles takes place, the use of informal helping networks, and the social workers' perception of the nature of their clients' problems. Rurality was conceived as the basic independent variable, and social work practice was conceptualized as the dependent variable. As

---

[24] Whitaker, "A Survey of Perceptions of Social Work Practice in Rural and Urban Areas. "

[25] Johnson, "Networking: A Means of Maximizing Resources."

[26] Austin et al., "Exploring the Base for Rural Social Work Practice."

explained below, both of these variables were operationally defined in several ways.

## Methodology

A survey was mailed to a random sample of the members of the North Carolina Chapter of the National Association of Social Workers (NASW). Students, retired members, and faculty members of graduate and undergraduate schools of social work were eliminated from the sampling frame because the authors' interest was in persons who were currently working as social workers. Two hundred ninety-five persons were included in the survey (25 percent of the systematic random sample). Five persons indicated that they were no longer members of this organization. Of the 290 remaining participants, a total of 177 returned questionnaires for a participation rate of 61 percent.

Degree of rurality was defined with regard to the county of employment of the respondents. Population, population density, and family farms were utilized as the operational definitions of rurality. Lower values on these variables indicated a higher degree of rurality. Respondents were asked to identify their counties of employment, and information concerning these independent variables was collected from statistical reports. [27] The variable related to family farms was computed by dividing the population of the respondent's county by the number of family farms in that county. Thus, this variable indicated the population figure per family farm. For example, a respondent in a county with a population of 100 persons per family farm would be considered to be working in a more rural county than would a respondent in a county with 200 people per farm.

In order to examine the potential influence of rurality on the various aspects of social work practice, several dependent variables were utilized. As mentioned above, issues related to social work roles, informal helping networks, and perceptions of client problems were examined.

To collect data concerning emphasis upon social work roles, a series of eight statements describing different roles were developed. These statements and the role labels are presented in Table 1. The statements were used in a Likert format with respondents indicating their emphasis on each activity on a seven-point scale ranging from "not at all" to "to a very great extent." Because certain role labels have traditionally been associated with rural social work practice, no role labels were attached to these statements in this questionnaire.

The extent to which respondents specialized in the above roles was conceptualized as a separate dependent variable. This variable was mea-

---

[27] *North Carolina State Government Statistical Abstract*, 5th ed., 1984, North Carolina State Data Center, Office of State Budget and Management, Raleigh, North Carolina.

sured by recoding the response to each of the role descriptions as either a 1 or a 0. A score of 1 was given to each role rated at a level 2 or higher and a score of 0 was assigned if the rating was 1. These new scores were then summed for each respondent. This total score has a possible range from 0 for those who emphasized none of the roles to 8 for those who emphasized all of the roles. Thus specialization was indicated by a low total score. For example, if a respondent reported an emphasis greater than 2 for broker, mobilizer, and clinician, but not for the other roles, that individual would receive a score of 3 on this dependent variable, whereas a respondent emphasizing these three roles plus advocate and data manager would have a score of 5. A respondent with a score of 3 would be considered more specialized than would the respondent with a score of 5. Alternative measures of this variable were calculated by summing the roles for which the respondent indicated an emphasis level of 3 or greater, 4 or greater, and 5 or greater. This procedure allowed the authors to test this variable at different levels of sensitivity to this definition.

Two activities related to informal helping networks were also employed as dependent variables. The questionnaire defined informal helping networks as follows: "Informal helping networks are sets of enduring relationships of a nonprofessional nature that provide emotional support, advice, mutual self-help, and, in some cases, even concrete assistance with

**Table 1. Descriptions of Social Work Roles**

| | |
|---|---|
| *Broker* | Guiding client systems toward existing services, helping them negotiate the service system, and/or linking components of the service system with one another. |
| *Mobilizer* | Working with groups or committees to create resources that relate to existing problems. |
| *Mediator* | Working with groups or individuals to resolve conflicts by mediating the interaction in an impartial manner. |
| *Advocate* | Attempting to obtain services or rights for an individual or a group by fighting for those services or rights in order to overcome obstacles. |
| *Clinician* | Working with individuals, families, or small groups to bring about specific change in their behavior patterns, symptoms, or perceptions, including imparting information in order to develop various skills. |
| *Data manager* | Collecting, classifying, and analyzing data generated within the social welfare environment in order to aid in the development of action plans. |
| *Manager* | Managing a program, organization, or service unit. |
| *Community organizer* | Working with large groups, organizations, or communities to help them increase their skills in solving social welfare problems. |

life problems such as finances and transportation." Using the same seven-point scale as noted for roles, respondents indicated the extent to which they (1) made use of informal helping networks and (2) worked directly with informal helping networks by helping get them started or helping to keep them going.

Finally, various perceptions of the employing agency's client problems were conceptualized as dependent variables. Included in the five categories of major problem areas confronted by the employing agency's clients were intrapersonal conflict, reactive emotional distress, interpersonal conflict, conflicts with formal organizations, and lack of economic or social resources. Using a seven-point scale, respondents indicated the extent to which their agency's clients exhibited each of these five problems as "major" problems. Table 2 presents the questionnaire definitions of these problems, which were developed as a synthesis of those definitions proposed by Helen Northen and William Reid and Laura Epstein. [28]

### Table 2. Description of Problem Areas

*Intrapersonal conflict:* A problem centered in the individual, which may include the desire for a specific change in a specific behavior or symptom, difficulties in role performance, problems in social transitions (for example, movement from one social role to another, such as divorce, leaving college, or changing jobs), or a lack of knowledge or experience, which, consequently, interferes with the social competence of the individual.

*Reactive emotional distress:* The occurrence of a precipitating event beyond the client's control or ability to cope, resulting in anxiety, depression, guilt, or other disturbed emotional state. This stress may be temporary or long-term. Examples include developmental or situational crises, illness or disability, loss of significant relationships, and so forth.

*Interpersonal conflict:* Distress is primarily located in conflicts between specific persons. Examples include conflicts in marital, parent–child, sibling, and employer–employee relationships.

*Conflicts with formal organizations:* Situations in which an individual, family, or group is in conflict with a representative of a formal organization. The issue is the policy, procedure, or function of the system, not the representative of the system.

*Lack of economic or social resources:* An individual, group, or family does not have available the tangible resources that are necessary for survival. Problems include those created by cultural constraints such as racism, sexism, or other forms of discriminations.

---

[28] Helen Northen, *Clinical Social Work* (New York: Columbia University Press, 1982); William J. Reid and Laura Epstein, *Task-Centered Casework* (New York: Columbia University Press, 1972).

## Results

The mean age of the respondents was 39.7 years. As expected, more females (81 percent) than males (19 percent) and more Caucasians (93 percent) than members of minority groups (7 percent) responded. Seventy percent of these respondents indicated that they were in direct service positions, whereas 6 percent indicated line supervision as their position and 18 percent indicated administration. The remaining 6 percent listed their position as "other."

Respondents came from 40 of the 100 counties in North Carolina; more populated counties tended to be overrepresented. For example, the mean county population for the state is approximately 60, 000, [29] whereas the mean population of the counties of the respondents was 186,062. Of the respondents, 5 percent came from counties with a population less than 30,000, 10 percent from counties with a population between 30,000 and 49,999, 17 percent from counties with a population between 50,000 and 99,000, 39 percent from counties with a population between 100,000 and 249,999, and 29 percent from counties with a population between 250,000 and 420,000.

Mean scores on the seven-point scales for each of the eight roles were computed as follows: clinician (5.74), broker (4.71), manager (3.81), mediator (3.81), advocate (3.32), mobilizer (2.99), data manager (2.63), and community organizer (2.19). The mean rating for using informal networks was 4.91, whereas the mean for development of networks was 3.41. The mean ratings of problems presented by clients to the respondents' agencies were as follows: reactive emotional distress (6.08), interpersonal problems (5.49), intrapersonal problems (5.45), lack of economic resources (4.15), and problems with organizations (3.40).

Regarding specialization among roles, fully 87 percent of the respondents reported they emphasized three or more roles at the level of 3 or more on the seven-point scale. Two-thirds (68 percent) of these individuals reported they emphasized four or more roles at the level of 3 or more. Respondents varied considerably, however, regarding the degree of specialization as indicated by standard deviation scores computed for the average number of roles emphasized at the various levels. A mean of 6.10 and a standard deviation of 1.77 were computed for the number of roles emphasized at the level of 2 or more. The comparable means for each of the other levels of emphasis are as follows: mean number of roles emphasized at the level of 3 or more=4.78 (SD=1.93), roles emphasized at the level of 4 or more=3.77 (SD=1.94), roles emphasized at the level of 5 or more=3.05 (SD=1.73).

To examine the relationships between the three independent variables representing rurality and the dependent variables, the Spearman rank

---

[29] This figure is based upon the population as of 1982 *North Carolina Statistical Abstract.*

correlation coefficient was employed. Table 3 presents the correlations between the three independent variables and the eight dependent variables related to roles. Of these 24 correlations, only 1 was significant at the .05 level, and that was a weak correlation of .17 between population density and the broker role.

The dependent variable of specialization was measured at several levels of sensitivity as discussed above. The results of the analysis of the relationship of specialization and the independent variables are presented in Table 4. Specialization was not found to be significantly correlated with rurality even at the lowest sensitivity level, as indicated by the correlations of each of the three independent variables with specialization measure 1. All these correlation coefficients were nonsignificant. It follows that the correlations for the more sensitive measures of specialization were also nonsignificant.

As reported in Table 5, a similar pattern was found in the correlations of the independent variables with the five categories of client problems. None of the five perceptions of the clients' problems was found to be correlated with rurality as defined by the three independent variables.

### Table 3. Correlation Coefficients among Practice Roles and Measures of Rurality

| | | County of employment | |
| --- | --- | --- | --- |
| Role | Population | Population density | Family farms |
| Broker | .07 | .17* | .14 |
| Mobilizer | .06 | .03 | .02 |
| Mediator | .06 | .00 | .03 |
| Advocate | .05 | .04 | .04 |
| Clinician | .12 | .10 | .10 |
| Data manager | .04 | −.06 | −.07 |
| Manager | .09 | .08 | .08 |
| Community organizer | −.01 | −.07 | −.05 |

*$p < .05$

### Table 4. Correlation Coefficients between Levels of Specialization and Rurality

| | | County of employment | |
| --- | --- | --- | --- |
| Specialization measures | Population | Population density | Family farms |
| 1 (emphasis > 1) | .00 | −.06 | −.05 |
| 2 (emphasis > 2) | .10 | .06 | .03 |
| 3 (emphasis > 3) | .05 | .02 | .04 |
| 4 (emphasis > 4) | .11 | .08 | .08 |

This pattern of nonsignificance was also found in the analysis of the relationship of rurality and informal helping networks. Table 6 reveals that only one of the independent variables was correlated with either the use of informal helping networks or with the development of informal helping networks. This significant correlation was a weak relationship between population and the use of networks (r=.18; $p<.05$). The relationship was in the direction opposite of that expected. This correlation indicated that persons in more populous counties were more likely to use informal helping networks than were persons in less populated counties.

Two additional analyses of subgroups were undertaken within the sample. Spearman rank correlation coefficients were computed for these same variables for persons in direct practice roles only and another set of correlations were computed for persons employed only in mental health agencies. This analysis was designed to ascertain whether the grouping of all respondents together, rather than by employment setting, had led to an oversight of possible relationships between rurality and practice. Neither of these analyses produced a noteworthy difference from the pattern that emerged in the total sample.

For the direct-practice group, neither of the three measures of rurality was found to be correlated with any of the eight practice roles, the five client problems, or the four measures of specialization. Statistically signifi-

**Table 5.** Correlation Coefficients between Perception of Client Problems and Rurality

| Perception of problem | Population | County of employment | |
| | | Population density | Family farms |
|---|---|---|---|
| Intrapersonal conflict | .07 | .02 | .04 |
| Reactive emotional distress | .04 | .04 | .08 |
| Interpersonal conflict | .13 | .13 | .13 |
| Conflicts with formal organizations | .03 | .01 | .05 |
| Economics and social resources | .02 | .03 | .01 |

**Table 6.** Correlation Coefficients between Helping Networks and Rurality

| | Population | County of employment | |
| | | Population density | Family farms |
|---|---|---|---|
| Use of informal helping networks | .18* | .14 | .09 |
| Development of networks | .14 | .07 | .01 |

*$p<.05$

cant but weak correlations were found between the use of informal helping networks and each of the three measures of rurality, but the direction
of these correlations was opposite of that which was expected. Persons
working in more highly populous counties were found to be more likely to
employ informal helping networks than were persons in counties with a
smaller population (r=.24; $p<.01$). Population density was also found to
have a positive but weak correlation with the use of networks (r=.23;
$p<.05$), as was the number of persons per family farm (r=.19; $p<.05$). A
similar pattern emerged in the analysis of the relationship between the
development of networks and each of the three measures of rurality.
Positive coefficients were computed for the correlations between this variable and population (r=.29; $p<.01$) and between this variable and population density (r=.22; $p<.05$). It was not, however, significantly correlated
with family farms.

The separate analysis of the 58 respondents who were employed in
mental health agencies produced even less eventful results. None of the 57
correlations between each of the 3 dependent variables and each of the 19
independent variables was statistically significant.

A clear pattern emerged from this analysis of the relationship of rurality with various aspects of social work practice. Social workers in rural
areas were generally not found to be different from social workers in urban
areas with regard to their reports of emphasis upon various social work
roles, specialization among those roles, use of informal helping networks,
and perceptions of the kinds of problems that their clients brought to their
agencies.

## Discussion

The findings of this study are consistent with the research of Whitaker[30]
in Maine and with the results of a study regarding services for the aged in
Wisconsin. [31] There appear to be few differences in social work practice
between rural and urban settings. In particular, the consistency of the
findings reported here with those of Whitaker provides substantial evidence for the generalizability of these conclusions, because both studies
were undertaken with a random sample of social workers representing two
different state chapters of the National Association of Social Workers.

In the explanation of these findings, several alternatives can be offered. First, it is conceivable that social workers do not perceive differences
between rural and urban communities and, thus, have no reason to practice differently. This explanation, however, has been refuted by a compan-
ion study of the same population in which social workers differed along
the rural–urban continuum regarding their perceptions of their communi-

---

[30] Whitaker, "A Survey of Perceptions of Social Work Practice in Rural and
Urban Areas."
[31] Austin et al., "Exploring the Base for Rural Social Work Practice."

X

ties. Rural and urban social workers reported differences in their perceptions of their communities in relation to formality of community decision-making processes, pace of life, stability of lifestyle, emphasis upon traditional values, informal support systems, individualism, and emphasis upon education. [32]

If rural communities are perceived as being different, why do social workers not practice in different ways? One possible answer to this question is that these differences are not relevant to social work practice. Such reasoning undergirds Richard Dewey's discussion of the relevance of these differences for sociology. Dewey argues that differences along the rural–urban continuum are real but relatively unimportant in the understanding of social organization and individual behavior. [33]

Conceivably these perceived differences in community dynamics are relevant to social work practice but not to practice as defined by the variables explored in this study. If this is true, some new lines of investigation must be established in order to identify these aspects of practice, because the study reported here is reflective of the dominant literature on social work practice as it relates to the rural–urban continuum.

Finally, the possibility exists that social workers perceive relevant differences between rural and urban communities but are not prepared to practice in ways that encompass these differences. Most schools of social work are located in urban areas. Perhaps these schools focus their training predominantly upon urban practice issues and are not appropriately preparing students for rural practice. In response to this concern, several schools of social work in recent years have been established with the rural agenda as a major part of their missions. Additionally, a journal has been established that focuses upon rural human services *(Human Services in the Rural Environment)* and a growing literature has emerged in the past decade.

Interpretations of the results of this study must consider the limitations of both the nature of the sample and the methods of measuring the variables of practice and rurality. The sample consisted of the members of NASW within one state. Perhaps social workers who are not members of this organization are different from other social workers. Perhaps members of NASW in other states are different from those in this state. However, the consistency of the findings of this study with the findings of studies undertaken in other states does not bear out these suppositions.

The fact that no differences were found between social work practice in rural and urban areas need not be interpreted as meaning that no

---

[32] Roy T. Denton, Regional O. York, and James R. Moran, 'The Social Worker's View of the Rural Community: An Empirical Examination," *Human Services in the Rural Environment* 11 (Winter 1988): 14-21.

[33] Richard Dewey, "The Rural–Urban Continuum: Real But Relatively Unimportant," *American Journal of Sociology* 66 (July 1960): 60-66.

differences exist. Differences may exist that are too subtle to be uncovered by the methods used in the present study to define the variables. Even if little difference exists in the degree of emphasis among practice roles from rural to urban populations, there may be differences in the way these roles are played. Differences could exist in the social influences upon behavior and the kinds of institutions that must be taken into consideration. In the rural South, religion may play a more significant role in the lives of people than in other geographical areas and may need to be taken into consideration in the social worker's approach to the client.

Research concerning rural social work should now be directed to the relevance of rural–urban differences to social work practice. Further research should also focus on specific aspects of social work practice that could be relevant to the rural–urban continuum. Finally, social work education must continue its effort to identify how social workers who expect to practice in rural areas should be trained differently from their urban counterparts.

# 8

# Community-Oriented Practice in Rural Social Work

by Emilia E. Martinez-Brawley

O ne of the most recent developments in social work practice has come to be known as community social work or community-oriented social work. This movement, not to be confused with traditional community organization, has been the object of much recent attention in the United Kingdom and has also gathered some followers in the United States. In a short "Comments on Currents" in *Social Work,* Harrison commented:

> Post industrial social change has led to new emphases in social work on networks, self-help, volunteerism, social support and social care. The new emphases often involve people caring for and about one another, usually in community settings. . . . The models of practice that put these social care ideas into action are not as well articulated as therapeutic models. Sometimes community social care work is seen as marginally professional case management work that does not merit serious professional attention, yet many successful innovations have not been examined systematically to determine how they might be used by others. (Harrison, 1989, p. 73)

Since 1989, the community-oriented social work movement has gathered momentum on this side of the Atlantic, as government and volunteer agencies struggle to make their dollars go further in securing services for their clients. The original intent of the community-oriented social work movement was to promulgate a philosophy of working rather than focusing on fiscal considerations. However, because proponents of community-oriented social work have delivered good value for the money, fiscal considerations have added to the movement's appeal.

During a recent Annual Program Meeting (APM) of the Council on Social Work Education (CSWE), Smale, Hearn, and Harrison (1992) conducted a session to show why community social work is effective and how it could be developed. A number of social workers responded with interest. Yet, there was a clear underlying belief that perhaps community-oriented social work could not operate within the context of the categorical, specialized, and often turf-protecting agencies that are most common in the United States. While the caution of most of the academics and practitioners attending the APM session was undoubtedly well founded, it might be more appropriate to envision community-oriented practice not necessarily as an avant-garde or newly conceived dimension in social work, but rather as the legitimization of one of the most successful ways in which practitioners, working in the context of small communities, have often practiced effectively.

A basic, albeit limited, definition of community social work or community-oriented social work is useful here. While many definitions could be quoted, the one developed by Smale and Bennett (1989) addresses the major ingredients which are our concern.

> Community social work is a phrase coined to emphasize the need for social workers and social service deliverers to strive to make their services more relevant and effective with the population they serve. The aim is to move away from a service which is unintentionally bureaucratic and removed from the population, towards a greater dovetailing of formal help with the majority of care, support and control to be found in our society. The process has been referred to as the interweaving of formal and informal caring or working partnerships with natural helping networks. The logic of the argument for community social work based on this premise of partnership is that no universal blue prints for practice can be drawn up: each social work team[1] will develop its own approaches to the work depending upon the circumstances of their area and the partnerships they form within their sphere of work. (Smale and Bennett, 1989, p.11)

Three basic ingredients are implicit in this definition: debureaucratization, egalitarianism and partnership between providers and consumers (or clients in more traditional models), and high levels of autonomy in practice. The second and third ingredients interact, inasmuch as autonomy is limited not by traditional bureaucratic rules and procedures, but by responsiveness to the consumers in the local or communal context in which most helping takes place.[2]

The rural social work literature has always included an orientation to the community in which the practice takes place as an essential ingredient.

---

[1] Here, the authors are referring to the "social work teams" as they have existed in social services departments in England and Scotland since the Seebohm organization. A team is a suborganizational unit within the local (county or region) social service or social work department. A team, usually headed by a senior social worker, includes generalist and specialist social workers, home-help organizers, home helpers, occupational therapists and other ancillary personnel, depending on the area and the particular local authority.

[2] For a discussion of helping as an activity that takes place in the local community context, see Martinez-Brawley (1990), *Perspectives on the small community*, particularly chapters 2 and 7. For a discussion on debureaucratization and the philosophy of patchwork as local units of service delivery, see Hadley (1983) and Cooper (1983).

Through the decades, this orientation to the community has been identified by various labels such as "locality specific work," "community based work," or "preventive and enhancing work." In other words, an orientation to the community has always been an integral component of rural social work practice, although it often lacked some of the ingredients of current conceptualizations.

In the first edition of this book, Ginsberg (1976) suggested that "generalist preparation [is] essential for rural and small town community workers...." Additionally, he acknowledged that "nontraditional models of education such as supervision by nonprofessional, with professional consultation and periodic consultation..." were essential to practice in *small* or rural environments (p.11). In the same edition, Buxton (1976) suggested that social workers must remind themselves that "the ultimate responsibility for solving community problems lies with the whole community, not just the social worker and agency" (p.36). Accurately and eloquently, Buxton emphasized,

> We must work on the assumption that we are not alone in our concerns. It is an illusion, it seems to me, to feel that social workers are isolated in their commitment to help people in trouble. This is a tempting conclusion, especially easy to come by if we have narrow community contacts. The growing ranks of volunteers belie this, however, and for years, effective workers have enlisted local leaders to make suggestions and to give leadership. (Buxton, 1976, p. 36)

In a 1984 article in *Small Town,* this author concluded that "neither social workers nor other human service professionals can successfully work in community if they continue to hold fast to the idea that their major work is accomplished within the confines of bureaucratic agencies" (Martinez-Brawley, 1984, p.19). Clearly, these and other references drawn from the rural social work literature were not just the ingredients of much that we now conceptualize as community-oriented social work practice in the United States but, to a large extent, essential antecedents of the new movement.

Given what the seminal textbooks in rural social work have stated about rural practice (Brown, 1933; Ginsberg, 1976; Johnson, 1980; Martinez-Brawley, 1981) and given the proximity that has always existed between clients and providers in rural areas, good rural social work has always encompassed some of the basic elements of the recent Smale and Bennett (1989) definition. The pertinent questions to be asked in this chapter are whether and to what extent rural social work has been successful in incorporating all of those ingredients. Have some of the ingredients been accommodated in practice while others are still only latent or proposed in theory?

My thesis is that the three ingredients of community-oriented social work, namely, debureaucratization, partnership with clients or consumers, and autonomy in practice, have been present for some time, at least in the theory of rural social work. It must be acknowledged, however, that through the decades, rural social work has struggled with varying degrees of success in translating its theory into practice. Furthermore, rural social work has often struggled to validate its own principles of commitment to craftsmanship and community rather than therapy, against the tide of the profession in general, which appears to have been moving in the opposite direction (Fabricant, 1985). For example, the autonomy of the social worker in the local context has often been severely limited by the bureaucratic demands of agencies that stress standardization. Yet, rural workers have always acknowledged the difficulty of practicing in small communities without considering the local context and the need to adjust the practice to unique local conditions (Johnson, 1983; Jacobsen, 1986). For example, how can a worker adhere to strict limitations on the award of general assistance benefits in areas with chronic unemployment or underemployment? Most workers find that they must interweave formal with informal resources in order to respond to real need.

Another illustration is provided by the struggle of the best rural practitioners to maintain a holistic perspective—that is, to keep *from* succumbing to unrealistic specialization. Repeatedly, rural workers comment that it is easier to serve rural clients in agencies where practice is conceptualized in global or holistic terms rather than in specialist terms. Yet, the social work profession has become more and more specialized in recent years. This specialization of function, in itself a bureaucratic requirement, fuels a great many social work tasks, which, unfortunately, are often highly rewarded and draw a great deal of social work talent. However, in spite of limitations of degree, the most innovative rural social workers have been attempting to practice something akin to community-oriented social work, though perhaps not by that name.

This chapter will examine the ways in which social work in general has moved away from a community orientation. Then, the case for working in community with natural networks will be built. The unique predisposition of small communities and small-town people to work in a community-oriented fashion will be explained. Finally, tips for practitioners who want to develop a community-oriented approach will be provided.

## Social Work and the Local Community

By and large, and from the inception of the practice, social workers have felt more at ease in vertical than in horizontal communities[3]; they have tended to emphasize national rather than local organizations and

---

[3] During the 1960s, conceptualizations of community were developed to recognize the impingement of national forces on the local level. Some theorists of the 1960s went so far as to state that the national forces had absolutely overshadowed the historical centrality of local forces (Vidich and Bensman, 1968). Others, like Warren (1963), pointed out that local units have two distinct types of systemic ties: the vertical, national, or external and the horizontal or local. It was not until the Reagan years that social workers began to refocus, albeit for working reasons, on local ties.

have related to the cosmopolitans rather than to the localites[4] in the towns and cities where they work. The reasons for this may have been understandable at the inception of a practice that was interested in establishing institutional or universal responses to need. To establish its domain, social work needed to become a profession, to institutionalize helping as the undertaking of professionals rather than laypersons. Furthermore, social workers needed to embrace an agenda of reform which was most likely to be carried out through the efforts of the cosmopolitans. The establishment of social policies that would supplant individual benevolence was a task for the cosmopolitan influentials of the community who, in Merton's words, "had a following because they knew" (Merton, 1957, p. 403) rather than because they understood, as was the case of the localities. Thus, social workers developed close alliances with the cosmopolitan influentials who were more likely to support social causes that transcended local parameters, to run for political office, or to believe in universal or institutional[5] rather than personal responses to people's needs.

The alliance of social work to vertical ties has always been strong. Even today, the social work profession spends a great deal of time and effort endorsing national political candidates, for example, but pays little attention to local ones. Historically, even in small communities, social workers have been committed to and have endorsed institutional responses to needs because they believed that such responses were more universal and avoided the nepotistic tendencies of individuals. However, as Hadley and McGrath (1985) have noted,

> The compartmentalism and rigidity of the bureaucratic structure reinforces the emphasis on qualification and narrow interpretation of professionalism held by many social workers. It encourages a view in which care is seen as the prerogative of the professional, in which the unqualified should be relegated whenever possible to routine tasks and in which volunteers should be confined to marginal, *dogsbody* roles. (Hadley & McGrath, 1985, p. 7)

---

[4] Merton (1957) distinguished two types of influentials in communities, the local and the cosmopolitan. The scope of activity of the *localite* is the local or geographic community; the scope of activity of the *cosmopolitan* is the national or international community. These two types co-exist in all towns, however small. Merton believed that the prototypical impersonal welfare worker could never become a local influential, but that community-oriented social work would necessitate that the worker understand and respect the localite. (For a full discussion of this topic, see Martinez-Brawley, 1983, pp. 78-79.)

[5] In the context of this chapter, *universal* or *institutional* responses are those that provide measures based on perceived rights of individuals rather than on the nature of social relationships. For example, political leaders who struggle for a nationally guaranteed minimum income would be supporting universal or institutional measures, while local leaders who might be struggling for a very accessible and local food bank would be focusing more on *personal* responses.

In attempting to standardize policies and services, social work often distanced its response from the community context of the individuals for whom such responses were intended. In small communities, however, it is hard to ignore the fact that most caring is carried out by lay people in their roles as kin, neighbors, or friends (Collins & Pancoast, 1974; Wenger, 1984, 1992) and cannot be standardized. Even when professionals care, their caring cannot be devoid of personalism[6] and is often received and acknowledged in the spirit of reciprocity that characterizes helping among neighbors.

A successful rural worker will always take into account the sum of helping resources available to people in need in rural communities; these resources may be formal in sponsorship and provision or informal, that is, provided by friends or neighbors. Over a decade ago, Johnson commented on this matter:

> In a time of decreasing fiscal resources it is essential that social workers maximize the use of all resources at hand, including informal networking. The contemporary political climate gives little hope that government funds and services will meet existing needs. In fact, some existing government services are an "endangered species." (Johnson, 1983, p. 27)

Because need is always greater than resources, ignoring the informal in one case serves only to drain the resources available for the total community. Successful rural workers have always practiced in this community-oriented fashion. Rural workers require further opportunities and greater legitimization in order to spread this practice of community-oriented social work.

A problem that emerges in dovetailing the formal and informal resources of a community is that the informal sector is, by its very nature, very local. The notion of kin helping kin and neighbor helping neighbor requires a degree of geographic proximity or a local setting. Yet, the idea that nonlocal is more sophisticated and consequently better has viciously permeated practice. Agencies have not only tended to define practice within an agency rather than a community context, but also to validate good practice as practice done at the center, in other words, in the county seat not the local village. The best workers are rewarded with positions at the central location of the agency (wherever it might be) or with more specialized jobs, thus further removing them from the community context.

---

[6] I first encountered the term *personalism* when attempting to describe the way in which ethnics, particularly Hispanics, related to the world of help. It was evident that Hispanics wanted to identify individual persons who provided help (personalism), not helping offices or positions in the helping bureaucracy. Many years of experience studying rural people cause me to conclude that rural and small-town people share this intense need for personalism. It is perhaps this personalism in helping and other spheres of life that counteracts anomie in small towns and villages.

Upward mobility on the job tends to mean more intensive work with other professionals rather than with community citizens.

In validating its own theory, rural social work must reject these centralistic tendencies. If good practice requires work in the local community, then the most sophisticated and best practitioners must receive those assignments. In validating their own practices, rural workers must show their commitment to a power shift in helping relationships (Barr, 1989). In involving laypersons and citizens in the provision of care, professionals must be committed to respecting and abiding by the community members' wisdom.

> Community-oriented social work emphasizes a more egalitarian environment in which local people plan and participate in providing services. Such an environment might open professionals and agencies to closer scrutiny, and, potentially, to criticism, but also might open them to the possibility of attaining the local support they never had before. Social workers and other professionals need to be prepared to handle these situations. Community-oriented services are as much an attitude as a collection of techniques. Because communities and local people vary, community-oriented social services will have their own unique aspects in each local community. (Martinez-Brawley, 1990, P. 239)

## Working in Community: Social Work and Natural Networks

The evidence that helping takes place within the context of the natural and/or informal networks of communities has been growing steadily since the 1960s when sociologists of the mass society school proposed that community, as it had been known through the centuries, was no longer important in modern industrial societies. During the 1970s and 1980s, evidence to the contrary was amassed and reported in the press and the social science literature ("America's small town boom," 1981; "Going home," 1989). In *The Pursuit of Loneliness: American Culture at the Breaking Point,* Slater (1976) identified some of the natural human desires that are satisfied through communal ties. One was the desire for community, that is, solidarity or cohesiveness—the wish to live in a total and visible collective entity. Another was the desire for engagement, that is, significance—the wish to confront one's surroundings and find meaningful extensions of one's ego. Another, and perhaps the most meaningful in this context, was the desire for dependence, that is, security—the wish to satisfy and be satisfied.

Whittaker and Garbarino (1983), for example, documented the importance of a variety of natural helping networks to help people cope with the problems of living. Harrison (1989) discussed the need to stress social interaction and interdependence in any quest for community. Martinez-Brawley and Blundall (1989, 1991) surveyed the attitudes and behaviors of farm families in two states and found that, in spite of researchers' and clinicians' concerns about the permanency and nature of natural networks in contemporary times, most families turned to them, or preferred to turn to them, when faced with stressful situations.

The centrality of natural networks of care is particularly true in relation to the elderly, who tend to be the least mobile group in almost any locality. Wenger (1988) developed a rating scale to assess the nature of social and communal relationships among the elderly and found that most elderly live in settings where social relationships are very satisfying and that the help they need tends to be for the short term, whenever a particular set of events prevents them from managing with existing networks. Attesting to the importance of natural interrelationships in communities when help is needed, Wenger (1988) also found that attempts to put relationships on a reciprocal basis and to ensure continuity of relationships characterized the elderly's dealings with the helping agents closest to them, home helpers (pp. 64, 66, and 90).

The tendency in social work, however, has been to view natural networks in fairly traditional terms. Social workers have concentrated on family and friends rather than extending their analysis to include all other community social support systems. Frequently, paid support mechanisms, which are considered formal in some sense, extend their roles to become unpaid or informal helpers. For example, mail carriers in small towns might call on long-time residents along their routes when they notice that the mail is not being collected.

In small communities, extensive informal networks of support can be energized to rally around issues that might be seen as everyone's responsibility (Johnson, 1983). This sense of communal responsibility can perhaps be most frequently used in relation to the elderly, where, for example, a great many members of a community would be willing to lend a hand to resolve individual and collective problems, such as transportation. Since old age is viewed as a condition that will, sooner or later, affect all members of the community, the natural networks of the elderly need not be circumscribed to those who are related.

Many social workers, however, still worry about the negative connotations of any approach that appears to resemble turn-of-the-century days in the profession, when social workers, eager to retain the support mechanisms of early immigrants, advised people to remain in what might have been ghettoized conditions. Furthermore, social workers also struggle against the implications of approaches that rely on people's awareness of similarities and sense of belonging to a particular group rather than on people's commitment to the diversity of the human condition. However, as prejudice and other barriers fall, a community-oriented approach to social work might begin to be viewed, not as a narrow path, but as a means of capturing the synergy that exists between the well-being of the inner self and the outer self, or the fit between the private self and the collective ethos.

While no one would argue that formal services are required in all environments, the case for using the formal sector as a vehicle to energize the natural or informal care networks can be made without apology.

Helping services, consequently, are becoming more concerned with and focused on helping consumers or recipients of services, either individuals or communities, make easier transitions between times of satisfactory and supportive social relationships and periods when those relationships are not enough or fail.

### Interweaving the Formal and Informal in Rural Areas

In arguing the importance of interweaving any formal help provided with the natural networks of people in their communal environments, we can turn to a recent study by Fitchen (1991), which addresses this mesh within the context of rural areas. Fitchen found that among the young, who constituted the most mobile group of people in her study of 16 counties in rural New York state (p. 6), the radius within which they moved was not very extensive. In other words, although some might argue that the young and poor are mobile and thus might fail to develop supportive social relationships to help them through stressful times, the reality was rather different. In Fitchen's account, these young people moved within circumscribed parameters wherein those networks were still operational. Some of Fitchen's case examples provide useful illustrations:

> *Case A.* One couple with two preschool children has moved eleven times in the six years of their marriage. Tomorrow, they would be moving again, but this would be a "good move" and an easy one to an adjacent apartment that would have the two bedrooms the Department of Social Services requires the family to have if it is to continue receiving support for a child with special needs. (Fitchen, 1991, p. 144)

> *Case B.* One young single mother had moved seven times in one year since she and her baby had fled from a violent boyfriend, staying temporarily with different relatives housing, moving into a condemned building, then into an apartment she could not afford, and then living with her girlfriend until the welfare department ruled that out, and eventually ending up in a roadside cluster of trailers. (Fitchen, 1991, p. 144)

> *Case C.* A young couple and their toddler had just recently moved into the largest apartment they had ever had. They had obtained it with the help of the county's community action program, which also obtained federal rental assistance for them. The couple had moved back and forth in the county and nearby, quite often living with his or her parents, grandparents or siblings. . . . (Fitchen, 1991,p. 144)

Fitchen's accounts bring to life two essential points. First, the case stories show the importance of functional natural networks that provide support, even among the poorest and neediest. Secondly, they show that in times of extreme need, natural networks alone are not enough. In making the case for community-oriented social work, the argument is not one of community social work versus access to formal resources; the central argument in community-oriented social work is the dovetailing of formal and informal resources in the community (O'Hare, 1988, p. 6; Porter, 1989, p. 26). The crux of the argument lies in the successful determination of what should be made available through the formal sector without eroding the informal.

Drawing on Fitchen's examples, one might suggest that a community oriented social worker involved with the young mother in Case B would need to be fully aware that the relatives and girlfriend who took the young mother into their already overcrowded homes were the mother's first line of assistance. Those relatives should be included in the mother's future plans because they are a support source for her and because they will be there when the welfare social worker or the community action worker is not. Fitchen's examples provide an important message to the community-oriented social worker: While the bureaucratic rule of the welfare department might not allow this young mother to live in such overcrowded accommodations, the fact that someone was willing to take her in when she needed help is a major asset that must be acknowledged and protected by social workers.

The community social work approach applied in Cases A, B, and C would also suggest that any agents from the formal sector who intervene on behalf of those clients would have to do so in consultation with the clients. In other words, before any action was taken in Case B, the social workers, using a community-oriented approach, would have explored at least the following questions:

- What did the young mother think about living with her girlfriend?
- Did she find the overcrowded conditions preferable and more supportive than living alone at a time of distress?
- What were this young mother's relationships with her various relatives?
- What did she want for herself and her child?
- How would she go about securing what she wanted?
- Was there anyone else in the community with whom she wanted to connect?
- Given that her mobility was circumscribed to one county, what additional people and networks could have been helpful to this client and this community?
- Could the young woman's problems have been defined as community problems that affected all residents, poor and nonpoor alike?
- What different types of interventions might result from such definition?

The continuing and worsening poverty for the rural areas of the United States, documented by recent statistics (O'Hare, 1988, p. 6; Porter, 1989, p. 26), indicates that the problems people are facing today are often not individual problems but community problems. The worsening poverty in rural and small communities is the result of the complex interaction of forces such as employment inadequacies, housing shortages, schooling concerns, and others. Each force in itself is not the cause, but the destabilizing interaction of these forces frequently creates chaos and erodes the very fabric of the small community. As Fitchen (1991) has stated, the combination of destabilizing forces "explain[s] why rural poverty is becoming qualitatively worse" (p. 150) and affecting not just individuals but the total rural environment.

Community social work is particularly relevant because it is not just about helping communities deal with these destabilizing forces in holistic ways. Community-oriented social work is about inventorying what the community has to offer; it is about helping communities take ownership of their concerns and problems (Higginson, 1990; Joslin, 1980).

In community-oriented social work, the type of work suggested by social support system theorists (Maguire, 1991; Maguire & Biegel, 1982; Whittaker & Garbarino, 1983) is expanded beyond the realm of the personal. The networking in community-oriented practice is not just relegated to family and friends but expands to neighborhood helping and community empowerment. All these levels of social support intervention are recognized by various authors who, in fact, share the views of many community-oriented practitioners in suggesting that social support development often results in the reexamination and redefinition of the role of professionals.

One of the advantages of working in small communities is that most social work clients are likely to know one another. Anomie and disengagement with the rest of the community are not common. Misengagement and even punitive engagement (if the community finds a person's problems particularly upsetting) are more common than anomic or disengaged relationships. This sense of interconnection makes the community-oriented approach an appropriate avenue for exploration. Most rural clients have extensive networks operating in their lives (Collins & Pancoast, 1974), although not all are supportive. The role of the skillful rural worker then becomes to transform existing networks into supportive and problem solving ones. Whether the problem is a person in need or a group of people who are underserved, the challenge for the rural worker is to help the community define the problem in communal terms and take appropriate action. This work, more often than not, involves not just the clients of social work but the community leaders.

In most of the United States, personal social services such as child welfare, mental health, and aging services require local matches that vary according to the funding formulae of the particular state. In order to maintain a local commitment to formal services, local leadership must feel a sense of ownership of those programs. Unless the local leadership is involved in generating community solutions for community problems, social workers will continue to apply Band-Aid solutions that do not last and are often not welcome. To be effective in a community, social workers in small towns and counties must realize that they are political. Local government is in a state of flux, and social work risks losing ground unless new approaches to social problems are tried. The community-oriented social work approach offers the opportunity for creating partnerships within the various layers of the social structure.

## Conclusion

Over 60 years ago, Laski (1930) pointed out:

> It is one thing to urge the need for expert consultation at every stage in making policy; it is another thing to insist that the expert's judgment must be final. For special knowledge and the highly trained mind produce their own limitations, which, in the realm of statesmanship, are of decisive importance. Expertise, it may be argued, sacrifices the insight of common sense to intensity of experience. It breeds an inability to accept new views from the very depth of its preoccupation with its own conclusions. It too often fails to see round its subject. It sees its results out of perspective by making them the center of relevance to which all other results must be related. Too often, also, it lacks humility; and this breeds in its possessors a failure in proportion which makes them fail to see the obvious which is before their very noses. (Laski, 1930, p. 102)

In Laski's analysis, the "intensity of vision" associated with expertise, specialization, and professionalization "destroys the sense of proportion." In the domain of the human services and social work, the community-oriented movement appears as an attempt to recapture that sense of proportion. It is an attempt to stop the erosion of the value or the contributions of the citizen and the consumer. Other movements have struggled to do similar things, that is, to make social services more commonsensical and accessible to the average citizen, and to reduce the complexity, particularly the bureaucratic complexity, of the organizations that deliver expertise and professionalism. These were not anti-professional movements but pro-proportion undertakings. An example of such a movement, which had some common elements with rural social work, was the services integration movement. Services integration was popular in the1960s and, like rural social work, was related to generalism and single-door efforts to serve people in community. Despite great effort and federal monies allocated to the pursuit of integration, a 1972 HEW Task Force identified size and complexity as two of the major obstacles to the success of that movement.

> The number of doors to open; the professional keys to open them; the mazes of paperwork and human interaction; the length of time between conception of an idea and fulfillment; the budgetary uncertainties. . . . All of these, in the aggregate, create a specter that is a challenge to the most sophisticated local advocate of integration. (HEW, 1972, p. 17)

In the end, and even today, services integration, a very humane attempt to make accessibility a more valued characteristic of services, has remained at the periphery of social work. Professionalization and bureaucratization have proven too powerful to conquer. Supporters of community-oriented practice are concerned that, once again, professional specialties, turf protection, and entrenched bureaucratic procedures might prove to be extraordinarily adamant.

On the brighter side, however, small-scale integrative gems, very entrepreneurial in nature, continue to interest administrators and workers in *Gemeinschaftlich* environments (Martinez-Brawley & Delevan, 1991). Small rural counties have risen to the challenge of scarcity by attempting to do things differently. In many ways, rural counties are pioneering integrative efforts to increase access to human services in what are very underserved environments. Community-oriented efforts might also find fertile ground within the context of small communities, where bureaucratic ways of working do not really make sense and where providers and recipients have always interacted with a certain degree of intimacy (Fenby, 1978).

Although resource constraints are generally viewed as deleterious to innovation and creativity, current concerns about resources might make the testing of community-oriented alternatives a mandate for survival. In this sense, social workers might be readier than ever to explore ways of interweaving all existing resources, formal and informal, professionally advanced or traditional and folk, to resolve current human problems. Rural communities have been particularly constrained, yet their needs have increased considerably. Survival will demand that all of the strengths of a community, including the close relationships among localites, be seen not as impediments to the actions of professionals but as resources to be used by them. More egalitarian relationships between providers and recipients, a trademark of community-oriented social work, will, out of necessity, be pursued.

Rural social workers need not wait for external circumstances to worsen to embrace this new way of working. The community orientation of social work practice, as discussed here, is not new or avant-garde in rural social work. Rural workers have always been instinctively familiar with the tenets of what is now being described as community-oriented practice. Consequently, as we formalize and institutionalize community-oriented practice in social work, rural practitioners can lead the way and set the tone for future decades.

## References

America's small town boom. (1981, July 6). *Newsweek*, pp. 26-37.

Barr, A. (1989). New dogs-new tricks? Some principles and implications for community social work. In G. G. Smale & W. Bennett (Eds.), *Community social work in Scotland. Pictures of practice: Volume 1* (pp. 163-183). London: National Institute for Social Work.

Brown, J. (1933). *The rural community and social casework.* New York: Family Welfare Association of America.

Buxton, E. B. (1976). Delivering social services in rural areas. In L. Ginsberg (Ed.), *Social work in rural communities: A book of readings* (pp. 29-40). New York: Council on Social Work Education.

Collins, A., & Pancoast, D. (1974). *Natural helping networks: A strategy for prevention.* Washington, DC: National Association of Social Workers.

Cooper, M. (1983). Putting philosophy into practice. In I. Sinclair & D. N. Thomas (Eds.), *Perspectives in patch* (Paper #14) (pp. 9-11). London: National Institute of Social Work.

Department of Health Education, and Welfare. (1972, June). *Report of the Task Force on Administrative and Organizational Constraints to Services Integration.* Washington, DC: Author.

Fabricant, M. (1985). The industrialization of social work practice. *Social Work, 30*(5).

Fenby, B. (1978). Social work in a rural setting. *Social Work, 23,* 162-163.

Fitchen, J. M. (1991). *Endangered spaces, enduring places: Change, identity, and survival in rural America.* Boulder, CO: Westview.

Ginsberg, L. (Ed.). (1976). *Social work in rural communities: A book of readings.* New York: Council on Social Work Education.

Going home. (1989, December 18). *U.S. News and World Report,* pp. 44-73.

Green, R. (1989). The Badenoch and Strathspey social work team of Highland. In G. G. Smale & W. Bennett (Eds.). *Community social work in Scotland. Pictures of practice: Vol. 1* (pp. 109120). London: National Institute for Social Work.

Hadley, R. (1983). The philosophy of patchwork and its implementation. In I. Sinclair & D. N. Thomas (Eds.), *Perspectives on patch* (Paper #14) (pp. 4-6). London: National Institute of Social Work.

Hadley, R., & McGrath M. (1985). Introduction. In R. Hadley & M. McGrath (Eds.), *Going local–Neighbourhod social services. NCVO Occasional Paper 1* (pp. 1-15). London: Bedford Square.

Harrison, W. (1989). Social work and the search for postindustrial community. *Social Work, 34*(1), pp. 73-75,

Higginson, J. (1990). Partners not problems: Developing new roles for staff and consumers. In G. Darvill & G. Smale (Eds.), *Partners in empowerment: Networks of innovation in social work. Pictures in practice: Vol. 2* (pp. 77-102). London: National Institute for Social Work.

Jacobsen, M. (1986). Working with communities. In *The social services: An introduction* (2nd ed.). Itasca, IL: Peacock.

Johnson, H. W. (Ed.). (1980). *Rural human services: A book of readings.* Itasca, IL: Peacock.

Johnson, L. (1983). Networking–A means of maximizing resources. *Human Services in the Rural Environment, 8*(2), 27-31.

Joslin, J. (1980). Islington: Essex road team–A community based team adopts a patch system. In R. Hadley & M. McGrath (Eds.), *Going Local–Neighbourhood Social Services. NCVO Occasional Paper 1* (p. 63-69). London: Bedford Square.

Laski, H. (1930, December). The limitations of the expert. *Harper's*, pp. 101-110.

Maguire, L. (1991). *Social support systems: A generalist approach.* Silver Spring, MD: National Association of Social Workers.

Maguire, L., & Biegel, D. (1982). The use of social networks in social welfare. In *Social Welfare Forum.* New York: Columbia University Press.

Martinez-Brawley, E. (1981). *Seven decades of rural social work: From country life commission to rural caucus.* New York: Praeger.

Martinez-Brawley, E. (1984). Working with the local community. *Small Town, 14*(5),14-21.

Martinez-Brawley, E. (1990). *Perspectives on the small community: Humanistic views for practitioners.* Silver Spring, MD: NASW Press.

Martinez-Brawley, E., & Blundall, J. (1989). Farm families' preferences towards the personal social services. *Social Work, 34*(6), 513-522.

Martinez-Brawley, E., & Blundall, J. (1991). Whom shall we help? Farm families' beliefs and attitudes about need and services. *Social Work, 36*(4), 315-321.

Martinez-Brawley, E., & Delevan, S. (1991). *Considerations on integrative structures, conditions and alternative models for county human services delivery.* University Park: Pennsylvania State University, Pennsylvania Rural Counties Human Services Project.

Merton, R. (1957). *Social theory and social structure.* Glencoe, IL: Free Press.

O'Hare, W. P. (1988). *The rise of poverty in rural America.* Washington, DC: Population Reference Bureau.

Porter, K. H. (1989). *Poverty in rural America: A national overview.* Washington, DC: Center on Budget and Policy Priorities.

Slater, P. (1976). *Pursuit of loneliness: American culture at a breaking point.* Boston: Beacon.

Smale, G., & Bennett, W, (1989). Introduction. In G. Smale & W. Bennett (Eds.), *Community social work in Scotland. Pictures of practice: Vol. 1.* London: National Institute for Social Work

Smale, G. G., Hearn, B., & Harrison, W. D. (1992, March). *Toward a practice theory for community social work: Britain's practice and development exchange.* Paper presented at the38th Annual Program Meeting of Council on Social Work Education, Kansas City, MO.

Vidich, A., & Bensman, J. (1968). *Small town in mass society: Class power and religion in a rural community.* Garden City, NJ: Anchor.

Warren, R. (1963). *The community in America* (3rd ed.). Chicago: Rand McNally.

Wenger, G. C. (1984). *The supportive network: Coping with old age.* London: Allen & Unwin.

Wenger, G. C. (1988). Old people's health and experiences of the caring services. In *Occasional papers. The Institute of Human Aging.* Liverpool, England: Liverpool University Press.

Wenger, G. C. (1992). *Help in the old age—Facing up to change: A longitudinal network study.* Liverpool, England: Liverpool University Press.

Whittaker, J., & Garbarino, J. (1983). *Social support networks: Informal helping in the human services.* New York: Aldine.

# 9

# Rural Poverty and Rural Social Work

by Janet M. Fitchen

**P**overty is a significant factor in the lives of many rural individuals, families, and communities and is often part of the context for the practice of rural social work. In many rural communities, poverty shapes the problems and service needs of individuals and families, defines the kinds of institutional human service responses that are needed, and, at the same time, may limit the array of service resources available.

This chapter is intended to provide an overview of rural poverty, to indicate its pervasiveness and its tenaciousness, to explore reasons why it is increasing, and to suggest implications for rural social work practice. To provide background on rural poverty throughout the nation, I will present a broad overview, summarizing recent data on trends, causes, and characteristics. To complement this macro-level overview, I will present a more descriptive close-up view of rural poverty at the local level, drawing on my field research in upstate New York. Finally, I will indicate particular aspects of rural poverty that appear to have the greatest consequence for the practice of social work in rural settings. But before turning to this substantive material, it might be helpful to consider first why rural poverty, though prevalent and increasing, is still largely overlooked.

## Clarifying Some Myths About Rural Poverty

As a society, we tend not to see rural poverty. It is invisible partly because it exists "out there" in places where few Americans live or travel and partly because it is overshadowed by urban poverty. The large concentrations of poor people, the despair, and the riots of inner cities that command popular and political attention are decidedly absent in rural places. But rural poverty is also invisible because of our national mental imagery. Collectively, we perceive rural America as the place of "the good life," and poverty as an inner-city phenomenon. In these equations, pov-

The New York State research for this chapter was conducted with support from the Ford Foundation through the Aspen Institute's Rural Economic Policy Program. Additional U.S. research is being conducted under the auspices of the National Rural Studies Committee and the Western Rural Development Center, with funding from the Kellogg Foundation.

erty and rurality are not associated, and the very concept of rural poverty strikes the collective mind as an oxymoron. In reality, however, the terms are neither contradictory nor mutually exclusive: Rurality and poverty frequently coexist. In fact, poverty rates are just as high in rural areas as they are in central cities, as we shall document in the next section.

If we are to recognize and deal with the reality of rural poverty, both in formulating policy and in carrying out social programs, a more accurate conceptualization is required. Towards this end, it may be useful to confront explicitly three common misperceptions about rural poverty.

- *Rural poverty is quite different from urban poverty.* The dispersed nature of rural poverty not only keeps it hidden from outsiders, but also means that poor people in rural areas live under a different set of circumstances from those of poor people in inner cities, with different relationships to land, to community institutions, and to each other. The rural poor have a different set of stresses, and different options and opportunities. Most obvious of all, rural poverty differs from urban poverty in the absence of the concentration effect, meaning that in rural areas poor people are small-scale populations, existing in isolated pockets in the open countryside or marginally enclaved within small communities or on their edges. Rural poverty is usually part of an economically mixed setting that includes the full spectrum of socio-economic statuses. This differs from ghettoized urban poverty in which a large, closely packed population lives in a confined area where nearly everyone is poor. This point is so obvious, perhaps, that it is never really recognized consciously, but its role in the lives of poor people and its consequences for the practice of rural social work can hardly be overestimated. Overcoming the misperception that poverty is only a city problem may pave the way for reducing the reluctance of many rural community leaders to admit to the poverty in their midst and to spend public funds on human service programs.

- *Rural poverty is not necessarily connected with the farm economy or the farm crisis.* Our collective thinking still features an agrarian myth that equates rural with agriculture and defines rural America as an agricultural place. A corollary of the myth suggests that if there is such a thing as rural poverty, it is surely connected to the farm economy. By this reckoning, the recent rise in rural poverty is assumed to be the result of the farm crisis of the mid-1980s. Such a misdiagnosis becomes enshrined in policy and institutionalized in programs. But in reality, only a tiny percentage of rural Americans became poor as a result of the farm crisis or the general restructuring of agriculture, in which more midsized family farms were lost and the remaining farms were further consolidated into larger operations. Most rural Americans, in fact, do not derive their employment income from agriculture. Although politicians and agricultural interests in many states, including New York, are fond of saying that agriculture is the number one rural industry, their claims to its major employment role include a large portion of jobs only very indirectly related to agriculture, such as retail food sales. In some regions where agriculture does dominate the local economy, as in parts of the Midwest and Northern Plains, its role in the employment and economic well-being of the population is much smaller than generally assumed. Nationwide, less than one quarter of all rural counties are "agriculture dependent" (meaning that 20% or more of the total labor and proprietor income comes from farming). At most, 10% of the nation's rural population live on farms; the other 90% are classified as nonfarm rural residents. Only about 2% of the nation's poor are farm residents. However, many thousands of people who work on farms as agricultural laborers live in counties not designated as rural or nonmetropolitan, yet these people may be desperately poor, as is the case in parts of California and the Southwest. But, overall, persistent and cyclical economic difficulties in agriculture play a much smaller role in creating rural poverty than is generally perceived. Recognizing the relatively weak and specific connections between agriculture and rural poverty will enable development of more appropriate antipoverty strategies for rural areas and will better attune social agencies and practitioners to the real issues of rural poverty.

• *Rural poverty is not geographically limited or uniform, but widespread and varied.* While the public and the media are reasonably cognizant of poverty in a few "famous" spots, such as Appalachia, the Mississippi Delta, and in the fields harvested by migrant laborers, rural poverty is actually much more pervasive. Also, there are many rural poverties, each with different etiologies and different expressions reflecting differences in regional or local economies, in demographic and social patterns, and in ethnic and racial factors. Proximity to metropolitan areas or, conversely, geographic isolation, is an additional variable shaping the particular nature of poverty in any specific locale. The concept of a multiplicity of rural Americas is important for social workers training for or practicing in rural America because strategies and efforts must be adapted to the situations and needs of particular rural places.

## A National Overview

### Statistics and Trends in Rural Poverty

Poverty rates have always been higher in rural (or nonmetropolitan) areas than in metropolitan (or urban/suburban) places. The difference diminished in the 1960s and 1970s as the result of several federal antipoverty initiatives and a generally strong rural economy; but after 1980, rural poverty rose more rapidly than urban poverty. By 1986, the nation's nonmetropolitan poverty rate had reached 18%, which was 50% higher than the metropolitan poverty rate of 12% and virtually equaled the poverty rate in the nation's inner cities. In the late 1980s, the increase in rural poverty slowed a bit while the inner-city poverty rate remained stable. The 1990 census shows a rural poverty rate of 16.3%, which translates to over 9 million poor people in rural America, as compared with a metropolitan poverty rate of 12.7% or 24.5 million people.

In examining trends among subgroups of the rural poor population, we find that poverty in rural America is no longer as concentrated among the elderly and the farm population. While farm poverty accounted for 20% of all nonmetropolitan poverty in 1960, it now accounts for approximately 10%. Among the rural elderly, the poverty rate has come down from 22.5% in 1973 to 16.1% in 1990; but even with this drop, poverty is more common among the rural elderly than the metropolitan elderly, for whom the poverty rate is 10.8% (U.S. Bureau of the Census, 1991, pp. 53, 56). In contrast, rural poverty rates have grown in two population subgroups, the young and the employed or "working poor," mirroring similar trends in urban poverty. In rural America now, the rate of poverty among children under 18 is 22.9%, even higher than the national rate of 20.6% (U.S. Bureau of the Census, pp. 56, 24).

Poverty rates among minority groups have not changed much in recent years. The total population of poor people in 1990 is still predominantly white and nonethnic: 71.3% of the rural (nonmetropolitan) poor are white, 25% are black, and 5.6% are Hispanic. However, poverty rates differ markedly among rural population subgroups: the poverty rate for rural whites is 13.5%; for rural blacks, 40.8%; for rural Hispanics, 32.0%; and for rural Native Americans, at least 30%. In each population subgroup, nonmetropolitan poverty rates are substantially higher than metropolitan poverty rates, as shown in Table 1.

Given the high rates of poverty among minority groups, it is not surprising to find that rural regions with larger minority populations also have higher poverty rates: Poverty of persons and poverty of place often coincide. Indeed, rural counties with persistently high poverty rates and persistently low income levels are found almost entirely in the South. Here the nonmetropolitan poverty rate was 21.2% in 1987, as compared with 13.6% in the rest of rural America. In the South, the rural poor are predominantly black; whereas in the persistently poor counties scattered in the upper Midwest and the Southwest, the populations with the highest poverty rates are American Indian or Hispanic.

*Table 1.* Poverty Rates by Race/Ethnicity and by Metropolitan/
Nonmetropolitan Residence, 1990

|  | Whites | Blacks | Hispanics |
|---|---|---|---|
| Nonmetropolitan | 13.5 | 40.8 | 32.0 |
| Metropolitan | 9.9 | 30.1 | 27.8 |

*Note:* From *Current Population Reports* (Table 8, pp. 53, 56). U.S. Bureau of the Census, 1991, Series P-60, No. 175, Poverty in the United States: 1990. Washington, DC: U.S. Government Printing Office.

## Causes of Increasing Rural Poverty

For rural America as a whole, increasing poverty is attributable to a variety of macroeconomic trends that have also occurred in urban areas but have had particularly detrimental effects on rural economies. Rural resource-based economies (e.g., those based on timber, mining, and oil) were hard hit in the 1980s, and to the extent that the farm crisis disrupted local retail businesses, it caused a ripple effect in rural nonfarm economies, especially in the Midwest. However, the poor performance of the rural economy in most regions during the last decade is primarily attributable to the loss of manufacturing. The downsizing of American manufacturing and the loss of plants to overseas locations has affected the nation's rural population particularly because nearly 40% of the rural population live in counties where manufacturing contributes the major share of local employment earnings.

In the postindustrial U.S. economy, and especially while the nation is in the throes of adjustment to a global economy, rural areas have been particularly vulnerable. Countless small cities and towns have recently suffered the loss of large or midsized manufacturing plants that had provided the backbone of their employment and local economy. In areas with a relatively small number of plants, when one or two factories leave an area, the remaining few are unable to take up the slack by hiring the displaced workers. Few new factories have replaced those lost; at best smaller scale routine manufacturing branch plants have decentralized to depressed rural regions in search of cheap labor—before they move on again to the cheaper labor markets of the Third World. Meanwhile, the growth of service-sector employment has only partially compensated for manufacturing job losses. Because the service sector tends to pay just above minimum wage and to offer only part-time hours, the substitution of service-sector jobs for manufacturing has reduced the income levels of rural workers and swelled the ranks of the working poor (Shapiro, 1989). Low-end service-sector jobs are an inadequate substitute in terms of health and retirement benefits as well. Additionally, small communities can create or sustain only a limited number of service jobs, such as retail work. While rural communities have been shortchanged by this employment shift, the situation has been exacerbated by the fact that the rural economy is more vulnerable to recession. In the 1980s, rural areas fell into deeper recession and recovered more slowly than metropolitan areas, a pattern that may be repeated in the 1990s.

Within this broad picture of rural economic decline, regional and local vulnerability to poverty varies considerably. At the local level, rural economies are affected by fluctuations in the economic health of the nearest urban centers. For example, when U.S. steel production lost its position in the global economy, many small towns lost their economic base, as well. Although the mills that shut down were located in urban areas, their demise robbed such towns of employment in ancillary, supportive, and spin-off manufacturing tied to the steel industry in the urban center.

Superimposed on economic differences are demographic and migration patterns that may also affect local poverty rates. Population migration may redistribute poverty and wealth over the landscape. Migration of people from rural to urban places has tended to impoverish rural communities because, in general, people with lower incomes or lower earning potentials remain in rural areas, while better prepared rural people with higher earning potential move to urban or suburban areas (Lichter, McLaughlin, & Cornwell, 1990). Differential migration also leaves a residual rural population that is older and less likely to be in the labor force because as much as one-third of the net loss from rural areas is in the young adult group of 18 to 24 year olds (O'Hare, 1988).

On the other hand, urban-to-rural migration has reduced poverty in some rural areas. The clearest examples come from rural areas situated close to metropolitan areas, some of which have benefited from decentralization of jobs outward from the cities and from a movement of middle-income commuter people to the countryside. This centrifugal migration pattern was common all across the nation during the 1970s and constituted what demographers call the "nonmetropolitan turnaround," for it represented a major change in the historic direction of internal migration in the U.S. In the 1980s, however, the turnaround reversed, and urban-to-rural migration was greatly reduced and much more localized. Where this movement to rural areas still continues, as in the Northeast, it has direct effects in elevating the local median income and the total local income and in decreasing the poverty rate. An indirect poverty-reducing effect may also be created when the influx of more affluent people increases housing and land prices and drives lower income people out of the locality in search of less expensive, more remote rural areas, which, again, creates increased poverty rates in the receiving communities.

Population migration to small towns, spurred by economic changes in both the city and the countryside, may cause increased poverty in some rural places. In the Midwest, for example, the decentralization of the meat-packing industry from cities to rural areas where the feed lots are located has brought a number of jobs to some rural communities. But in the new generation of packing plants, jobs are lower skill and wages are considerably less, making the new plants unattractive to local populations and providing an impetus for in-migration of low-skilled minority populations. Because many of the minority workers, who are often of Southeast Asian and Central American origin, were poor when they moved to the new packing-plant town and because they receive low wages, the advent of new jobs in these towns has resulted, ironically, in increased poverty and increased demands on local human services and assistance.

A different impoverization phenomenon is occurring in some places in the Northeast: migration of poor urban people outward to small towns. As urban housing costs have risen steadily and the supply of low-cost urban housing has fallen far behind demand, and as city living conditions for low-income families have steadily deteriorated, some people with inadequate incomes, whether from welfare or from low-paid employment, are attracted to the lower housing costs and safer living conditions of rural areas. Although few jobs are found in the rural communities, they have surplus housing and low rents as well as public assistance, food stamps, Medicaid, and other transferable benefits, and part-time low-wage jobs are more tolerable when they can cover a greater portion of living expenses. The net result, in these cases, too, is an increase in poverty in the receiving communities and often an increase in the racial and ethnic complexity of the local population. This migration pattern also creates stress, sometimes quite suddenly, on small-town schools and social services.

### Changing Characteristics of the Rural Poor

Traditionally, the rural poor have exhibited characteristics that distinguish them from the urban poor. Nationwide, the rural poor are more apt to be employed than are the urban poor, and they participate less in various public assistance programs. They are more likely to live in two-parent families or owner-occupied housing than the urban poor. Outside of the South and a few counties of the northern Midwest and Southwest, the rural poor are less frequently members of minority groups. Additionally, rural poverty has been more persistent and intergenerational than urban poverty.

Now, however, economic and social changes occurring throughout the nation are diminishing these differences between rural and urban poverty. Unemployment is an increasingly important contributor to rural poverty, especially where there are whole cohorts of young, discouraged workers no longer looking for jobs. The growth of part-time employment in the service sector, on the other hand, has increased the poverty rate among those who are employed.

The rural-urban marriage difference is also diminishing, mostly as a result of changing marriage patterns among the rural poor. Traditionally, a large majority of rural households in poverty have been composed of married couples, but today 39% of rural poor households are headed by women (Porter, 1989, p. 30). Although the prevalence of "female-headed households" is much lower in rural areas than in central cities, where 58% of the poor live in households headed by women (Porter, 1989, p. 30), the incidence of single parenthood has grown significantly in rural America and continues to increase. This trend has even greater implications than one might suppose because the economic disadvantage of single parenthood is particularly severe in rural America. Although the majority of poor rural families are not single-parent households, those that are face a triple poverty vulnerability: They are more apt to be poor than are single-parent families in the city; they are more apt to be in deep poverty (less than 75% of the official poverty line [Lichter & Eggebeen, 1991, Table 1, p. 11]); and they are apt to stay poor for a longer time (Ross & Morrissey, 1989, p. 65). Moreover, since 1980, the rate and depth of poverty for rural single-parent families have grown worse (Lichter & Eggebeen, 1991, p. 15).

Importantly, these economic and social changes interact so that the effect of each is multiplied. The trend towards female-headed households intersects with the conversion of local employment to part-time, service-sector jobs largely held by women, and together they explain a significant share of the recent rise in rural American poverty. To understand the nature of these changes in rural poverty, their interactions, their effects on communities, and their implications for rural social work, I turn now to the local-level research that I have been conducting.

## A Closer View: Poverty in Rural Upstate New York

Although New York is neither the most rural nor the poorest of states, it provides a suitable geographical locus for exploring rural poverty. Using as a baseline the findings I gained from a decade of ethnographic research in some of the state's rural pockets of poverty during the 1970s (Fitchen, 1981), and adding findings from a recent broad-based study ranging over 17 rural New York counties (Fitchen, 1991), I now have the in-depth perspective, the time span, and the geographic coverage to offer additional insight on changes in rural poverty in the last twenty years within the context of a single state.

For all its "urbanness," New York contains a dispersed rural population of 3 million rural residents and, in some places, serious and tenacious poverty. As a result of the same economic, demographic, and social changes occurring in rural areas nationwide, poverty in rural New York is now undergoing significant change and, in some places, is increasing quite rapidly. The worsening rural poverty has major consequences for individuals, families, and affected communities and for the whole spectrum of human services, including social work.

Distribution and rates of poverty around the state are currently in flux. In the past, of the state's 44 rural counties (from a total of 62 counties), the most remote have generally had the highest poverty and unemployment rates and the lowest median incomes. Some of the more remote counties made employment gains during the mid-1980s, but these gains were short-lived in most cases. Some municipalities situated near metropolitan areas are becoming less poor through suburbanization; but at the same time, other not-so-remote areas are getting poorer. As the 1990s began, several rural counties were reporting major, unanticipated increases in welfare rolls, far outpacing the growth rate of urban welfare rolls, as more poverty was being added to the old base of rural poverty. Governmental and nonprofit groups operating emergency services in small towns now report significant increases in caseloads, emergency requests, new clients, and repeat clients. Caseworker interviews and agency records indicate that clients are poorer now than in the past. For example, records of a community action agency show that an increasing number of program participants fall below 75% of the federal poverty level. Agency workers also report that poverty is qualitatively worse now and that their clients' problems seem deeper and more intractable than in the past.

The increasing population of poor rural people appears to consist of three subpopulations or "poverty streams": (1) rural people who were raised in poverty or have been poor for many years and have been unable to improve their position and so are now raising the next generation in poverty; (2) rural people who had previously not been poor but who have recently fallen into poverty; and (3) urban poor people who have been driven out of cities by the high cost and deteriorated quality of life there. The proportions of increased poverty coming from each of these three streams has not been measured, and it varies in different communities and different parts of the state.

I have conducted lengthy open-ended interviews with low-income rural residents from all three poverty streams, residing in several of the counties under study. These interviews indicate the common aspects of people's situations and help to identify certain location-specific patterns in the relative contributions from the three sources. They also indicate the need to use different, "stream-specific" approaches and intervention strategies. People who have been raised in entrenched intergenerational poverty may need special multifaceted assistance to overcome deleterious physical, psychosocial, and educational deficits resulting from long-term poverty. Rural residents who have recently fallen into poverty as a result of employment or family changes, on the other hand, are likely to get out of poverty quite quickly and with minimal long-term damage if they receive prompt, coordinated assistance in job re-training or education, housing, and medical and child care. Poor people who have come to a rural community seeking relief from urban slum conditions may require extra help in making social and institutional connections in their new community, as well as requiring preparation for employment and various supports and financial assistance until they can become adequately employed.

Regardless of the sources of the poor population, the physical or visual expression of rural poverty takes only a limited number of forms. I have identified four basic residential or settlement patterns in which poor rural people live. Because rural social work must adapt to local situations, familiarity with these distinct types of settlement may be advantageous.

### Poverty on Farms

Farm people compose only a relatively small fraction of New York State's rural poor population and are inadequately counted and often neglected. The farm-based poor are a varied population, with differing service needs. Some are dairy farmhands, often called "dairy migrants" because they circulate from one dairy farm to another, moving every year or two, but generally within one or two counties. Their wages may leave their families below the poverty line and cash-poor, although housing, milk, and firewood are usually provided by the farm operator-employer. As farming in New York has been undergoing consolidation into the state's more favorable areas and into larger, more mechanized farm units, some of these dairy migrants have been displaced, which leaves them with no marketable skills and no employer-provided housing. Thus, they are poorer and more needy than before. Another segment of the farm-related poor is the more truly migrant population, the nondairy laborers, traditionally blacks based in Florida, who circulate through the state and the region on a seasonal basis and usually live temporarily in grower-provided housing on fruit and vegetable farms. Sometimes they are caught in the harvest area for a longer period of time than expected with no income and no job-related housing, as when a crop is delayed or when anticipated employment falls through, or perhaps because a new pool of migrants from Mexico or the Caribbean has been imported to do the work for lower wages.

Probably the largest component of poor people living on farms is made up of elderly owner-operators living on marginal farms that are no longer commercially viable but that still yield a limited subsistence, when combined with a meager pension from earlier off-farm employment, and provide a cheap place to live. Though unable to afford adequate amenities and services as they live out their later years in crumbling farmhouses, most of these elderly farm people are unwilling to ask for assistance of any kind.

In some places, a younger generation is also living on marginal farms and in poverty. These situations, which have turned up in several of my interviews, typically involve a young family living on a farm that belongs to grandparents or a surviving widowed grandmother. These are not professional, ex-urbanite back-to-the-land enthusiasts, but local people who grew up in marginal circumstances or who have recently fallen into poverty. Instead of living in a village apartment and struggling to meet the rent from meager wages in low-level service-sector jobs, they are trying to make their living and raise their children on a grandparents' small farm, perhaps supplemented by a modest off-farm income. Although marginal farms usually provide a below-poverty income, these young families are living inexpensively or rent-free in fairly secure family-owned housing. They are also more connected than their grandparents to the agencies and services of the villages and county seats: For example, their children may attend Head Start, they may participate in the Special Supplemental Food Program for Women, Infants, and Children (WIC), and they may use food stamps. Most of the New York farm-based poor have been poor throughout their lives; and with the exception of migrant crop workers, the farm-based poor are long-time local residents.

### Poverty in Isolated Open-Country Depressed Neighborhoods

Chronic and tenacious intergenerational poverty has long plagued back valleys and uplands of New York and surrounding Northeastern states, especially in areas where marginal soils prevent efficient modern agriculture. Small pockets of intergenerational poverty usually include up to a dozen families clustered together (Fitchen, 1981). Most households in these depressed neighborhoods have at least one regularly employed adult, working in the lower-paying jobs on highway and public works crews and in low-skill construction, maintenance, janitorial, and manufacturing jobs in the region's larger towns. Families are frequently pushed below or farther below the poverty line by accident, illness, or the primary earner's loss of job. Residents must travel 15 miles or more in old, unreliable cars in order to work, to attend adult educational or job-training programs, to shop, and to tend to matters involving county offices and service agencies. Their housing, for the most part, is seriously inadequate: run-down farmhouses, very old trailers encased in wooden additions, and shacks made of used lumber and covered in black sheathing material. But the fact that this housing is owner-occupied and located in remote areas has worked to the advantage of residents. By using traditional makeshift strategies and relying on ingenuity and kin ties, many families in these depressed neighborhoods have remained housed and residentially quite stable. But their poverty continues.

The stigmatized and socially isolated open-country pockets of poverty I studied intensively through the 1970s are still there today. The number of houses and people has grown, however, and new offshoot or satellite neighborhoods have also appeared. Initial follow-up indicates that while a few individuals and families have moved away and some have overcome their poverty, most households have continued a pattern of just getting by but never getting ahead. Many of the youngsters included in the earlier sample eventually settled close to the parental home, some in trailers placed in the side yard. Some became parents very early, and now their children are growing up in these same pockets of poverty, already identified by schools, public health officials, and family courts as children at risk. While the older people may receive little except transfer payments from community and governmental programs, their children and grandchildren are increasingly connected to services and agencies of the county seat.

Residents of these depressed neighborhoods are almost entirely long-term poor and long-term locals. Most grew up in poverty in the very same neighborhood or in similar neighborhoods nearby. They are rooted by connections of kinship and connections to place.

### Poverty in Trailer Parks and Informal Trailer Clusters

Throughout the nation, trailers (officially mobile homes) are the hallmark of limited rural incomes. Indicative of the dramatic growth in this type of housing in poorer rural areas, mobile homes accounted for 52% of the additional housing between 1986 and 1990 in one of the counties I studied. In another county, 13.6% of households were living in mobile homes in 1980; but in the poorer and most remote townships, 20 to nearly 30% of households were living in mobile homes.

The less expensive mobile home parks are located at the edge of villages and along country roads, often squeezed onto an undesirable piece of land, such as a little parcel between the highway's edge and a river. People may rent either a trailer or a lot on which to place their own trailer. As mobile home parks are zoned out of some municipalities or eliminated when more profitable uses for the land become available, pressure mounts on some existing parks to expand: New tiers of pot-holed driveways lead to new rows of trailers, and more trailers are squeezed in between existing ones, overtaxing water and sewer systems and leading to further deterioration of the social environment. Some mobile home parks could more accurately be described as private-sector low-income housing projects. For example, in one park where I conducted interviews, 38 of the 39 households were at least partially supported by public assistance. The park is in an isolated valley, with no town and no employment within about 15 miles. Thirty miles away is the county seat, a small dynamic city with a relatively strong economy. There, rents have risen sharply, low-cost apartments are virtually nonexistent, and low-income families are being squeezed out to places such as this trailer park. Residents readily voiced their unhappiness with living in the park and their desire to move out soon; some actually had moved out but had been forced to return because they were unable to find or keep a place elsewhere. Like many other trailer parks, this one is characterized by social pathology: Nighttime marital conflicts reverberate into adjacent trailers less than a car's length away; the high level of interhousehold sex and violence is exceeded only by rumors and stories of even more sex and violence; and "hot lining your neighbors" (telephoning the state child protective network on the anonymous hot line) is a regular pastime.

Increasingly common now are small, informal trailer clusters, which usually contain too few trailers to be registered officially as mobile home parks. Some are family compounds, but more are simply rental arrangements in which the landlord's trailers are mostly old and the tenants are mostly poor. Most tenants would prefer to purchase a second-hand trailer and have their own piece of land, but this ideal is not usually attainable by young families with meager incomes, unless they are able to purchase, perhaps from relatives, an inexpensive parcel of land. For those who do achieve this goal, distance to jobs and services, transportation problems, and, in some cases, social isolation may exacerbate the problems of limited income.

Residents of the low-rent trailer parks and clusters are quite diverse. They include long-term local people and relative newcomers to the area. The adult residents may have been raised in poverty or may only recently have fallen into poverty as a result of family and employment changes. The proportion of households composed of single mothers and their children is generally much higher in these trailer parks than in the surrounding communities.

## Converted Apartments in Small Villages and Hamlets

In many of the rural counties of New York, one or two hamlets or villages now have an increasing number of low-income families living in rented apartments scattered among the community's owner-occupied houses. This phenomenon, while not new, has become increasingly apparent in places where long-term economic decline, job loss, and population exodus have created a local housing surplus. As elderly village homeowners have given up their homes or died, and as young adults have left town, houses have become vacant and may remain so for years, unmarketable as single-family homes because no new home-buying families are moving to the village. Eventually, family heirs or outside investors convert the vacant houses to apartments, often with minimal renovation or updating, and rent them out at rates just low enough to attract people on welfare or at the low end of the local wage scale. Similarly, vacant store buildings, the excess commercial space of small towns, are also converted. Because regional demand for low-rent housing exceeds supply, as apartments in such a village are filled, more vacant houses and stores are converted, and more low-income families, local or from higher rent communities, move in. Some of the smaller hamlets and villages undergoing this conversion pattern are located on the peripheries of rural counties, remote from the more prosperous central towns or county seats. Conversion is also occurring in villages located along train lines emanating from cities as much as 100 miles away.

Most of the tenants in these village apartments are poor. Many are parents (including single mothers, married couples, and loose pairs) still in their teens and early 20s who want independence from their parents, but who cannot afford better housing. Household membership fluctuates and may be quite unstable. Employment is problematic, as the villages undergoing such housing conversion tend to be places with stagnant or declining economies. Tenants with jobs earn low wages, and others are without work or without reliable transportation to get to a job if they had one. Many tenant households are supported partially or completely by welfare.

Residents of converted village apartments are a rather diverse population coming from all three poverty streams. Some are long-term rural poor people who grew up in the depressed pockets of poverty in the open countryside or right in the village; some are lifelong village residents who have only recently fallen into poverty; and some have recently arrived from urban areas and have few ties to the community except to other recent arrivals. Tenants of these cheap apartments may be quite heterogeneous in racial or ethnic traits, as well. What they all have in common, though, is their poverty and their tenuous hold on a place to live and a means to pay for it.

## Trends of Special Significance for Rural Social Work

Wherever it is found, whether on farms, in open-country pockets of poverty, in cheap trailer parks, or in depressed villages, increasing and worsening rural poverty presents major challenges to rural human service programs. In particular, my research has identified four major characteristics or trends that may be particularly significant for rural social work. The first two reflect more macro-level structural problems in the society as a whole and are hardly amenable to direct social service intervention; but they frame the daily life experiences of low-income rural residents and shape the problems that put them in contact with human-service professionals. The second two characteristics are more within the purview of social work.

### Detachment from the Labor Force

In the deteriorated and changing rural economies, some people cannot work or find jobs. Some of the unemployed people in their 20s and 30s have barriers to employment such as physical disabilities, alcoholism, health conditions, meager education, lack of transportation, young dependent children, serious family problems, and attitudinal and self-esteem problems. Men who were unable to find work during the years of high unemployment in the early 1980s have now been out of the work force so long that local employers consider them unemployable. Unless they receive extra employment preparation, job training, and supervision in their first regular jobs, many of these men will remain dependent on Home Relief assistance. Women who have been on Aid to Families with Dependent Children (AFDC) for a decade or more while they had small children at home may also be difficult to place in jobs. For older people, in their 40s and 50s, the barriers to employment reflect not only age and individual problems but also shifts in the local economy. Older farm laborers displaced by the diminishing number of farms and farm jobs are unable to obtain nonfarm employment. Even long-term factory workers with good work records have difficulty finding replacement jobs after their plants shut down. Line workers who are over 40 have a particularly difficult time finding substitute employment, especially if they lack a high school diploma. However, few of them wish to break ties with family and community to seek jobs elsewhere. And few can afford to give up their local housing, perhaps an inexpensive rented trailer or a modest home with no mortgage, to move to a larger community that has better job opportunities—but more expensive housing.

For the never-employed and the underemployed, and for displaced workers as well, the main solution lies in rural economic development: There is no substitute for adequate local employment. But even if jobs do become available, enhancing people's employability requires more than job-training programs. Integrated, multifaceted programs that include basic and specialized education and personal and family counseling are also needed. Beyond that, the situation also calls for community development in its broader sense, including initiatives that address deficiencies in such areas as childcare and public transportation, because these barriers prevent or limit people's employment even when jobs are available.

### Deterioration of the Rural Housing Situation

Poor rural people have always had to accept poor quality housing because they could afford no better; and many consciously make sacrifices in the quality of their housing as a way to minimize cash expenses and remain independent of welfare. But the quality of rural low-cost housing stock has been deteriorating recently as a result of reduced public and private investment, as well as further deterioration of an already-old housing stock. Much of the owner-occupied housing in the open-country pockets of poverty is structurally unsound, and some still lacks adequate wiring, heating, running water, or plumbing. Low-cost trailer parks and cheap converted apartments are notorious for health and safety hazards, but landlords are rarely challenged by local authorities.

Deterioration of the rural housing situation involves more than just physical decay of buildings, however. It is a problem of access as well. In the past, poor people in villages and the open countryside had the security and limited cash expense of owning a place to live, even if it was just a crumbling farmhouse, an old trailer, or a village home in sad need of repair. Recently, however, especially in areas close to growing metropolitan centers, booming real estate markets for housing development and second homes, as well as a tightening of local land use regulations and state housing codes, have combined to make it harder for low-income residents to acquire and keep their own homes. Young families are no longer so free to set their own trailers or shacks on their relatives' property or to add onto or modify their homes when and as needed, with used materials and intermittent work. As a result of these interacting forces, the security of ownership is increasingly being replaced by the precariousness of tenancy.

While small-town rents are still lower than urban rents, incomes in poorer rural counties may be only 60% of urban incomes, so that the rent burden is about the same. In addition, rural rents rose significantly in the late 1980s. Only a small amount of publicly funded low-income housing has been created in rural communities in the last decade, except for senior citizen housing. In communities that received an influx of low-income people from elsewhere or those where a new industry or state prison has come in, growing demand for housing has pushed rents up considerably. Competition for existing low-cost rental housing units is further exacerbated by the growth of single-parent households. The erosion of workers' incomes and the failure of welfare shelter allowance levels to keep up with inflation have left economically marginal people especially vulnerable if they do not own their homes or do not have relatives who can help provide them with a place to live. And fewer of the poor now have these options.

Serious as the housing situation is, however, its impact is even greater because it occurs in conjunction with and tends to exacerbate the problem of inadequate jobs. It is also connected with two other trends to be discussed in this chapter: family instability and residential mobility. To tackle the problem of people's insecure tenancy in a situation of inadequate supply of low-cost housing, rural social workers must network with other agencies and community groups, and together they can contribute to both the welfare of their clients and the welfare of the community.

### Destabilization of Family Relationships

In rural America as in urban, the status of the nuclear family is increasingly insecure, especially among low-income populations. The national trend towards more female-headed households among the rural poor has been found at the local level in my research in rural New York. It is remarked upon by case workers of all sorts; indicated in the records of Head Start, elementary schools, and WIC; and figures prominently in the programming efforts of community action agencies. Household histories that I gathered in home interviews revealed many situations of instability and flux, with sudden dissolutions of marriages or partnerships causing interpersonal disruptions that reverberated even into relationships between children and grandparents. But marital instability and single parenthood carry an even greater impact in rural communities now than in the past because individuals and families are no longer as effectively cushioned within an extended family support system.

In contrast to the findings of my earlier ethnographic study in open-country pockets of poverty, my current research indicates that younger poor adults, especially those living in village apartments and trailer parks, tend to have weaker networks of extended family. Individuals who still have such anchoring networks report that they call on their mothers and sisters for help, especially for assistance with babysitting and transportation and to provide a temporary place to stay while looking for apartments of their own. But for many, relatives are less accessible, less effective, or less willing to help with the difficulties and emergencies of daily life.

For rural social work, erosion of marriage and nuclear-family ties has significant implications, especially in the context of the weakening of informal kin-based social structure. Rural human services must catch up with this changed rural reality. We can no longer assume the traditional or mythic stability of the rural nuclear family and can no longer expect that the network of the extended family and kin-based neighborhood is in place to cushion individuals in need of social support and to compensate for destabilization of the nuclear family. However, rural human service practitioners must not overlook kinship and neighborhood ties that are still functioning, for where and when they exist, they are a priceless resource available to rural social workers and may play a key support role for individuals in crisis. In fact, proactive and community-oriented social work in small communities may help rebuild kin-based social ties or create new non-kin substitutes, including neighborhood- or community-based groups, social networks, and support groups based on common needs and interests.

### Decline of Residential Permanence

Residential stability appears to be diminishing significantly, and movement within and between rural communities is increasing. In some village apartments and many trailer parks, turnover of residents is very high, as is apparent in enrollment records of elementary schools and address records of participants in Head Start, WIC, welfare, and other programs. Some families move three or four times a year; some disappear in the night and turn up later in another apartment or another nearby town. Residential history interviews with young single mothers and young couples, married or unmarried, show that economically marginal families easily become overwhelmed by their personal and financial situations and fall behind in rent payments, which leads to eviction and forces them to look for cheaper places to live. The inadequacy of the housing they find, their continued financial problems, and the upheavals in their personal relationships are likely to prompt still other residential moves in the near future. This increased mobility leads to further destabilization of the family, disrupting education of children and adults, treatment or services for family members, and ties to supportive social networks. The high-frequency movers, in many cases, are people already characterized by instability and disorganization, people often subsumed under the label "dysfunctional families." A high level of residential turnover also leads to deterioration of the communities in which people circulate.

The impact of residential impermanence on the delivery of services to troubled and impoverished families is patently obvious. From school teachers to the full spectrum of human service professionals, the concern voiced is that high-frequency moving not only interferes with effective progress in tackling the problems of individuals and families, but it also causes inefficiency and frustration for service providers, teachers, and case workers. Response to this mobility must be of two kinds: first, devising new ways to keep up with the movers by expediting record transfer, by smoothing integration into new schools and new service agencies, and by ensuring that benefits are transferred with minimal delay and disruption; and second, helping to stabilize people where they are by reducing their vulnerability to eviction from housing, by assisting them in finding jobs they can keep and that can support them adequately, and by helping them to develop personal and interpersonal skills that will make relationships with friends, family, and partners less volatile.

## Conclusion

Increasing rural poverty is caused by the interaction of changes in rural employment, family relationships, and housing. Each of the several causes must be tackled, but the efforts must be integrated in a comprehensive approach. For example, to reduce poverty levels among rural children living in single-parent families, more is needed than just job creation, critical as that is. Child-care and transportation problems must also be tackled, as these are particular problems for single mothers and cause some to quit their jobs and return to welfare. While meeting such community-level needs is clearly beyond the scope of social work, rural social workers can effectively engage in–or lead–local advocacy and community organizing and can also assist community leaders in working towards community development in its broadest sense.

Increased rural poverty includes not only impoverization of people but also impoverization of communities. Some communities may be less able to stem their economic decline and assist their needy residents. Communities with insecure economies have special difficulty preventing social-institutional decay and meeting the needs of their impoverished residents. One critical problem in communities with growing poverty rates is the stigmatization and exclusion of poor people by more affluent and politically powerful residents. Despite the persistent idealization of classlessness and friendliness in a small community where everybody knows everybody, the lower-income residents of rural communities are socially distanced, especially if they have moved in from other communities or are racially or ethnically "different." Negative attitudes toward low-income residents are frequently translated politically and fiscally into inadequate funding and leadership support for local human services. Effective approaches to overcoming this attitudinal and funding problem must be carefully worked out at the local level by a coalition of service providers and practitioners working with local leaders and must appeal to the community's long-range interests.

Although rural poverty does not exist as a free-standing problem independent of what is happening in urban America, it has its own particular contexts, expressions, and needs. Rural poverty is sufficiently different from urban poverty to require different approaches and strategies. For example, the dispersed, low-density nature of the rural service-needy poor population offers major challenges to social work and other human services. But the rural community also presents opportunities for action and resources for response that should not be overlooked or wasted. Trailer parks and converted apartments of small towns do offer a higher client density to make service delivery more efficient. In addition, they provide a special opportunity: Through creative social engineering, such residential concentrations of poor people can be transformed into social communities, making them socially healthier places for people to live and greatly enhancing the effectiveness of social services.

Some rural communities may weather the current recession and may benefit by continuing to draw a more affluent in-migrant population, whereas other communities may lose still more employment and may gain more low-income residents. If deterioration of rural employment contin-ues through the decade, and if the trend toward more female-headed families also continues, then, from both sources, many rural communities will experience a rise in poverty rates. Some places will have an even sharper increase in poverty because, in addition, they will be affected by adverse migration trends as poverty is redistributed around the state and the nation. Places with multiple poverty risks should most concern the social work profession, for the continued downward spiral can become a cycle of poverty from which neither people nor communities will escape for many years. The need for rural social work to serve impoverished people in distressed communities in rural America is critical, the opportu-nities are endless, and the time is now.

## *References*

Duncan, C. M. (Ed.). (1992). *Rural poverty in America.* New York: Auburn.

Fitchen, J. M. (1981). *Poverty in rural America: A case study.* Boulder, CO: Westview.

Fitchen, J. M. (1991). *Endangered spaces, enduring places: Change, identity, and survival in rural America.* Boulder, CO: Westview.

Lichter, D. T., & Eggebeen, D. J. (1991, August). *Children among the rural poor: 1960-1990.* Paper presented at the annual meeting of the Rural Sociological Society, Columbus, OH.

Lichter, D. T., McLaughlin, D. K., & Cornwell, G. T. (1990). Migration and the loss of human resources in rural America (Working Paper No. 1990-37). University Park, PA: Population Issues Research Center.

O'Hare, W. P. (1988). *The rise of poverty in rural America.* Washington, D.C.: Population Reference Bureau.

Porter, K. H. (1989). *Poverty in rural America: A national overview.* Washington, D.C.: Center on Budget and Policy Priorities.

Ross, P. J. & Morrissey, E. S. (1989). Rural people in poverty: Persistent versus temporary poverty. *Proceedings of National Rural Studies Committee* (pp. 59-73). Corvallis, OR: Western Rural Development Center.

Shapiro, I. (1989). *Laboring for less: Working but poor in rural America.* Washington, D.C.: Center on Budget and Policy Priorities.

U.S. Bureau of the Census. (1991). *Current population reports, 1991* (Series P-60, No. 175, Poverty in the United States: 1990). Washington, D.C.: U.S. Govern-ment Printing Office.

# 10

# Religion and Spirituality: A Long-Neglected Cultural Component of Rural Social Work Practice

by Leola D. Furman and Joseph M. Chandy

*Religion and spiritual values are important to most Americans, particularly rural cultures. However, these dimensions are rarely discussed in social work literature or curriculum. A random sample of licensed social workers residing in a rural frontier state was surveyed to obtain their perceptions about issues of religion and spirituality; the impact of religion and spirituality on themselves, their clients, and their practice; and their preparedness to deal with these issues.*

A major theme of rural social work is that social work practice should be culturally sensitive. It has been noted that religion plays a very important role in all cultures (Jacobsen, 1993). Hence, we cannot talk about a culturally sensitive rural social work practice without understanding the influence of religiosity and spirituality in rural human lives.

However, the role of religion and spirituality in the lives of clients has been neglected both in social work curricula and in practice (Canda, 1992) in spite of the fact that the desire to treat the whole person in his or her environment has been a part of social work goals and objectives for decades. This omission is possibly due to the highly personal and sensitive nature of the subject, the desire of professionals to be scientific and there-

Major funding for this research was provided by a grant from the Faculty Research Committee, University of North Dakota. Partial funding was provided by the Alumni Office, University of North Dakota. Special thanks to Kee Tan for assistance with statistical analysis.

Reprinted from *Human Services in the Rural Environment* (Winter/Spring 1994), with permission of the Eastern Washington University School of Social Work and Human Services.

fore not to deal with the mystical, and the confusion surrounding the definitions of spirituality and religion.

## Definitions

Definitions of religion and spirituality are imprecise at best and often contradictory. Titone (1991) defines religion as a "relationship between a superhuman power and humanity" (p. 7). Joseph (1988) calls it the external expression of faith. Religion is the institutionalization or formalization of spiritual concepts, according to Dudley and Helfgott (1990). For the sake of this study, religion is defined as an organized set of beliefs and practices of a particular faith community.

Since religion deals with specific beliefs, it is often exclusive. Conversely, spirituality is inclusive. It is an internal process which may or may not include a belief in God. Although there are numerous definitions of spirituality, Canda's (1990) definition of spirituality covers all eventualities:

> It is the gestalt of the total process of human life and development, encompassing biological, mental, social, and spiritual aspects...the spiritual relates to the person's search for a sense of meaning and totally fulfilling relationships between oneself, other people, the encompassing universe, and the ontological ground of existence, whether a person understands this in terms that are theistic, atheistic, nontheistic, or any combination of these. (p. 13)

These definitions, however, do not reflect the use of the terms religion and spirituality by the general population. They are often used in combination or interchangeably. This study made no attempt to differentiate between these terms since its purpose was to assess the degree of religious and spiritual commitment of the social workers surveyed and the importance of religious and spiritual issues in the lives of their clients.

## Review of the Literature

### Reasons for Social Work's Neglect of Religion and Spirituality

Although the social work profession historically has had strong ties to religious groups, it has neglected issues of religion and spirituality among its consumers. Fears of converting clients to the religious doctrines of those helping them steered the profession away from religion and spirituality toward more scientific approaches (Canda, 1992).

Seplowin (1992) describes this shift in emphasis quite clearly:

> As social work professionalized, it became eager to rank as a science and replaced its religious roots with secular values, skills, and dependency on government (Canda, 1988b). This thrust away from religion gave way to clinical theories that fostered ego-centered functioning and relationships. (p. 2)

The social work profession became concerned with the separation of church and state and concentrated on non-sectarian democratic values. Therefore, even though social workers themselves might follow religions or spiritual practices, they often failed to fully appreciate the effect this might have in their professional lives. Lost in their attention to impartiality and nonjudgmental attitudes, social workers have been described as radical, libertarian, irreligious, and even anti-religion (Siporin, 1985), often substituting the profession for a religious belief system. This professional stance has resulted in a lack of integration of religion and spirituality in education and practice (Canda, 1988, 1989; Cornett, 1992; Loewenberg, 1988).

### Social Work Client System Inherently Religious and Spiritual

Although social work has been distancing itself from religion and spiritual issues, Seplowin (1992), Brandon (1976), and Delgado (1977) indicate a need within society to rediscover spirituality and religion along with an emphasis on self-awareness, cultural diversity, and social responsibility. There is evidence indicating that clients continue to attach a deep meaning to the religious and spiritual dimensions of their lives. For example, Neuhaus (1985) reported that 94 percent of Americans profess a belief in God, and a 1985 Gallup report indicated that 7 out of 10 Americans are members of a church or synagogue, a proportion that has remained more or less constant in the past 50 years.

Religious congregations and clergy also serve as solid referral systems and resources to clients by providing a support network after therapy has been completed (DiBlasio, 1988; Meystedt, 1984). In rural communities, in particular, the religious organizations have traditionally assumed many of the health, welfare, and social functions that closely parallel the roles of the social work profession. While human service professionals have a tradition of waiting for people to come to them with problems, religious communities have greater natural access to people through their ongoing participation in church or synagogue life and have greater social sanction to reach out to people in need. In fact, congregation members allow clergy and others to reach out to them during the initial stages of difficulty before crisis occurs (Pargament, Maton, & Hess, 1992). Therefore, to ignore those resources may diminish social work effectiveness with clients who are religious both in rural and urban areas (Meystedt, 1984).

### Rural Families: Fundamentally Religious Families

Since, according to Meystedt (1984), rural families tend to be more religiously oriented than other groups, religion's prevalence, influence, usefulness as a resource, and implication for treatment are important variables to examine in relation to rural communities. In longitudinal case studies on the impact of the rural crisis on two-generational, farm families, Furman (1991) found that during a life crisis, rural people preferred discussing their problems with their clergy rather than with mental health personnel or social workers, indicating a need for human service workers to collaborate closely with rural community priests or pastors in order to best serve rural populations.

Denton's (1990) research on the culture of fundamentally religious families found that religion is not incidental to life or the family system but is an integral part of that system. God plays as important a role in those families as any other family member. Therefore, if a therapist displays anti-religious feelings, very likely these families will withdraw from therapy. Family treatment with rural families and with fundamentalist families requires sensitivity to their cultural beliefs and the use of a set of unique assessment and intervention skills. Clearly, this calls for the integration of religiously and spiritually sensitive social work practice into a culturally diverse educational curricula.

## Functional and Dysfunctional Aspects of Religion and Spirituality

Religion, however, is not an unmixed good. History is an eloquent witness to the fact that religion can become dysfunctional for some people and functional for others. Religions have a long tradition of acting as a resource, by supporting people in times of stress and aiding them in their return to normal functioning.

What has been overlooked has been the fact that these various belief systems do not simply offer direction to people after problems arise. Instead, they offer a framework for living, with its implications for anticipating, avoiding, or modifying problems before they develop (Pargament et al., 1992). Indeed, both religious and spiritual norms and values can stimulate ethical relations with others which can provide the believer with emotional support and a source of positive mental health (Loewenberg, 1988). In addition, religion and spirituality as personal and social forces have been closely associated with significant life passages, providing a set of rituals that mark life events such as birth, transitions to adulthood, marriage, divorce, tragedy, and death (Pargament et al., 1992).

On the other hand, dysfunctional use of religion can be viewed as an attempt to anesthetize the individual, relieving him or her from life responsibilities. It can also activate burdensome, even crippling, roles in the lives of some individuals (Pargament et al., 1992) while promoting fanaticism, intolerance, and prejudice. For some, the practice of religion can become pathological (Loewenberg, 1988). The profession needs to acknowledge these vital issues and encourage an active discussion about functional and dysfunctional aspects of religion and spirituality in education and practice.

## Need for Professional Preparation

In recent years, the social work profession has recognized the need to develop a coherent body of knowledge assessing the impact of religion and spirituality in determining people's attitudes towards society and philosophies of life (Sheridan, Bullis, Adcock, Berlin, & Miller, 1991). This calls for specific professional preparation in spiritual and religious matters if the social worker is to respond effectively to help clients with spiritual orientations appropriate to their cultures. Loewenberg (1988) argues that since social workers interact with clients as whole persons, deliberately avoiding one important segment of a person's culture, such as religion and spirituality, could handicap the professional relationship between client and social worker.

Few studies have been conducted on social workers' perceptions of religious and spirituality issues. Sheridan et al. (1991) presented a study of 328 licensed clinical social workers, psychologists, and counselors suggesting that though religion and spirituality offered a positive contribution in their own lives and in their clients' lives, it was an area many of the practitioners struggled with in practice, given the relative lack of direction provided by their clinical training. Joseph (1988) surveyed clinical field instructors for a church-related MSW program and reported that practitioners viewed religious and spiritual concerns as being within the parameters of social work practice, demonstrating a need for more training in this area in social work education. These studies are limited either in sample size, special affinity of the respondents to the Church as their employer, lack of rural subjects, or inclusion of non-social work professionals in the study sample.

## Study Design

### Purpose of the Study

In order to enhance knowledge in this controversial area and to discover how rural social workers view theses issues, the present authors undertook a study of the licensed social workers in the state of North Dakota. Considered to be one of the most rural areas in the nation, North Dakota, along with six other states has been federally designated a frontier state. A frontier state is so designated if half or more of its population density has less than six persons per square mile. Thirty-four of North Dakota's 53 counties, approximately two-thirds of this rural state, are defined as frontier.

A representative sample of all the licensed social workers in North Dakota was surveyed in order to understand the role religion and spirituality play in their own personal lives and in their practice. The study was exploratory/descriptive in design and dealt with the following research questions: 1) What is the religious and spiritual commitment of these social workers? 2) What are the perceptions of the social workers regarding the importance of religious and spiritual issues in the lives of their clients? 3) How do social workers perceive their competence in dealing with the spiritual and religious issues of their clients? 4) Were the social workers prepared professionally to deal with spiritual and religious concerns of their clients?

## Methods

Two hundred licensed social workers were selected, using a systematic random sampling method, from a list of all licensed social workers of North Dakota provided by the Board of Social Work Examiners, the licensing body in the state. State law requires that all social workers must be licensed by this board at one of two levels: Licensed Social Worker (LSW) and Licensed Certified Social Worker (LCSW). The former is available to those who hold a BSW degree. The LCSW is available only to those who hold MSW degrees. The practicing social workers with nonsocial work degrees were grandfathered into the social work profession at the time licensure became mandatory in the state of North Dakota about 10 years ago.

The randomly selected licensed social workers were contacted by a mailed questionnaire. Approximately 71 percent of the workers (142 persons) responded to the questionnaire. The sample consisted of 83.8 percent LSWs and 14 percent LCSWs; 2.2 percent did not respond to the question about type of licensure. This proportion roughly corresponded to the proportion of all social workers in the state: 87.5 percent LSWs and 12.5 percent LCSWs.

## Findings

With respect to educational background, 46.5% of these social workers (66 persons) were BSWs; there were 19 (13.4%) MSW-level social workers. Seventeen of the respondents had a MA degree and 36 had a BA degree. The latter two categories are the group of practicing social workers who were grandfathered into the profession. There was one social worker in the sample with a PhD.

A majority of social workers in this sample (68 or 47.9%) had a practice experience of over 10 years. About 17.6 percent (25) had less than 2 years of practice experience. The remaining 49 social workers (34.5%) had a practice experience that ranged between 2 and 10 years. They were working with a variety of employers. The major employers included the Department of Human Services (24.6%), County Social Services (16.9%), private social service agencies (12.7%), group care facilities (16.9%), hospitals (9.2%), and schools (5.6%). About 10 percent were not currently employed.

A majority (94%) of the respondents belonged to a church, with Lutheran church affiliation representing the largest membership (45.8%) and Catholic the second largest (28.2%). Only 1.4 percent professed to be atheist, and 5.6 percent said they did not belong to a church.

### Religiosity in the Lives of Social Workers

The religious and spiritual orientation of the social workers were measured on the 7-item scale displayed in Table 1. Each of the scale items required an answer on a 5-point ordinal Likert scale with 1 referring to the lowest rating and 5 referring to the highest rating. These survey items represented a modified version of King's scale for measuring religiousity (1967).

The social workers scored moderately high on most of the survey items. Private prayer was the component most frequently engaged in (66%). This was followed by participation in ritual activities (52%), commitment to credal tenets or teachings (49%), active participation in congregational activities (25%), readings of religious books (25%), and generous contribution to the church or spiritual community (19%). The lowest response was talking about faith in God to others (7%). Thus, about one-half of the social workers subscribed to a belief system, with almost two-thirds engaging in private prayer. This indicated that though the social workers held a belief system and regularly kept in touch with a spiritual reality through prayer, they tended not to speak about it to others.

## Religiosity and Client Populations

As can be seen from Table 2, a large number of social workers, though not the majority, perceived that religiosity or spirituality had positive effects on their client populations and considered religion or spirituality important in the lives of their clients. Thus, over 43 percent of the social workers indicated that religion provided emotional support to their clients, and about 31 percent indicated that religious affiliation of their clients helped them solve their problems. They also were more likely to agree that religion was functional (48.6%) than to agree that religion was dysfunctional (17.6%) in the lives of their clients. This finding was corroborated by the relatively low percentage of the social workers who reported that their clients perceived problems as punishment from God (14.1%) or as willed by God (22.5%).

Social workers' perceptions regarding the role of religion in the lives of clients was further analyzed by correlating these perceptions with the social worker's religiosity, length of practice, and education. As can be seen from Table 3, positive correlations existed between the religiosity of the social workers and the perception of positive contributions of religion in the lives of clients. Thus, social workers with higher religiosity scores

**Table 1. Religiosity of Social Workers (N=142)**

| Items | Percent | n |
|---|---|---|
| 1. Frequency of private prayer | 66.2 | 94 |
| 2. Participation in ritual services | 51.7 | 73 |
| 3. Commitment to credal tenets | 48.6 | 69 |
| 4. Activeness in congregation/ community programs | 25.4 | 36 |
| 5. Frequency of reading religious books | 24.6 | 35 |
| 6. Generosity of contributions to church | 19.0 | 27 |
| 7. Talking about faith in God to others | 7.7 | 6 |

*Note:* The responses represent percentage of social workers who reported 4 or above on a 5-point scale for these items.

tended to perceive that a belief system provided emotional support to clients ($r=.1905; p<.05$); that a belief system is functional for clients ($r=.2803; p<.001$); that religious affiliation was helpful in solving clients' problems ($r=.2031; p<.05$); and that religion was important in the lives of clients ($r=.2172; p<.01$).

One interesting note here is that length of practice ($r=.2008; p<.01$) and education of the social workers ($r=.1760; p<.05$) were positively correlated with the social workers' perceptions that a belief system was dysfunctional in the lives of their clients. Thus, the more experienced and educated social workers were more likely to perceive that a religious or spiritual belief system was dysfunctional to clients.

## Professional Training and Religiosity

When these social workers were asked about their competency in dealing with issues of religion and spirituality with their clients, 33 percent reported that they felt they were not at all competent or only a little competent to deal with those issues. Further, as Table 3 indicates, 76 percent reported that they had received very little or no professional

*Table 2.* **Religion and Spirituality in the Lives of Clients (N=142)**

| | | | Correlations with the worker's | | |
|---|---|---|---|---|---|
| Items | Percent | n | Religiosity | Length of practice | Education |
| 1. Belief system provides positive emotional support to clients | 43.0 | 61 | .1905* | .1155 | .0880 |
| 2. Belief system is functional to clients | 48.6 | 69 | .2803*** | .0002 | -.0048 |
| 3. Religious affiliation was helpful in solving clients' problems | 31.0 | 44 | .2031* | .0919 | .1082 |
| 4. Religion is important in the lives of clients | 41.6 | 59 | .2172** | -.0414 | .0164 |
| 5. Belief system is dysfunctional in the lives of clients | 17.6 | 21 | .0640 | .2008** | .1760* |
| 6. Clients see problems as punishment from God | 14.1 | 20 | .0770 | -.0643 | .1229 |
| 7. Clients see problematic situations cannot be changed because they are willed by God | 22.5 | 32 | .0976 | -.0976 | -.0952 |

*Note:* The responses represent percentage of social workers who reported 4 or above on a 5-point scale for these items. *=<.05 **=<.01 ***=<.001

training in this area. About 52 percent felt that it was important that social workers be prepared to deal with religious and spirituality issues. Finally, 50 percent of the social workers felt that religion and spirituality should be made part of the social work curriculum. Further analysis showed a positive relationship of the social workers' own religiosity with their competency in dealing with the religious and spiritual issues of their clients ($r=.1790$; $p<.05$), their perception of the importance of social workers being prepared to deal with spiritual issues ($r=.2834$; $p<.0001$), and their recommendation to make religious and spiritual issues part of the curriculum ($r=.2961$; $p<.001$).

## Religion and Spirituality in Practice

The social workers in the sample were asked to respond to several facets of social work practice where religion and spirituality interfaced with practice (see Table 4). One third reported that they frequently came across issues of religion and spirituality in practice, which again stresses the importance of these issues for client populations. A majority of the respondents did not report any conflict between their practice and their religious spiritual values, whereas only 2 percent reported such a conflict. On the other hand, 50 percent of the social workers indicated that a spiritual orientation was indeed helpful in working with clients. This perception was positively related to their religiosity ($r=.3036$; $p<.001$) and their education ($r=.1772$; $p<.05$). Compatibility with clients' religious and spiritual

*Table 3.* **Competency of Social Workers to Deal with Religious Issues (N=142)**

| Items | | | Correlations with the worker's | | |
|---|---|---|---|---|---|
| | Percent | n | Religiosity | Length of practice | Education |
| 1. Competency dealing with religious/spiritual issues of the clients | 33.1 | 47 | .1790* | -.1117 | .0877 |
| 2. Professional training received to deal with religious and spiritual issues | 76.1 | 108 | .1124 | -.0447 | .0677 |
| 3. Importance of being prepared to deal with religious and spiritual issues | 52.1 | 74 | .2834*** | -.1205 | .0020 |
| 4. Whether religious/spiritual issues need to be part of the social work curriculum | 50.0 | 71 | .2961*** | -.0727 | .0013 |

*Note:* Responses indicate percentage of social workers who reported 1 (not all) or 2 (very little) on 5-point scale regarding questions 1 and 2. For questions 3 and 4, responses indicate those who reported 4 or above on a 5-point scale.
\* = <.05  \*\* = <.01  \*\*\* = <.001

values made a small percentage of social workers (21.9%) feel comfortable in working with clients ($r$=.3328; $p$<.001). However, non-compatibility with clients' religious or spiritual orientations made the work of only 3.5 percent of the social workers difficult. Finally, about 25 percent of the social workers involved the client's pastor or religious leaders in the helping process. The more religious or spiritual social workers tended to do this more often ($r$=.1623; $p$<.05).

## Discussion

The results of this study of rural social workers are consistent with other more urban-oriented studies indicating that issues of religion and spirituality are of importance to social work. It has revealed that social workers consider religion and spirituality to be of significance in their own lives and the lives of their clients, and that religion and spirituality provide a positive resource for persons in solving their problems. Only in a minority of instances was religion believed to have a dysfunctional impact on clients. In a rural state such as North Dakota, it is not surprising that 90

*Table 4.* **Influence of Religion on Social Work Practice (N=142)**

| | | | Correlations with the worker's | | |
| Items | Percent | n | Religiosity | Length of practice | Education |
|---|---|---|---|---|---|
| 1. Comes across in practice issues of spirituality | 33.3 | 96 | .0749 | -.0159 | .1147 |
| 2. Personal religious/spiritual values come into conflict with practice | 2.1 | 3 | .0703 | -.0401 | .0426 |
| 3. Religious/spiritual orientation is helpful in helping the clients | 50.0 | 71 | .3036*** | .0544 | .1772* |
| 4. Compatibility with client's religious/spiritual values makes one feel comfortable to work with them | 21.9 | (31) | .3328*** | .0065 | .0938 |
| 5. Non-compatibility with religious/spiritual values of the clients | 3.5 | (5) | .0483 | .0293 | .0440 |
| 6. Involves the pastor or religious leader of the client in practice | 25.3 | (36) | .1729* | -.0972 | -.1623* |

*Note:* The responses represent percentage of social workers who reported 4 or above on a 5-point scale on these items. *=<.05  **=<.01  ***=<.001

percent of this sample claimed church membership, almost a requirement in a rural culture where practicing a religious faith continues to be of value and have positive social rewards.

An interesting conclusion of this research is that more experienced social workers and those with an MSW degree find religion and spirituality somewhat less functional in the lives of their clients than those with an undergraduate degree. A possible reason for this finding could be that more complex cases are assigned to more experienced or advanced degreed social workers which would include those clients who use religion in a dysfunctional manner.

In addition, the MSW social workers reported less collaboration with clergy on assigned cases than did those with BSW degrees. This could occur in North Dakota because MSW social workers are located in the state's larger, more urban settings where they are able to use the resources of psychologists and psychiatrists and are not as likely to access the services of clergy. BSW social workers, on the other hand, tend to work in smaller rural counties where the only other professionally educated helping resource would be a priest or pastor. In the rural cultures of states like North Dakota, the church is as much a center for social interaction as it is for spiritual growth and development and therefore has more active church membership. Consequently, in these subcultures, the pastor becomes an integral part of the community, often serving on school boards, human service boards, and having memberships in service organizations. Because these are often the same boards and organizations with which social workers are involved, opportunity exists for interaction between clergy and social workers which eventually also could lead to professional collaboration on behalf of clients.

In this study, the more strongly religious the social worker, the more competent she or he felt to deal with religious and spiritual issues with clients. However, caution should be taken when intrepreting this finding. Religious and spiritual experience and practice may sensitize a professional to these issues but is no substitute for professional training and education in specific methods for dealing with religious and spiritual issues with clients. This special training may be necessary before one feels qualified or competent to professionally deal with these complex issues. Because the finding showed that one out of three social workers admitted they frequently came across issues of religion and spirituality in their practice, and that 78 percent of the sample reported very little or no professional training in religious or spiritual matters, it is clear that additional training is needed to deal with issues of religion or spirituality in practice.

This study supports the findings of previous research indicating that the social work profession does perceive a need to deal appropriately with religion/spirituality in the lives of their clients. The findings of this research indicate that in order to be culturally sensitive to the diverse needs of a rural state, information about religion and spirituality need to be integrated in a professional manner both in social work curricula and in practice. Curriculum development is needed to determine appropriate ways of providing training about religious and spiritual issues in higher education, continuing education conferences, and workshops.

Some issues that the profession needs to grapple with in the future include the following:

1. There is a need within the profession to define and delimit the concepts of religion and spirituality as they apply to social work education and practice. Because issues of religion and spirituality transcend present-day organized religion, these terms may be separated. Should the profession identify and emphasize some common threads within all the religions that represent helping aspects? Should social work maintain its secular identity without identifying a particular religion as the embodiment of spirituality? Or could there be a process of identifying common elements in religions that can be specifically helpful in the practice of social work?

2. Can social work be completely secular? Often the secular stand of social work is defined as irreligious or antireligious. Since many social work clients and professionals maintain some kind of spiritual identity, is it possible to compartmentalize and separate practice from religion and spirituality?

There are no easy answers to these questions. However, the profession needs to acknowledge these vital issues and encourage an active discussion within the profession. In this era of knowledge of and sensitivity toward cultural diversity, the integration of religion and spirituality into the social work curriculum will provide a holistic approach to the client and his or her unique environment. It will allow the social worker to provide interventions that are not only culturally appropriate but spiritually sensitive to the client's individual needs.

## References

Brandon, D. (1976). *Zen in the art of helping.* New York: Delta.

Canda, E. R. (1992). In network news: Social workers seek spiritual roots. *Common Boundary Between Spirituality and Psychotherapy, 10*(3), 17.

Canda, E. R. (Ed.). (1990). Afterward: Spirituality re-examined. *Spirituality and Social Work Communicator,* School of Social Welfare, University of Kansas, *1*(1), 13-14.

Canda, E. R. (1989). Religious content in social work education: A comparative approach. *Journal of Social Work Education, 25,* 36-45.

Canda, E. R. (1988). Spirituality, religion, diversity, and social work practice. *Social Casework, 69,* 238-247.

Cornett, C. (1992). Toward a more comprehensive personalogy: Integrating a spiritual perspective into social work practice. *Social Work, 37,* 101-102.

Delgado, M. (1977). Puerto Rican spiritualism and the social work profession. *Social Casework, 58*(8), 457-458.

Denton, R.T. (1990). The religiously fundamentalist family: Training for assessment and treatment. *Journal of Social Work Education, 26,* 6-14.

DiBlasio, F. (1988). *Beliefs, attitudes, and values.* San Francisco, CA: Jossey-Bass.

Dudley, J. R., & Helfgott, C. (1990). Exploring a place for spirituality in the social work curriculum. *Journal of Social Work Education, 26*(3), 287-293.

Furman, L. E. (1991). The impact of the rural crisis on two-generational farm families. *Family Practice Quarterly Journal, 17*(1), 26. University of North Dakota, Department of Family Medicine, Grand Forks.

Gallup, G., Jr. (1985). *Religion in American–50 years.* (The Gallup Report, 236). Princeton, NJ: Princeton Religion Research Center.

Jacobsen, M. (1993, July). *Rural culture and ethnicity: Culturally appropriate rural social work practice.* Presentation at the National Institute on Social Work and Human Services in Rural Areas. Oxford, GA.

Joseph, V. M. (1988). Religion and social work practice. *Social Casework, 69,* 443-453.

King, M. (1967). Measuring the religious variable: Nine proposed dimensions. *Journal for the Scientific Study of Religion, 6,* 173-190.

Loewenberg, F. (1988). *Religion and social work practice in contemporary American society.* New York: Columbia University Press.

Meystedt, D. M. (1984). Religion and the rural population: Implications for social work. *Social Casework, 65,* 219-226.

Neuhaus, R. J. (1985). What the fundamentalists want. *Commentary, 79,* 41-46.

Pargament, K. I., Maton, K. I., & Hess, R. E. (Eds.). (1992). *Religion and prevention in mental health: Research, vision, and action.* Binghamton, NY: Haworth.

Seplowin, V. M. (1992). Social work and karma therapy. *Spirituality and Social Work Journal, 3*(2), 2-8.

Sheridan, M. J., Bullis, R. K., Adcock, C. R., Berlin, S. D., & Miller, P. C. (1991). Practitioners' personal and professional attitudes and behaviors toward religion and spirituality: Issues for education and practice. *Journal of Social Work.*

Siporin, M. (1985). Current social work perspectives for clinical practice. *Clinical Social Work Journal, 13,* 198-217.

Titone, A. M. (1991). Spirituality and psychotherapy in social work practice. *Spirituality and Social Work Communicator, 2*(1), 7-9. School of Social Welfare, University of Kansas.

# 11

# Treating Religious Fundamentalist Families: Therapists' Suggestions from a Qualitative Study

by Roy T. Denton and Martha J. Denton

*Human service workers, particularly in rural areas, frequently encounter families with religious fundamentalist belief systems. There exists, however, little systematically researched information to assist the practitioner working with fundamentalist families. This study was conducted using a random sample of the certified marriage and family therapists in North Carolina and soliciting from them practice suggestions which work with fundamentalist families. These practice suggestions were analyzed using a qualitative research procedure. Four major categories of responses were developed with several subcategories. Examples and implications of the suggestion categories are discussed, and directions for future practice model-building and research are set forth.*

The clients of rural human service workers often belong to a fundamentalist religion. A study of the certified family therapists in North Carolina found that an average of twenty-three percent of their case load were religious fundamentalists (Denton and Denton, 1992). Even though this demand for service exists, there is a reluctance on the part of helping professions to deal with clients' religious beliefs in general and Christian fundamentalism specifically (Faver, 1987; Goldstein, 1984; Loewenberg, 1988; Prest and Keller, 1993).

For a variety of ethical and paradigmatic reasons, the human service professions have sidestepped the issue of religion as an area of study or work. The profession's efforts to align itself with the empirically and rationally based sciences have pushed toward the exclusion of systematic research and practice development of those human phenomena which cannot

Reprinted from *Human Services in the Rural Environment* (Winter/Spring 1994), with permission of the Eastern Washington University School of Social Work and Human Services.

be easily measured or are grounded in personal belief systems. Stalley (1978) asserted that the profession's insistence upon nonjudgmental practice has led to an avoidance of dealing with the client's bases of judging. Paradoxically, the use of the ecological or general systems theoretical perspective impels practitioners and researchers to consider the spiritual and religious dimension as part of the holistic view of the client (Loewenberg, 1988; Vincentia Joseph, 1988; Prest and Keller, 1993).

There is a significant body of empirical findings and theoretical propositions to support the conclusion that meaning systems, including religion, have a significant impact upon one's attitudes and behaviors (Burnett, 1979; Wuthnow, 1976). In an extensive discussion of the "New Christian Right's" view of the family, McNamara (1985) argued that evangelical beliefs and practices meet the cognitive, emotional, and interpersonal needs of believers. In Warner's (1979) opinion, the fundamentalists' need for reassurance, reduction of uncertainty, control over the environment, and relief of existential anxiety are unmet by the broader society. Summarily, the impacts of these beliefs are so comprehensive on the individual, family, and community that the fundamentalist movement can be perceived as a subculture (Whipple, 1987; Denton, 1990).

Since this subculture is a significant part of the rural context, it is imperative that practitioners have available reliable knowledge about this group. However, attempts to empirically study this population have generated considerable controversy. Hood, Morris, and Watson (1986) assert that the fundamentalistic paradigm differs from that of the social sciences and efforts to investigate fundamentalism have been flawed by an antireligious bias because of the negative presuppositions built into the research instruments. Responding to a similar argument by McNamara (1985), Goettsch (1986) set forth the viewpoint that while the theoretical propositions on which fundamentalism rest cannot be tested empirically within the social sciences paradigm, the consequences of religion on people's cognitions and behaviors are appropriate topics for research.

Using a descriptive, phenomenological methodology, this study gathered from family therapists practice suggestions based on their experience in working with religious fundamentalist families. This method was used to lessen both researcher and instrument bias.

## Religious Fundamentalism

Used here, fundamentalism is defined as a class of Christian religious sects falling within the purview of McNamara's (1985) "New Christian Right"—fundamentalists, charismatics, evangelicals, pentecostals—which have some dogma variations but share a body of common beliefs (Loewenberg, 1988). Arising among the rural population as a reaction against the Protestant denominations of that time, it continues to reflect a traditional orientation (Sandeen, 1970). However, its constituents are no longer predominantly rural (Hood, et al., 1986). This traditionalism requires the assertion of the authority of the church over the family and of the family over the individual (Hargrove, 1983). The traditional perspective is further reinforced through a literal interpretation of the Bible.

Holding twin beliefs—dominance of the church over the family and men over women—fundamentalist families have a particularly rigid patriarchal hierarchy (Dobash and Dobash, 1979). Whipple (1987) stipulated five major factors complicating the work with battered fundamentalist females which seem to partially define the subculture of the fundamentalist church. These are: (1) A strong "we versus them" mentality which encourages members to seek help only from the church; (2) Reliance on faith leading to a passive approach to life; (3) A demand for forgiveness which tends to confirm aggressive behavior among family members; (4) Dominance of males over females; and (5) Strong prohibitions against divorce or remarriage.

To achieve a balanced picture of fundamentalism requires that one understands its two sides. These are the polemical (argumentative, we versus them mentality) and the private-faith nurturing side (emphasis on love and support). The faith nurturing side is the one most neglected in the literature (Marsden, 1983). In York's (1987) review of the literature and clinical experience, fundamentalism provided families with opportunities for socialization, belongingness, increased status and role opportunities, forgiveness, ability to relinquish responsibility for one's actions and problems, and spiritual guidance in the form of rules, values, and rituals. In a similar discussion, Ness and Wintrob (1980) concluded that participation in a fundamentalistic church led to a reduction in emotional distress.

## The Fundamentalist Family

There is a considerable body of clinical studies and anecdotal commentary on fundamentalist families; however, the number of empirical studies is limited particularly in identifying practice strategies that work. As McNamara (1985) has stated, "There are woefully few social sciences studies of New Christian Right families from the inside; and to this extent our understanding of how they actually work, as contrasted with ideal portraits painted by pastoral theologians on the one hand and critical commentary from social scientists on the other, is severely limited."

Those empirical studies which have been conducted confirm that there are distinct effects of fundamentalism upon the family. Larson (1978) concluded that while fundamentalist families are frequently treated similarly to nonfundamentalist families, they are different in distinct ways. In his study of fundamentalist families experiencing problems with adolescent children, he found that they took either an authoritarian stance or a spiritualizing one—both resulted in ambiguous communication. Other researchers have found that fundamentalists tend to evidence a high degree of guilt, dependency, and reliance upon authority, with females accepting a submissive role as defined by their church (Peteet, 1981; Maranell, 1974; Kucznski, 1981).

In a comparative study of therapists' ratings of fundamentalist and nonfundamentalist families in therapy, Denton and Denton (1992) found that fundamentalist families differ significantly from nonfundamentalist families on four of eight dimensions of family health. Fundamentalist families were rated as having significantly clearer expectations of how family members were to behave in relation to each other. Conversely, nonfundamentalist families in therapy demonstrated significantly more flexibility in dealing with change, in allowing and encouraging family members to assume age appropriate responsibilities, in using information to make their own judgments, and in maintaining appropriate family boundaries. Furthermore, nonfundamentalist families as compared to fundamentalist families were rated as significantly more emotionally close as families.

Consequently, it can be concluded that religion and the church have clear behavioral effects upon the fundamentalist family. This is a system whose boundaries, acceptance of feedback, control functions, role performances, and information exchanges with its environment are monitored by the church and its concomitant belief structure. Religion and church may well function as a steady-state stabilizer at step points of system transition (Denton, 1990).

Given the unique nature of the fundamentalist family, the development of congruent practice principles is a relevant task. Therefore, this study gathered suggestions for working with these families from certified family therapists so that a set of practice principles could be systematically developed.

## Methodology

According to the literature, the development of practice principles relevant to working with fundamentalist families has relied upon single case studies and anecdotal commentary. Little effort has been devoted to the systematic compilation of descriptive data leading to the development of testable hypotheses. Preliminary empirical groundwork for the construction of a practice model with this population has not been conducted. Consequently, these families are relatively uncharted "social terrain," so the authors started from the subjective viewpoint of therapists regularly working with these fundamentalist families. An exploratory qualitative methodology was appropriate for this level of knowledge building and was respectful of the phenomena being studied (Grinnell, 1988).

The particular phenomenological methodology used was developed by Adrian van Kaam (1969). Summarily, this method focuses on the response to one question aimed at obtaining spontaneous descriptions of experience. There is a four-stage process: (1) All of the respondents' statements are given to judges (in this study, two experienced family therapists) to be placed in categories; (2) The researchers formulate summary statements that capture the essence of each category; (3) The respondents' statements are scrutinized for any elements not directly related to the phenomena, and these are eliminated.

The summary statements are then reevaluated; (4) Finally, all respondents' statements are examined to see if they are subsumed within the abstracted categorical statements.

This study was one piece of a two-part research project comparing fundamentalist and nonfundamentalist families in therapy. The sample was drawn from the population of all certified marriage and family therapists in North Carolina listed in the State Marriage and Family Therapists' Certification Board roster (N=372). After randomly dividing the sample into two equal groups, each group received an instrument to which they were to respond either in terms of fundamentalist families or nonfundamentalist families, respectively. The quantitative portion of the study has been published previously (Denton and Denton, 1992). Within the instruments delivered to the therapists who were rating fundamentalist families was a qualitative question: "It will be appreciated if you will note any methods or practice suggestions which you have found to be helpful in working with religiously fundamentalistic families." Upon receipt of the completed questionnaires, the transcribed responses were forwarded to the judges.

## Results

The number of therapists responding to this survey was 188 (51%). Twenty were deleted because they were primarily in administrative or non-clinical positions, retired, or failed to complete the instrument. This left a total of 168 (45%) respondents. Of this number, 91 (54%) were therapists in the fundamentalist group, and of these 78 (46%) answered the qualitative question.

The respondents were middle-aged (x=46.9, s.d.=8.79), experienced as professionals (x=17.9, s.d.=7.57), experienced as family therapists (x=13.3, s.d.=6.89), and possessed varied experience regarding fundamentalist families (% of caseload x=23.4%, s.d.=21.17, range 0-80%). While fundamentalist families comprised, on the average, 23.4% of the therapists' caseloads, the variability was quite large within the sample. There were more males (55%), predominantly white (99%), and they were trained mainly in either social work or psychology (cumulative 68.5%). The majority were in private practice (56%) with the remainder distributed between public human services agencies (25%) and private human service agencies (19%).

The study's findings are presented in Table 1. Four major categories were developed, many of which contain multiple subcategories. All categorical statements are abstracted generalizations based upon many individual comments from respondents. Following the category title is stated the number of comments from which the statement is derived.

According to the therapists in this study, working with fundamentalist families required the same knowledge gathering as in working with any other subculture, i.e., the worker must be familiar with the characteristics of the subculture. The category drawing the largest number of practice sug-

**Table 1.** Categories and Summary Statements of Therapists' Responses by Descending Frequency

I. Therapy methods (N=85)

A. Practical use of beliefs (N=29)

1. First gain an understanding of the fundamentalist family's belief system and then frame interventions which use these beliefs to reinforce treatment recommendations.

2. Since religion can be used as a defense mechanism, it must not be taken away without replacing it with alternatives.

3. Bridges must be built between issues and beliefs.

4. While showing respect for the family's own beliefs, the therapist can suggest other methods of coping, especially in areas where the beliefs are not working.

B. Use of scriptures (N=28)

1. Being well versed scripturally enhances the therapists's skills while it increases the family's sense of being understood and accepted.

2. One can use biblical metaphors to expand the family's coping strategies.

3. Selectively quoting scriptures using those that allow for flexibility helps to reframe family behavior.

4. Prayer or a certain religious ritual can be used if it is appropriate to the situation and especially if the family requests it.

C. Problem solving (N=13)

1. Since most fundamentalists seem to be concrete thinkers, a problem solving approach seems to work best because the method is clear-cut, gradual and specific.

2. Get each family member to agree to an investment in the well-being of the family, then put in a written contract specific behaviors expected from each member.

3. Ask questions using plain, common sense and everyday language rather than making statements and attacking dysfunctional methods of dealing with change.

D. Defocus off religion (N=6)

1. Use dilemmas relative to areas other than religion in order to find similarities conducive to positive identification with other family members and to develop the formation of cognition at higher levels.

2. While maintaining your own objectivity, listen for the meaning behind the religion and try to understand what it is doing for the family.

E. Family structure: Use of males in the family (N=5)

1. Since the male parent holds the central power and control in the family and interprets information for the entire family, building a relationship with this person or eliciting his support is of vital importance even though contact may have to be in writing or by telephone.

F. Focusing on family feelings (N=4)

    1. Since feelings are largely ignored or discounted in fundamentalist families, recognizing and working with their emotions as individuals and as a family can be the most important and challenging task that the therapist can undertake.

II. Nonconfrontation about belief systems (N=25)

    A. Be nonconfrontive, nonjudgmental and never argue or debate with a religious fundamentalist client about religious faith.

    B. Do not directly challenge or attempt to change the family's religious beliefs or defend your own. If you are unable to do this then you must refer to another therapist.

    C. Convey understanding of religious fundamentalist beliefs

        1. The therapist must manifest a genuine basic understanding of religious fundamentalist assumptions and deal honestly with differing views from those of the client.

        2. All fundamentalist families are not dysfunctional. Many are no different from other families seeking therapy in that their problems are related to the level of defensiveness, not necessarily due to their religion.

        3. Many forms of fundamentalism promote beliefs which are family centered and supportive, and family beliefs are not rigid in all areas.

        4. There are certain fundamentalistic religions that include in their written dogma rules and regulations specific to the family while in others these teachings are "creatively interpreted".

    D. The therapist should be comfortable with his or her own religious beliefs and aware of his or her bias toward fundamentalism.

III. Relationship building (N=22)

    A. Although a slow process, building a relationship of trust is of vital importance; however, trust is often an issue with fundamentalists.

    B. Frequently fundamentalist families are so dogmatic in feelings and thoughts that one must minimize perceived threat and enhance the perception of the therapist as ally.

    C. Fundamentalists are frequently difficult clients in that the use which they make of their faith can be in the form of a primary symptom (suspiciousness, rigidity, or magical thinking) which reality or paradoxical maneuvers will not affect.

IV. Use of outside support (N=10)

    A. If the family agrees, contact the family's minister early in treatment.

    B. Establishing both of you as collaborators in helping the family and eliciting the minister's support eases treatment.

    C. Gaining the support of the minister is often a difficult process.

    D. Any outside exposure to family and marriage support groups or skill development courses is helpful even if only with people presenting other fundamentalist positions.

gestions was the use of the family's religious beliefs to support the treatment process. While there were some differences of opinion about the particular approach, there was unanimity that this would have to be addressed by the worker. A typical comment was, "It seems constructive to try to understand the importance of the belief system to the individual and to respect its purpose."

More than understanding the belief structure, however, was the orientation to the use of the belief system in the change effort. The majority of the respondents emphasized the need for respect and care in approaching the family's beliefs. But, they felt that in those situations in which the beliefs were being used as a defense or were supporting and maintaining the dysfunctional behavior (spouse abuse or child abuse as an example), the worker would have to find a method for using the belief system to support change. Some illustrative comments were:

> Whenever possible, I use their beliefs as constructively as I can to undergird any treatment recommendations, i.e., "I want you to help your wife with this problem by being as patient and forgiving as you understand Jesus to be," or I might ask, "What are you comfortable with doing in view of what your family and church friends want you to do?"

> I have found that the reframing of actions within their belief system, shifting emphasis from judgement and rigidity toward tolerance and acceptance works well with these families.

> When they come to the agency for service, they are already dissatisfied with their beliefs, values, and methods of problem solving to some extent and are often uncomfortable with this awareness. Being supportive of their doubts and using their familiar language/phrases to offer a different framework of what they have been taught is often helpful.

Consistent with approaching the family within their perspective is the therapists' emphasis upon the use of scripture (if the therapist is comfortable with it) as a method of establishing a relationship, expanding the family's concept of God and coping mechanisms available within that paradigm, and also modifying the family's boundaries and receptivity to feedback from the therapist. This position is congruent with that proposed by Prest and Keller (1993) in stressing the importance of language in establishing meaning systems for religious families. To implement this procedure requires the therapist to be knowledgeable of those relevant scriptures. Frequently, fundamentalist families are familiar with only a limited number of Bible verses repetitively quoted from the pulpit.

Using scripture, prayer or religious ritual, however, has to be congruent with the context and the therapist's comfort level. One therapist stated, "I have found the use of prayer and scripture helpful when requested by the family or it is appropriate to the situation." Familiar language helps the family feel understood and couches change efforts in terms acceptable to them. One of the major functions of the therapist's use of scripture is to encourage the family to develop a different perception of faith in areas where the family is using religion as a defense or where their interpretation of scripture is confounding change efforts. This is particularly true in husband/wife and parent/child relationships where male dominance is being reinforced by selective biblical passages.

Whipple's (1987) discussion of the biblical roots of male domination of wives agreed with the comments of the therapists in this study. One suggested that the best approach is to expand the perceptions of the family members by using scriptures that contradict the ones supporting male dominance, and then being puzzled by the apparent paradoxes. An example is the scripture most quoted in support of husband domination over the wife: Ephesians 5:22, "Wives, submit yourselves unto your husbands, as unto the Lord." When this verse is placed in the context of the entire chapter of Ephesians, a different picture emerges. The preceding verse (v.21) states, "Submitting yourselves one to the other in the fear of God," implying a mutual submission process, a symmetrical relationship as opposed to a complementary one. Similarly, Ephesians 5:28-29 states, "So ought men to love their wives as their own bodies. He that loveth his wife loveth himself. For no man ever yet hateth his own flesh but nourisheth and cherisheth it even as the Lord the church" (King James Version).

An even more direct statement is found in the discussion of sexual relationships between partners in I Corinthians 7:3-4, which says, "Let the husband render unto the wife due benevolence: and likewise also the wife unto the husband. The wife hath not power of her own body, but the husband: and likewise also the husband hath not power of his own body, but the wife" (KJV). Again, the scriptures have postulated a contradictory position, but this confusion can be utilized to expand the perception of the fundamentalist family in order to gain a picture of a "bigger God."

Divorce, overcoming a passive approach to life, forgiveness (when it is preventing movement), and relationships with children can be dealt with scripturally to free the family from a rigid position and allow change. This overall approach emphasizes the message of love and acceptance as opposed to a legalistic adherence to narrowly defined rules. This point is scriptural in that Jesus averred that justice, mercy, and faith were more important than legalistic rigidity (Matthew 23:23, KJV). However, it is important not to argue or threaten the family's beliefs but to expand their perceptions in those areas which cannot be dealt with otherwise. Helpful expositions of useful scriptures can be found in Whipple (1987), Griffith (1986), Lovinger (1979), and Prest and Keller (1993).

Therapists found biblical metaphors to be useful. One example was an enmeshed family struggling with a nineteen-year-old daughter over separation issues. The therapist was able to use the prodigal son metaphor to teach the family that loving sometimes means letting go. Summarily, language consistent with the internal frame of reference of the family provides feedback information in a mode acceptable to the family system.

Among the therapists commenting on therapeutic methods, thirteen stipulated the need to deal with fundamentalist families from a concrete problem-solving approach. These families responded best to a highly structured, step-by-step procedure with specific written contracts for all members. While this concept is congruent with fundamentalists' need for structure, the therapist must be aware of overreliance upon authority figures and must consistently refuse to be drawn into the position of decision-maker.

The last three sub-categories of "Therapy Methods" garnered a total of 14 statements. Therapists found that initially building a success base with fundamentalist families by focusing as much as possible on issues not tinted by religion established positive linkages between family members and between the family and the therapist. Getting a picture of the relationship network of the family included gaining an understanding of the meaning of the relationship to God for various family members.

Five therapists addressed the importance of respecting the family hierarchy. The male is the "head of the house," and successful approaches include building a relationship with this person and eliciting his support. If the worker's own theoretical or personal philosophy is so in conflict with this stance that they are unable to respect this subcultural structure, then they must refer. This family structure, as perceived by the therapists, may be related to the statements of those therapists who perceived fundamentalist families as being emotionally cold. It might be that the rigidity of the role performance among family members is such that boundaries are closed to each other, which constricts the expression of feelings. One of the therapist's tasks, then, is to help the family open the boundaries to allow expression of their feelings.

Twenty-five respondents' statements were directed to the need for a nonconfrontive and respectful approach. They were particularly emphatic about the avoidance of debating, arguing, or challenging the religious beliefs of fundamentalists; furthermore, they were quite specific about not being drawn into a defensive stance about one's own belief structure. Working with fundamentalists requires the therapist to manifest a genuine understanding of the fundamentalist religious assumptions and an appreciation of the positive contributions of the family's faith. This stance neither approves nor disapproves of the belief structure, but it is an honest appraisal of its role in the ecology of the family.

One of the assumptions to which therapists fall victim is that the problems of the family are related to their religious beliefs. Several of the respondents strongly stated that fundamentalist families in therapy frequently present with the same problems as nonfundamentalists which may or may not be supported by their faith. It is only when the problems are supported by religious beliefs or when these beliefs are being used as a defense mechanism against change that they must be approached directly.

It is necessary to know to which specific fundamentalist organization the family belongs. Some of the larger groups have written rules and regulations specific to the governance of family life. In these instances, the therapist is dealing not with just the family but also with a community. Conversely, in some smaller independent churches, the rules may be arbitrary ones issued from the pulpit by the minister; therefore, the therapist is dealing mainly with the family's feelings toward the minister rather than the rules.

In working with beliefs, it is imperative that the therapist be comfortable with his or her own religious beliefs and with his or her own biases toward fundamentalism. In general, using religious beliefs to enhance treatment poses paradigmatic and ethical problems for human service workers. Several authors have addressed the antireligious bias in psychotherapeutic literature, theories, and test instruments (Ethridge & Feagin, 1979; McNamara, 1985; Larson, 1978; Goettsch, 1986). In social work, Loewenberg (1988) has produced an excellent summary of the trends which bias against working with a client's religious feelings. These ethical dilemmas are exaggerated when the therapist holds presuppositions which are derogatory toward the particular religion (Denton, 1990). The respondents in this study thought that being very clear about their own biases toward fundamentalism is even more important than their biases toward other religions since part of the fundamentalist's code is a heightened sensitivity to perceived persecution.

This sensitivity complicates the topic of the fourth category, "Relationship Building." Twenty-two comments pointed out the vital importance of a slow and thoughtful development of trust with the fundamentalist family. Be aware that different members of the family adhere differently to the religious dogma; consequently, the response rate of family members will vary. For work to progress, the therapist must be viewed as ally. In very fundamentalistic families, trusting anyone outside the church community is suspect. Therefore, the previous discussions concerning the use of language and respect for families' beliefs are also very relevant in relationship building.

One method of facilitating a relationship with the family is to solicit the support of the minister. Success rate estimates from the respondents in gaining positive minister cooperation averaged 40%. The effort, even if only by letter or telephone (with the family's permission), tends to be seen as conferring legitimacy on their beliefs and as an act of respect by the therapist. Support from the minister greatly enhances interventions.

It is possible to open family boundaries by exposure to other opinions through family and marriage support groups, skill development courses, or parent training workshops. This feedback is often received more readily from other fundamentalists than from an outsider. Since there are many varieties of fundamentalists, it is frequently possible to find a resource offering a different perspective more functional for the family. This is true with literature as well as with groups.

## Conclusion

In this qualitative study of religious fundamentalist families, 78 randomly selected certified family therapists responded to a question soliciting their practice wisdom about working with these families. Their statements fell into four broad categories: (a) suggestions about therapy methods, (b) being nonconfrontational with the family, (c) relationship building, and (d) the use of outside resources. Within each of these four areas, there were subcategories of specific practice suggestions which clarified and elaborated practice cues found in the anecdotal literature.

According to therapists in this study, the boundaries and meaning systems of fundamentalist families were governed by their religious belief systems to the extent that any attempt to enter their system required specific knowledge and use of belief-congruent techniques. Further, therapists need to be fully conscious of their own theoretical and religious biases in order to avoid counter-transference difficulties.

There are two main arguments for the continuance of research and theory development regarding religious fundamentalist families in therapy. First, if the profession of social work is to continue to utilize the ecological or general systems perspective with its holistic orientation, then the dimension of spirituality must be a part of that perspective (Sullivan, 1992; Denton and Denton, 1992; Loewenberg, 1988). Second, the argument has been advanced that this is a distinct subculture with characteristics which, as with any other subculture, require the therapist's understanding (Denton, 1990). Given the size—approximately 40 million (PBS, 1989)—of the subculture and its relevance to rural communities, continued efforts to establish validated practice principles are of great importance.

Exploratory, qualitative studies can only provide a description of the perspectives of the respondents at the moment of response. Consequently, the generalizability of the results is limited. In this study, there is the additional limitation that all the respondents were answering from a biased (either pro or con) stance about a topic which elicits emotional reactions. Further complicating the results is that all the respondents have been trained in theories which are inherently biased. Given these limitations, this study has practical value in beginning the process of systematically gathering information about practice with religious fundamentalist families that can be replicated in further research and quantified for comparative studies.

In summary, the size and impact of the religious fundamentalist subculture is such that practitioners must become familiar with effective methods of entering and intervening in these family systems. The suggestions from experienced therapists developed in this study can act as guides for practice as well as the launching point for future research.

## References

Burnett, D. W. (1979). Religion, personality, and clinical assessment. *Journal of Religion and Health*, October, 308-312.

Denton, R. T. (1990) The religiously fundamentalist family: Training for assessment and treatment. *Journal of Social Work Education 26*(1), 6-14.

Denton, R. T., & Denton, M. J. (1992). Therapists' ratings of fundamentalist and nonfundamentalist families in therapy: An empirical comparison. *Family Process, 31*, 175-185.

Dobash, R. E., & Dobash, R. P. (1979). *Violence against wives*, New York: Free Press.

Ethridge, F. M., & Feagin, J. R. (1979). Varieties of "fundamentalism": A conceptual and empirical analysis of two Protestant denominations. *Sociological Quarterly, 20*, 37-48.

Faver, C. A. (1987). Religious beliefs, professional values, and social work. *Journal of Applied Social Science, 11*(2), 207-219.

Goettsch, S. L. (1986). The new Christian right and the social sciences: A response to McNamara. *Journal of Marriage and the Family, 48*, 447-454.

Goldstein, H. (Ed.). (1984). *Creative change: A cognitive-humanistic approach to social work practice.* New York: Tavistock.

Grinnell, R. M. (1988). *Social work research evaluation* (3rd ed.). Itasca, IL: Peacock.

Griffith, J. B. (1986). Employing the God-family relationship in therapy with religious families. *Family Process, 25*, 609-618.

Hargrove, B. (1983). The church, the family, and the modernization process. In W. V. D'Antonio & J. Aldous (Eds.), *Families and religion: Conflict and change in modern society.* Thousand Oaks, CA: Sage.

Hood, R. W., Morris, R. J., & Watson, P. J. (1986). Maintenance of religious fundamentalism. *Psychological Reports, 59*, 547-559.

Joseph, M. V. (1988). Religion and social work practice. *Social Casework, 69*, 443-452.

Kucznski, K. (1981). New tensions in rural communities. *Human Services in the Rural Environment, 6*, 48-56.

Larson, J. A. (1978). Dysfunction in the evangelical family: Treatment considerations. *The Family Coordinator, 27,* 261.

Loewenberg, F. M. (1988). *Religion and social work practice in contemporary American society.* New York: Columbia University Press.

Lovinger, R. J. (1979). Therapeutic strategies with "religious" resistance. *Psychotherapy: Theory, Research, and Practice,16,* 419-427.

Maranell, G. M. (1974). *Responses to religion.* Kansas: University of Kansas Press.

Marsden, G. (1983). Preachers of paradox: The religious new right in historical perspective. In M. Douglas & S. Tipton (Eds.), *Religion in America.* Boston: Beacon.

McNamara, P. H. (1985). The new Christian right's view of the family and its social science critics: A study in differing presuppositions. *Journal of Marriage and the Family, 47*, 449-457.

Ness, R. C., & Wintrob, R. M. (1980). The emotional impact of fundamentalist religious practice: An empirical study of intergroup variation. *American Journal of Orthopsychiatry, 50,* 302-315.

Peteet, J. (1981). Issues in the treatment of religious patients. *American Journal of Psychotherapy, 35,* 559-564.

Prest, L. A., & Keller, J. F. (1993). Spirituality and family therapy: Spiritual beliefs, myths, and metaphors. *Journal of Marital and Family Therapy, 19*(2), 137-148.

Sandeen, E. R. (1970). *The roots of fundamentalism.* Chicago: University of Chicago Press.

Stalley, R. F. (1978). Nonjudgmental attitudes. In N. Timms & D. Watson (Eds.), *Philosophy in Social Work.* London: Routledge & Kegan Paul.

Sullivan, W. P. (1992). Spirituality as social support for individuals with severe mental illness. *Spirituality and Social Work Journal, 3,* 7-13.

van Kaam, A. (1969). *Existential foundations of psychology.* New York: Image Books.

Warner, R. (1979). Theoretical barriers to the understanding of evangelical Christianity. *Sociological Analysis, 40,* 1-9.

Whipple, V. (1987). Counseling battered women from fundamentalist churches. *Journal of Marital and Family Therapy, 13,* 25-258.

Wuthnow, R. (1976). *The consciousness reformation.* Berkeley: University of California Press.

York, G. Y. (1987). Religious-based denial in the NICU: Implications for social work. *Social Work in Health Care, 12*(4), 31-45.

# Part 3

## Rural People and Special Populations

P art 3 describes some of the population groups that constitute rural America. An article on minorities in rural society, taken from a socio-logical journal, sets the stage. Long-time rural specialist Wilburn Hayden, Jr. writes about the special population of Appalachian African Americans. Chapters on elderly black farm women, minorities in rural areas, and the aging rural population are also included.

Although the book does not include special chapters on many other rural population groups, their needs and characteristics are also special. All are discussed in one or more chapters in various contexts. Two of the larger rural minority groups, for example, are Hispanics (particularly Mexican Americans) and Native Americans, the most rural minority group in the United States. However, there are also many Asian American rural people and many rural communities whose citizens have long-term connections with Eastern and Western Europe. These communities, scattered throughout the United States, are populated by those of German, Scandinavian, Polish, Czechoslo-vakian, and Romanian descent.

Although some may think of rural communities as having little or no diversity—as places with exclusively white populations or small African-American populations—the reality is that rural America has historically been every bit as diverse as metropolitan America.

# 12

## Minorities in Rural Society

by Gene F. Summers

The United States is not a Third World country, but poverty is stalking the American landscape and appears to be capturing more victims every day (Barancik 1990; Duncan 1991; Gorham 1990; O'Hare 1988; Porter 1989). This is happening in what is perhaps the richest nation in the world. It is not a new thing; America has known poverty for many generations (Fitchen 1981; Levitan and Shapiro 1987). From time to time the architects of public policy have attempted to contain this social disease, but they have not succeeded. Poverty persists! It is malignant, and it is spreading (Brown and Warner 1989; Palerm 1988; Thurow 1987).

### The Third World in Rural America

The agony and debilitating effects of this social cancer fall most heavily on racial and ethnic minorities, especially rural minorities (Ghelfi 1986; Palerm 1988; Sandefur and Tienda 1988; Snipp 1990; Snipp and Summers 1991). We are all familiar with statistical reports of poverty running at 50 percent or more in many Third World nations. We carry with us the television images of malnourished and starving children, dilapidated housing, make-shift health clinics, and ill-clothed men and women with faces etched by age long before their time. Sadly, one does not need to send television camera crews to the Third World to film such human degradation (Hoppe 1989; Shotland et al. 1988a, 1988b).

The Third World exists in rural America, especially among families and communities of racial and ethnic minorities. In any nation poverty is unacceptable; but in a nation as rich as America, it is inexcusable—even immoral (Deavers 1989).

To understand my position on poverty, it may be helpful to know more about me and my vocabulary of emotions. I was born and raised on a 40-acre farm in the swamps of Southeast Missouri on the northern rim of the Mississippi Delta. My father was illiterate, my mother finished 8th grade, and I have one brother who is illiterate. We lived in a two-room,

Reprinted from *Rural Sociology* (*56*[2], 1991, pp. 177-188), with permission from the Rural Sociological Society.

tin-roofed shack one mile from the nearest gravel road, with no electricity or indoor plumbing. We had no gasoline powered equipment, no newspapers, and no books except the family Bible.

In May of 1989 I revisited the Delta as a member of the National Rural Studies Committee. We listened to speeches and toured the region around Greenville and Stoneville on a Greyhound bus (Castle and Baldwin 1989). We saw the Delta's soybean fields, its catfish farms, its cooperative feed mills, its roadside cafes, and its public housing estates.

At breakfast in Greenville, I met a black colleague from Mississippi who spoke eloquently about the problem. What he said seemed to expose the spirit and soul of all rural minorities who live in poverty. He said to me, "Gene, the wealth of these Delta planters and their families was made by the sweat and labor of my grandparents and my parents. I am determined that my children will get their share of the estate. These white folk owe their wealth to the work and toil of my ancestors. That is 'value added,' and we have a right to our share. But that's my problem."

Friend from Mississippi, the problem is not *your* problem. It is not a problem of the Delta; it is not a problem of Mississippi; it is *our* problem.

I joined the Rural Sociological Society (RSS) in 1970 because it has a history of concern for the plight of rural minorities. For example, in 1969 the Rural Sociological Society responded positively to a call from Dr. R. D. Morrison, President of Alabama A&M University, to assist the Black Land Grant Universities. A committee was formed to call upon the U.S. Secretary of Agriculture and request an allocation of USDA research funds for these historically black institutions. Working together and with others, Congress was persuaded two years later to appropriate $12 million for the Black Land Grant Universities and Institutions.

When I returned from the Delta, I resolved to do all I could to encourage the RSS to take a position of leadership in dealing with the persistent poverty that burdens so many rural minorities. The RSS has done this through the formation of a task force on persistent rural poverty.[1]

---

[1] This task force has been formed with the collaboration and support of the Kellogg Foundation and the four Regional Centers for Rural Development; a National task force began work on November 1, 1990 under the leadership of the Rural Sociological Society.

The goals of the task force are to be achieved through a two-phase project covering a three-year period. The first two years will provide a conceptual clarification regarding the factors and dynamics of society which precipitate and perpetuate rural poverty. We expect this will lead to significant reinterpretation of existing theory. The third year will be devoted to the dissemination of results and policy implications through a national workshop on rural poverty and a series of publications.

The task force will consist of eight working groups, each chaired by a member of the Rural Sociological Society, and will include social scientists from other

Below, I will do two things: first, describe what I see as the challenge in addressing rural poverty and, second, call attention to seven barriers to achieving a clearer understanding of poverty among rural minorities. The purpose of this discussion is to clarify the nature of poverty, eliminate the rationalizations often used to avoid or delay action, and encourage social scientists to resolve anew to determine the causes and develop solutions which will eliminate poverty in rural America.

## The Challenge

It should be very clear that we are dealing with a problem of social structure, not a problem of social misfits (Colclough 1988, 1989; Lichter and Constanzo 1986; Tickamyer and Duncan 1990; Tomaskovic-Devey 1987). Our task is to discover why a rural poverty class exists and why it is so heavily populated by rural minorities (Duncan and Tickamyer 1989; Wilson and Aponte 1985).

Because the sources of poverty very likely lie in the social fabric of rural society and because many rural sociologists know the evils of rural poverty from personal experience, they are particularly well suited to respond to the challenge, even though the task of discovery and clarification is not limited to rural sociologists.

The challenge to rural sociologists is to identify the barriers that prevent rural minorities from claiming their rights of citizenship in this prosperous land. As citizens they have a right to adequate education, sufficient income, decent housing, adequate health care, and full employment. We need to examine the origins of barriers to access, study their structure and dynamics, and offer visions of how the barriers can be overcome (Christenson and Flora 1991; Deavers 1989; Duncan 1991; Duncan and Tickamyer 1988).

---

disciplines as well. The groups and their leaders are: Fred Buttell–State Policy and Rural Poverty; Leonard Bloomquist–Work Structures, Labor Market Dynamics, and Rural Poverty; Nina Glasgow–The Rural Elderly and Poverty; Craig Humphrey–Natural Resources and Rural Poverty; Dan Lichter–Human Capital Investments, Labor Supply, and Rural Poverty; Thomas Lyson and William L. Falk–Spatial Location of Economic Activities, Uneven Development, and Rural Poverty; C. Matthew Snipp–Racial and Ethnic Minorities and Rural Poverty; Ann Tickamyer–Rural Women and Poverty.

I will chair the task force as Past-President of the Rural Sociological Society, and an advisory board of nonsociologists will guide the work of the Task Force. Sandra Batie (President, American Agricultural Economics Association); Emery Castle (Oregon State University); Kenneth Deavers (Economic Research Service, USDA); Barbara Stowe (Dean, College of Human Ecology, Kansas State University); and Julian Wolpert (Princeton University).

## The Barriers

The persistence of poverty among rural minorities and others in spite of dozens of government programs and the expenditure of billions of dollars calls into question the theories social scientists have constructed to guide these programs and efforts.

Are social scientists part of the problem? Have they constructed inaccurate or incomplete conceptual maps that were appropriate for society as it existed 50 or 75 years ago, but are dated because of the global economic and political restructuring of the past decade? Or have such maps always been inadequate?

The search for barriers must begin with a careful self-examination. We must acknowledge the possibility that it is the belief system of social science itself which creates barriers to a clearer understanding of persistent rural poverty. There are seven elements of this belief system which may function as conceptual barriers and which need to be scrutinized.

### Barrier One: The Belief that Poverty Can Be Reduced by Merely Improving the Marketable Skills of Minorities

This belief rests solidly on human capital theory which claims that the limited success of minorities in rural labor markets is due to their lack of human capital: basic education, specialized skills, and industrial experience (Becker 1971, 1985). There is evidence to support the view that education and job training are positively associated with success in labor markets (Hauser and Featherman 1977; Kurz and Mueller 1987) and that rural minorities have less formal education than nonminority cohorts (Farley and Allen 1987; Sandefur and Tienda 1988; Snipp 1990). Because of this evidence, greater investment in human capital seems to be a plausible solution to rural poverty among minorities.

However, this solution makes no provision for the resources necessary for greater investments and comes dangerously close to leaving the escape from poverty up to the will and resources of the victims. The poverty-stricken must make investments to enhance their income-producing capacity. But the poor do not have the resources, even if they may have managed to maintain the will (Beaulieu 1988; Lyson 1989).

Human capital theory is also silent regarding demand factors. It assumes that a demand will exist for the labor services of rural minorities who have education and job skills. Make no mistake—education is essential, but it is not sufficient to erase poverty. An educated labor force without jobs is an educated, unemployed labor force. Attention must be given to creating a demand for labor, including educated labor (Brown et al. 1988; Pollard and O'Hare 1990).

Human capital theory also ignores important aspects of the organization of work, the interrelations among work structures (industries, firms, and locations), and the impact of these interrelations on the operation of labor markets (Farkas and England 1988; Kalleberg and Berg 1988; Osterman 1988; Whitener 1985). These institutional factors may create formidable barriers for rural minorities, even those who are educated, job trained, and experienced. Kalleberg and Berg (1983:3) assert "that many work-related inequalities among individuals are generated by correlates of such work structures as firms, industries, occupations, classes, and unions."

### Barrier Two: The Belief that Persistent Unemployment and Poverty Can Be Reduced by Making American Industries More Competitive in World Product Markets

This belief rests on a rapidly deteriorating model of industrial organization—a model characterized by very large factories with hierarchically structured internal labor markets (Osterman 1988). Clearly, American industry is facing stiffer international competition and changes in product markets. These changes create additional market uncertainties and fluctuations.

In response, firms often search for greater flexibility (Harrison and Bluestone 1988). This is achieved through innovations in technology or by down-sizing the internal labor market to an essential core of workers and externalizing the remainder of the workforce (contracting work out to other firms or hiring workers on a temporary or part-time basis to fill the surges in demand) (Osterman 1988).

Labor costs also can be saved by relocating jobs from the internal to the external or peripheral labor market. Part-time and temporary workers almost always earn less per hour in wages, are seldom covered by contract seniority rules governing lay-off and recall, almost never receive a benefit package equal to that of full-time, permanent employees, and seldom receive health care benefits (Gorham 1990; Morrissey 1990; Palerm 1988; Porter 1989; Shapiro 1989; Snipp 1990; Tickamyer and Duncan 1990).

It appears that a more competitive American industrial sector is being purchased by forfeiting the job security and social insurances of a large and increasing portion of the workforce. Indeed, it seems that the poverty machine is most effective during upturns of the economy (Shapiro 1989). Clearly, all ships do not rise with the tide.

### Barrier Three: The Belief that the Creation of a Peripheral Labor Force Affects Urban Minorities But Not Rural Minorities

The most frequent use of part-time and temporary workers is in the service and retail sectors. Health care and medical service providers employ many part-time workers. Part-time employees are not limited to orderlies and nurses aids. Many nurses and technicians are also employed part-time.

In the retail sector, peripheral workers are not limited to fast-food shops. Virtually all supermarkets, discount stores, department stores, banks, and real estate and insurance sales firms employ predominantly part-time workers. It is quite common to find 80-90 percent of the employees in these sectors in the peripheral labor force.

These businesses are the fastest growing sources of rural employment (Brown et al. 1988) and are often the primary sources of employment for rural minorities—especially women and youth (Killian and Hady 1988; O'Hare and Pauti 1990; Tickamyer and Duncan 1990).

### Barrier Four: The Belief that the Informal Labor Market is Largely a Third World Phenomenon

Industrial homework may sound like an artifact of bygone days, an activity left behind in America's early industrial days along with the Model "T" Ford. That does not seem to be the case (Portes et al. 1989). Beginning in the 1970s, the popular press began exposing the resurgence of "illegal sweatshops" and "cottage industries" in the long-established garment-making industry and in the newer clerical and electronics industries. Urban centers are usually mentioned as the locations where industries employ most homeworkers. More recently, however, some press attention has centered on "farm-factories," the relocation of industries to depressed rural areas, and the employment of rural families in farm-based assembly work (Davidson 1989; Gringeri 1990).

That informal labor relations are "at home" in rural areas should come as little surprise. The greater prevalence of routine manufacturing jobs and the documented growth in low-wage and low-skill work in rural areas suggest that the line between formal and informal activities in this context may indeed be quite fine. The depressed rural economy means greater numbers of people seeking work—people who may be willing to accept low-wage rates, job insecurity, and no benefits in exchange for a somewhat increased household cash flow.

### Barrier Five: The Belief that Labor Market Participation Will Eliminate Poverty

If asked to offer a solution to poverty among rural minorities, there is no doubt many social scientists would say, "Put them to work." Social scientists place an overwhelming emphasis on labor markets and labor market participation. But labor markets could be functioning perfectly and still fail to address poverty among 30 percent or more of rural minorities (Glasgow 1988). There are people who cannot participate in the labor market—the elderly, the disabled, the sick and injured, and single parents who cannot afford childcare. The children of these persons also suffer from poverty because their parents cannot enter the labor market (Shotland et al. 1988b).

Some say, "Let them work." But many of these people have years of experience in the labor market and still find themselves in poverty. Why? Because the jobs they had were not covered by Social Security or any other social insurance program. Rural minorities are often victims of this loophole.

Moreover, the recent growth of the peripheral and informal labor markets, where there are virtually no social insurances, is likely to increase the size of the army of the working poor (Colclough 1989; Lichter 1989; Oliveria 1986; Shapiro 1989; Summers et al. 1990; Tomaskovic-Devey 1987). It also spells poverty for yet another generation who will not have earned a right to consumption after leaving the labor market.

### Barrier Six: The Belief that the Problems of Rural Minorities Are Due to Failures of Rural Social Institutions and Inferior Human Resources

The problems of rural areas are often attributed to failures of schools, local government, the family, poor business leadership, and/or bad management of natural resources. Implicitly, if not explicitly, the goal is to make rural institutions more like those of urban areas. This was the conclusion of the Country Life Commission in 1906 and is still accepted by a great many people, but this goal completely disregards the fact that many of the problems of rural areas are precisely the same as those found in the inner cities of the nation.

Focusing on the social institutions as the *cause* of rural problems keeps social scientists from asking why they are so ineffective. Social scientists seldom examine the possibility that rural resources (natural, human, and social) are being exploited for the benefit of urban interests, external investors, or even a local ruling class. For exceptions examine Caudill (1962), Dill et al. (1988), Gaventa (1980), and Snipp (1986).

Social science has seldom explored the possibility that pockets of unemployment, poverty, school attrition, poor health, and concentrations of minority populations coincide and persist for reasons other than "loss of comparative advantage" in regional, national, and international markets. It is possible that these things exist because they create and support a comparative advantage for *other* segments of society.

### Barrier Seven: The Belief that Merely the Good Will and Social Conscience of the Powerful Will Overcome Poverty

The search for barriers to equality must not disregard the systems of racial, ethnic, class, and gender relations. These are systems of deferential relations based on uneven distribution of social power and characterized by a great deal of paternalism and discrimination.

Attempts to alter these systems have been resisted by those holding dominant social power. Moreover, in the few instances where policy instruments *have* been put into place, their effects have been minimal because the system adapts.

For example, federal legislation which forbids discrimination in the housing markets based on race, age, gender, etc. has been largely ineffective in providing better housing for minority families with income. Landlords and financial institutions have either introduced or raised the income requirement for would-be renters and home-buyers. For example, a black mother providing care for six children cannot find housing in the market-place even though she has a full time job with the state of Wisconsin and earns $20,000 per year. Her annual income would have to be $27,000 in order to qualify for housing adequate for her family's need. In the mean-time, she and her children must live in temporary housing for the home-less. Income requirements in housing markets are presently perfectly legal. They have the effect of maintaining the status quo of power relations in the housing markets.

One strategy for changing power relations is to draw upon the social bonds inherent in these relations. It is proposed that conscience and the sense of civic obligation among those in power be challenged to make concessions for improving the welfare of those with little power. Such challenges must not have the character of demands, but are required to preserve the symbolic values of gemeinschaft (the paternalistic system).

This voluntary approach allows particularistic criteria to take prece-dence over universalistic standards. The result is that the authority of power holders is not really challenged, but is accepted and legitimated.

It is in these dynamic systems of social power that rural minorities likely face the most formidable barriers to equality. New theories are needed to explicate the changing strategies of finance and industrial capi-tal which operate in a deregulated economy. These strategies tend to repro-duce (and could not prosper without) systems of exploitation and poverty at the local level.

## Conclusion

For me, there is no more important task facing rural sociologists than discovering the roots of poverty among rural minorities. No group in American society suffers the burdens of poverty more severely. No group in society has suffered the depth of poverty for so long.

The intensity of such poverty is not the worst of it. The system also treats minorities differently. Solving poverty among white folks will not erase poverty among minorities.

Finding the factors which precipitate poverty and allow it to persist among rural minorities is our greatest challenge. I believe that by working together, we can and will discover the causes of persistent rural poverty. When we do, we will have taken a giant step toward solving poverty in America and for the poor elsewhere in the world.

## References

Barancik, Scott. (1990). *The rural disadvantage: Growing income disparity between rural and urban areas.* Washington, DC: Center for Budget and Policy Priorities.

Beaulieu, Lionel J. (Ed.). (1988). *The rural south in crisis.* Boulder, CO: Westview.

Becker, Gary S. (1971). *Human capital: A theoretical and empirical analysis with special reference to education* (2nd ed.). New York: Columbia University Press.

——. (1985). *Human capital.* New York: National Bureau of Economic Research.

Brown, David L., & Warner, Mildred. (1989). Persistent low income areas in the United States: Some conceptual challenges." In Emery Castle & Barbara Baldwin (Eds.), *National Rural Studies Committee: A proceedings of Stoneville, Mississippi meeting May 17–18, 1989* (pp. 47-58). Corvallis, OR: Western Rural Development Center.

Brown, David L., Reid, J. Norman, Bluestone, Herman, McGranahan, David, & Mazie, Sara M. (Eds.). (1988). Rural economic development in the 1980s: Prospects for the future. (Rural Development Research Report No. 69.) Washington, DC: U.S. Department of Agriculture, Economic Research Service.

Castle, Emery, & Baldwin, Barbara. (Eds.) (1989). *National Rural Studies Committee: A proceedings of Stoneville, Mississippi meeting May 17–18, 1989.* Corvallis, OR: Western Rural Development Center.

Caudill, Harry. (1962). Night comes to the Cumberlands: Biography of a depressed region. Boston: Little Brown.

Christenson, James, & Flora, Cornelia. (Eds.). (1991). *Rural policy for the 1990s.* Boulder, CO: Westview.

Colclough, Glenna. (1988). Uneven development and racial composition in the deep South. *Rural Sociology, 53*(1), 73-86.

——. (1989). Industrialization, labor markets and income inequality among Georgia counties: 1970-1980. In William W. Falk & Thomas A. Lyson (Eds.), *Research in rural sociology and development, Vol. 4* (pp. 207-222). Greenwich, CT: JAI Press.

Davidson, Osha Gray. (1989, July). Rural sweatshops: doing homework down on the farm. *Nation, 17,* 87-90.

Deavers, Kenneth. (1989). Rural America: Lagging growth and high poverty. . . Do we care?" *Choices, 2,* 4-7.

Dill, Bonnie, Timberlake, T. M., & Williams, Bruce. (1988). *Racism and politics in depressed, rural Southern communities.* Presented at Aspen Institute Rural Poverty Conference, Wye, MD.

Duncan, Cynthia M. (Ed.). (1991). *Rural poverty in America.* Westport, CT: Greenwood.

Duncan, Cynthia M., & Tickamyer, Ann R. (1988). Poverty research and policy for rural America. *American Sociologist, 19*(3), 243-59.

——. (1989). The rural poor: What we need to know. *Northwest Report, 7*(March). St. Paul, MN: Northwest Area Foundation.

Farkas, George, & England, Paula. (Eds.). (1988). *Industries, firms, and jobs: Sociological and economic approaches.* New York: Plenum.

Farley, Reynolds, & Allen, Walter R. (1987). *The color line and the quality of life in America.* New York: Russell Sage Foundation.

Fitchen, Janet. (1981). *Poverty in rural America: A case study.* Boulder, CO: Westview.

Gaventa, John. (1980). *Power and powerlessness: Quiescence and rebellion in an Appalachian valley.* Urbana: University of Illinois Press.

Ghelfi, Linda. (1986). *Poverty among Black families in the nonmetro South.* (Rural Development Research Report No. 62.) Washington, DC: U.S. Department of Agriculture, Economic Research Service.

Glasgow, Nina. (1988). *The nonmetro elderly: Economic and demographic status.* (Rural Development Research Report No. 70.) Washington, DC: U.S. Department of Agriculture, Economic Research Service.

Gorham, Lucy. (1990). *Working below the poverty line: The growing problem of low earnings in rural and urban areas and regions across the United States.* Washington, DC: Aspen Institute.

Gringeri, Christina. (1990). The nuts and bolts of subsidized development: industrial homeworking in the heartland. In Emery Castle & Barbara Baldwin (Eds.), *National Rural Studies Committee: A proceedings of Cedar Falls, Iowa, meeting May 17-18, 1990* (pp. 81-88). Corvallis, OR: Western Rural Development Center.

Harrison, Bennett, & Bluestone, Barry. (1988). *The great U-turn: Corporate restructuring and the polarizing of America.* New York: Basic Books.

Hauser, Robert M., & Featherman, David L. (1977). *The process of stratification.* New York: Academic Press.

Hoppe, Robert A. (1989, December). *Poverty in rural America: The statistical evidence.* Presented at the Professional Agricultural Workers Conference, Tuskegee University, Alabama.

Kalleberg, Arne L., & Berg, Ivar. (1988). Work structures and markets: An analytic framework. In G. Farkas & P. England (Eds.), *Industries, firms, and jobs: Sociological and economic approaches* (pp. 3-17). New York: Plenum Press.

Killian, Molly Sizer, & Hady, Thomas F. (1988). The economic performance of rural labor markets. In David Brown, Norman Reid, Herman Bluestone, David McGranahan, & Sara M. Mazie (Eds.), *Rural economic development in the 1980s: Prospects for the future. rural development* (pp. 181-200). (Research Report No. 69.) Washington, DC: U.S. Department of Agriculture, Economic Research Service.

Kurz, Karin, & Mueller, Walter. (1987). Class mobility in the industrial world. *Annual Review of Sociology, 13*(4), 17-42.

Levitan, Sar, & Shapiro, Isaac. (1987). *Working but poor: America's contradiction.* Baltimore, MD: Johns Hopkins University Press.

Lichter, Dan. (1989). Race, employment hardship, and inequality in the American nonmetropolitan South. *American Sociological Review, 54*(3), 436-46.

Lichter, Dan, & Constanzo, J. A. (1986). Nonmetropolitan underemployment and labor-force composition. *Rural Sociology, 52*(3):329-44.

Lyson, Thomas A. (1989). *Two sides to the Sunbelt: The growing divergence between the rural and urban South.* New York: Praeger.

Morrissey, Elizabeth S. (1990). Poverty among rural workers. *Rural Development Perspectives* (June-September), 37-42.

O'Hare, William. (1988). *The rise of poverty in rural America.* Washington, DC: Population Reference Bureau.

O'Hare, William P., & Pauti, Anne. (1990). Declining wages of young workers in rural America. Washington, DC: Population Reference Bureau.

Oliveria, V. J. (1986). *Distribution of rural employment growth by race: A case study.* (Rural Development Research Report No. 54.) Washington, DC: U.S. Department of Agriculture, Economic Research Service.

Osterman, Paul. (1988). *Employment futures: Reorganization, dislocation, and public policy.* New York: Oxford University Press.

Palerm, J. V. (1988). *The new poor in rural america: Chicano–Mexican communities and agribusiness in rural California.* Presented at the Aspen Institute Rural Poverty Meeting, Wye, MD.

Pollard, Devin, & O'Hare, William P. (1990). *Beyond high school: The experience of rural and urban youth in the 1980s.* Washington, DC: Population Reference Bureau.

Porter, Kathryn H. (1989). *Poverty in rural America: A national overview.* Washington, DC: Center on Budget and Policy Priorities.

Portes, Alejandro, Castells, Manuel, & Benton, Lauren. (Eds.). (1989). *The informal economy.* Baltimore, MD: Johns Hopkins University Press.

Sandefur, Gary D., & Tienda, Marta. (Eds.). (1988). *Divided opportunities: Minorities, poverty, and social policy.* New York: Plenum.

Shapiro, Isaac. (1989). *Laboring for less: Working but poor in rural America.* Washington, DC: Center on Budget and Policy Priorities.

Shotland, Jeffrey, Loonin, Deanne, & Haas, Ellen. (1988a). *Patterns of risk: The nutrition status of the rural poor.* Washington, DC: Public Voice for Food and Health Policy.

–––––. (1988b). *Off to a poor start: Infant health in rural America.* Washington, DC: Public Voice for Food and Health Policy.

Snipp, C. Matthew. (1986). The changing political and economic status of the American Indians: from captive nations to internal colonies. *American Journal of Economics and Sociology, 45*(2), 457-74.

–––––. (1990). *American Indians: The first of the land.* New York: Russell Sage Foundation.

Snipp, C. Matthew, & Summers, Gene F. (1991). American Indians and economic poverty. In Cynthia M. Duncan (Ed.), *Rural poverty in America.* Westport, CT: Greenwood.

Summers, Gene F., Horton, Francine, & Gringeri, Christina. (1990). Rural labour market changes in the United States. In Terry Marsden, Philip Lowe, & Sarah Whatmore (Eds.), *Rural restructuring: Global processes and their responses* (pp. 129-164) London: Fulton.

Thurow, Lester C. (1987). A surge in inequality. *Scientific American, 256*(5), 30.

Tickamyer, Ann R., & Duncan, Cynthia M. (1990). Poverty and opportunity structure in rural America. *Annual Review of Sociology, 16,* 67-86.

Tomaskovic-Devey, Don. (1987). Labor markets, industrial structure, and poverty: A theoretical discussion and empirical example. *Rural Sociology, 52*(1), 56-74.

Whitener, Leslie A. (1985). Migrant farmworkers: differences in attachment to farmwork. *Rural Sociology, 50*(2), 163-80.

Wilson, William J., & Aponte, R. (1985). Urban poverty. *Annual Review of Sociology, 11,* 231-58.

# 13

# African-American Appalachians: Barriers to Equality

by Wilburn Hayden, Jr.

**F**our conditions or barriers confront all minorities and act to reduce the quality of their lives. These are poverty, low social status, discrimination, and inequality. These conditions are also the primary elements that define any group as a minority. This definition is fluid, not static, and it can be applied in both contemporary and historical contexts.

A historical example is the millions of European immigrants who settled in northeastern U.S. cities between 1880 and 1910. They experienced overcrowded conditions, poor housing and sanitation, and low wages—poverty. The new arrivals were held to low-level jobs and designated residential areas—discrimination. They were not allowed equal citizenship (because of their legal status as nonvoting aliens) and were denied membership in social gatherings of the day—inequality and low social status. As these immigrants, mostly through their children, moved out of poverty, discrimination became less of an issue. By the 1920s, their third-generation descendants, born into full citizenship and a redefined social order, were no longer minorities.

Unlike European immigrants, minorities of color and women have historically remained victims of the four conditions, which act as permanent barriers that only a few individuals can overcome. Acknowledgment of these conditions makes it easy to understand why assimilation is an unlikely goal for many minorities. The goal should be instead to create a diverse society that recognizes each group as a distinct part of the common whole of society.

There are two possible forms of diversity. One form will not end poverty, low status, discrimination, or inequality. Traces of this form are evident in a segment of black society today. Many African Americans in their mid-20s to late 40s have risen above poverty and, to a great extent, above discrimination, by attending and graduating from colleges and universities (a large majority from predominately white institutions). They also work in fields and institutions that were not open to their parents in the larger white society, and they live in residential areas that would have been defined as white-only 30 years ago. Yet inequality and low social status still plague their group, from exclusion from social groups (e.g., the country club) and other private associations (especially the places of worship) to a lack of social interaction outside of the job. Hence, this group of young African Americans is not seen as equal and is forming a separate social order within a diversity framework—a separate social order that appears to be much like the former institution of segregation. The major difference, perhaps, is that before the 1960s segregation was a result of racist policies. In the 1990s, it is the result of many blacks giving up on the larger white society ever accepting blacks as equals. What whites have yet to understand, and what blacks and other minorities have always known, is that the majority of whites are heavily invested in locking minorities into poverty, low status, discrimination, and inequality.

The other form of diversity is manifested by the acceptance of differences among groups. Although differences may be visible or acknowledged by all, minority groups are viewed as important members of the society based on their ability to participate and contribute. Thus this form of diversity fosters an open society, with minorities viewed as equals, held free from discrimination, and able to improve their economic status.

## Black Invisibility

It is a common belief that blacks living in the Appalachian region are so few that there is little need to identify them; to account for their heritage and contributions; to provide services for them; or to include them in decision-making processes, cultural programs, or the economic well-being of the region. One reason blacks are ignored is that they tend to live in the small towns and cities rather than in the rural areas of Appalachia. However, few attempts have been made to delineate the location of blacks, to establish demographic patterns and trends, or to recognize that there are blacks living and working in the region. In fact, so little attention has been given that some authors view blacks as being invisible within the region.

Black invisibility as an institution in Appalachia will be defined as the view that Appalachia is predominantly a white region with concomitant formal and informal collections of customs, practices, beliefs, and attitudes that have led and will lead to ignoring the plight, contributions, and experiences of blacks, and to unequal social and economic conditions for blacks as a group. The linkage of two constructs—view and group—is important to understanding the definition. *View* is the holding to and acting on an unsubstantiated judgment or opinion. The importance of the construct *group* may be understood by looking at a phenomenon: When a majority member develops a close friendship with a minority individual, the majority member may see the minority individual as separate from the minority group. As one moves throughout the Appalachian region it is clear that individual blacks appear to escape unequal treatment by whites because they are treated as separate from blacks *as a group*. Both blacks and whites have learned to accept the institution of black invisibility that fosters the appearance of a high level of tolerance for blacks as individuals. The tolerance level quickly shifts to unequal treatment, however, when the institution is challenged.

For example (this example is to illustrate a point, not to negate the many exceptions), even today there are hollows, communities, or counties in Appalachia that demonstrate and maintain that blacks are not welcome. The white residents of these hollows, communities, or counties may work daily alongside a black individual and develop a positive relationship. The nonwork association is maintained in a neutral setting or in the black community; seldom is social contact allowed within the white residents' setting. If the black raises the issue, the friendship begins to shift. The white resident now sees the black individual as a member of a group—a visible group—desiring to be an equal.

The invisible institution of blacks is seen by some as positive. This view holds that invisibility is important to the lack of racial tension and to the perception of greater freedom in the region for blacks. By being invisible, blacks are not singled out as a significant threat to the order of the white domain, and are thus able to co-exist. But this institution causes many blacks to suffer discrimination as individuals. Invisibility means that blacks can be ignored by the institutions of the region (particularly employment). The invisibility of blacks may well be singled out as the major cause for poorer housing, a higher proportion of poverty and unemployment, less ownership of large land parcels, a smaller voice in the political and governmental decisions or services, and a lesser social status for black than for white Appalachians.

## Census Data

An examination of the 1980 census data reveal the extent to which black invisibility has been institutionalized in the region. The census identifies 1,575,368 blacks living in 397 counties in the region; the total population for the region was 20,359,082. Thus, blacks comprised 7.8% of the region's population. Table 1 is a distribution by race for the 13 states that make up the region. American Indians represented 0.1% of the region (numbering 29,373). "Others"—primarily individuals who failed to be identified by race—represented 0.5% (numbering 110,146).

Alabama had the largest number of blacks at 486,438 and third largest percentage at 19.9%. The largest percentage of blacks was 27.8% in Mississippi, which had the fourth largest black population at 133,569. The state with the smallest percentage was New York at 1.5% (15,592) and the state with the smallest number of blacks was Maryland at 6,419. Table 2 shows rankings for each state by the number and percentage of blacks in the population.

For most scholars and people living in the region, these statistics are no surprise, yet blacks remain an invisible institution. Why? A closer took at the census data sheds some light on the question.

The mean number of blacks per county was computed at 3,968. County maps for each state were used to plot counties with near or more than 3,968 blacks. Twenty concentrations, consisting of 62 of the 397 counties, were plotted. Kentucky and Virginia were the only states in which all regional counties had fewer than 4,000 blacks. Table 3 shows the number of concentrations and number of counties for each of the 13 states. Table 4 shows the 62 counties that make up the 20 concentrations.

As shown in Table 5, the concentrations were correlated with three settings and two combinations of the three settings: (1) a coal or industrial site,

*Table 1:* **State Population Distribution in the Appalachian Region as Defined by 1980 Census Data**

| States and Percentages | Total | Whites | Blacks | American Indians | Others |
|---|---|---|---|---|---|
| Alabama | 2,448,121 | 1,926,125 | 486,438 | 2,721 | 32,837 |
| Percentage | 100.0 | 78.7 | 19.9 | 0.1 | 1.3 |
| Georgia | 1,104,081 | 1,027,236 | 71,048 | 2,387 | 3,410 |
| Percentage | 100.0 | 93.0 | 6.5 | 0.2 | 0.3 |
| Kentucky | 1,078,076 | 1,056,048 | 18,394 | 809 | 2,852 |
| Percentage | 100.0 | 98.0 | 1.7 | 0.1 | 0.3 |
| Maryland | 220,132 | 212,358 | 6,419 | 171 | 1,184 |
| Percentage | 100.0 | 96.5 | 2.9 | 0.1 | 0.5 |
| Mississippi | 481,717 | 346,080 | 133,569 | 654 | 1,414 |
| Percentage | 100.0 | 71.8 | 27.8 | 0.1 | 0.3 |
| New York | 1,082,794 | 1,053,887 | 15,592 | 3,950 | 9,365 |
| Percentage | 100.0 | 97.3 | 1.5 | 0.3 | 0.9 |
| North Carolina | 1,217,514 | 1,094,682 | 112,137 | 7,041 | 3,654 |
| Percentage | 100.0 | 89.9 | 9.2 | 0.6 | 0.3 |
| Ohio | 1,262,503 | 1,229,540 | 26,715 | 1,944 | 4,034 |
| Percentage | 100.0 | 97.4 | 2.1 | 0.2 | 0.3 |
| Pennsylvania | 6,103,923 | 5,741,637 | 332,121 | 4,608 | 25,557 |
| Percentage | 100.0 | 94.1 | 5.4 | 0.1 | 0.4 |
| South Carolina | 835,095 | 654,155 | 176,481 | 675 | 3,784 |
| Percentage | 100.0 | 78.3 | 21.2 | 0.1 | 0.2 |
| Tennessee | 2,090,517 | 1,955,618 | 120,775 | 2,506 | 11,618 |
| Percentage | 100.0 | 93.5 | 5.9 | 0.1 | 0.5 |
| Virginia | 505,487 | 493,412 | 10,618 | 352 | 1,098 |
| Percentage | 100.0 | 97.6 | 2.1 | 0.1 | 0.2 |
| West Virginia | 1,929,122 | 1,853,437 | 65,061 | 1,555 | 9,069 |
| Percentage | 100.0 | 96.0 | 3.4 | 0.1 | 0.5 |
| **Total** | **20,359,082** | **18,644,215** | **1,575,368** | **29,373** | **110,146** |
| **Percentage** | **100.0** | **91.6** | **7.8** | **0.1** | **0.5** |

(2) a major university or military base, (3) an urban center, (4) a combination of 1 and 3, and (5) a combination of 2 and 3. Five of the 20 concentrations were found in the first two settings; 12 concentrations were found in urban centers; and 3 concentrations were found in urban centers that were coal/industrial sites or university/military settings. Thus, 75% of the concentrations were located in urban centers.

The total number of blacks in these concentrations was 1,157,986, which represents 73.5% of the total black population. In contrast, only 36.6% of all whites were found in the counties that formed the 20 concentrations. According to an Appalachian Regional Commission (ARC) report, 74% of the

*Table 2:* **Ranking for Each State by Number and Percentage of Blacks**

| States | Number | Percentage |
| --- | --- | --- |
| Alabama | 1 | 3 |
| Georgia | 7 | 5 |
| Kentucky | 10 | 12 |
| Maryland | 13 | 9 |
| Mississippi | 4 | 1 |
| New York | 11 | 13 |
| North Carolina | 6 | 4 |
| Ohio | 9 | 10 |
| Pennsylvania | 2 | 7 |
| South Carolina | 3 | 2 |
| Tennessee | 5 | 6 |
| Virginia | 12 | 10 |
| West Virginia | 8 | 8 |

*Table 3:* **Number of Concentrations and Counties for Each State**

| States | Number of Concentrations | Number of Counties |
| --- | --- | --- |
| Alabama | 2 | 19 |
| Georgia | 1 | 6 |
| Kentucky | 0 | 0 |
| Maryland | 1 | 1 |
| Mississippi | 2 | 9 |
| New York | 1 | 1 |
| North Carolina | 3 | 4 |
| Ohio | 1 | 1 |
| Pennsylvania | 3 | 7 |
| South Carolina | 1 | 6 |
| Tennessee | 2 | 2 |
| Virginia | 0 | 0 |
| West Virginia | 3 | 6 |
| **Total** | **20** | **62** |

total 1980 U.S. population lived in urban environments while only 48% of the total Appalachian population lived in urban environments. The report concluded: "Appalachia remains essentially a region of small towns and rural areas" (ARC Staff, 1984, p. 5). Clearly, though this conclusion was accurate for white Appalachians, it was not for black Appalachians. The ARC report reinforced the institution of black invisibility. Most black Appalachians lived in urban environments in 1980; in fact, only 26.5% of black Appalachians lived in non-urban settings.

*Table 4:* **Counties for the 20 Concentrations, by State**

| **Alabama** | **Mississippi** | **Pennsylvania** |
|---|---|---|
| Concentration: 1 | Concentration: 5 | Concentration: 12 |
| Lauderdale | Marshall | Erie |
| Lawrence | | |
| Limestone | Concentration: 6 | Concentration: 13 |
| Madison | Chickasaw | Mercer |
| Morgan | Clay | |
| | Kemper | Concentration: 14 |
| Concentration: 2 | Lee | Allegheny |
| Pickens | Lowndes | Beaver |
| Tuscaloosa | Noxubee | Fayette |
| Walker | Oktibbeha | Washington |
| Jefferson | | Westmoreland |
| St. Clair | **New York** | |
| Etowah | Concentration: 7 | **South Carolina** |
| Calhoun | Chemung | Concentration: 15 |
| Talladega | | Anderson |
| Shelby | **North Carolina** | Cherokee |
| Randolph | Concentration: 8 | Greenville |
| Tallapoosa | Buncombe | Oconee |
| Chambers | | Pickens |
| Coosa | Concentration: 9 | Spartanburg |
| Elmore | Forsyth | |
| | | **Tennessee** |
| **Georgia** | Concentration: 10 | Concentration: 16 |
| Concentration: 3 | Rutherford | Knox |
| Floyd | Burke | |
| Bartow | | Concentration: 17 |
| Polk | **Ohio** | Hamilton |
| Carroll | Concentration: 11 | |
| Gwinnett | Jefferson | **West Virginia** |
| Hall | | Concentration: 18 |
| | | Fayette |
| **Maryland** | | McDowell |
| Concentration: 4 | | Mercer |
| Washington | | Raleigh |
| | | |
| | | Concentration: 19 |
| | | Cabell |
| | | |
| | | Concentration: 20 |
| | | Kanawha |

Realizing that most blacks in the region are found in the same environments as most blacks in the nation, it is not difficult to see why the institution of black invisibility exists. The social and economic conditions for blacks in the region are very different from whites. To acknowledge and respond to the difference requires the visibility of blacks. Recognizing the difference, blacks as a group may be able to do in the region what has not occurred in the rest of the nation—attain the second type of diversity. This means shifting some of the resources and services to the urban struggle, to the social and economic conditions of the visible black Appalachians.

Urban dwellers in Appalachia are not exclusively black; with 48% of the region's population living in urban environments in 1980, it is clear that many Appalachians of both races are located in cities and towns. Thus, resources are needed by white as well as black urban Appalachians.

### Land and Inequality

Land is at the core of white Appalachians' investment in maintaining black minority status. Land ownership is the underlying factor for white domination and black inequality within Appalachia. One only has to look at cases in which family members are disputing over the inheritance property left by the parent or grandparent. The property may have 32 heirs, most of them renting their homes or living at a poverty level. Yet they refuse to agree to a sale. They are not concerned about money or longago family disagreements; they are concerned about land ownership. As long as they can lay claim to a piece of land, they will be viewed as contributing

*Table 5:* **Number of Concentrations for Each State, by the Five Factors**

| State | Coal or Industrial Site | University or Military Base | Urban Center | 1/3 | 2/3 | Total |
|-------|------|------|------|------|------|------|
| | 1 | 2 | 3 | 4 | 5 | Total |
| Alabama | 1 | | | | 1 | 2 |
| Georgia | | | 1 | | | 1 |
| Kentucky (none) | | | | | | 0 |
| Maryland | 1 | | | | | 1 |
| Mississippi | | 1 | 1 | | | 2 |
| New York | | | 1 | | | 1 |
| North Carolina | | 1 | 2 | | | 3 |
| Ohio | | | 1 | | | 1 |
| Pennsylvania | | | 2 | | 1 | 3 |
| South Carolina | | 1 | | 1 | | 2 |
| Tennessee | | | 2 | | | 2 |
| Virginia (none) | | | | | | 0 |
| West Virginia | | | 2 | | | 2 |
| **Total** | **2** | **3** | **12** | **1** | **2** | **20** |

members of the region. "Land has attributes of wealth, status in the community, equality, power, and piety" (McGee & Browne, 1973, p. ii). The Appalachian culture is very much centered around ownership of land. In his 1979 book preface, Fisher discussed the importance of land to the sanity and survival of the Appalachian people. He traced the Appalachian closeness and attachment to the land as a dominant theme in the literature of the region. Fisher concludes: Who owns the land in rural areas such as Appalachia clearly affects the options available for economic development and has a profound impact on the nature of work, culture and community life" (Fisher, 1973, Preface).

Pinkney noted that even when land was sold to blacks, the white landlord often profited on two counts. First at the time of purchase, and second when the land was taken back by illegal means (Pinkney, 1987, p. 56). There is mounting evidence that blacks were frequently losing land without fair compensation due to title disputes, heir property sales, or profiteering on the part of land speculators who learned of changes in local land values well before the black landowners. As a result land tended to remain in black hands only so long as it was economically marginal; when it became valuable, it was acquired, often unfairly, by whites (Salamon, 1976, p. ii). McGee and Brown (1973, p. 101) cite another reason for declining land ownership among black Appalachians: legal trickery perpetrated by southern white lawyers, land speculators, and county officials. This group often took advantage of unsophisticated rural blacks who did not fully understand the importance of land. Thus even when blacks managed to buy land, they often found it difficult to hang on to it.

This loss of land is more than an economic issue—it is also linked to keeping African-American Appalachians in a minority status. In Appalachia, land ownership contributes to social status. In fact, individuals without it, whether white or black, will find themselves on the lower end of the social scale. Blacks, unlike poor whites, had to fight hard to hold on to their land, and their place in the community.

Another barrier to black land ownership in the region is that, even in the 1990s, most of the rural residential areas are off-limits to blacks who want to own or rent land. Through the use of intimidation, threats, sometimes physical attacks, and white-only codes, African Americans are limited in residential choice. In a *Sylva Herald* editorial ("Letter to the Editor," 1990) a woman (married to an African American) complained that she, her husband, and children had been forced to move five times as a result of racists acts. Although no legal discriminatory practices exist in Appalachia, most blacks and whites know where blacks are accepted or excluded.

Blacks were once victimized by city and county ordinances that legalized white-only residential areas. Although these were finally struck down by the U. S. Supreme Court in 1913 (Johnson, 1922, pp. 35–36), what remained for a time were legalized realtor practices of maintaining racially segregated communities. An official 1939 National Association of Real

Estate Board (NAREB) publication defined an "objectionable" purchaser in a "respectable" neighborhood:

> He might be a bootlegger who could cause considerable annoyance to his neighbors, a 'madam' who had a number of call girls on her string, a gangster who wanted a screen for his activities by living in a better neighborhood, or a colored man of means who was giving his children a college education and thought they were entitled to live among whites. (Atkinson and Frailey, pp. 16–17)

This definition was supported in the NAREB *Code of Ethics.* The selling to a non-white of a home in a white neighborhood was considered unethical practice. One could be expelled from the local real estate board. The code was clear:

> A realtor should never be instrumental in introducing into a neighborhood a character of property or occupancy, members of any race or nationality, or any individuals whose presence will clearly be detrimental to property values in that neighborhood. *(Code of Ethics,* 1946, Article 34)

When the code was finally changed, decades of practice continued to keep many areas racially segregated. The Federal Homeowners Administration also aided in the acceptance and perpetuation of race restrictive covenants and residential segregation prior to World War II (Weaver, 1967, pp. 217–218).

Maintaining low or no black ownership of Appalachian land was an objective ingrained in the minds of many of the area's whites. The prevailing view was that land in the mountains was for whites only. A survey of white public officials in western North Carolina conducted by Oxley in the 1920s found that some officials felt that blacks should not be allowed to own land (Bell, 1990, p 4). The survey also found local laws in Jefferson and Morganton that prohibited ownership of land within the town's limits and reported that whites in Graham and Mitchell counties were hostile toward blacks, encouraging visiting blacks to depart before sundown (Bell, 1990, p. 5).

Discouraging or excluding blacks from land ownership is directly related to inequality. Equality is the acceptance of individuals as equals into the established social order. In Appalachia, land is a major factor for determining social status. As a group, African Americans in the mountains are held at a lower status resulting from their lack of land or limited ownership. Thus, social inequality, as linked to land, remains a reality. As Pinkney (1987) concludes: "Unlike the situation among white Americans, blacks are segregated residentially for racial reasons alone. . . poor blacks and rich blacks alike are, usually, confined to the same residential areas" (p. 57).

## Social Contact and Inequality

Still another aspect of the inequality issue is found in the social contact between blacks and whites. Although many have cited the lack of a civil rights movement surfacing in Appalachia in the 1960s and the few incidents arising from public school desegregation as evidence of the generally low level of racial tension in the region, these examples are due more to the limited social contact between the races than to racial harmony. Black–white interactions can best be described as economically rather than socially or politically based.

Examples of economically based contact would be a black housekeeper or cook in contact with a white employer—an interaction that would put blacks on an unequal footing with whites. Social contacts do exist, of course, but they often have limited acceptance beyond the individuals involved and do not carry into the larger question of equality. Pinkney (1987) asserts:

> Social relations between black and white communities on a basis of equality have never existed. Law and custom have decreed that a rigid caste line separates the two communities socially and that no association between blacks and whites, as equals, take place. In matters of economics the black community, with few exceptions, has been totally dependent on the white community for survival. (pp. 53-56)

Inequality may also be seen as the result of discrimination within the social arena. Johnson (1943) defined it as "the unequal treatment of equals either by bestowal of favors or the imposition of burdens" (p. xvii). Johnson views inequality as stemming from arbitrariness, unfairness, and injustice.

> It involves the inclusion or exclusion of groups or individuals by an infinite number of arbitrary lines of demarcation drawn on the basis of the most varied marks of similarity or dissimilarity. Differential treatment of individuals based upon accepted differences in rank or status is the result of a similar process. . . . Distinctions in law or custom, based solely upon race or other disadvantage are discriminatory and, to be understood, must be referred to the underlying schemes of social values prompting the distinctions. (pp. xvii–xviii)

When it comes to equality in Appalachia, James and Williams (1989) conclude that racism and the continuing discriminatory treatment of blacks precludes equality. Despite genuine progress, there remain significant forms of resistance to a variety of proposals for reducing inequities. At the heart of the resistance are a number of traditional values, which although they are not strictly race-related, result in blacks receiving unequal treatment.

## Racial Attitude and Inequality

Perhaps the final point to be made concerning inequality in Appalachia concerns what appears to be a hardening of the racial attitudes of whites toward blacks. Equality in other parts of the nation—as it is demonstrated in inter-racial gatherings and opportunities to participate freely—does not exist in Appalachia. Few white social gatherings include blacks. This fact, especially when combined with the isolation or segregation (even voluntary) of blacks, indicates that negative racial attitudes have found fertile soil. In a 1986 report on testimonies received throughout the region, CORA cited a rise in racial violence, especially in areas where blacks compete with low-income whites for jobs and economic survival (p. 10). CORA noted an increase in the activities of the Klan, the White Patriot Party, the white supremacy movement, and other hate groups in the region. Such actions have been documented in increasing numbers of incidents of harassment and discrimination against blacks.

As seen here, Appalachian blacks have not been treated with equality, resulting in an increasing, not decreasing, distance between the races. The net result is a continuation of inequality in the mountains.

## Employment and Discrimination

Many believe that discrimination resulting from racism in the South is declining in the 1990s. Few overt acts are being recorded or reported; conflicts between the races seem minimal. Within most areas, blacks exercise an increasing amount of opportunity and access to the larger society. Whereas there still remain clear divisions in interpersonal and social interactions, blacks are not generally being subjugated to or intimidated by racist acts or attacks. Even the Klan has sugar-coated its racist nature, turning instead to issues such as abortion and prayer in schools.

Perhaps the major struggle for African Americans in the 1990s is racism that surfaces as institutional discrimination. Institutional discrimination may be defined as intentional or unintentional acts resulting from prejudicial or racist views held by majority members of a societal unit or organization toward a minority group or individual. One result of institutional discrimination is the income gap between blacks and whites. The causes of racial wage differentials are complex, but evidence suggests that lower black incomes result not so much from joblessness or lower wages as from a number of other variables that maintain black productivity at a low level. These variables can best be described as institution discrimination.

### Income and Status

In the south, employment is the simplest overall measure of status differences between the races. Employment translates into income. The more income one has, the more one can participate in the benefits found within the social structure. Thus, employment is linked to one's "life chances."

Life chances of both races in the south, as reflected in income, fall short of the rest of the nation. Smith and Welch (1986) calculated the wage differences for white and black adult males in terms of percent of wages in the North (see Table 6) and the wages of both southern white and southern black males in terms of percent of wages received by whites (see Table 7). Although white and black wages in the Nouth made gains on those of their counterparts in the North from 1940 to 1980, both groups were shown to have fewer life chances, as expressed in terms of income, than their northern counterparts. For southern blacks, life chances appear very restricted. Their gain in wages over the 40 years is impressive, yet they still lag significantly behind southern whites. In theory, the next generation will benefit from their parents' income gains, but their parents' achievements have resulted from struggle against discrimination rather than the exercise of their life chances.

Tables 6 and 7 reveal the large gains blacks made during the 1980s. The preceding decades showed no clear trend. The movement of industries to the Sunbelt and the implementation and enforcement of affirmative action programs began to pay off for blacks during the 1970s. Table 8 shows Appalachian per capita income in relation to U.S. per capita income. For the entire region, per capita ranged between 80.3% (1969) and 84.9% (1979) of that for the entire U.S. And projecting from the wage differentials of blacks in the South, blacks in Appalachia are in relatively worse shape than their white counterparts.

In short, the level of income is directly related to status. Blacks in the South have fewer life chances because they have lower incomes. The

*Table 6:* **Wage Differential for Southern White and Black Males 1940–80, Expressed in Percentage of Northern Wages**

| Year | Black/White | White | Black | Differences between Black/White |
|------|-------------|-------|-------|--------------------------------|
| 1940 | 77.7 | 91.2 | 70.9 | 20.3 |
| 1950 | 78.8 | 87.7 | 69.1 | 18.6 |
| 1960 | 76.4 | 88.8 | 67.8 | 21.0 |
| 1970 | 79.5 | 91.2 | 72.5 | 18.7 |
| 1980 | 90.3 | 93.5 | 84.6 | 8.9 |
| Mean | | 90.5 | 73.0 | 17.5 |

*Note:* Adapted from Smith and Welch (1986), p. 48.

*Table 7:* **Wage Difference between Southern White/Black Males 1940–80, Expressed in Percentage of White Wages**

| Year | % of White Wages |
|------|------------------|
| 1940 | 80.2 |
| 1950 | 81.3 |
| 1960 | 79.1 |
| 1970 | 81.2 |
| 1980 | 90.9 |

*Note:* From Smith and Welch (1986), p. 49.

thesis of the remaining chapter is that this difference in income has not occurred by chance, but has resulted from racism in the South, and in Appalachia specifically. Institutional discrimination has systematically maintained blacks in relative poverty with fewer life chances. The lack of employment opportunities affect the psychological and cultural determinants of black Appalachians' ability or willingness to participate in the social structure. Simply stated, a message is given to the black community: "Do Not Bother to Apply for White-Only jobs." Because the only jobs available to black Appalachians are black jobs, each black person seeking employment has two choices: yield to inferior status or resist. Sometimes resisting may require seeking greener pastures, but more often it results in unemployment or dependence on society through social programs or the criminal justice system. This drama is continuously being played out within black families, and it is at the core of family problems, stress, and break up.

As well as acting as a disincentive for black Appalachians, job discrimination reinforces a negative stereotype in the larger Appalachian community. These stereotypes take the form of: "We cannot find any good black workers." "They do not want to work." "They cannot handle the job." Franklin and Resnick (1973) state:

> Whites' image of the black population is derived from the black population's over-representation in the less skilled, lower-ranked occupations, which has been a result of systemic discrimination by all segments of the white population. (p. 55)

**Table 8: Per Capita Income, Appalachia and United States, 1969–79**

| | Per Capita Income in Dollars | | Percentage of U. S. Income | |
|---|---|---|---|---|
| | 1969 | 1979 | 1969 | 1979 |
| Appalachian Alabama | $2,430 | $6,147 | 77.9% | 83.9% |
| Appalachian Georgia | 2,419 | 6,301 | 77.6 | 86.0 |
| Appalachian Kentucky | 1,732 | 4,856 | 55.5 | 66.2 |
| Appalachian Maryland | 2,599 | 6,327 | 83.3 | 86.3 |
| Appalachian Mississippi | 1,861 | 4,956 | 59.7 | 67.6 |
| Appalachian New York | 2,845 | 6,135 | 91.2 | 83.7 |
| Appalachian North Carolina | 2,437 | 6,095 | 78.1 | 83.2 |
| Appalachian Ohio | 2,443 | 6,073 | 78.3 | 82.9 |
| Appalachian Pennsylvania | 2,790 | 6,770 | 89.5 | 92.4 |
| Appalachian South Carolina | 2,571 | 6,473 | 82.4 | 88.3 |
| Appalachian Tennessee | 2,340 | 5,983 | 75.0 | 81.6 |
| Appalachian Virginia | 2,050 | 5,614 | 65.7 | 76.6 |
| West Virginia (whole state) | 2,333 | 6,179 | 74.8 | 84.3 |
| Appalachian Region | 2,505 | 6,221 | 80.3 | 84.9 |
| United States | 3,119 | 7,330 | 100.0 | 100.0 |

*Note:* From Appalachia (1982), p. 33.

## Forms of Institutional Discrimination

Wachtel's 1965 literature review identified three major methods of discrimination in employment. Each method had sub-categories. Institutional discrimination in Appalachia is linked to two of these methods:

1. Complete exclusion from employment regardless of qualification and previous experience.

   (a) Outright refusal to hire.

   (b) Recruiting workers through associations and agencies with membership limited to whites[1]

2. Partial restriction on employment opportunities.

   (a) Limitation of employment to menial and unskilled jobs or to those involving little public contact.

   (b) Demotion from mechanical to menial jobs. (Wachtel, 1965, pp. 11–12)

Wachtel's analysis suggests several reasons for unequal employment opportunities in Appalachia. It may be that Appalachian employers have always hired whites for some jobs and blacks for others. From the employer's viewpoint, this system appears to have worked; thus, they see no reason to change. Employers, as victims of a discriminatory environment, act as they are expected to act, that is, they only hire blacks for black positions. Employers may believe that discrimination will divert white hostility that might otherwise be directed at their company by other employees, by their customers or suppliers, or by the community at large. (This was evident in the coal strikes when blacks were brought in to replace white workers.) Last, employers may believe that blacks will be unable to do the job or will seek special privileges.

These reasons may seem valid, but in reality, not hiring blacks or hiring them only for certain positions is institutional racism. Rungeling's (1977) analysis of rural labor market behavior revealed indirect evidence of racial and sexual discrimination. He found "occupational segregation" directed toward blacks, female heads of household, and married females. Thus black families and female-headed families suffer lower earnings due to sexism and racism (Rungeling et al., 1977, pp. 38-39).

Boston (1988) discusses three related forms of labor market discrimination. In the first form, discrimination is evident when two individuals or

---

[1] For the region this is played out through the informal white network that keeps members informed about job possibilities. Unfortunately blacks are not members of the network. This is probably not from malice, but because there are very few biracial informal networks in the mountains.

groups who differ racially do identical jobs, but one group receives a smaller remuneration for its efforts than the other.

> The second type [of labor market discrimination] has to do with differential and unequal access to employment. In this case Group B possesses similar attributes to A but is more likely to be unemployed simply because of its race; other things are again held constant. Finally discrimination exists if the job offers made to A are superior to those of B, and in addition the former experiences greater on-the-job mobility because of race. (Boston, 1988, pp. 58–59)

The second and third forms, asserts Boston, "are the most prevalent and historically significant forms of discrimination against blacks" (Boston, 1988, p. 59). Federal laws seem to have made it difficult in the 1990s, at least at the time of hiring, to pay different wages. In Appalachia, labor market discrimination is evidenced by the lack of black employees in certain jobs and their over-representation in others. For example, the requirements for a cashier at a supermarket, fast food restaurant, or department store are usually a high school education and little or no past job experience. Since the 1970s, blacks and whites have attended the same Appalachian schools, but seldom are black students found in these positions. More often blacks can be found cleaning up spills in the supermarket, cooking or cleaning in the fast food restaurant, and stocking shelves in the department store.

The jobs with the lowest salaries and status, that are flat in terms of potential for promotion or advancement opportunities, are often filled by blacks. (For example, to what higher level can a housekeeper rise?) On the other hand, jobs filled by whites have levels, and thus a better chance for higher incomes. For example, a maintenance worker could become a supervisor.

Each area of the region has its own distribution of white jobs and black jobs. Appalachia, especially in the non-urban areas, is unique from the South because of its smaller black population. Institutional racism can be masked by hiring whites for positions that are traditionally earmarked as black jobs. This phenomenon occurs in areas where few blacks live.

In general, jobs paying hourly wages require minimum education. Using the U.S. Bureau of the Census "Current Population Survey" (CPS) microdata tapes for the month of January 1983, Boston illustrates the point. He found that hourly wages were lowest in the three southern regions (South Atlantic, East South Central, and West South Central) in which blacks were most heavily concentrated in low-income jobs. In three of the remaining six regions (East North Central, Mountain, and Pacific) the average hourly wages for blacks exceeded those of whites, even though the annual earnings of blacks did not exceed those of whites in any region (Boston, 1988, p. 70).

## A Case in Point

An examination of employment data supports the thesis that black income, as determined by bottom-level jobs, is a means for locking black Appalachians into a lower status within the larger social structure. The Office for Civil Rights Annual Report from 1977–88 on a large employer within the 397 counties that define Appalachia is illustrative. The employer is a major hotel and conference center. Overall, the hotels have two occupational groups: hourly wage earners (minimum education requirements, labor-intensive jobs) and professionals (higher educational requirements, more specialized functions). Only hourly wage positions are analyzed here.

Table 9 lists the 237 hourly wage positions at the hotel in 1987. Twenty of these positions (8.4%) are held by black workers. The lowest salary grade at the hotel is 50 and the highest is 71. The hiring rate for pay grade 50 was $10,880 in 1990; for the position of Cook I, pay grade 52, the hiring salary was $11,760; General Utility Worker, pay grade 53, paid $12,194; Clerk Typist II, pay grade 54, paid $12,674; Waste Water Plant Operator, pay grade 60, paid $16,114; Police Officer II, pay grade 64, paid $18,994; and Food Service Director I, pay grade 67, paid $21,566.

### Table 9: All Hourly Wage Positions, by Race/Sex in 1987

| Pay Grade | Position | White | Black | Native Amer. | Asian | Male | Female |
|---|---|---|---|---|---|---|---|
| | Duplicating Unit. | | | | | | |
| – | Supv. II | | 1 | | | | 1 |
| – | Truck Driver | 1 | | | | 1 | |
| – | Unk. Craftsman | 1 | | | | 1 | |
| – | UNKN | 4 | | | | 4 | |
| 50 | Food Service Asst. I | 37 | 6 | | 1 | 16 | 28 |
| 50 | Housekeeping Asst. | 31 | 8 | | | 21 | 18 |
| 50 | Sales Clerk I | 2 | | | | | 2 |
| 51 | Commercial Cashier I | 1 | | | | | 1 |
| 52 | Baker I | 1 | | | | | 1 |
| 52 | Cook I | 6 | 1 | 1 | | 4 | 4 |
| 52 | Food Service Asst. II | 6 | | | | 5 | 1 |
| 52 | Housework | 1 | | | | | 1 |
| 53 | Floor Maint. Asst. | 7 | | | | 7 | |
| 53 | General Utility Worker | 12 | 1 | | | 13 | |
| 54 | Clerk Typist II | | 1 | | | | 1 |
| 54 | Housekeeping Supv. I | 4 | | | | 3 | 1 |
| 55 | Baker II | | 1 | | | 1 | |
| 55 | Cook III | 2 | | | | 1 | 1 |
| 55 | Security Guard | 1 | | | | 1 | |
| 55 | Stock Clerk II | 3 | | | | 3 | |
| 56 | Grounds Worker | 6 | | | | 5 | 1 |
| 56 | Mail Clerk II | 1 | | | | 1 | |

| Pay Grade | Position | White | Black | Native Amer. | Asian | Male | Female |
|---|---|---|---|---|---|---|---|
| 57 | Clerk Typist III | 6 | | | | | 6 |
| 57 | Cook Supervisor I | 1 | | | | | 1 |
| 57 | Head Baker | 1 | | | | | 1 |
| 57 | Mach. Operator III | 1 | | | | 1 | |
| 58 | Housekeeping Supv. II | 2 | | | | 2 | |
| 58 | Labor Crew Leader | 2 | | | | 2 | |
| 58 | Maint. Mechanic I (none) | | | | | | |
| 59 | Boiler Operator II | 5 | | | | 5 | |
| 59 | Electrician I | 1 | | | | 1 | |
| 59 | Print. Pho. Typeset. | 1 | | | | 1 | |
| 59 | Records Clerk IV | 1 | | | | | 1 |
| 59 | Secretary IV | 2 | | | | | 2 |
| 60 | Maint. Mechanic II | 8 | | | | 8 | |
| 60 | W/W Wa PLTOP | 2 | 1 | | | 3 | |
| 61 | Painter | 4 | | | | 4 | |
| 61 | Sales Manager III | 1 | | | | | 1 |
| 61 | Warehouse Mgr. I | 1 | | | | 1 | |
| 62 | Food Service Supv. III | 3 | | | | 2 | 1 |
| 62 | Grounds Wk. Supv. I | 1 | | | | 1 | |
| 62 | Locksmith II | 1 | | | | 1 | |
| 62 | Maint. Mechanic III | 3 | | | | 3 | |
| 63 | Mechanic II | 2 | | | | 2 | |
| 63 | Boiler Operator I | 5 | | | | 5 | |
| 63 | Carpenter Supv. I | 1 | | | | 1 | |
| 63 | Const/Renov. Tech. II | 1 | | | | 1 | |
| 63 | Electrician II | 2 | | | | 2 | |
| 63 | Painter Supv. | 1 | | | | 1 | |
| 63 | Plumber II | 5 | | | | 5 | |
| 63 | Police Officer I | 7 | | | | 6 | 1 |
| 63 | Steam Plant Supv. I | 1 | | | | 1 | |
| 63 | Welder II | 1 | | | | 1 | |
| 64 | Police Officer II | | 1 | | | 1 | |
| 65 | HVAC Mech. | 3 | | | | 3 | |
| 65 | Mechanic Supv. I (none) | | | | | | |
| 66 | Electrician Supervisor I | | 1 | | | | 1 |
| 66 | Police Officer III | 3 | | | | 3 | |
| 66 | W/W Water Plnt. Chf. I | 1 | | | | 1 | |
| 67 | Food Svc. Dir. I | | 1 | | | | 1 |
| 67 | HVAC Tech. | 1 | | | | 1 | |
| 68 | Electrician Supv. II | 1 | | | | 1 | |
| 68 | Plant Maint. Supv. I | 1 | | | | 1 | |
| 68 | Police Chief | 1 | | | | 1 | |
| 71 | Plant Maint. Supv. II | 1 | | | | 1 | |
| | Total=237 positions | 214 | 20 | 2 | 1 | | |

Blacks were found in the lowest paid positions: food service assistant and housekeeping assistant. Fourteen of the 20 black employees (70%) were found in salary grade 50 jobs. Of the 214 positions held by whites, 70 (33%) were at pay grade 50. Only 3 (15%) of black positions were *above* pay grade 60, while whites held 52 (22%) jobs in the same category. Table 10 illustrates the positions blacks held in the hotel from 1977 to 1989. Black workers were employed primarily in the two lowest positions. These data illustrate institutional discrimination, wherein blacks are systematically held in certain positions. The old argument that few qualified blacks are in the area has no logical basis.

## Conclusion

So, where do we go from here? Certainly the starting point is to recognize the existence of the barriers confronting all minorities that act to reduce their quality of life. In terms of employment discrimination, employers should then examine the potential for currently employed blacks to be promoted to other areas in which blacks have never been employed; develop a mandatory sensitivity training program for all employees who make hiring decisions; include in the performance criteria for supervisors the hiring and retention of black workers; and create an outreach program for the white and black communities that seeks to clarify and redefine the employer's commitment to hiring blacks in an open market.

*Table 10:* **Position Categories for Blacks, 1977–89**

| | '89 | '88 | '87 | '86 | '85 | '84 | '83 | '82 | '81 | '80 | '79 | '78 | '77 |
|---|---|---|---|---|---|---|---|---|---|---|---|---|---|
| 00[1] Truck Driver | — | — | — | — | — | — | — | — | 1 | — | — | — | — |
| 50 Food Svc. Asst. I | 6 | 5 | 6 | 8 | 5 | 7 | 7 | 8 | 7 | 6 | 6 | 6 | 7 |
| 50 Hskpng Asst. | 23 | 13 | 8 | 9 | 9 | 9 | 9 | 8 | 11 | 17 | 26 | 25 | 24 |
| 52 Baker I | — | — | — | — | — | — | — | — | — | — | 1 | 1 | 1 |
| 52 Cook I | 1 | — | 1 | 1 | 3 | 1 | 1 | — | — | 2 | 4 | 3 | 3 |
| 53 Gen. Util. Wrkr | 1 | — | 1 | — | — | — | — | 1 | 1 | 1 | 1 | 1 | — |
| 54 Clerk Typist II | — | — | 1 | — | — | — | — | — | — | 1 | 1 | — | — |
| 54 Hskpng Spv. I | — | — | — | — | — | — | — | — | — | 2 | 2 | 2 | 2 |
| 55 Cook 11 | — | — | — | 1 | — | — | 2 | 2 | 3 | 4 | 3 | 4 | 4 |
| 57 Cook Spv. I | — | — | — | — | — | 1 | 1 | 1 | — | — | — | — | — |
| 60 Water/Waste WTR PLTOP | — | — | 1 | 1 | 1 | 1 | 1 | 1 | 1 | 1 | 1 | 1 | 1 |
| 62 Food Svc. Spv. III | — | — | — | 1 | 1 | 1 | 1 | — | — | — | — | — | — |
| 64 Police II | 1 | 1 | 1 | 1 | 1 | 1 | 1 | 1 | 1 | 1 | 1 | 1 | 1 |
| 66 Police III | — | — | — | — | — | — | — | — | — | — | 1 | 1 | — |
| 67 Food Service Dir. | — | — | — | — | — | — | — | — | — | — | — | — | — |
| Total Black | 32 | 19 | 20 | 22 | 20 | 21 | 23 | 22 | 25 | 34 | 47 | 44 | 43 |
| Yearly Total | | 234 | 237 | 203 | 181 | 204 | 192 | 192 | 207 | 228 | 216 | 205 | 191 |

[1] Salary classification 50 is the first grade in the salary classification.

One final note: Hiring a single black in a traditionally segregated unit is doomed to failure and will reinforce arguments for maintaining the white-only unit. About 15 years ago, a black man was hired at the hotel/conference center in a traditionally all-white unit. With no support from the supervisor, the black worker was exposed to racial slurs, harassment, and unfair work assignments. In time the black worker's performance dropped and he began to come to work late or missed days. After giving the black employee many opportunities to change his behavior, the supervisor had *no choice* but to terminate him, completing the cycle of inequality, discrimination, and poverty. Other African-American Appalachians, like the above individual, are caught in this cycle.

## References

ARC Staff. (December 1984). Appalachia: The economic outlook through the eighties. *Appalachia, 16.*

Atkinson, C. F., & Fraley, B. D. (1939). *Essentials of real estate practice.* Washington, DC: NAREB.

Bell, J. *(1990). Lawrence A. Oxley and social services for blacks in North Carolina's Appalachian counties.* (Unpublished paper.)

Boston, T. O. (1988). *Race, class and conservatism.* Boston: Unwin.

Commission on Religion in Appalachia. (1986). *Economic transformation: The Appalachian challenge.* Knoxville, TN: Author.

Franklin, B., & Resnik, S. (1973). *The political economy of racism.* New York: Holt, Rinehart and Winston.

Johnson, C. S. (1922). *Negro housing: Report of the Committee on Negro Housing.* New York: Negro University Press.

Johnson, C. S. (1943). *Patterns of Negro segregation.* New York: Negro University Press.

Letter to the editor (1990, December 12). *Sylva Herald,* p. 6.

McGee, F., & Browne, R. S. (1973). *Only six million acres: A decline of black owned land in the rural South.* New York: Black Economic Research Center.

National Association of Real Estate Boards. (1946). *Code of ethics.* Article 34. Washington, D.C.: Author.

Pinkney, A. (1987). *Black Americans,* 3rd ed. Englewood Cliffs, NJ: Prentice Hall.

Rungeling, B., et al. (1977). *Employment, income and welfare in the rural south.* New York: Praeger.

Salamon, L. M. (1976). *Land and minority enterprise: Crisis and the opportunity.* Washington, DC: U.S. Department of Commerce.

United States Census Bureau. (1967). *General social and economic characteristics.* Washington, DC: Government Printing Office.

Wachtel, D. *The Negro and discrimination in employment.* Ann Arbor, MI: University of Michigan.

Weaver, R. C. (1967). *The Negro ghetto in the United States.* New York: Russell and Russell.

## Selected Readings on Black Appalachians

ARC Staff. (1984, December). Appalachia: The economic outlook through the Eighties. *Appalachia, 16*, p. 5.

Cabbell, E. J. (1980). Black invisibility and racism in Appalachia: An informal survey. *Appalachian Journal, 16*(Autumn), pp. 48-54.

Campbell, J. D. (1969). *The Southern Highlander and his homeland.* Lexington, KY: University Press of Kentucky.

Carlton-LaNey, I. (1989). *Elderly Black farm women: As keepers of the community and the culture.* Charlotte, NC: University of North Carolina-Charlotte.

Clowes, W. Laird. (1970). *Black America: A study of the ex-slave and his late master.* Westport, CT: Negro University Press. (originally published in 1891)

Cobb, J. C. (1984). *Industrialization and Southern society, 1877–1984.* Lexington, KY: University of Kentucky Press.

Cornman, J., & Kincaid, B. K. (1984). *Lessons from rural America.* Washington, DC: Seven Locks.

Davis, A., Gardner, B., & Gardner, M. (1941). *Deep South.* Chicago: University of Chicago Press.

Feagin, J. R. (1989). *Racial and ethnic relations.* Englewood Cliffs, NJ: Prentice Hall.

Franklin, R., & Resnik, S. (1973). *The political economy of racism.* New York: Holt, Rinehart and Winston.

Frazier, E. F. (1940). *Negro youth at the crossroads, 1894–1962.* Washington, DC: American Council on Education.

Frazier, E. F. (1964). *The Negro church in America.* New York: Schocken.

Genovese, E. D. (1974). *Roll Jordon roll: The world the slaves made.* New York: Pantheon.

Good, P. (1968). *The American serfs: A report on poverty in the rural South.* New York: Putnam.

Hayden, W. (1991). Rites of death and burial of blacks in Appalachia. *Appalachian Heritage*, Winter.

Hayden, W. (1986, March). *The contemporary Appalachian: Urban or rural.* Paper presented at the Ninth Annual Appalachian Studies Conference, Boone, NC.

Hayden, W. (1986). Blacks an invisible institution in Appalachia? In J. Lloyd & A. Campbell (Eds.), *The impact of institutions in Appalachia: Proceedings of the Eighth Annual Appalachian Studies Conference.* / Boone, NC: Appalachian Consortium.

Herskovits, Melville J. (1958). *The myth of the Negro pasts.* Boston: Beacon.

Higgs, Robert. *Completion and coercion: Blacks in the American economy, 1865–1914.* New York: Cambridge University Press.

Johnson, J. W. (1973). *Negro Americans: What now?* New York: DaCapo.

Katz, I, & Gurin, P. (Eds.). (1969). *Race and the social sciences.* New York: Basic Books.

Keefe, S. E. (1988). *Appalachian mental health.* Lexington, KY: University Press of Kentucky.

Lewis, J. A. (1976). *White and minority small farm operators in the South.* Washington, DC: U.S. Department of Agriculture.

Lewis, R. L. (1987). *Black coal miners in America: Race, class and community conflict, 1780–1980.* Lexington, KY: University Press of Kentucky.

Lovingood, P., & Reiman, R. (1985). *Emerging patterns in the Southern Highlands: A reference atlas, vol. 1.* Boone, NC: Appalachian Consortium.

Marshall, ,R., & Christian, V. L., Jr. (1978). *Employment of Blacks in the South.* Austin: University of Texas Press.

Marshall, R., et al. (1978). *Employment discrimination: The impact of legal and administrative remedies.* New York: Praeger.

McAdoo, H. P. (1988). *Black families.* Newbury Park, CA: Sage.

McCummings, L. (1969). *The Black family.* Philadelphia: National Conference of Black Social Workers.

McDonald, M., & Wheeler, W. B. (1985). *Knoxville, Tennessee: Continuity and change in an Appalachian city.* Knoxville: University of Tennessee Press.

Owsley, F. L. (1965). *Plain folks in the old South.* Baton Rouge: Louisiana State University Press.

Rungeling, B, Smith, L., Briggs, V., Jr., & Adams, J. (1977). *Employment, income and welfare in the rural South.* New York: Praeger.

Smith, J., & Welch, F. R. (1986). *Closing the gap: Forty years of economic progress for blacks.* Rand.

Taeuber, K. E., & Taeuber, A. (1965). *Negroes in cities.* Chicago: Aldine.

Trends in per capita money income: Appalachia and United States. (1982). *Appalachia, 15/16,* 33.

Turner, W. H., Cabbell, E. J. (1985). *Blacks in Appalachia.* Lexington, KY: University Press of Kentucky.

*U.S. Census Report, 1970 and 1980: General Social and Economic Characteristics.*

Wachtel, D. (1965). *The Negro and discrimination in employment.* Ann Arbor, MI: University of Michigan.

Walker, J. L. (1977). *Economic development and black employment in the nonmetropolitan South.* Austin: University of Texas.

Wright, C. (1978, August 6). Black Appalachian invisibility–Myth or reality? *Black Appalachian Viewpoints,* pp. 1-3.

# 14

# Elderly Black Farm Women: A Population at Risk

by Iris Carlton-LaNey

Elderly black farm women are an invisible segment of the elderly population; their contributions to their families, communities, and the larger society have often been overlooked. Their work and resourcefulness have been ignored because their production was generally for use, rather than for exchange. Moreover, planners, policymakers, and service providers seldom consider this group's needs when they develop policies and programs. For example, the *North Carolina Aging Services Plan* (North Carolina Division of Aging, 1991) only briefly acknowledged the dearth of information and lack of documented formal research about the quality of life of elderly blacks and Native Americans and did not distinguish between the needs of women of color and white women. If elderly black women are combined with all other elderly women or minorities, their specific needs may never be addressed within a cultural context. To its credit, the *North Carolina Aging Services Plan* identified obtaining information about aged minority groups in the state as a first step to serving them better. In line with this goal, it is important to understand who these elderly farm women are and how their histories have affected their current positions in society.

A search for demographic data on this population is complicated by the fact that information on minority elderly people is not usually broken down by sex, and data on older women do not include cross-classifications by minority or nonwhite status. Furthermore, demographics on farmers generally exclude this population because they have retired and their farm earnings fall below the agricultural cash-earnings cutoff of $1,000. Given these limitations, the data that are available are not revealing. Nevertheless, the 1980 census reported that 603,181 North Carolina residents were aged 65 and older. In 1990, 825,377 residents, or 12.5 percent of the state's population, were aged 65 years and older. It is expected that this group will reach nearly 1.2 million by 2010. More than two-thirds of the state's older residents live in rural areas in 56 of the state's 100 counties (North Carolina Division of Aging, 1991).

---

Reprinted from *Social Work* (November 1992), with permission from the National Association of Social Workers.

## Background

Duplin County, a moderately populated rural county, was the site for the current study. In 1990, more than 5,947 people, or 30 percent of that county's residents, were nonwhite. In North Carolina's inner coastal plain counties, including Duplin County, there are considerably fewer black men than black women aged 65 and older. Furthermore, at age 65, minority women have a life expectancy of 73.4 years. Half those who survived to be age 65 in 1980 could expect 17.3 additional years of life, and half those who were 85 in the same year could expect to live an additional 6.7 years. With the long tradition of farming in these counties, the sex ratio of women to men, and the life expectancy of elderly minority women, one can assume that more than half the minority residents aged 65 and older who are classified as rural nonfarmers in Duplin County are women who have work histories as farmers (Birdsall, Comer, Ullman, & Wilson, 1989; North Carolina Division of Aging, 1991). These data argue for the development of services and programs to ensure the health and well-being of this growing population of women.

Approximately three-fifths of all black farmers in the South are concentrated in Alabama, Mississippi, North Carolina, and South Carolina. The majority of these farmers are located along the Mississippi Delta or in the bright-tobacco area of North Carolina (Schulman, Garrett, & Luginbuhl, 1985; Wadley & Lee, 1974). This research focuses on elderly black farm women, aged 65 and older, who have spent most of their lives in the bright-tobacco area of North Carolina. Among black farmers, the elderly constitute the largest portion of the population.

The term *farmer* usually refers to men, yet from information about farm families in general, it is known that women were and often continue to be a significant part of the farm communities (Bokemeier & Garkovich, 1987; Coughenour & Swanson, 1983), functioning as agricultural producers or as partners in production (Pearson, 1979). Although some studies have focused on farm women as decision makers (C. Jones & Rosenfeld, 1981; Sawer, 1973) and as performers of many specific farm tasks (Boulding, 1980; J. Pearson, 1979), they have revealed little about black farm women. The literature search is further complicated when one searches for information on elderly black women. An extensive literature search revealed virtually nothing about this group.

This article presents some initial insights into the lives of elderly black farm women, based heavily on the author's illustrative interviews with elderly black farm women, who were engaged in farm work for most of their adult lives before their retirement, and on her lifetime exposure to countless black male and female farmers in Duplin County. The material presented is exploratory. It provides information and describes the impressions of 10 elderly black farm women in only this one county. In semistructured, tape-recorded interviews, the author asked each woman generally about her life as a farm woman, the years of the Great Depression, her marriage (and wedding day), her needs, and the things that have given her the most pleasure and joy in life. These oral histories ran from two to more than five hours. The 10 women were selected through the snowball sampling method—that is, because they were identified by the author or by each other and because they would be willing participants.

These oral histories encouraged the women to structure their accounts and ideas of what they considered relevant and gave them an opportunity to reminisce. Through reminiscence, these women conducted a mental and oral review of their lives, and their awareness of personal strengths and a positive sense of self may have been revived. Throughout their lives, these qualities provided an impetus for their resourcefulness and mutual aid. These same qualities must be considered as programs are developed to meet this population's needs and to ensure an adequate quality of life during old age.

The author's inferences and summations are also based on her protracted and intimate relationships with this group of women. It was easy for the author to overcome many of the barriers inherent in the oral history method because she has had a lifelong rapport with the participants. The respondents trusted her to be respectful of them and of the frank and detailed content they presented and expressed confidence that she would use discretion and judgment in revealing intimate details about their lives. Although the information gleaned from this research may not be generalizable to a larger population, it is hoped that the depth of the material will offset this problem.

## The Women's Relationship to Farm Production

To understand these women, it is important to understand their relationship to farm production. For these women, agricultural production primarily meant flue-cured tobacco. Historically, other crops, such as grain, fruits, or vegetables, were never major crops among black farmers. Although cotton was the predominant crop for many years, it was replaced by tobacco. The production of tobacco lends itself to family labor and has traditionally been one of the most labor-intensive crops in the United States. The federal government intervened in the production of tobacco in the 1930s by assigning acreage allotments to landowning tobacco farmers that granted farmers the right to grow tobacco in specified areas. Acreage allotments were later replaced by poundage quotas. This change allowed the lease and transfer of allotments-poundage quotas from one farm to another within the same county. Essentially, the farmers' chances of economic success are based on their access, by ownership or rental, to a special government-controlled productive resource—tobacco allotments (Schulman et al., 1985; Wadley & Lee, 1974). The participation of black farm women in the production of flue-cured tobacco was multidimensional and included labor roles that were linked to a larger system of allocating labor in the farm family.

According to J. Pearson (1979), farm women perform four roles in agricultural production: independent producers, agricultural partners, farm helpers, and farm homemakers. The independent producer manages the farm largely by herself. The agricultural partner shares work responsibilities and decision making with her spouse. The farm helper does not generally participate in production unless it is a busy time on the farm and extra help is needed. The farm homemaker contributes to production only indirectly by running errands and preparing food for the workers.

Few of the women interviewed could be classified as independent producers, nor did they fit neatly into the remaining three categories. Their roles as farm wives included some combination of partner, helper, and homemaker. They have been joint decision makers with their husbands in many business matters. Both their small-scale farms and their heavy commitments to tobacco production forced them to be more involved in farm operation than are women on larger farms.

On occasion, some women would "cross over" to do what was considered men's work. In describing her role on the farm, one woman took pride in her ability to do so:

> I'd hitch up the mule and ply all day. I'd crop tobacco; I'd hang tobacco. I've done everything just about on the farm. I've cut ditch bank. Everything on the farm to be done, except work the tractor, I've done.

Another woman recalled bittersweetly, "I've worked just like a man on this farm."

In addition to farm labor, these women were heavily involved in production for home consumption. Their tasks included gardening, preserving foods, and preparing meals for their family members and hired day workers. Illustrating this point, one woman recalled her role this way:

> We grew most of our food. . . canned everything, peaches, beans, string beans, okra, and cabbage. . . . We'd kill 10 or 11 hogs in December. We had to salt it [the pork] down and then wash it and hang it up in the smokehouse. I canned sausage in lard. We also had a hundred head of chickens, and we sold the eggs for groceries.

This woman's homemaking duties did not preclude her intense involvement in farm work. Instead, the typical practice included a combination of helper and homemaker. Her role as helper was especially intense during the tobacco-harvesting season. She described her role this way:

> I had never worked on a farm until we came here, and then I had to cook three meals a day, feed the help, and then go to the field when they [her husband and the hired workers] went. And then I'd be given out, but I'd have to cook supper when I came in from work.

Although these women were a significant part of their small-scale farm operations and actively participated in joint decision making with their husbands, clear sex-role definitions still remained. Tradition designated the man as the farmer and the woman as the helper. Janiewski (1985) noted that as the "tobacco-growing region around Durham [NC] affirmed into the late 1930s, men, not women, 'toted the pocketbook'" (p. 29). Women seldom questioned the patriarchal system that dictated this sexual division of labor between spouses; rather, they saw it as a complementary division of labor. Furthermore, these farm women were not involved with the mechanization of agriculture once it occurred. The women vividly recalled a much simpler and harder time when most farm work was done manually. As they gradually acquired farm equipment, such as tractors, their husbands took responsibility for operating the equipment.

These women were also excluded from another aspect of farming—deciding which crops would be planted where, which was the men's role. Likewise, the men did not participate equally in housekeeping or child rearing. Powers, Keith, and Gordy (1981) found that farmers spent less time interacting with their families than did members of any other occupational category. The black farm women added housekeeping and child-rearing responsibilities to their other chores. One woman recalled her child care arrangements when her children were young:

> My first baby was born in 1935. At that time we stayed with my father-in-law, and he had some young children. The young children would take care of the smaller babies at the end of the row and in the middle of the field or under a shade tree. The babies were in the field until my oldest girl got big enough to stay in the house with the baby and younger children.

## Attributes of Elderly Black Farm Women

These women all shared certain characteristics that allowed them to cope with the rigors of their lives as farmers. They had a strong work orientation, effective links with farm and nonfarm organizations and activities, a strong family orientation, and a definite system of mutual aid.

### Strong Work Orientation

All the women had a positive work orientation. They expected a life of hard work and rarely complained as they reminisced. Although they do not maintain the pace of their earlier years because of their advanced ages, they continue to work, particularly at those tasks related to production for family consumption. It is not unusual for farmers to continue to work long after many others have retired (Coward & Lee, 1985). For these women, work is such an integral part of their existence that poor health or, as they phrased it, "being no account" is the major impetus for retreating from farm labor. The following comments were typical and reflected these farm women's love of farm work and adherence to the work ethic:

I've worked on the farm all of my life. I love working on the farm. I really love it.

We made ourselves useful through the years from one thing to the other.

I've always been on the farm, and I just enjoy it. Anyway, I'd rather be on the farm than anywhere else. I love the work.

For these women, work was more than a way to accomplish specific tasks for monetary or other material gain. The cooperative nature of farm work also held a strong emotional commitment that emphasized mutual affection and sisterhood.

### Links with Farm and Nonfarm Organizations

These elderly black farm women were all active members and leaders in church, farm, and fraternal organizations. This finding is consistent with research findings that elderly women in general attend religious services more often, are more likely to be church members, and report a higher degree of religiosity than do elderly men (Taylor, 1986). Research further shows that rural blacks attend services more frequently than do their urban counterparts and are more likely to be church members (Langford, 1974; Taylor, 1986). The rural church and the black church have historically been significant in helping to organize the lives of their parishioners. The black church is a place not only for worship through celebration, but for affirmation, rejoicing, and recognition (Dancy, 1977). The following comment reflects the women's general attitude toward the church:

Our main goal during those days was going to church and Sunday school. That's where you saw everybody.... [You'd] get out of church and everybody would be talking, shaking hands... everybody would be glad to see each other.

Membership in secret, fraternal orders was another characteristic that these women shared and that provided them with a great source of sisterhood and comradeship. The majority held membership in one or more of these groups: the Eastern Star, the Grand Order of Salem, or the Knights of Giddeon. With long traditions in the black community, these organizations provided opportunities for socializing, holding leadership positions, developing support networks, and receiving and giving mutual aid.

Eight of the 10 women were members of the same chapter of the Home Demonstration Club—a community-based organization that is part of the Agricultural Extension Service and that provides educational services to rural farm families. This organization has a long, credible history and is solidly integrated into the social fabric of the community. For these women, the monthly meetings of the club gave them an opportunity to socialize with each other and to learn better or different ways to meet their families' needs, such as preserving food, sewing, and flower arranging. The meetings also gave them an opportunity to prepare and enjoy a meal together. Several women commented that the eating together was the most enjoyable part of the meetings. Preparing and sharing food has traditionally symbolized the spiritual component of collective survival (J. Jones, 1985). In general, the club meetings reinforced the sense of sisterhood that the church initiated. They also demonstrated the women's commitment to grow and develop in their roles as farm wives and mothers.

### Strong Family Orientation

Children were an essential part of these women's lives. Of the 10 women who were interviewed, only one had no biological children and had not adopted any. However, this woman lives across the road from her sister, who has four children, and has been intimately involved in the children's lives. Her living room is filled with photographs of her nieces and nephews, and she shows them off with a mother's pride. Three of the 10 women had adopted children either formally or informally. There were a total of 34 children between the 10 women.

All the women discussed their children and grandchildren during the interviews, and three of them stated that their children were their most important contribution to society. One woman who has no biological children has spent much of her time since her husband's death as a foster mother. In addition, she informally adopted a son while she and her husband were young and told the story of the neglectful teenage mother and the "sickly" infant's circumstances that led her to adopt the baby. She also formally adopted a daughter, who came into her home as a foster child. She told the following story of one foster child:

> Sammie...I kept Sammie a long time cause he was a little tiny baby when they brought him here and he was talkin' and goin' with me anywhere I wanted to go before they came and adopted him out. I told them [the child welfare workers], I said, "You get people to raise the younguns and get them up so they can enjoy them then you come and sell them just like you sell cows and hogs" (she laughed)....It hurt when they came and got Sammie cause you see he was so close to me and I was to him, too.

> Well, Miss Dent called and said she didn't think the people was going to adopt him. But anyway she said, "We'll bring him back this evening." Carried Sammie away that morning....They came back about this time of evening...that same man that Sammie loved is the one who came back. He got out the car and I said, "Where's Sammie?" He said, "Miss C, the people saw him and like him and they carried him on home with them."

> The water went to flying. I couldn't help from crying to save me. He said, "Miss C, he'll be alright and probably they'll bring him back to see you." I said, "That ain't the thing of it...and you go back to

Kenansville and tell Miss Dent that I said she lied!"....Did you know those people come out here everyday for a long time...checking on me. They did.

This is one woman's account of her love for a foster child, and it is also a reflection of the commitment that all these women had toward children and family.

A majority of these women also spoke of the importance of education to success in life. They have firsthand experience with life's hardships and recognize the affliction of being black and uneducated. They did not want their children to suffer as they had done and were determined to give their children the advantage of an education. Therefore, they encouraged their children to attend college, which for them was a major investment well worth the sacrifices and hard work involved. For several of these women, the education of their children represented the fulfillment of their own dreams of achievement. The following comment illustrates the women's general attitude toward education:

I'm so proud of my children. I ain't got a bad one in the bunch. I've always tried to help my children to get a good education and make something of themselves. We sent them to college...well, they sent themselves, but we did what we could to help them.

Sixteen of the 34 children attended college, and several have master's and doctoral degrees in such fields as business, education, social work, and journalism. Ironically, most of these children now live in urban centers and will probably never become farmers. Another consequence of their children's educational achievements is that they are unavailable to advocate, on a regular basis, for their aging parents.

## Definite System of Mutual Aid

According to these women, group survival rests on the idea of mutual support. The women have developed a system of mutual aid and social support that has taken them through crises of family illnesses and death to general activities of farm life, such as barn raisings and hog killings. For these women, the social support network is a coping mechanism that is permanent and provides them with esteem, support, and encouragement. Preston and Mansfield (1984) found that the closeness among rural elderly people in a support network promotes feelings of security, which, in turn, help to reduce stress. Older blacks, moreover, have not been able to count on formal support systems of service. A history of injustices, supported and often initiated by "the government," has caused elderly blacks to develop a healthy sense of paranoia. To avoid the expected humiliation of racism that is often inherent in formal helping systems, they have established and relied on their own network of helpers. Chatters, Taylor, and Jackson's (1986) research on elderly black people in the South showed that the "helper network" includes spouses, children, siblings, friends, and neighbors. Furthermore, Taylor (1985) found that elderly blacks prefer to receive help from a particular group and that their help-seeking journey includes, in order of frequency, children, kin, nonkin, and formal organizations.

The elderly black farm women in this study indicated that they often gathered for work in small groups of relatives and neighbors. Consistent with Janiewski's (1985) findings, talking and socializing was an integral part of their work. The following comments illustrate the sense of mutuality and community support inherent in their world of work:

> Some parts of farm work we enjoyed because we worked with other people. When we'd barn tobacco, we enjoyed it because we'd always be with community people. Neighbors worked together. If it had not been for the neighbors working with one another, I don't see how we would have made it. But they would come and help us, and we'd help them.

## Implications for Practice

Although these women have histories as "survivors and effective copers" (Chatters & Taylor, 1989), many of the resources that were traditionally available to them no longer exist. Poor health, decreased mobility, and advancing age put their quality of life at risk. The at-risk population has been described as individuals aged 60 and older who have fewer physical problems than do the high-risk group but who experience impairment in their social, economic, mental, physical, or home and community functioning (North Carolina Division of Aging, 1991).

Elderly black farm women are at risk in at least four important ways: economic security, health, their caregiving responsibilities, and social isolation and dependence.

### Economic Security

North Carolina had the eighth highest rate of poverty among the elderly in the nation for 1987, and nonwhite women aged 75 and older had the highest rate at 47.7 percent (North Carolina Division of Aging, 1991). With such a high rate of poverty, it is alarming that so few of the state's elderly people participate in any economic security programs. In 1988, for example, only 6.7 percent received Supplemental Security Income (SSI), and only 7.2 percent received food stamps (North Carolina Division of Aging, 1991). The low participation rate in such programs may be attributed to the lack of information on and understanding of these programs. Another explanation may be that the elderly fear that they will lose their land if they apply for and receive means-tested services.

These farm women can be described as land rich. Their lives have revolved around farming and agricultural activities. Although their livelihoods may not remain tied to their farming efforts, the values embodied in landownership and involvement in the community provide them with an identity, stability, and continuity (Brown & Larson, 1979). Land, according to Beaver (1982), is symbolically associated with family. The farms on which these women reside have been in their families for more than 100 years. Many can trace their land acquisitions from inheritances and small purchases from siblings, other relatives, or others. Several of the women laughingly recalled that their husbands referred to the most recently purchased parcels of land as the "new ground," although they may have been purchased 20 to 30 years ago.

Landownership gives the women not only a sense of stability but some semblance of power and control. To sell their land to younger family members or, what is less desirable, to people outside their families could devastate and dehumanize these women. Their quality of life would likely be negatively affected, both economically (with the loss of a financial base) and emotionally (in that discontinuity would probably cause undesirable or pronounced personality changes that would lead to dependence, reduced self-esteem, and depression). The very qualities that have helped these women to cope would be destroyed because low self-esteem destroys resourcefulness, self-reliance, and independence.

Landownership also makes these farm women ineligible for many means-tested social programs, particularly if the land is not contiguous to their residence, which it often is not because of the haphazard method of acquiring small parcels throughout the years. Furthermore, many of these women have paid limited social security taxes and are, therefore, eligible for only small monthly social security payments. Few of them or their spouses did off-farm work and, therefore, are not recipients of private pensions. Essentially, although these women have worked continuously, they are experiencing the growing poverty shared by all small-scale farmers.

In sum, the significance of this study's findings is underscored by the context of information on the financial status of elderly black adults. The higher incidence of poverty among elderly black individuals is a reflection of the disparity between the income levels of black and white adults. Of the four race-sex groups (black men, black women, white men, and white women), black women have the lowest median income (Chen, 1985).

In dealing with the problems of economic security, social workers and other advocates for the elderly need to become more tenacious in social change efforts by lobbying for legislative changes to consolidate eligibility requirements for programs, such as food stamps, SSI, and the low-income energy-assistance program, or a system that increases the value of homestead exemptions as property values increase. The change involving the value of homestead exemptions would provide some protection to landowners and help to allay anxieties associated with landownership and the acceptance of social services.

## Health

Most of the women in this study did not report chronic health problems that inhibited their functioning, but health issues were of major concern to them. The women realize that their health is tied closely to the social and economic aspects of their lives. When discussing health, they described themselves as being "no good" or "no account." In general, they suffer from physical health problems, such as vision impairments, hearing loss, arthritis, memory loss, hypertension, and stroke.

By age 65, 82 percent of black women suffer from hypertension, compared with 66 percent of their white counterparts (B. P. Pearson & Beck, 1989). Hypertension, sometimes referred to as the "silent killer," requires early diagnosis and treatment, including a low sodium diet, which is often inconsistent with the traditional eating habits of black farm women (Dancy, 1977). Other leading physical health problems include heart disease and stroke. Strokes are the third leading cause of death among women and hypertension is a major risk factor for stroke (B. P. Pearson & Beck, 1989). Shortly after the interviews for this study, one woman suffered a massive stroke that left her unable to care for herself. At the time of the stroke, she was the primary caregiver for an ill adult son who lived at home with her. Her concern about the care of her disabled son could further complicate her own recuperation.

### Caregiving Responsibilities

Living arrangements and caregiving responsibilities present another risk factor for this group. Of the 10 women who were interviewed, only four live with their husbands. The remaining six either live alone or with someone other than a spouse. These living arrangements may mean that they have caregiving responsibilities for their spouses or for other older kin. One 76-year-old woman is living with her husband and caring for his frail elderly aunt whom she "took in." In discussing her caregiving role, she stated,

> I'd like to be remembered for the life I've lived and the service I've given, 'cause I always helped sick people in any way that I could. My mama always did that and...I think that would be 'bout the proudest thing about myself...is caring for other people.

It is not unusual for elderly women to assume caregiving responsibilities for impaired family members. Furthermore, society has come to rely on women to provide the majority of care for dependent family members who can no longer care for themselves (Wilson, 1990). In caring for others, elderly women often neglect their own health in the belief that they have no other choice but to care for those in need.

### Social Isolation and Dependence

The impact of the caregiving role, along with some physical health problems, has meant that many of these women have had to give up their social and community functions. Their complaints of vision impairments and "nerves" have caused most of them to stop driving. The fact that they no longer drive, combined with the lack of public transportation in rural areas, has meant that these women must depend on others to transport them. Because they are dependent, most travel only when necessary and hence attend church less regularly. This finding is consistent with Taylor's (1986) finding that poor health and difficulty in getting around account for elderly people's decreased attendance at religious services. Furthermore, these women no longer participate in the activities of their clubs or secret orders. Although most maintain their membership in the secret orders, they do not attend meetings or other related activities. Even the chapter of their Home Demonstration Club, a source of pleasure and reward to them for more than 30 years, is now defunct. The women who were members stated that they were no longer "able" to prepare for the meetings or attend related county and regional meetings. With limited outside contact and the loss of personal freedom and mobility, these women are more dependent on their families and others for social stimulation. Hence, they are at risk of social isolation, which is an additional threat to the quality of their lives.

Aggressive outreach must form the foundation for services offered to this population, and tapping into existing rural community resources could make the process both efficient and effective (Carlton-LaNey, 1991). Because the Home Demonstration Club once served such a useful function for this group, establishing a similar in-home program under the auspices of the Extension Homemakers Association may help to provide continuity and decrease isolation. Blau (1973) noted that peer relationships, rather than filial relationships, determine morale in old age; therefore, a community-based in-home women's group could provide the women with an opportunity for information sharing and education about social services and economic security programs. Even if they are unable to retain all the information, they at least will have the advantage of knowing a resource to call upon in times of need. The group meetings could focus on a specific service each month by drawing on expertise from the local department of social services (DSS), the health department, the mental health agency, councils on aging, and so on.

Given that eating together was an important aspect of the Home Demonstration Club's meetings, homemakers or chore workers from DSS could purchase and prepare light meals that are based on the club members' preferences and dietary needs. The menus of the Home Demonstration Club usually consisted of meat or chicken salads, crackers, cake, and coffee. Another option may be for the congregate-meals programs to deliver meals to the homes where the meetings are scheduled to take place. Volunteers who deliver meals to the homebound are more likely to travel to rural homes when they are delivering several meals within the same area. The spouses or other eligible individuals could also receive meals with the same delivery.

These in-home monthly meetings would be reminiscent of the pleasure that these women experienced learning and sharing with women friends in their clubs and lodges in previous years. As Berzoff (1989) noted, groups are beneficial to women who have suffered losses of self-esteem and self-worth. Furthermore, these groups provide both corrections of self-perception and ties to other women. These elderly women's clubs would be multifunctional, giving participants opportunities to interact with each other; to gain information about available services, programs, and resources; to share nutritious meals; and to develop new kinds of healing ties with other women.

## Conclusion

The development and implementation of culturally sensitive programs and services for this population require that social workers first become aware of the culture and values of elderly black farm women and understand and respect the ways that these women deal with problems. Social workers must also capitalize on the distinct qualities of the culture. These findings suggest that social programs and services for elderly black farm women must be free of means-testing whenever possible; have an outreach component; utilize natural helpers, such as family members, neighbors, and friends; be church or community based; and be sensitive to the women's rurality, work histories, and feelings of sisterhood and mutuality. Given services that incorporate these components, elderly black farm women will be able to enjoy old age with a heightened sense of security and a greater sense of continuity.

## References

Beaver, P. D. (1982). Appalachian families, landownership, and public policy. In R. L. Hall & C. B. Stack (Eds.), *Holding on to the land and the Lord: Kinship rituals, land tenure, and social policy in the rural South.* (pp. 146-154). Athens: University of Georgia Press.

Berzoff, J. (1989). From separation to connection: Shifts in understanding women's development. *Affilia, 4,* 45-58.

Birdsall, S., Comer, L., Ulhnan, M., & Wilson, J. (1989). *Geographic patterns of North Carolina's elderly population.* Chapel Hill: University of North Carolina Press.

Blau, Z. (1973). *Old age in a changing society.* New York: New Viewpoints.

Bokemeier, J., & Garkovich, L. (1987). Assessing the influence of farm women's self-identity on task allocation and decision making. *Rural Sociology, 52,* 13-36.

Boulding, E. (1980). The labor of U.S. farm women: A knowledge gap. *Sociology of Work and Occupations, 7,* 261-290.

Brown, M. M., & Larson, O. F. (1979). Successful black farmers: Factors in their achievement. *Rural Sociology, 44,* 153-175.

Carlton-LaNey, I. (1991). Some considerations of the rural elderly black's underuse of social services. *Journal of Gerontological Social Work, 16,* 3-17.

Chatters, L. M., & Taylor, R. J. (1989). Life problems and coping strategies of older black adults. *Social Work, 34,* 313-319.

Chatters, L. M., Taylor, R., & Jackson, J. (1986). Aged blacks' choices for an informal helper network. *Journal of Gerontology, 41,* 94-100.

Chen, Y. (1985). Economic status of the aging. In R. Binstock & E. Shanas (Eds.), *Handbook of aging and the social sciences* (2nd ed., pp. 641-665). New York: Van Nostrand.

Coughenour, C. M., & Swanson, L. (1983). Work statuses and occupations of men and women in farm families and the structure of farms. *Rural Sociology, 48,* 23-43.

Coward, R. T., & Lee, G. A. (1985). *The elderly in rural society.* New York: Springer.

Dancy, J. (1977). *The black elderly, a guide for practitioners.* Ann Arbor: Institute of Gerontology, University of Michigan.

Janiewski, D. (1985). *Sisterhood denied: Race, gender, and class in a new South community.* Philadelphia: Temple University Press.

Jones, C., & Rosenfeld, R. A. (1981). *American farm women: Findings from a national survey.* Chicago: National Opinion Research Council.

Jones, J. *(1985). Labor of love, labor of sorrow.* New York: Vintage Books.

Langford, C. (1974). Church attendance and city size. *Journal for the Scientific Study of Religion, 13,* 361-362.

North Carolina Division of Aging, North Carolina Department of Human Resources. (1991). *North Carolina aging services plan: A guide for successful aging in the 1990s.* Raleigh, NC: Author.

Pearson, B. P, & Beck, C. M. (1989). Physical health of elderly women. *Journal of Women and Aging, 1,* 149-174.

Pearson, J. (1979). Notes on female farmers. *Rural Sociology, 44,* 189-200.

Powers, E. A., Keith, P. M., & Gordy, W. J. (1981). Family networks of rural aged. In R. T. Coward & W. M. Smith, Jr. (Eds.), *The family in rural society* (pp. 421-447). Boulder, CO: Westview Press.

Preston, D. B., & Mansfield, R K. (1984). An exploration of stressful life events, illness, and coping among rural elderly. *The Gerontologist, 24,* 490-494.

Sawer, B. J. (1973). Predictors of the farm wife's involvement in general management and adoption decisions. *Rural Sociology, 38,* 412-425.

Schulman, M. D., Garrett, P., & Luginbuhl, R. (1985). Dimensions of the internal stratification of smallholders: Insights from North Carolina Piedmont Counties. *Rural Sociology, 50,* 251-261.

Taylor, R. J. (1985). The extended family as a source of support to elderly blacks. *The Gerontologist, 25,* 488-495.

Taylor, R. J. (1986). Religious participation among elderly blacks. *The Gerontologist, 26,* 630-636.

Wadley, J. K., & Lee, E. S. (1974). The disappearance of the black farmer. *Phylon, 35,* 276-283.

Wilson, V. (1990). The consequences of elderly wives caring for disabled husbands: Implications for practice. *Social Work, 35,* 417-421.

# 15

# The Health and Well-Being of Rural Elders

by Raymond T. Coward and Jeffrey W. Dwyer

This chapter examines the health status and health care utilization patterns of older people who reside in small towns and rural America. It is not a detailed, academic enumeration of the existing research literature; rather, it is a summary of existing knowledge highlighting those aspects of aging in rural environments which are critical to the development and delivery of services. The materials are organized in a question and answer format. The questions are illustrative of those that we have heard our colleagues, both academic and service-providing, ask over the years.

The chapter begins with a brief section describing the population size and distribution of elders in rural America. The second section summarizes our current state of knowledge about the health status of rural elders, with particular attention to the status of their health, relative to that of older persons who live in more urban and suburban contexts. Finally, the concluding section describes the access that rural elders have to health and human services and reviews our best understanding of the factors that influence the use of services by older rural residents.

## The Elderly in Rural America

### Who Are the Rural Elderly?

At one time it was a relatively easy task to identify the rural elderly. They lived on farms far removed from urban areas, their income came from farm-

Portions of this chapter originally appeared in a 1991 monograph authored by Raymond Coward and Jeffrey Dwyer entitled *Health Programs and Services for Elders in Rural America* and distributed by the National Resource Center for Rural Elderly. The development of that document was supported, in part, by a grant from the Administration on Aging to C. Neil Bull of the University of Missouri-Kansas City. Partial support for the revisions to produce this chapter were provided under a grant from the National Institute of Aging to the senior author. The authors want to express their gratitude to Angela Hightower for her assistance in the preparation of the final manuscript and to C. Neil Bull for permission to incorporate portions of the earlier monograph.

ing-related activities, and they were often the hub of a large family network. This basic description characterized the vast majority of elderly persons in the United States until the first or second decade of the 20th century and, perhaps accurately at the time, implied that the rural elderly were a relatively homogeneous population.

We now know, however, that such portrayals are no longer accurate. Instead, we are aware that there is considerable heterogeneity among the rural elderly and that the rural/urban or metropolitan/nonmetropolitan dichotomies that were so often used in the past do not capture the full range of unique characteristics and life circumstances that currently exist in rural America.

At the conceptual level, there is general agreement that a *continuum* of residence (rather than dichotomous categories) is a better representation of the social, cultural, life style, and economic differences that exist among communities of varying sizes (Coward & Cutler, 1988). Unfortunately, although we can agree that this is the best way to conceptualize area of residence, there is little consensus about the specific elements or characteristics of a community that should be used to distinguish among different points along the continuum. This failure to adopt a common definition or typology of rurality makes it difficult, but not impossible, to compare research findings from different studies and to develop and implement public policies that address the specific needs of rural elders. Indeed, characterizing this dilemma, Hewitt (1989) has said that:

> It is difficult to quantify rural health problems and to make informed policy decisions without a clear definition of what and where "rural" areas are. Small population, sparse settlement, and remoteness are all features intuitively associated with "rural." These features exist on a continuum, however, while federal policies usually rely on dichotomous definitions. (p. 1)

### How Many Rural Elders Are There in the United States?

Depending on the definition of rural that is used, approximately one in four older persons in the United States lives in a small town or rural community (Clifford, Heaton, Voss, & Fuguitt, 1985) or, in 1990, a total of 8.2 million nonmetropolitan elders (U.S. Senate Special Committee on Aging, 1992). The rural elderly are not, however, evenly distributed throughout the United States. For example, a comparison of the four census regions reveals that while 17.1% of the total population in the north-central states are elders living in all-rural, nonmetropolitan counties, the comparable proportions are noticeably lower in the northeastern (14.9%), southern (13.2%), and western (10.6%) regions (Clifford, Heaton, Voss, & Fuguitt, 1985).

When individual states are compared, these differences are even more pronounced. In Maryland, Louisiana, Colorado, Nevada, New Mexico, and Alaska, the elderly account for less than 10% of the population of all-rural, nonmetropolitan counties. In contrast, the proportion of elders in comparable counties in Iowa, Kansas, Missouri, and Nebraska exceeds 18%. Indeed, there is an almost five-fold difference in the proportion of these elders in Kansas (19.7%) compared to Alaska (4.1%).

In addition, there have been significant regional differences in the growth of this population (Clifford, Heaton, Voss, & Fuguitt, 1985). Specifically, the southern and western regions have experienced an increase in the percentage of elders living in all-rural, nonmetropolitan counties (19.8% and 13.5%, respectively), while both the north-central (-1.4%) and northeast (-3.2%) regions have experienced declines.

Just as we have learned not to clump all older people together (because of the tremendous differences among them), so, too, must we remember not to heap all rural settings together as if they were one homogeneous group. Rural New England is not the same as the back hollows and valleys of Appalachia–which, in turn, is different from the rural Mississippi Delta or the open country of the Great Plains. Although these settings have many things in common, they are *not* carbon copies of each other.

### Health Status of Rural Elders

This section of the chapter summarizes our understanding of residential differences in the health status of older persons. It begins with simple comparisons of the incidence and prevalence of certain conditions and proceeds to a discussion of the factors that may account for these observed differences.

#### Is the Health of the Rural Elderly Different from That of Older People Who Live in More Urban Settings?

The health of the rural elderly differs from their urban counterparts, but the differences are not universal, nor do they always place the rural elderly at a disadvantage (Coward, Miller, & Dwyer, 1992). In general, the rural and urban elderly experience the same kinds of health problems, although rural elders may have a greater prevalence of chronic health conditions (such as arthritis, cardiovascular disease, hypertension, and diabetes) (Dwyer, Lee, & Coward, 1990). At the same time, however, there are some significant differences *within* the rural population–particularly between farm and nonfarm elders–in a number of specific health dimensions (Cutler & Coward, 1988).

#### Are There Differences in the Medical Conditions Experienced by Rural Elders?

Limited information is available about differences in medical conditions that may exist between rural and urban elders. Moreover, what is available is inconsistent. For example, even though farm elders in one study experienced the most acute and chronic conditions, they had the fewest days of restricted activity and total days in bed, when compared to all other elders (Palmore, 1983-1984). Older farmers, however, did spend more days in bed from injuries than did others their age.

More recent studies raise still further questions about the relative disadvantages of rural elders (Cutler & Coward, 1988). This latter work reminds us that we have a great deal to learn about differences between rural and urban areas and about differences within rural environments with respect to the experience of specific diseases and conditions. For example, Cutler and Coward (1988) examined the total number of certain medical conditions experienced by all elders in a national sample (16 medical conditions were examined, including broken hips, hardening of the arteries, Alzheimer's disease, and arthritis). Their results indicate that the number of medical conditions experienced by elders was lowest among nonmetropolitan-farm elders (1.43) and highest among nonmetropolitan-nonfarm elders (1.81). Both metropolitan elders living in central cities (1.73) and outside central cities (1.65) had a mean number of medical conditions that was between the two extremes found in the nonmetropolitan categories.

Similar research by Coward, Miller, and Dwyer (1992), using a slightly older sample, explored nine specific medical conditions and found that while there were residence differences in the number of elders who reported six of these conditions (i.e., hypertension, cancer, arthritis, a fall within the past 12 months, difficulty controlling bowels, and difficulty controlling urination), rural elders were "disadvantaged" in only four of the six cases (they fared better than elders residing in more urban environments on cancer and difficulty controlling bowels).

The results of both of these studies underscore the notion that there is a great deal of diversity in the experience of specific medical conditions by area of residence, but variation by residence does not place one group of elders (i.e., rural elders) *always* at a disadvantage.

### Do the Differences in Existing Medical Conditions Affect How Older Persons from Rural Areas Are Able to Perform Tasks of Daily Living?

Many gerontologists think that assessing an elderly person's ability to function effectively in everyday daily activities is a better measure of their long-term care requirements than the specific medical conditions with which they have been diagnosed (Katz, Ford, Moskowitz, Jackson, & Jaffee, 1963). Research has documented residential differences in the ability of older persons to perform such everyday tasks (Coward & Cutler, 1988; Cutler & Coward, 1988). Specifically, differences have been observed in the difficulty that elders have performing activities of daily living (ADL), such as bathing and eating, or instrumental activities of daily living (IADL), such as shopping and doing housework, and in their functional limitations, such as walking for a quarter of a mile or walking up ten steps without resting.

These comparisons also illustrate, however, the diversity that exist within rural populations. That is, while rural elders not engaged in farming enterprises were found to have the most difficulty performing everyday activities, those elders who were still farming had the least difficulty performing such tasks (Coward & Cutler, 1988; Cutler & Coward, 1988).

This variation within rural populations should not, however, divert attention away from the greater difficulty that older rural persons as a group have performing such tasks. Most rural elders, after all, are *not* engaged in farming. Elders who still farm represent a very small minority of the overall elderly population in the United States (about 2-3%) and are even a small minority of the elders who live in nonmetropolitan places (less than 10%). The proverbial bottom line is that the better health of older farmers simply does not counterbalance the prevailing poorer health status of the much larger group of rural elders who are not farmers.

### Do these Differences Affect How Sick the Elderly from Rural Areas Feel?

Another important measure of health, in addition to medical conditions and functional limitations, is how a person feels. In the health literature, this is called "perceived health" or "self-reported health." Although our knowledge in this area is also limited, some evidence suggests that rural elders seem to perceive themselves to be in worse health than urban elders. Specifically, both rural farm and rural nonfarm elders perceived their health to be poorer than their urban counterparts (Cutler & Coward, 1988).

Again, the distinction between farm and nonfarm responses among rural elders is worth mentioning. Because nonfarm elders have the largest number of medical conditions and the largest number of functional limitations, it is not surprising that they report the poorest perceived health. That seems both logical and consistent. What is paradoxical, perhaps, are the responses of the farm elders. Even though they reported the fewest number of medical conditions and the second fewest number of functional limitations, they reported the second poorest perceived health. In objective comparisons to the other groups, older farmers seem to be relatively healthy; yet, in their own subjective judgment, they perceive their health as poorer. Why? Some have suggested that life on a farm is more physically demanding, and, as a consequence, smaller amounts of disability are perceived as more onerous. A variation of this explanation suggests that because farm elders are still working, any health impairment will be perceived as a greater impediment to performance. Unfortunately, we do not yet have the information that will allow us to solve this paradox. What we can say with assurance is that nonfarm elders (again, the largest group among rural elders) have more medical conditions, more functional limitations, and a poorer perception of their health than any other group of elders.

### Are There Background and Demographic Characteristics That May Explain Residence Differences in Medical Conditions, Functional Health, and Perceived Health?

This question reaches the heart of one of the most difficult aspects of doing research on the health of rural elders—namely, being able to isolate that part of health which can be attributed to residence *per se* from that which is due to other factors operating simultaneously. Stated differently, many of the other factors that influence health (like income, medical insurance coverage, or level of education) also vary by residence—e.g., rural people have lower incomes, are less likely to have medical insurance, and have less schooling. As a consequence, when differences in health are observed among people living in different sized communities, we have difficulty knowing how much of the variation is due to life in those different settings and how much is due to these other factors that covary with residence.

Only a small number of studies have attempted to control for other variables when looking at the relationship between area of residence and health indicators among a sample of elders. For example, as described previously in this section, Cutler and Coward (1988) reported differences by residence in the total number of medical conditions, in three indicators of daily functioning (i.e., ADLs, IADLs, and functional limitations), and in perceived health status. That research, however, probed beyond this surface difference and used a multivariate analysis in order to isolate that portion of the variance that could be attributed to residence directly. As depicted in Figure 1, the differences for ADLs and IADLs disappeared when controls for sex, living arrangement, age, and education were introduced. In other words, one or more of the background or demographic variables that were used as controls accounted for *all* of the differences that were being observed—residence per se was not a significant contributor. In contrast, for the remaining three health measures (number of medical conditions, functional limitations, and perceived health), all of the variance could not be explained by the control variables, and, as a consequence, residence exerted a significant independent effect in these cases.

### What Residential Differences in Population Characteristics Might Have the Greatest Effect on the Health of Elders?

Historically, rural America has been described as an idyllic environment, free of the problems of urban living. By extension, rural residents, including the elderly, were almost universally characterized as individuals living the good life. Recent research suggests, however, that the rural elderly are sometimes disadvantaged in sociodemographic comparisons with their urban counterparts and that there is a great deal of diversity in the characteristics of rural residents. Identifying residential differences in population characteristics is important for health care providers and planners because many of these characteristics are also associated with health and access to health services.

In the sections that follow, we briefly review rural-urban differences in four of the most significant sociodemographic influences on the health of elders: race, poverty, marital status, and age.

**Race, Ethnicity, and Culture.** These three population characteristics are important factors for health care providers to consider because minority status has been associated with poorer health and reduced health and human service utilization (Braithwaite & Taylor, 1992). In certain rural areas, minorities compose a significant proportion of the overall population. For example, in rural areas of the South, blacks constitute a large segment of the elderly. In a similar manner, in some parts of the Great Plains and the Southwest, Native American elders represent a large potential clientele, as do Hispanics in the Southwest and West. Beyond these commonly recognized minorities, rural areas often serve as enclaves for smaller groups—the Amish in Pennsylvania, Filipinos in California, Vietnamese in Texas and Louisiana, and Haitians in Florida. Rural America is not solely white—it is, instead, a mosaic of colors, languages, and cultures. As a consequence, when attempting to understand the health of rural America, such racial, ethnic, and cultural variations must be taken into account.

*Figure 1.* **The Effect of Controlling for Key Sociodemographic Characteristics When Examining the Relationship between Residence and Selected Health Status Indicators**

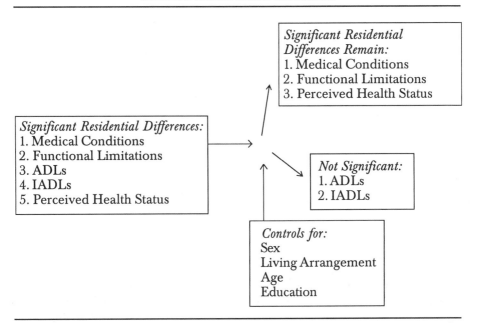

Adapted with permission from "Residence Differences in the Health Status of Elders," by S. J. Cutler and R. T. Coward, 1988. *Journal of Rural Health, 4*(3), pp. 11-26.

**Poverty.** Poverty is also associated with poorer health among the elderly and with the decreased use of formal services (Kingston, Hirshorn, & Cornman, 1986). In 1985, the overall poverty rate was 11.3%, but the rate for persons over age 65 was 12.6% (U.S. Senate Special Committee on Aging, 1987). Historically, poverty rates have been higher among the rural elderly compared with their urban counterparts. In fact, the interaction of age and residence combines to produce poverty rates that are particularly high. Some researchers suggest that as many as 50% of the elderly with income levels below the poverty level live in small towns and rural areas (Glasgow & Beale, 1985). Looked at another way, in 1985, the median incomes of older farm and nonfarm families were, respectively, 71% and 65% of that of older urban families (U.S. Senate Special Committee on Aging, 1987).

**Marital Status.** Marital status is an important indicator of the availability of informal resources. Many millions of older, disabled persons, both male and female, are cared for primarily by their spouses (Coward, Horne, & Dwyer, 1992). Analyses of the 1980 census reveal residential differences in the marital status and household composition of elders (Coward, Cutler, & Schmidt, 1988). Elderly rural farm residents, for example, were much more likely to be married (69.7%), compared with rural nonfarm (59.3%) and central city elders (47.8%). On the other hand, they were less likely to be widowed (22.6% versus 32.6% and 38.1% for rural nonfarm and central city elders, respectively) or to live alone (16.5% versus 26.5% and 33.6% for rural nonfarm and central city elders, respectively).

Residence differences in marital status by gender were even more revealing. Data from the 1980 census indicate that the proportions of married elderly males is essentially the same across residential categories (ranging from 80.6% for males on rural farms to 72.1% among central city males), but the differences for females are substantial (ranging from 58.2% among females on rural farms to 32.7% for central city females) (Coward, Cutler, & Schmidt, 1988).

**Age.** Age is the final personal characteristic to be considered because levels of impairment and the need for formal services increase with age (Manton & Soldo, 1985). In 1980, greater proportions of both farm and nonfarm rural elders were 65 to 74 years of age, compared with their counterparts in more urbanized environments (Clifford, Heaton, Voss, & Fuguitt, 1985). Conversely, central cities had the highest percentage of elders over 80 years of age. These age differences also help to explain some of the differences in other characteristics which have been observed among elders across areas of residence. For example, residential differences in marital status are substantially reduced at the upper age categories. The difference between rural farm and central city females who are married at ages 65 to 74, for example, is nearly 30%, but this difference declines to 18.6% among those age 75 to 84 and falls still further to only 4.3% among women age 85 or over (Coward, Cutler, & Schmidt, 1988).

## Do These Differences Affect How Long Older Persons from Rural Areas Live?

We are not sure. Comparisons between rural and urban populations, in general, have indicated that residents of small towns and rural communities have higher crude death rates. However, like earlier conclusions in this section, the residential differences in crude death rates have been largely a result of other factors that covary with residence (like age, race, and sex) (Miller, Stokes, & Clifford, 1987).

With regard to the specific mortality patterns of elders, we have no solid information. Some work has been done to explore mortality rates among the elderly, but the work has not included residential comparisons. And, as cited previously, some research has examined residential comparisons, but that work has not concentrated exclusively on the elderly. As a consequence, we are left to wonder about the specific mortality rates of rural elders as compared with their urban peers.

## If Many of the Differences in Health between Rural and Urban Elders Are Due Not to Residence, but to Other Factors that Covary with Residence, Can We Ignore Rurality as a Factor in Health Planning?

No. From a planning and advocacy perspective, residence offers an easy means of aggregating the differential distribution of a range of health risks. In some ways, it is a convenient marker or proxy for a collection of interrelated factors that appear to covary in unison.

Residence and rurality remain important dimensions of policy and planning because, ultimately, the location of health services must be thought of in geographic terms—i.e., services must be located in a particular place. At this most fundamental level, residence is a critical indicator for health services planning.

Once the location of a service is determined, however, the focus of planning shifts to deciding what services will be offered. In this context, the causes of sickness and disability become the primary issues for health care planners and direct service providers. Residence *per se* may recede as an important element of planning, and those characteristics that directly predict illness (like age, poverty, and gender) should assume greater importance.

Finally, once the "where" and the "what" of services have been decided, the question of "how" emerges—i.e., how the health services will be delivered. In this context, the issue of residence again becomes meaningful. Clearly, the physical and social contexts that together form a community—e.g., its topography; its industry, employment patterns, and economy; its health care infrastructure and manpower; its housing stock; and its land use—will all, in concert, dictate what can and cannot be done.

## Access to Health and Human Services for the Rural Elderly

In this final section of the chapter, we examine residential differences in the availability and use of health and human services. Although uncertainty exists about the precise magnitude and etiology of residential differences in the health status of older persons there is no doubt that rural elders have access to a smaller number, and narrower range, of formal services (Coward & Cutler, 1989). Indeed, deficits in the health care system for rural elders have been documented among in-home services (Nelson, in press), community-based services (Krout, in press), ambulatory-care services (Wallace & Colsher, in press), and institutionalized services (Shaughnessy, in press).

### Do Rural Elders Use Formal Health and Human Services as Much as Their Urban Counterparts?

Most comparisons of service use have found that elders from small towns and rural communities are less apt than their urban counterparts to use formal service providers (Coward, Cutler, & Mullens, 1990; Krout, 1986). This does not mean that no rural elders are using formal services, only that at any one point in time a smaller percentage of rural elders use them when compared with elders who live in more urban and suburban environments. Indeed, there is some recent research which suggests that even when you are able to hold constant the influence of other variables (e.g., the health of the individual or the composition of the household in which the person is living), rural elders are still less likely to receive a service from a formal agency or provider (Coward & Dwyer, 1991).

This pattern of lower use is not true, however, for every single community service nor for all subgroups of elders. For example, research has indicated that a higher proportion of rural elders attend senior citizen centers than do elders who live in large cities or the suburbs (Krout, Cutler, & Coward, 1990). Yet rural elders who live alone have service utilization patterns that are indistinguishable from their counterparts who live alone in more urban settings (Coward, Lee, Dwyer, & Seccombe, 1992). But, in each of these cases, these patterns tend to be exceptions to the rule. In general, elders who live in small towns and rural communities do not use formal health and human services to the same degree as their more urban peers.

### Do Rural Elders Have the Same Access to Formal Services as Their Urban Counterparts?

No. One reason that rural elders do not use formal services as often as their urban counterparts may be that they do not have as many services available to them. As one 74-year-old Vermonter commented, "I don't use them, because they're not there!"

In most rural communities, with some notable exceptions, elders simply do not have as many or as large a range of formal services available for them to use (Krout, 1986; Nelson, 1980, 1983). Although we witnessed important improvements in the number of services that were available to rural elders during the 1980s, these advances did not eliminate completely the significant differences that exist between rural and urban social networks (Coward & Rathbone-McCuan, 1985).

In fact, one comparison of the services available in different-sized places across the nation found that the most significant differences that remained between rural and urban social service networks were in those services most needed by frail, severely impaired older persons who were struggling to maintain their independent living status in the community (Nelson, 1983). Thus, some of the biggest gaps between rural and urban social service networks are found in services like adult daycare, homemaker-chore services, hospice and respite programs, foster care, and home health nursing. Indeed, some have suggested that, because of the deficiencies in these vital services for the home-bound elderly, rural older people may be at greater risk of institutionalization or premature institutionalization. In fact, there is some scanty, but nevertheless disturbing, evidence that rural elders who enter nursing homes are younger and less disabled than their urban counterparts (Greene, 1984).

### Are Services Accessible?

Accessibility is a problem that goes beyond the simple availability of services. That is, even if a service is available in a rural area, elders may not be able to get to it. In that sense, distance and transportation are twin, interrelated obstacles to the use of services by rural elders. Indeed, one author has insisted that distance "represents the most formidable barrier to the development of programs for rural areas," arguing that it "complicates the delivery of every service" (Parkinson, 1981, p. 227).

In many rural areas, the effects of distance are compounded by harsh weather, poor road conditions, and the absence of public transportation. Nevertheless, even though distance is a major determinant of accessibility, it is not the only factor that contributes to determining whether a service is considered accessible. Service planners and providers, when judging the overall accessibility of a program, must also consider the public's knowledge of a service, the standards that are used to determine if a client is eligible, the cost of services, psychological constraints that influence the use of a service (like the stigma attached to seeking mental health services), and administrative practices that may be seen by rural residents as meddlesome and intrusive.

### Is It True that Rural Elders Do Not Need the Same Level of Formal Services Because They Have Access To Stronger Family Networks?

Little evidence supports this popular, and widely accepted, notion that rural elders have family networks that are stronger and more able to respond to their needs than urban elders (Lee & Cassidy, 1985). Rural families are not weaker or less responsive than urban families; they are just not particularly different in this regard. In truth, regardless of the type of community in which an elder lives, family members are the main source of aid and assistance in times of need (Coward, Cutler, & Mullens, 1990).

In some aspects of family life, however, rural elders do seem to have an advantage. For example, rural elders may experience a slight advantage with regard to the availability of both spouses and adult children. This greater availability of spouses and children may be particularly critical for elders with impairments, because those family members are the most frequently used sources of personal care and assistance when an elder is disabled (Coward, Horne, & Dwyer, 1992). For example, we know that spouses are often the "first line of defense" in the lives of elders. That is, an available and able spouse is often the first person to whom an elder turns in times of need. In that regard, rural elders do seem to experience a slight advantage over their urban counterparts because they are more likely to have a marital partner (Coward, Cutler, & Schmidt, 1988).

Two observations about these marital differences need to be mentioned, however, to help place them in perspective. First, the rural-urban differences are more pronounced for women than for men—that is, a higher proportion of rural women have husbands, whereas, among men, approximately equal percentages have wives. Second, the rural-urban difference in the availability of marital partners disappears by age 85. Thus, any advantage that rural elders might have is no longer present among the oldest, who are most apt to need help and assistance with the activities of daily living.

In a similar manner, research has demonstrated residential differences in the availability of adult children (Lee, Dwyer, & Coward, 1990). However, such differences do not vary systematically along a rural-urban continuum. Specifically, older residents of large cities are more likely to live with children than elders from any other place. Large-city and farm residents are also more likely than small-city or rural nonfarm residents to live near children (i.e., at least one child who was as close as a 30-minute drive from the elder). Thus, to the degree that proximity improves the ability of children to be of help to their parents, important differences do seem to exist between rural and urban older people.

### Do Rural Elders Depend More Heavily on Help from Family Members than Urban Elders?

One piece of evidence which is often used to defend the notion that rural families are stronger is the fact that more rural elders depend on family members as sources of aid. That is, research has indicated that a greater proportion of rural elders are likely to be dependent *exclusively* on family members for the help they receive—whereas, more urban elders will be using formal service providers (Coward, Cutler, & Mullens, 1990; Coward & Dwyer, 1991).

The difficulty with this argument is that we do not know which came first. Do rural elders use fewer formal services because their family systems are stronger? Or do rural elders depend more heavily on family members because the formal service network available to them is deficient and, thus, they have nowhere else to turn?

The first interpretation emerges from a conceptualization of the relationship between formal and informal networks as hierarchical—that is, that formal service providers are used only after the resources of the family network have been exhausted. The second interpretation argues for a more complementary relationship between formal and informal providers—one that hinges on maximizing the effectiveness of each through coordination and case management. Unfortunately, the latter only works where there are formal providers with which to share the workload and formal services to manage it. In some rural areas, elders and families do not have that choice.

In reality, we do not have sufficient evidence to choose between these two competing interpretations, even though their implications for public policy are quite different.

### Do Rural Elders Have Less Access to Formal Health Care Providers than Do Urban Elders?

Comparisons of physician distributions have long shown a rural–urban difference. In 1986, nonmetropolitan areas had 44% fewer physicians, medical doctors (MDs), and doctors of osteopathy (DOs) per 100,000 residents than did metropolitan areas (Hicks, 1990). Despite some predictions of a "physician glut" during the 1980s (which was expected to help small towns because some physicians would practice in such places), nonmetropolitan areas have actually fallen further behind. Between 1983 and 1986, the number of metropolitan physicians increased 11.0%, while the number of nonmetropolitan physicians increased only 3.5% (Hicks, 1990).

In addition, comparisons of overall physician supply mask significant differences in the make-up of the physician pool. In 1986, DOs accounted for only 4.5% of the total physician supply in the United States, but they represented 20.3% of all nonmetropolitan physicians. Indeed, between 1983 and 1986, DOs accounted for 92% of the increase in nonmetropolitan area physicians (Hicks, 1990, p. 488).

### Do Rural Elders Have Access to Home Health Services?

Once again, rural elders appear to be disadvantaged, compared with their urban counterparts. In general, studies have found that rural elders are less likely to have access to home health services, and, where available, the range of services offered is narrower (Nelson, in press).

This conclusion, however, must be taken with a large grain of salt. Frankly, we do not have good information on such comparisons. Studies to date have either focused on one particular sector of the aging network, e.g., services provided through Area Agencies on Aging (AAA), or on one particular service, e.g., visiting nurses. As a consequence, we have not yet grasped the whole picture (i.e., private and public sources of home health care that cross a full range of services). Nevertheless, in no comparisons to date have rural elders, as a group, been shown to have an advantage over urban elders–although there are reports of individual small towns and rural communities with impressive arrays of in-home services.

### Do Rural Elders Have Access to Hospitals?

The news is not good here, either. First of all, there are fewer hospital beds per capita in small towns and rural communities (Moscovice & Rosenblatt, 1985). Indeed, a comparison of the number of hospital beds with the number of elders in an area shows that large metropolitan areas have 67% more hospital beds per 1,000 elders than do small nonmetropolitan areas. Furthermore, many of the hospital beds that do exist in rural America are in danger of being lost. The U.S. Congressional Research Service found that, between 1981 and 1988, 190 rural hospitals closed (Merlis, 1989).

In addition, we must remember that rural hospitals are different from urban ones–they are not simply scalded-down versions of their urban cousins (Hart, Amundson, & Rosenblatt, 1990). On average, rural hospitals have fewer beds (more than 1,000 rural hospitals have fewer than 50 beds); operate older facilities; have lower occupancy rates; and are more dependent on Medicare reimbursement as a source of revenue. As a result, although rural hospitals are often the source of core medical services for their communities, they provide services of relatively low complexity.

A number of factors, all working in combination, have recently threatened the rural hospital (Mick & Morlock, 1990). Foremost among them are: (1) low profit margins relative to urban hospitals; (2) aging facilities in need of renovation; (3) low occupancy rates and relatively wide fluctuations in occupancy over short periods of time; (4) the vulnerability of small rural hospitals due to physician relocation; (5) hospital administrators and managers who do not have as much training as their urban counterparts and who change jobs more frequently; (6) disproportionate uncompensated care burdens; (7) some facilities which are geographically isolated and inaccessible; and (8) the siphoning off of patients by urban hospitals through their rural primary care referral centers.

Finally, studies by the National Center for Health Services Research have indicated that rural elders (over the age of 75) are much more dependent on their local facilities when they require hospitalization (Hogan, 1988). Severely ill young rural residents (including persons aged 65-74) are much more likely to bypass their local facility and seek treatment in urban hospitals or in rural referral center hospitals (i.e., hospitals which have qualified for Medicare rural referral center status under criteria used by the Health Care Financing Administration). For the oldest residents, however, this is not the pattern. Instead, they are much more likely to rely on their local, rural hospital for the care they need. As a consequence, the changes that are occurring in rural hospitals—in terms of their existence or in the nature of their operations—have tremendous implications for our oldest residents.

### Do Rural Elders Have Access to Nursing Home Beds?

With respect to the availability of nursing home beds, there is mixed information. On the one hand, there is some evidence, and certainly a popular belief, that rural elders have less access to nursing home beds than urban elders. For example, using information from the Area Resource Files of the Bureau of Health Manpower (a source which contains information on the health manpower and resources available in each county in the United States), Coward (1991) has reported that large metropolitan areas have 23% more nursing home beds per 1,000 elders than small nonmetropolitan areas. But at the same time, those same analyses showed that the highest ratios of nursing home beds to elders were found in large nonmetropolitan counties. Describing this contradiction, Wiener (1987) has written that:

> Although there is a perception of shortages of nursing home care in rural areas, it should be noted that rural states have some of the highest ratios of nursing home beds to populations in the country. For example, compared with a national average of 57.5 beds per 1,000 people age 65 and over in 1980, predominantly rural South Dakota had 94.2 beds per 1,000 elderly, Iowa had 86.4, Kansas had 81.5 and Colorado had 69.4. These are among the highest nursing home bed ratios in the country. (p. 22)

Despite the lack of solid, irrefutable evidence of the relative advantage or disadvantage of rural elders and their families, the general perception of a rural shortage (and its certainty in some rural communities) has precipitated a major innovation in the delivery of skilled nursing care—the development of so-called "swing-beds" (Shaughnessy, 1991). The swing-bed concept was introduced to permit small rural hospitals in communities with a frequent excess of acute care beds and a scarcity of nursing home beds to use their beds interchangeably to provide either acute care or nursing home care. This approach has two advantages: it provides services to elders in their own community (thus keeping them nearer their natural caregiving network of family and friends), and it avoids the significant costs of constructing new nursing home beds.

The swing-bed concept was first initiated in the early 1970s in 25 hospitals in Utah, but it soon expanded to all regions of the nation. By July 1985, approximately 700 small hospitals in 30 states were certified to provide swing-bed services, or about four out of every ten eligible rural hospitals. Although information on the success and impact of this alternative form of care is continuing to emerge, we do not know much about where, when, and for whom swing-bed care is most effective and most efficient.

## Do Rural Elders Have Access to Other Community Services?

The Older Americans Act funds a wide range of community services for persons over the age of 60 through the nationwide system of Area Agencies on Aging (AAA). Unfortunately, the precise set of services which are available to any one elder, through this network, is highly variable among communities. Thus, 77-year-old Mrs. Elizabeth Miller, who lives in Round Mountain, Nevada, a small town of about 400 located 140 miles east of Carson City, has a different set of services available to her as a result of the Older Americans Act than does 81-year-old Mrs. Janet Sitefield, who lives in Cherry Hill, New Jersey, a Philadelphia suburb with a population of approximately 70,000.

Indeed, Krout (1991), who surveyed a sample of AAAs in 1987-1988, found wide variability in the services offered through this network. He observed that among the most rural AAAs in his sample:

> 33% indicated that adult day-care was not available; 18% reported no respite care; 20% no guardianship; 58% indicated adult day-care and respite services were extremely limited; and 38% said transportation was extremely limited. (p. 18)

## To What Extent Do Rural Elders Use Mental Health Services?

To begin with, elders, regardless of where they live, do not use formal mental health services in proportion to their representation in the general population. Although elders represent approximately 12% of the overall population, they account for a much smaller percentage of the people who use formal mental health services. Similarly, people who live in small towns and rural communities do not use formal mental health services to the same degree that urban and suburban people do (even though some investigators have argued that rural areas suffer from higher rates of psychopathology). At the juncture of these two trends are the rural elderly—and, as a consequence, the mental health service utilization rates of rural elders are among the lowest of any subpopulation in the country.

Once again, we are faced with the dilemma of not knowing to what degree these lower utilization rates are due to the resistance of rural elders to seeking formal help with personal problems or to the simple absence of services. Clearly the latter is true, there are fewer services available. Whereas almost two-thirds of metropolitan counties (63.4%) have inpatient psychiatric services, less than 13% of the nonmetropolitan counties have such services available to their residents (Wagenfeld, 1990). Indeed, Wagenfeld (1990) has suggested that "nonmetropolitan counties with [inpatient psychiatric] services were likely to be those with urban population centers. Services were virtually nonexistent in the most rural and isolated metropolitan counties" (p. 515).

One innovation that has attempted to bring more mental health services to rural people, and to make them more palatable to rural people, is the linking of the mental health and primary health sectors. In the early 1980s, 100 primary health care clinics, funded by the Bureau of Community Health Services, were given grants by the National Institute of Mental Health to establish linkages with mental health facilities. Although a number of different strategies were tried, evaluations found that the direct provision of mental health and consultation services in the primary care centers was a more effective mechanism of linkage than referrals to a separate mental health facility (Burns, Burke, & Ozarin, 1983). The investigators also suggested that shared funding between the health and mental health centers was important to success, as were certain characteristics of the linkage worker. They also said that transportation and space were factors in a thriving program. No negative consequences were reported.

Thus, we have successful models to follow in order to improve mental health services for rural people. Unfortunately, this does not appear to be a major health priority of state or federal governments.

## The Future of Health Services for Rural Elders

The major health care problems facing the rural elderly in the 1990s can be divided into two primary categories: (1) issues of access and availability, and (2) issues of quality of care. First and foremost is a simple need to improve the number and variety of services which are available to rural elders and their families as they attempt to cope with changing health needs. In general, the rural health system for elders is acutely deficient in at least three major categories of services: (1) the availability and accessibility of primary-care physicians (who are the linchpin of our current system of health care for elders); (2) the availability and accessibility of home health services; and (3) the availability and accessibility of affordable health care services. Unless improvements are made in each of these three areas, rural elders and their families will continue to be constrained in their choices of health care, and our system will continue to place older persons from small towns and rural communities at greater risk of early institutionalization, poorer health status, or a diminished quality of life.

In addition, when and where services *are* available, we face the challenge of ensuring that rural services are "the best that they can be" (to paraphrase a U.S. Army slogan). In that context, new innovations in rural health care (meant to maintain or improve service access to rural residents) must be carefully monitored to ensure that rural people are not being shortchanged with inferior quality of service. As the American health care system continues to evolve, newly emerging strategies for health care delivery must be watched carefully to be sure that the search for financially viable organizational structures does not have deleterious, latent consequences for the health of rural people, particularly older rural residents.

## References

Braithwaite, R. L., & Taylor, S. E. (Eds.). (1992). *Health issues in the black community*. San Francisco: Jossey-Bass.

Burns, B. J., Burke, J. D., & Ozarin, L. D. (1983). Linking health and mental health services in rural areas. *International Journal of Mental Health, 12*(1-2), 130-143.

Clifford, W. B., Heaton, T. B., Voss, P. R., & Fuguitt, G. V. (1985). The rural elderly in demographic perspective. In R. T. Coward & G. R. Lee (Eds.), *The elderly in rural society* (pp. 25-55). New York: Springer.

Coward, R. T. (1991). Key facts about rural elders. *Perspectives on Aging, 20*(1), 10-11.

Coward, R. T., & Cutler, S. J. (1988). The concept of a continuum of residence: Comparing activities of daily living among the elderly. *Journal of Rural Studies, 4*(2), 159-168.

Coward, R. T., & Cutler, S. J. (1989). Informal and formal health care systems for the rural elderly. *Journal of Health Services Research, 23*(6), 785-806.

Coward, R. T., Cutler, S. J., & Mullens, R. A. (1990). Residential differences in the composition of the helping networks of impaired elders. *Family Relations, 39,* 44-50.

Coward, R. T., Cutler, S. J., & Schmidt, F. E. (1988). Residential differences in marital status and household type among the elderly. In R. Marotz-Baden, C. B. Hennon, & T. H. Brubaker (Eds.), *Families in rural America: Stress, adaptation and revitalization* (pp. 104-115). St. Paul, MN: The National Council on Family Relations.

Coward, R. T., & Dwyer, J. W. (1991). A longitudinal study of residential differences in the composition of the helping networks of impaired elders. *Journal of Aging Studies, 5*(4), 391-407.

Coward, R. T., Horne, C., & Dwyer, J. W. (1992). Demographic perspectives on family caregiving. In J. W. Dwyer & R. T. Coward (Eds.). *Gender, families, and elder care* (pp. 18-33). Newbury Park, CA: Sage.

Coward, R. T., Lee, G. R., Dwyer, J. W., & Seccombe, K. (1992). *Rural elders living alone*. Washington, DC: American Association of Retired Persons.

Coward, R. T., Miller, M. K., & Dwyer, J. W. (1992). The role of residence in explaining variation in reported health and dysfunction of the elderly in the United States. In National Rural Health Association (Eds.), *Study of models to meet rural health care needs through mobilization of health professions education and services resources* (pp. 529-582). Kansas City, MO: National Rural Health Association. (Prepared under contract HRSA-240-89-0037)

Coward, R. T., & Rathbone-McCuan, E. (1985). The development and delivery of human services for the rural elderly. In R. T. Coward & G. R. Lee (Eds.), *The elderly in rural society*. New York: Springer.

Cutler, S. J., & Coward, R. T. (1988). Residence differences in the health status of elders. *Journal of Rural Health, 4*(3), 11-26.

Dwyer, J. W., Lee, G. R., & Coward, R. T. (1990). The health status, health services utilization, and support networks of the rural elderly: A decade review. *The Journal of Rural Health, 6*(4),379-398.

Glasgow, N., & Beale, C. (1985). Rural elderly in demographic perspective. *Rural Development Perspectives, 2*(1), 22-26.

Greene, V. L. (1984). Premature institutionalization among the rural elderly in Arizona. *Public Health Reports, 99*(1), 58-63.

Hart, L. G., Amundson, B. A., & Rosenblatt, R. A. (1990). Is there a role for the small rural hospital? *Journal of Rural Health, 6*(2), 101-118.

Hewitt, M. (1989). *Defining rural areas: Impact on health care policy and research.* Washington, DC: U.S. Government Printing Office.

Hicks, L. L. (1990). Availability and accessibility of rural health care. *The Journal of Rural Health, 6*(4), 485-505.

Hogan, C. (1988). Patterns of travel for rural individuals hospitalized in New York State: Relationships between distance, destination, and case mix. *The Journal of Rural Health, 4*(2), 29-41.

Katz, S., Ford, A. B., Moskowitz, R. W., Jackson, B. A., & Jaffee, M. W. (1963). Studies of illness in the aged, the index of ADL: A standardized measure of biological and psychosocial function. *Journal of the American Medical Association, 185,* 94-101.

Kingston, E. R., Hirshorn, B. A., & Cornman, J. M. (1986). *Ties that bind: The interdependence of generations.* Washington, DC: Seven Locks Press.

Krout, J. A. (1986). *The aged in rural America.* New York: Greenwood Press.

Krout, J. A. (1991). Rural area agencies on aging: An overview of activities and policy issues. *Journal of Aging Studies, 5*(4), 409-424.

Krout, J. A. (in press), Rural aging community-based services. In R. T. Coward, C. Neil Bull, G. Kukulka, & J. A. Galliher (Eds.), *Health services for rural elders.* New York: Springer.

Krout, J. A., Cutler, S. J., & Coward, R. T. (1990). Correlates of senior center participation: A national analysis. *The Gerontologist, 30*(1), 72-79.

Lee, G. R., & Cassidy, M. L. (1985). Family and kin relations of the rural elderly. In R. T. Coward & G. R. Lee (Eds.), *The elderly in rural society* (pp. 151-169). New York: Springer.

Lee, G. R., Dwyer, J. W., & Coward, R. T. (1990). Residential location and proximity to children among the impaired elderly. *Rural Sociology, 55*(4), 579-589.

Manton, K., & Soldo, B. (1985). Dynamics of health changes in the oldest old: New perspectives and evidence. *Milbank Memorial Fund Quarterly, 63,* 206-285.

Merlis, M. (1989). *Rural hospitals.* Washington, DC: U.S. Congressional Research Service.

Mick, S. S., & Morlock, L. L. (1990). America's rural hospitals: A selective review of 1980S research. *The Journal of Rural Health, 6*(4), 437-466.

Miller, M. K., Stokes, C. S., & Clifford, W. B. (1987). A comparison of the rural-urban mortality differential for deaths from all causes, cardiovascular disease and cancer. *The Journal of Rural Health, 3*(2), 23-34.

Moscovice, I. S., & Rosenblatt, R. A. (1985). A prognosis for the rural hospital: Part I, What is the role of the rural hospital? *The Journal of Rural Health, 1*(1), 29-40.

Nelson, G. M. (1980). Social services to the urban and rural aged: The experience of area agencies on aging. *The Gerontologist, 20*(2), 200-207.

Nelson, G. M. (1983). A comparison of Title XX services to the urban and rural elderly. *Journal of Gerontological Social Work, 6*(1), 3-23.

Nelson, G. M. (in press), In-home services for rural elders. In R. T. Coward, C. Neil Bull, G. Kukulka, & J. A. Galliher (Eds.). *Health services for rural elders.* New York: Springer.

Palmore, E. (1983-1984). Health care needs of the rural elderly. *International Journal of Aging and Human Development, 18*(1), 39-45.

Parkinson, L. (1981). Improving the delivery of health services to the rural elderly: A policy perspective. In P. K. H. Kim and C. P. Wilson (Eds.), *Toward mental health of the rural elderly* (pp. 223-239). Washington, DC: University Press of America.

Shaughnessy, P. W. (1991). *Shaping policy for long-term care: Learning from the effectiveness of hospital swing-beds.* Ann Arbor, MI: Health Administration Press.

Shaughnessy, P. W. (in press), Changing institutional long-term care to improve health care in rural communities. In R. T. Coward, C. Neil Bull, G. Kukulka, & J. A. Galliher (Eds.), *Health services for rural elders.* New York: Springer.

U.S. Senate Special Committee on Aging. (1987). *Developments in aging, 1986.* Washington, DC: U.S. Government Printing Office.

U.S. Senate Special Committee on Aging. (1992). *Common beliefs about the rural elderly: Myth or fact?* Washington, DC: U.S. Government Printing Office.

Wagenfeld, M. O. (1990). Mental health and rural America: A decade review. *The Journal of Rural Health, 6*(4), 507-522.

Wallace, R. B., & Colsher, P. L. (in press), Improving ambulatory and acute care services for the rural elderly: Current solutions, research, and policy directions. In R. T. Coward, C. Neil Bull, G. Kukulka, & J. A. Galliher (Eds.), *Health services for rural elders.* New York: Springer.

# 16

## Crossing Cultural and Geographic Boundaries: Teaching Social Work Courses in Aboriginal Outreach Programs

by Michael Kim Zapf

Our hosts have selected "Crossing Boundaries through Outreach and Exchange" as the theme for the 1995 National Institute on Social Work and Human Services in the Rural Environment. Based on my own experiences as an instructor in outreach and campus-based social work programs, this paper examines the two themes of "outreach" and "exchange" and their application in the design and delivery of outreach social work courses in Aboriginal communities.

The paper begins with background comments on terminology and scope of the discussion prior to addressing the Institute's theme of "outreach." An exploration of the contract between the educational institution and the Aboriginal community is followed by consideration of specific issues encountered by instructors in outreach programs. Questions are raised about the appropriateness of distance education technologies in such outreach endeavors. The paper then considers the Institute's second theme of "exchange," with reflections on efforts to incorporate Aboriginal content into the central campus program.

### Background

It may be helpful for the reader if I begin with a brief explanation of the terminology I have chosen for this paper. Anyone writing in the general area of cross-cultural relations and the original inhabitants of North America must make a choice between competing and confusing labels. My selection of the term "Aboriginal" for this paper reflects the reality and preferences of the region in which I live. "Native" has become an ambiguous and contentious label in this area where descendants of the

Reprinted from *Human Services in the Rural Environment* (Spring/Summer 1995), with permission of the Eastern Washington University School of Social Work and Human Services.

early European immigrants may consider themselves to be "native Canadians" after several generations have been born in this country. "First Nations" and "American Indian" are terms that can exclude the large Metis group who are represented in the population and all of the outreach programs where I have taught.

I also determined to present this discussion in the first person rather than the conventional academic third-person voice. Many of the teaching adaptations I will discuss focus on learning to teach in a more subjective manner, teaching from my story. I remain consistent in this approach if I also write of those experiences in the first person.

The observations and examples discussed in this paper derive from my experience as an instructor in two Aboriginal outreach social work education programs contracted for on-site course delivery in northern Alberta:

1. The University of Calgary Faculty of Social Work Aboriginal BSW Program in Spruce Grove (contract with the Yellowhead Tribal Council); and

2. The Grant MacEwan Community College Social Work Outreach Program in High Level (contract with the High Level Tribal Council).

Because my observations and arguments apply to social work education outreach programs at both the community college and university levels, I have deliberately used the word "credential" rather than "degree" or "diploma."

While I have attempted to make appropriate reference to the developing literature on Indian education and distance learning, I want to emphasize that the material presented here is based on my experiences with specific social work outreach education programs in specific Aboriginal communities. These experiences are not intended as a blueprint to be replicated intact in other Aboriginal communities. I cannot tell anyone what must be done in their programs in other parts of the continent with different traditions and local circumstances. What I can do is offer some reflections from my experiences, connect those with the literature, and hope my observations will have some value for those who are designing and delivering similar programs in their own region.

## Contracts

Most urban-based social work programs feature a simple contract between the institution and the individual student who is accepted into the program. The student registers and pays a fee; the school agrees to provide certain courses and resources in a particular sequence leading to the desired credential. While the school commits to making accessible the opportunity to achieve the credential, the individual student is still responsible for his or her own engagement in the learning process. Failure to complete course requirements usually results in a failing grade with the subsequent options of repeating the course later or withdrawing from the program.

In Aboriginal outreach programs, the school–student contract is affected by the addition of another party to the negotiations (Zapf, 1993a). In effect, there is another client. Most of the time, a local organization (Tribal Council or Regional Council) contracts with the school to offer the social work program on a one-time basis for a particular cohort of students in their constituency. Typically these potential students are already community resource persons within the local social service network, either formally employed or informal caregivers. Through their Council, the Aboriginal community in effect is buying a program to upgrade their current workers and train a resource pool for the future. The community administrators and the school administrators negotiate a contract for the sale and purchase of the social work program as a package.

Obviously, the local Council cannot simply purchase the social work credential for their constituents; the school is selling an opportunity not a credential. Individual instructors must still assess students and apply standards to maintain the integrity of the credential and the profession. In the Aboriginal outreach context, however, there may be complications arising from the contract because the community is now in the picture as a client.

Ryan (1987) refers to the "fierce claims of ownership" between the host community and the educational institution "which funds and otherwise makes possible the program in the first place" (p. 72). Instructors in Aboriginal outreach programs, according to Ryan, are expected to satisfy the requirements of both groups: meeting the needs and expectations of the local community while maintaining the academic standards of the institution. DeMontigny (1992) argued that the cultural values of Aboriginal social work students are actually violated by the grading, competition, probing, and doubt inherent in conventional Western approaches to social work education. In the outreach programs where I have taught, I have found that this tension or conflict can have major implications at the level of the instructor and the students in the classroom. Some of the issues that arise and subsequent adaptations for course delivery will be explored in the next section.

## Couse Delivery Issues and Adaptations

### Course Outlines

In most urban campus-based academic programs, instructors prepare a Course Outline that is distributed to students during the first class. By this process, the students are told the course objectives, the resources they are required to use, and the basis on which they will be evaluated (Fox & Ziska, 1989). All of this structure has been worked out by the instructor in advance.

Social work courses differ from many other academic disciplines in that the material is context sensitive. Since our focus is on the person-environment interaction, the environment or context is crucial. Chemistry can be chemistry anywhere; algebra is algebra anywhere. Yet effective social work practice can look very different in different settings. Urban-based instructors may have enough familiarity with the social problems, issues, and resources in their community to design appropriate course outlines for students who will participate in on-campus classes and urban field placements; however, the instructor who is contracted to deliver a course in an Aboriginal outreach program cannot simply transfer that same course outline. He or she must first spend time with the students and community resource persons to develop an approach to the material that will reflect local issues and learning styles. Course Outlines in Aboriginal outreach programs tend to be a working contract in the true sense of an ongoing negotiated agreement between instructor and students with input from the host community that purchased the program.

### Grades and Standards

In most campus-based social work education programs, the instructor applies academic standards through grading practices that maintain the integrity of the credential. A student who fails a course has options such as repeating the course another term or withdrawing. Routine application of these standards, however, can be complicated in Aboriginal outreach programs.

I have already observed that the host community can purchase only the opportunity and not the credential for their students. Yet Aboriginal communities commit substantial resources toward the establishment of a local cohort social work program and they hold strong expectations about the learning opportunities that will be made available locally by the educational institution. In a sequenced outreach program where courses may be offered only once in a community, a failing grade in a prerequisite course can prevent a student from continuing on to other required courses. In effect, one failed core course can bump an outreach student out of the entire program. There may be no easy option to repeat the course next term or next year if each course is delivered only once in the community before the program leaves.

To appreciate the possible impact of these academic decisions in Aboriginal outreach programs, consider a situation where the student is a child welfare worker for the local Band and fails a first-year course that is a prerequisite for key courses offered in second year. Effectively, that student could be out of the program, unable to proceed in good standing with no opportunity to take the course over again. Is it desirable to fail the student and maintain the academic standards of the credential? Considering that this person will likely continue doing child welfare work in this community for the next twenty years, is it preferable that she be allowed to continue to have access to the special opportunity of the courses now being offered in the local community? Should this worker have the benefit of as much training as possible while it is available, or should she be dropped for failing to meet a standard of the institution? From whose perspective should these decisions be made? The community or the school? Should standards other than conventional academic criteria be applied? These questions need to be considered by those negotiating the original contract between community and school before the issues are played out at the level of instructor–student interaction in the classroom.

## Gatekeeping

Some have argued that social work faculty have a quality control responsibility as gatekeepers for the profession by screening out inappropriate students (Moore & Unwin, 1990; Peterman & Blake, 1986). In addition to grades, criteria have been proposed that include poor communication skills, inappropriate affect, and poor field performance. The role of gatekeeping is complicated in Aboriginal outreach programs. The criteria suggested are so culture-bound that I question whether a non Aboriginal outreach instructor has the perspective to make any meaningful judgment. How can a valid assessment be made of a student's communication skills in a language, culture, and context often unfamiliar to the instructor? Against whose standards will field performance be assessed, local conditions or the conventional urban-based criteria? How does a non-Aboriginal instructor assess appropriate affect in a foreign culture where verbal and non-verbal cues may not be understood, let alone the deeper cultural and historic patterns to which the community members may be reacting? Can an outside instructor presume to assess the "appropriate" response for people dealing with colonialism, addictions, and systematic devaluation?

It has been my experience that most Aboriginal outreach students in social work are not motivated by a desire to enter the profession as much as by a desire to understand the forces affecting their communities and to learn skills to help their people. Professional status may be a foreign concept in this setting. The application of culture-bound standards to screen out those who are perceived as unsuitable or unworthy to enter the profession ignores the community context of practice and could be seen as a further extension of colonialism.

## Co-Teaching

During my time with the Aboriginal outreach program in High Level, Alberta, I had the opportunity to co-teach a social work methods course with an Aboriginal instructor, Dr. Pam Colorado. Since we have both written elsewhere about this teaching experience (Colorado, 1993; Zapf 1993b, in press), I will attempt only to summarize the highlights here.

Although we had originally been hired to teach one section each of the methods course in High Level, we decided to combine the sections and teach together, giving the students both an Aboriginal and a Western perspective in the classroom at the same time. Material presented by one instructor was assessed and critiqued by the other.

The students responded very well to this approach. Having Dr. Colorado and me as models for the dialogue between the Aboriginal mind and the Western mind encouraged students to participate actively in the work. They watched us sort out differences and similarities between our two approaches, a process which was sometimes painful and sometimes very funny, in an atmosphere of trust and support.

Students told us they had previously been left to do this integration on their own. Aboriginal content had been presented by Aboriginal resource people when possible; Western content had usually been presented by non-Aboriginal instructors. Students described for us how they had learned to consciously "flip" between their Indian mind and their Western mind. The students had become quite adept at producing what was needed to pass a course from either perspective. Because the two minds seldom came together in the classroom, however, students felt split with a resulting lack of confidence in gaining proficiency in either system. Having students watch and then participate as their instructors explored these connections in the classroom was a profound learning experience for them and for us.

Each day began in a ceremonial manner with smudge, prayer, and affirmations. The first few days, Dr. Colorado led the ceremonies and taught about the circle, the directions, and respect for each other. Later, students assumed the various functions in the circle. In many ways, this tradition prepared us for our day's work. We dealt with many issues in the circle: the unfinished business from the previous day; overnight reflections and insights on our work; personal accounts of the fear, the pain, and the humor associated with our work; affirmations of the importance of our work and the value of each other. Gratitude was often expressed for the progress we were making, and appeals were made for guidance with the tasks ahead. When we were ready, we began our academic work. Most days the opening ceremony lasted about half an hour; some days much more time was needed.

We determined for this course that our theoretical focus would require examination of key concepts from both of our helping systems, with an emphasis on the bridges or connections between the two. We discovered, for example, that replacing the labels "Assessment, Implementation, Termination, and Evaluation" with "Vision and Transformation" served to connect the problem-solving process more closely with local conditions and traditional approaches to helping. Discussion of traditional concepts such as the Good Mind, Stream of Life, and the Still Quiet Place helped us explore the different approach to time, relations, and spirituality underlying the two helping models.

### Monitoring and Evaluation

Most on-campus social work courses include an evaluation component whereby students in their final class are presented with an instrument that allows them to evaluate the instructor and the learning experience. In the Aboriginal outreach co-teaching scenario just described, the course content and teaching approach were new to all of us, instructors and students. There was a need for ongoing monitoring and immediate feedback on each section of the course material; a summary evaluation conducted during the final class would not be adequate.

We gave students time to answer these questions in writing following each content section:

1. How will this be useful for me in my community?
2. What do I like most about this material?
3. What do I find most difficult or objectionable about the material?
4. Can I express these ideas in more useful words?

Dr. Colorado and I could then consider the student narratives as we developed our approach for the next section or determined to revisit material that had been difficult.

### Instructors as Counselors

It has been my experience that many Aboriginal students who want to be social workers have themselves been victimized and are engaged in a healing process of their own (often the entire community is involved in healing). While some personal development work may have preceded the social work courses, many students come to class in various stages of awareness and healing. Issues such as addictions, family violence, sexual abuse, and child welfare are not simply abstract course content areas; many of the students are or have been the victims of these experiences. Because of the limited resources available in the community for referral, the course instructor could well be the only resource person with any expertise and the class may be the only available forum for disclosure, sharing, and support related to these issues. You may be hired by the educational institution to teach these outreach courses on the basis of your expertise and credentials, but you will be a guest in the Aboriginal community and assessed for what you have to offer as a person, not just an instructor. You may be required to act as counselor and groupworker to an extent far beyond that expected of faculty members in urban campus-based programs.

### Learning Styles and Instructor Characteristics

Although there have been some attempts to characterize an Aboriginal Learning Style (Kaulback, 1984; Wauters, Bruce, Black, & Hocker, 1989), there are also arguments that this may not be a useful endeavor. The search for a single characteristic learning style could be seen as a product of the tendency in the literature to "construct generalizations about American Indian cultures and worldviews that create the impression of one unified American Indian reality" (Gross, 1995, p. 206) rather than recognizing the diversity of Aboriginal groups. More (1987) concluded in his review of the literature that "No, there is not a uniquely Indian Learning

Style" (p. 27).

In a recent study comparing the learning styles of Aboriginal and non-Aboriginal social work students in northern Alberta, Elliot (1994) found greater variation within the groups than between them. Weisenberg (1992) examined learner preferences and put forward a similar "evident conclusion that individual differences were as important as Native/ non-Native differences" (p. 82). Sawyer (1991) sums up the issue clearly:

> Native students are better served when we as instructors abandon the attempt to identify a definitive answer to the question "How do Native students learn?" for answers to the question "What teaching accommodations have proven most effective in helping Native students succeed in educational settings?" (p. 103)

From the research literature, Sawyer (1991) goes on to develop a list of suggested instructional practices that promote more effective and successful teaching in the Aboriginal classroom. These suggestions include:

- share classroom control and responsibility—negotiate a "culture of the classroom"
- reduce formal lecturing
- use experiential learning techniques
- utilize warmer and more personal teaching styles
- establish a pace and flow consistent with the students
- establish close personal relationships with the students
- become part of the community (p. 102-103)

Osborne (1989) strongly supports this last notion of connection with the local community:

> Mainstream teachers who want to deliver culturally congruent curriculum should be willing to spend considerable time in the local community learning about the culture. . . .Such preparation also needs appropriate inservice support from members of the local community so that locally appropriate curricula can be delivered in culturally sensitive ways. (p. 18)

### Time

The time factor is not a new consideration since this issue has been apparent throughout the preceding discussion, but I want to emphasize the importance of an increased time commitment in Aboriginal outreach social work education. It will take time to develop and continually renegotiate the Course Outline as I have suggested. The non-Aboriginal instructor should also allow considerable time for reflection and discussion with supportive colleagues regarding the tensions of grading and gatekeeping in an Aboriginal outreach program. Co-teaching demands a tremendous time commitment for the extensive preparation and debriefing sessions necessary. Structuring experiential learning experiences can take much longer than conventional lecturing. Establishing personal relationships with students can also be a lengthy and unhurried process. Becoming familiar with the local community and establishing contacts and supports demands considerable time in addition to conventional classroom hours.

All of these commitments are perceived as negatives only if the standard time constraints are placed on Aboriginal outreach courses. It would not be possible to take a 40-hour course from the main campus and effectively deliver the same material in an Aboriginal community within the same time frame. An instructor caught in such an unfortunate situation is forced to choose between two unattractive options: (1) transplant the 40-hour course intact from the main campus thereby sacrificing cultural relevance, or (2) make the necessary time-consuming adaptations but cut back on the course content. Either way, the learning experience is diluted or flawed.

The alternative is to assign more hours to Aboriginal outreach courses. For example, the social work methods course I taught in High Level was a 90-hour course whereas the same course on the Edmonton campus is 45 hours. The extra time is not because the students have deficits or lack intellectual ability; rather, the allocation of additional hours recognizes the importance of working to cross the cultural boundaries for effective course delivery.

## Distance Education Technology

The literature on distance education and Aboriginal students is relatively new and mostly anecdotal at this time. I have attempted to identify a few of the issues and discuss their implications for outreach social work education programs.

Using a qualitative methodology, May (1994) interviewed several women who were involved as distance education students with Athabasca University in northern Alberta. One of her respondents was an Aboriginal woman who described how teleconferencing actually discouraged her active participation because it was uncomfortable and intimidating for her. With respect to the pre-packaged course materials, she found it difficult "to question and be critical of the written word of experts" (p. 88) because this would be disrespectful and inappropriate within her culture. Feeling alienated by the experience, she eventually withdrew from the program.

There are indications that such feelings of isolation and alienation may be overcome when distance education students perceive a connection with the institution through some form of direct interaction (Fulford and Zhang, 1993). In their discussion of the role of distance technology in social work field instruction, Cochrane, Sullivan, and Bloom (1995) underscore the importance of regular face-to-face contact between distance students and "faculty from the on-campus program traveling at regular intervals to visit" (p. 5). English-Currie (1990) argues that the visual cues of face-to-face interactions are essential and necessary for effective communication in traditional Aboriginal cultures.

May (1994) also concluded from her study of distance learners that distance education may be "a significantly different experience for female learners than for male learners" because the women had to add the role of student to all the continuing family responsibilities.

> Distance learning was "easier for a man." For these women, family responsibilities remained the same as they took on the role of student. By necessity, study schedules were planned around the needs of others. (p. 94)

Tate and Schwartz (1993) described the typical Aboriginal student in social work as female and much older, with "numerous family and financial pressures" (p. 29). Such pressures (housing, daycare, family obligations, personal problems) emerged in their study as a major factor affecting the retention of Aboriginal social work students. This pattern would appear to be characteristic of the Aboriginal outreach programs where I have taught; 97% of the students were women (only one man in 36 graduates) and most were older than their on-campus counterparts.

The literature is suggesting that self-directed study time, a common component of distance education programs, may be a major problem for the group of students typically found in Aboriginal outreach social work programs. Family and community needs may make it very difficult to set aside the required personal study time. In this situation, a commitment to a regularly scheduled program of local classroom sessions may be easier for the family and community to accommodate and support.

Gruber and Coldevin (1994) report on the Atii pilot project to design and deliver management training to remote Inuit settlements across the Canadian North using distance education technologies. The project featured live instruction delivered by television to small groups of students gathered in local community learning centers. An evaluation of the project concluded overall that "decentralized group training through distance methods can be both effective and efficient in the aboriginal context in Northern Canada" (p. 33).

The apparent success of this project might appear at first to contradict the argument made thus far for face-to-face interaction as a crucial component of outreach education in Aboriginal communities. It is important to note, however, that each local learning center in the Atii project had an on-site group facilitator who received prior training and whose major responsibilities included "managing the site facilities and activities, which included group discussion, role playing and exercises, and generally keeping the learning process on track" (p. 24). Clearly there was a supportive face-to-face contact as a component of this successful endeavor.

Evaluators of the Atii pilot project recommend at least doubling the amount of time estimated for completion of all phases of such a project because

> the complexity inherent in working with several partners and their respective cultural contexts requires that significant time allowances be built into each phase of course development. This is particularly important for any non-aboriginal specialists assigned to such projects who have not worked in this milieu before. Cultural sensitivity to aboriginal priorities and values that differ from those of non-aboriginals is critical. (p. 30)

It would appear that distance education technologies may demand a commitment of extra time similar to what was proposed for face-to-face Aboriginal outreach programs if they are to be effective in the cultural context.

## *"Exchange"—Aboriginal Content in the Main Campus Program*

The discussion to this point has focused on the first part of the Institute's theme of "crossing boundaries through outreach and exchange." I have identified some of the issues involved in the design and delivery of outreach social work education courses in Aboriginal communities, but little has been said about the second component of our theme. What about "exchange"?

Aboriginal social work education in Canada typically consists of programs based in urban campus locations with outreach efforts then directed to distant Aboriginal communities. Obviously, this is a one-way effort focused on the task of getting our programs "out there." The notion of exchange complements this focus on outreach by challenging us to consider how Aboriginal content might effectively be incorporated into the main campus program. Most of the non-Aboriginal students on the main campus will eventually be working with Aboriginal clients and resource persons in the field. How can they be introduced to the world view, issues, and resources of the Aboriginal population?

As one example of how an educational institution can encourage this exchange, I have summarized a series of recent initiatives undertaken at the BSW level by the Faculty of Social Work at The University of Calgary.

**Policy:** Rather than leaving this exchange to the discretion of individual faculty members, the Faculty approved specific policy to support the initiative. A commitment was made to the development of elective courses addressing traditional helping approaches and the issues of social work in Aboriginal communities (these courses were developed by an Aboriginal faculty member). Not wanting to relegate Aboriginal concerns only to elective courses, Faculty Council also approved a policy that a minimum of one 3-hour session in each BSW core course be devoted to Aboriginal issues. For example, the Research course considers indigenous science, traditional knowledge, and other ways of knowing; the Groupwork class may experience sharing or healing circles; the Human Behavior Course includes material on Aboriginal family structures and child-rearing practices.

**Aboriginal Resource Directory:** To support instructors in their efforts to incorporate Aboriginal content and to connect students directly with local Aboriginal resources, the Faculty is currently assembling a Directory of Aboriginal Resource Persons. Elders, leaders, planners, helpers, and social workers from the Aboriginal community are being approached and invited to participate in the BSW program by meeting with classes of students. A directory is being produced that will identify these resource people and their particular areas of knowledge and skill so that instructors will be aware of whom to contact to invite as guests to their class.

**Faculty Workshop:** A four-day workshop was conducted on a local Reserve to encourage faculty members from Social Work and Nursing to encounter an Aboriginal world view outside the confines of the conventional academic setting. Designed by the Native Center at the university, the workshop was guided by a pipe-carrier and ceremonialists who led the faculty group through a number of ceremonies and discussions about the connections between professional helping and traditional healing approaches. Another powerful feature of this workshop was the presence of a group of Aboriginal BSW alumni who came back to share openly with faculty about their experiences in the program and the barriers they faced.

**Practicum Workshop:** A workshop on "Preparing for Work with Aboriginal Clients" was developed for all BSW students about to enter their senior practicum placement. Conducted over two days, this workshop allowed small groups of students to attend three concurrent experiential workshops (Aboriginal World View; Aboriginal Values; Unlearning & Reframing), concluding with a large pot-luck gathering and sharing circle at the Native Center.

**Spring Course/Camp:** An innovative elective course was designed and offered to 12 senior BSW students in the spring of 1995. A truly cooperative effort, this course featured three co-instructors: the director of the Native Center, the child welfare director from Tsuu T'ina First Nation, and myself as a faculty member from Social Work. At the center of the course was a four-day camp on a Reserve in the foothills of the Rocky Mountains under the guidance of a ceremonials and elder from the Hobbema Reserve and a Cree woman who is completing her BSW degree. Students were involved in assembling the teepees where they would live and the sweatlodge for their ceremony. In addition to much group discussion time in the circle, students had individual time with the elder. Two on-campus classroom sessions were also held: one several days prior to the camp for preparation, readings, and an assignment; one afterwards for debriefing, sharing, and a final assignment.

## Conclusion

My Western academic training tells me that I should end this discussion with some major conclusion or resolution following from the arguments I have presented. But that was not the nature or the intention of this commentary. I did not present a linear sequential argument that builds to a conclusion about how Aboriginal outreach education in social work should be conducted. Instead, I offered reflections on my own experiences in this area and attempted to make connections with developments in the current literature in the hope that these ideas might be useful to others who are involved with the design and delivery of such programs.

The Indian Nations at Risk Task Force (Charleston, 1994) alerted us to the pitfalls of "quasi Native education," those sincere and well-intentioned but temporary programs that only "teach about Native cultural topics" (p. 27), operating outside of the regular education program and subject to whimsical funding allocations. A model of culturally sensitive outreach delivery balanced with a true exchange between the systems may help us to offer genuine and relevant learning experiences to students in both our Aboriginal outreach and our main campus programs in social work education.

## *References*

Charleston, G. M. (1994). Toward true Native education: A Treaty of 1992 (Final Report of the Indian Nations at Risk Task Force). *Journal of American Indian Education, 33*(2), entire issue .

Cochrane, S., Sullivan, M., & Bloom, V. (1995, March). *The role of distance technology in the social work field program.* Paper presented at the Annual Program Meeting of the Council on Social Work Education, San Diego, CA.

Colorado, P. (1993). Who are you?: How the Aboriginal classroom sparks fundamental issues in human development. In K. Feehan & D. Hannis (Eds.), *From strength to strength: Social work education and Aboriginal people* (pp. 65-78). Edmonton: Grant MacEwan Community College.

DeMontigny, G. (1992). Compassionate colonialism: Sowing the branch plant. In M. Tobin & C. Walmsley (Eds.), *Northern perspectives: Practice and education in social work* (pp. 7382). Winnipeg: Manitoba Association of Social Workers.

Elliott, G. (1994). *Learning styles of Native and non-Native social work students.* Unpublished Masters Thesis, Faculty of Social Work, The University of Calgary.

English-Currie, V. (1990). The need for re-evaluation in native education. In J. Perreault & S. Vance (Eds.), *Writing the Circle* (pp. 47-60). Edmonton: Nuwest.

Fox, R., & Ziska, P. C. (1989). The field instruction contract: A paradigm for effective learning. *Journal of Teaching in Social Work, 3*(1), 103-116.

Fulford, C. P., & Zhang, S. (1993). Perceptions of interaction: the critical predictor in distance education. *The American Journal of Distance Education, 3,* 8-21.

Gross, E. R. (1995). Deconstructing politically correct practice literature: The American Indian case. *Social Work, 40(2),* 206-213.

Gruber, S., & Coldevin, G. (1994). Management training at a distance for Inuit administrators: The Atii pilot project. *Journal of Distance Education, IX*(2), 21-34.

Kaulback, B. (1984). Styles of learning among Native children: A review of the research. *Canadian Journal of Native Education, 11*(3), 27-37.

May, S. (1994). Women's experiences as distance learners: Access and technology. *Journal of Distance Education, IX*(1), 81-98.

Moore, L. S., & Unwin, C. A. (1990). Quality control in social work: The gatekeeping role in social work education. *Journal of Teaching in Social Work, 4*(1), 113-128.

More, A. J. (1987, October). Native Indian learning styles: A review for researchers and teachers. *Journal of American Indian Education,*17-29.

Osborne, B. (1989, January). Cultural congruence, ethnicity and fused biculturalism: Zuni and Torres Strait. *Journal of American Indian Education,* 7-20.

Peterman, P., & Blake, R. (1986). The inappropriate social work student. *Arete, 11*(1), 27-34.

Ryan, A. G. (1987). Tensions in trans-cultural Native education programs: Hurdles for the sensitive evaluator. *The Canadian Journal of Program Evaluation, 2*(1), 69-79.

Sawyer, D. (1991). Native learning styles: Shorthand for instructional adaptations? *Canadian Journal of Native Education, 18*(1), 99-105.

Tate, D. S. & Schwartz, C. L. (1993). Increasing the retention of American Indian students in professional programs in higher education. *Journal of American Indian Education, 33*(1), 21-31.

Wauters, J., Bruce, J. M., Black, D. R., & Hocker, P. N. (1989). Learning styles: A study of Alaska Native and non-Native students. *Journal of American Indian Education, Special Issue,* 53-62.

Weisenberg, F. P. (1992). Learner and task considerations in designing instruction for Native adult learners. *Canadian Journal of Native Education, 19*(1), 82-89.

Zapf, M. K. (1993a). Contracts and covenants in social work education: Considerations for Native outreach programs. *The Social Worker, 61*(4), 150-154.

Zapf, M. K. (1993b). Methods instruction as a two-way process. In K. Feehan & D. Hannis (Eds.), *From strength to strength: Social work education and Aboriginal people* (pp. 95-110). Edmonton: Grant MacEwan Community College.

Zapf, M. K. (in press). Bicultural teaching of helping approaches: Integrating Native and Western perspectives in the classroom. *The Canadian Journal of Native Education.*

# Part 4

## Social Programs and Problems in Rural Communities

This final part deals with a number of social programs that address social problems in rural communities. Perhaps the most notable change for rural areas is the passage and implementation of the new Personal Responsibility and Work Opportunity Reconciliation Act of 1996, which is being integrated into the rural social welfare landscape in 1998. Thus far, it is not clear what effect the program will have with sweeping changes such as the elimination of Aid to Families with Dependent Children and substitution of Temporary Aid for Needy Families; the wide latitude given to states to implement the new law; the time limits specified for receipt of social services; and the enforcement of stringent work requirements. Since the federal–state income maintenance program is the foundation of most rural services, it is clear that things will change.

Part 4 also provides information on rural crime and delinquency issues and on substance abuse and corrections programs, provided by rural scholar H. Wayne Johnson. The issue of helping people with AIDS in rural areas is also covered in Kathleen Rounds's article, "AIDS in Rural Areas: Challenges to Providing Care."

The special problems of limited health care for the rural poor is also covered, and the emerging problem of homelessness in rural areas is described in two articles.

Of course, most social services that exist in the United States—for example, vocational rehabilitation services, services for people with developmental disabilities, and services for people who are blind or deaf—are also available, in one form or another, to those in rural communities. However, the natures of the problems and of the service delivery systems in rural communities are often different from those in urban settings. They should be examined, therefore, in a light that reflects these differences. Part 4 thus closes the volume by looking at the special tasks associated with extending social services to rural people.

# 17

# Rural Crime, Delinquency, Substance Abuse, and Corrections

by H. Wayne Johnson

There is conventional wisdom about rural America which holds that it is clean, green, and problem free. This idealized view denies some or all of the social problems that exist in nonmetropolitan areas and associates these conditions more or less exclusively with the supposedly corrupt, wicked, and crime-ridden cities (Johnson, 1987). Although this myth has some basis in fact, substantial amounts of crime and delinquency do exist in the nation's nonurban regions, and they give reason for concern. The rural community is simply less idyllic than is sometimes assumed.

## Incidence of Rural Crime

The general statistical picture shows lower rates of crime and delinquency in rural areas than in urban or suburban communities. One indicator is the National Crime Survey, which has been ongoing since 1975 as an assessment of the number of households victimized by crime. In each of the last four years of the 1980s, one-fourth of the nation's 95 million households were victimized by a crime of violence or theft (Rand, 1990). In 1989, rural residents were less vulnerable than suburbanites who, in turn, were less likely to be victimized than urban dwellers. Incidence varied with type of offense. For example, the urban/suburban/rural differences were not extensive in the case of aggravated assault. In contrast, for robbery victims the differences were considerable: 1 in 59 urban households experienced robbery, compared with 1 in 133 suburban, and 1 in 280 rural (Rand, 1990). The rates of personal crime of both violence and theft and household crimes were higher in central cities than in suburbs. Nonmetropolitan areas had the lowest rates for these crimes (Johnson & DeBerry, 1990).

The Federal Bureau of Investigation (FBI) (1991, p. 51) estimated the rates and incidence of rural crime in 1990 as set forth in Table 1, based on the FBI's index of offenses.

In all cases except murder, the rural rate is lower than that for both Metropolitan Statistical Areas and for other cities. With regard to murder, the rural rate was lower than that for Metropolitan Statistical Areas but slightly higher than for other cities.

Another measure of crime, in addition to victimization studies and reports of offenses known to police, is arrest records. Arrests in rural counties in 1990 for the FBI's eight indexed offenses are reported in Table 2 (FBI, p. 218).

Property crimes, by far the most numerous offenses, vary little between cities, suburbs, and rural areas with regard to the percent of such offenses known to the police that are cleared by arrest. On the other hand, in the case of violent crimes (murder, forcible rape, robbery, and aggravated assault) higher cleared-by-arrest rate occurs in rural communities than in suburban areas or in cities (Maguire & Flanagan, 1991, p. 447).

Crime and delinquency occur in both farm and rural nonfarm areas., The same types of illegal activities that characterize urban locations are found in small town and countryside communities. In addition, because of the different nature of nonmetropolitan areas, certain kinds of rural deviancy occur. Small-town and farm homes and businesses are burglarized. Farm tools, equipment, grain, and seed are stolen. The theft of chemicals (fertilizer, pesticides, and herbicides) is somewhat seasonal, related to the

### Table 1. Index of Crimes, 1990

|  | Murder and Nonnegligent Manslaughter | Forcible Rape | Robbery | Aggravated Assault | Burglary | Larceny | Motor Vehicle Theft |
|---|---|---|---|---|---|---|---|
| U.S. Totals | 23,438 | 102,555 | 639,271 | 1,054,863 | 3,073,909 | 7,945,670 | 1,635,907 |
| Rate/100,000 inhabitants | 9.4 | 41.2 | 257.0 | 424.1 | 1,235.9 | 3,194.8 | 657.8 |
| Rural Counties Est. Totals | 1,929 | 7,561 | 5,318 | 55,028 | 226,601 | 345,954 | 40,908 |
| Rate/100,000 Inhabitants | 5.7 | 22.4 | 15.7 | 162.8 | 670.6 | 1,023.8 | 121.1 |

### Table 2. Arrests in Rural Counties, 1990

| | |
|---|---|
| Murder and Nonnegligent Manslaughter | 1,457 |
| Forcible Rape | 2,714 |
| Robbery | 2,037 |
| Aggravated Assault | 25,894 |
| Burglary | 30,465 |
| Larceny–Theft | 46,056 |
| Motor Vehicle Theft | 8,547 |
| Arson | 1,496 |
| Violent Crime | 32,102 |
| Property Crimes | 86,564 |
| Total Index | 118,666 |
| Total Crime | 848,248 |

time of the year when they are in greatest use and demand. Livestock is sometimes taken, both on a small scale and in large organized operations.

Family violence, substance abuse, assault, embezzlement, rape, murder, arson, and other offenses occur in rural as well as urban locations. For example, one offense, fraud, had rural arrest rates in 1989 that exceeded the rates of all other population categories (Maguire & Flanagan, 1991, p. 413). So it can be seen that crime is statistically present in rural areas, although on a generally lesser scale than in metropolitan centers. Furthermore, in a few kinds of crime the pattern shows disproportionately high rates for rural places.

The other significant observation is the relatively recent increase in rural crime. Hagan (1986, p. 83) reports that rural crime has increased more rapidly than urban crime since the 1960s. He attributes this rise to the fact that the urban way of life has become more generalized across the nation. He also speculates that the relatively high rates of violent crime in rural areas may be due to "frontier values" and a "subculture of violence" in the South and in southern Appalachia. That rural murder rates are higher than urban murder rates in Canada is also noted. According to a news story ("City Crime," 1992), reporting a U.S. Justice Department study, rates of violent crime were down in 1989 compared with 1981, but rural rates decreased less than suburban and city rates. One possible cause was the farm crisis of the mid-1980s, which brought increased suicide and also contributed to other tragedies. The case of one distressed farmer received national attention when he killed his wife, his banker, and a neighbor before shooting himself (Brown, 1989).

In discussing the reasons for the growth of rural crime in recent decades, Sagarin, Donnermeyer, and Carter (1982) suggest that there has been an increase in rural America of three interacting components essential to crime: suitable targets, opportunities, and motivated offenders. Changes in all three factors have contributed to the expansion of rural crime.

The problems of the rural elderly are dealt with elsewhere in this volume. A disproportionately large population of older persons lives in small communities. This age group is relevant to a study of crime partly because of its possible fear of being victimized. Yet in actuality, crime is mainly a matter of young perpetrators victimizing the young; hence, the elderly are less likely to be crime victims than are persons of other ages. But studies have shown, although with mixed results, that the elderly *feel* vulnerable, and the resulting fear is the important element (Alston, 1986, pp. 94-122).

Recent public opinion polls show that crime is one of the major fears of the general public, regardless of age. At the end of 1991, an annual poll was conducted in seven Midwestern states that are mainly rural (University of Iowa, 1992). The respondents manifested more concern about crime than they had just two and three years earlier, and there was a perception of increased crime. Although fear of crime is probably greater in the inner city, a significant change has occurred in rural communities on this matter. Often for the first time, people have begun to lock vehicles, doors, and windows particularly after a well-publicized offense has occurred in a rural area.

## Criminal Justice System

Our society has constructed a system (often more of a makeshift nonsystem) of responses to the problems of crime and delinquency made up of three subsystems: law enforcement, judiciary, and corrections. The social work role is primarily in corrections, but there are activities in the other two as well. Collectively, these subsystems aim at controlling or changing behavior and, hence, have social control features differing only in degree from those in several other social welfare enterprises (e.g., mental health and public welfare). The three subsystems interact and what occurs in one has impact in the other two.

### Law Enforcement Subsystem

Rural law enforcement involves a combination of town police officers, county sheriff's units, and state police, with the latter operating mainly on state and federal highways. Diverse patterns exist, even within one state. In some towns the police officer is a municipal employee, whereas in others the county sheriff provides law enforcement services to some or all of the towns in the county. Whatever the structure, rural law enforcement is generally less formal and sophisticated than that in metropolitan centers, although this situation is changing as law enforcement is upgraded and modernized and the states offer assistance through police academy training. As Wilson (1982) has indicated, change is the order of the day for rural law enforcement as much as for other facets of rural life.

The police are one of the few organizations that are available and on call 24 hours a day, 365 days a year. However, this availability has different meaning in a small, rural police office because there may not be enough officers to staff the unit around the clock. In this case, those officers may be "on call." Pepinsky and Jesilo (cited in H.W. Johnson, 1987) point out that four of five calls to the police are noncriminal in nature, which makes this subsystem especially relevant from a social work point of view.

Some small towns have organized to protect the community in ways similar to the Neighborhood Watch programs found in some cities. As noted by H.W. Johnson (1987), in one town of 567 residents, 61 people volunteered to take turns patrolling at night. Using their own cars, they worked in pairs, radioing the sheriff's office when there was questionable activity. A deputy was then sent to the scene. Two radios were purchased for this activity with money raised at a community benefit, an event characteristic of rural communities. This small community has created an inexpensive and informal way of maintaining order. It may possess the potential for unfortunate vigilante action, but this need not be an inevitable result.

One of the striking characteristics and problems of rural law enforcement is the large areas that must be covered. Sheriff's deputies travel considerable distances, and much time is consumed in the process. Frequently an officer is miles away from the nearest colleague who could provide back up, and this tends to create isolation, loneliness, and feelings of vulnerability (H.W. Johnson, 1983).

Another characteristic of law enforcement in the nonurban environment is the diversity of tasks performed by officers. A few of the many tasks noted by a criminal justice student (Gary, cited by H.W. Johnson, 1987) in a rural internship were: serving as bank escort for a small town's annual picnic and taking the proceeds to the bank, providing crowd control for grand openings and community suppers, removing farm animals from roads and putting them back into pastures, picking up walk-aways from a state mental hospital, attending school-merger hearings where violence had been threatened, checking hauled livestock to determine possible theft, handling traffic offenses, informing people of deaths, performing jail checks and other jail activities, and conducting "beer busts" in the countryside. There is a little place for specialization in this range of activities.

Police social work has developed in the United States since the 1970s. Within the context of law enforcement organizations, social workers provide various social services to the police and/or to people with whom the police come in contact, such as those in domestic-dispute situations (Treger, 1975). Much police social work has taken place in small cities, often in suburban contexts, but this work also has relevance, utility, and considerable potential for rural law enforcement units. Wilson's (1982) call for an emphasis on crime prevention and usage of a community development approach parallels Treger's idea of a police social work team.

## Judicial Subsystem

The adjudication of persons accused of committing an offense takes place within the judicial subsystem. As with law enforcement, in rural locations the judicial apparatus is often less elaborate and has less specialization than in metropolitan areas, although this is changing in both systems.

Some rural judges and magistrates serve a multicounty circuit and, hence, are available in court only part time. Prosecuting attorneys in small counties of ten serve only part time in their official capacity while carrying on private law practices. Similarly, rural attorneys may be less likely to develop the trial experience and expertise that characterize an urban criminal lawyer. It is possible, however, for a state attorney general to provide assistance or leadership in prosecuting a case anywhere in the state, just as it is for a defendant to retain an attorney with criminal law expertise from a city (H.W. Johnson, 1987). But both of these practices are probably the exception rather than the rule.

Defendants in criminal cases are often financially unable to provide attorneys for their own defense. Three systems of criminal defense have evolved for the poor: public defenders, counsel assigned by courts from lists of available attorneys, and contract systems in which, for example, a law firm or bar association contracts to provide services. A Justice Department report (cited by H.W. Johnson, 1987) indicates that in the 1980s the public-defender system was most commonly used, operating in 43 of the 50 largest counties and serving 68% of the nation's population. But a majority of rural counties used assigned-counsel systems. These arrangements, too, are changing over time, although it is not surprising to find the assigned-counsel system operating in rural areas as it requires less specialization than the public-defender system. Not known is how effective the assigned-counsel system would be for the nonurban setting. This is a subject for further research.

Rural juvenile courts vary considerably in quality and in disposition of cases. Pawlak (cited by Farley, Griffiths, Skidmore, & Thackeray, 1982) indicated that about half of the rural juvenile courts have part-time judges who preside in other courts as well. These rural-based juvenile courts average a fraction of one probation officer. In one rural state, 12 small counties with similar populations of approximately 19,000 to 23,000 each committed boys to the State Training School (1991) at highly diverse rates. From 1982 to 1992, commitments ranged from 2 to 38 per county. In 1989 alone, the range was from 0 to 8, reflecting in part, perhaps, differing local attitudes toward delinquency and its control. This diversity of commitment rates within one state is consistent with McGarrell's (1991) observation of state-to-state variations in incarceration of juveniles. He notes the simultaneous pressures to be severe with juvenile offenders and to deinstitutionalize them. The mix of factors impinging on incarceration rates results in diverse decisions "either supporting or disfavoring incarceration in public facilities" (McGarrell, 1991, p. 262).

## Corrections

Social work is most extensively involved in the criminal justice subsystem of corrections, which encompasses both community-based programs and institutions. Probation and parole are the large, traditional, community-based correctional services. They operate in both urban and rural settings and differ basically in the greater distances traveled by rural probation and parole personnel. In the past this was sometimes offset, at least partially, by smaller caseloads in the nonmetropolitan areas. In recent years, however, tight budgets and cutbacks in public-sector funding have reduced or eliminated this advantage, as caseloads have increased generally. The other major rural/urban difference in the probation officer's role is in the multiplicity of diverse duties required of rural officers.

In order to make probation a realistic option for more offenders and to increase the likelihood of successful completion of probation, some communities have instituted special *intensive probation* (Barton & Butts, 1990), a variation of traditional probation in which there is closer monitoring and more extensive input from correctional professionals. Programs of this sort are more likely to be instituted in cities where there is more specialization than in rural areas. If experience with them is positive, they are sometimes expanded statewide and become available in rural locations as well.

Another development in recent years is *house arrest,* in which persons accused of committing a crime await their trials at home or those found guilty are sentenced to serve a period of time at home under constraints (Petersilia, 1988). Since 1984, some places have used electronic technology and phone equipment to monitor an offender's location with devices attached to the wrists or ankles (Schmidt, 1991). This equipment is expensive but costs less than incarceration. It is used in rural (Rath, Arola, Richter, & Zahnow, 1991) as well as urban areas although there are limits on how this form of supervision can be maintained.

*Restitution* is another community-based sanction that has reemerged since the mid-1960s (MacDonald, 1986) and is used as effectively in rural as in urban sites (Rath et al., 1991). In part, restitution is a reflection of the growing concern for crime victims and the recognition that there can be restorative value for both the offender and the victim in this program. Whether administered by the courts or probation/parole officers, restitution can be a useful addition to corrections tools (H.W. Johnson, 1983).

Another new correctional measure is *community service.* In this provision, which can be an alternative to incarceration, the convicted person is ordered by a judge or some other agent of the court to do a specified number of hours of community service. Usually this service is done in a public or governmental organization or in the nonprofit private sector, such as in a social agency. Although there is some controversy (McKinney, 1992) related to this program, community service has substantial potential for improving the public's extremely negative view of offenders. And, like restitution, it has restorative value. Community-service arrangements are probably found more extensively in urban than in rural locations because cities are generally more liberally equipped for such measures. But these programs do exist in nonmetropolitan settings (Rath et al., 1991), and there is nothing inherent in rural settings to preclude them.

## Correctional Institutions

In addition to community-based programs, there are institutions for offenders. While the majority of convicted offenders are fined or have a community-based penalty imposed, many are incarcerated in correctional institutions, such as detention facilities and training schools for juveniles, and jails, reformatories, prisons, and other institutions for adult offenders. The major problem with America's correctional institutions, both rural and urban, is that they frequently do little more than warehouse offenders in mass-care, antiquated, overcrowded facilities with inadequate attention to constructive programming designed to facilitate behavioral change.

Juvenile detention is the temporary holding of young suspects and offenders who are awaiting hearings or the holding of those who have been committed to longer term institutions and are awaiting transportation/admission. Juvenile detention in adult jails has been an issue nationally, and has prompted a movement to reduce and prevent this form of incarceration. Many have expressed concern about juvenile suicides in jail, as well as the lack of constructive programs for juveniles. Reid (1987, p. 523) quoted one study indicating that "for every 100,000 juveniles placed in adult jails, 12 will commit suicide. This is eight times higher than the rate of suicide in secure juvenile detention centers." Federal legislation of 1974 requires "sight and sound separation" from adults for jailed juveniles who are not tried as adults (Stephan & Jankowski, 1991). According to further legislation in 1980, all juveniles, except those being tried for felonies as adults, must be removed from jail. In spite of these requirements, on a one-day count in 1990, over 2,000 juveniles were in jail, and there were 59,789 juvenile admissions in 1990, according to Stephan and Jankowski (1991).

Solving the problem of jail use for juvenile detention is of particular concern in rural areas. Many urban communities have specialized juvenile detention centers, but this is less feasible for the small numbers of rural delinquents requiring detention. One answer to this need is regional detention facilities that serve two or more counties or a judicial district (Santiago, 1992). In this case, transporting a juvenile a long distance to this center could be problematic, but it is preferable to the potential destructiveness of incarcerating the youngster with adults in jail. Newer jails are more likely to provide for genuine separation of adults and youth than the older jails, particularly some of the small rural ones.

Regional jails serving more than one county in rural areas can be as advantageous for adults as regional detention is for youth. For adults, jails are used not only to hold those awaiting trial or movement elsewhere but also for people who have been given short sentences, generally up to one year. When jail is used for this function, it is especially important that there be more positive programming for inmates than exists in many such facilities.

The remaining correctional institutions are training schools of various sorts for delinquents, and minimum-, medium-, and maximum-security prisons for adults. Many of these were placed in out-of-sight out-of-mind locations when they were established, sometimes over a century ago. Frequently, they were placed in rural sites. Today, when there is a proposal to build a correctional facility, there is often local opposition. But if it is suggested that an existing facility be closed, there is also opposition. It may be the largest employer in the area and central to the local economy. Its reduction or elimination may be viewed as economically devastating.

In the case of the infamous prison riot at Attica, New York, in 1971, it has often been noted that one cause was large numbers of urban minority inmates being confined in a distant nonmetropolitan area by largely rural, white staff. Other negative features existed as well, and the result was disastrous.

In state institutions such as prisons, mental hospitals, and facilities for people with other disabilities, two "classes" of staff have been observed: (1) the professionals and (2) the aides, attendants, guards (correctional officers), and other direct service workers. The professionals, who have the higher paying positions, often move into the community from elsewhere, whereas the group that receives less pay and status is employed from surrounding small towns and farms. This can make for strained relationships both within the institution and in the surrounding area. On the other hand, these state institutions can be a resource for their neighbors as some staff participate in the larger community, formally or informally providing consultation and other services. In rural areas lacking many services, a nearby state institution can be an invaluable resource.

Another new development related to institutions is the requirement that the first part of an offender's sentence be served in a jail-like institution, followed by a period of time on probation. Senna and Siegel (1987, p. 409) call this "split sentencing." A variation, "shock probation," involves a short prison stay prior to resentencing to probation in the community. Actually, shock probation is a misnomer in that the intended jolting of the offender derives from the incarceration, not the release on probation. As of 1989, eleven states had shock incarceration programs (MacKenzie & Ballow, 1989), often located in boot camps of a military style. Most are units located within a larger prison but they may be separate facilities. Emphasis is placed on hard labor, physical training, and strict discipline. These kinds of correctional measures are used in rural as well as urban settings and are equally applicable.

## Rural Substance Abuse

The subject of substance abuse is being included in this chapter because so many participants in the criminal justice system have illegal drug or excessive alcohol involvements and because of the societal response to this group of problems, which are defined as crimes. In spite of the fact that the abuse of alcohol and other substances can be called a victimless offense, our society continues to handle such matters extensively through the criminal justice system. Ever since the President's Crime Commission report of 1967 pointed out that one-third of America's crime was public drunkenness and proposed the decriminalization of this conduct, there has been some move in this direction with regard to alcohol (Senna & Siegel, 1987, p. 136).

On the other hand, the government has waged various "wars" on drugs, which have taken the form of stringent law enforcement and severe penalties for violations. One of the reasons for prison overcrowding is this effort to get tough with drug offenders. That the problem goes on seemingly unabated suggests that the actions aimed at preventing and curbing this conduct have not been particularly successful.

In 1990, the U.S. General Accounting Office (GAO, 1990) conducted a study of rural drug abuse at the request of federal legislators. At that time, the only national survey on this subject was over a decade old; it had found that about two-thirds as many rural as urban people would try illegal drugs during their lifetime. The 1990 research found that rates of total substance abuse are about the same in rural and urban locations, a finding consistent with the research of Mulford (personal communication, April 20, 1992), who studied drinking in a rural state and concluded that there has been a convergence of rural and urban problem drinking (Mulford & Fitzgerald, 1983).

According to the GAO (1990) study, there are differences in prevalence rates of various drugs. Cocaine use is lower in rural areas, whereas use of inhalants may be higher. By a wide margin, the most extensively abused substance is alcohol, which has the highest rates of treatment admissions and arrests. Rural and urban arrest rates for substance abuse are equally high. Most prisoners in rural states have abused alcohol, other drugs, or both. The study also found that the high rate of substance abuse among prisoners "completely overwhelms available treatment services" (GAO, 1990, p. 5). In rural states, over 80% of admissions for treatment are for alcohol abuse, despite a requirement that at least 35% of block grant funding in major federal sources of funds be directed to nonalcohol drug treatment. As a result, the GAO report (1990, p. 6) raises a question as to whether such requirements meet the needs of rural communities.

The GAO report (1990, p. 7) suggests that rural communities "pool resources and coordinate efforts" because rural health care personnel, teachers, and police are responsible for the provision of a broad array of health services and are unable to specialize in drug concerns. The importance of coordinating rural social service activities aimed at the alcohol/drug abuser is confirmed in the works of Maypole and Wright (1979). This team of social worker and physician succeeded in positioning multiservice centers in three rural Wisconsin county seats. These centers serve the emotionally troubled and developmentally disabled, as well as substance abusers, on an outpatient basis, bringing together the efforts of a private medical clinic and a community mental health center.

Alcoholism detoxification services are often a specific need in rural areas. Maypole (1981) describes how implementation of such services was accomplished in the rural three-county area alluded to above. Written agreements were developed between the mental health center and the existing small general hospitals so that the hospitals provided detoxification and the mental health center gave follow-up care. Added later were a halfway house and a community education program. As a result of these developments, the number of detoxification patients of a larger, more distant medical center declined significantly. This approach of using written agreements is more formal than is often characteristic of rural areas, but it was effective in this instance.

The GAO study (GAO, 1990, pp. 44-45) noted that rural program effectiveness might be limited by four factors identified in three earlier reports: funding with diseconomies of scale, lack of community agency and school system acceptance, lack of trained and experienced staff, and transportation of clients to programs and staff to clients. The study concluded that residential programs are as feasible in rural areas as elsewhere, but that outpatient and after-care programs are a greater challenge and suggested that routine monitoring for drug usage could be made a condition of probation or parole.

Poole (1987) reports another way in which rural counties can deal with alcohol problems, citing an example from a county in the Southeastern United States. In addition to community denial of the existence of social problems, various resistances to creating and supporting programs in response to human needs, as well as assorted vested interests and hidden agendas, are found in most communities, certainly in rural ones. But these forces can be overcome, as was demonstrated through this county's concern with repeat alcohol-related offenses. A 6-month pilot program was implemented by the local mental health agency in order to assist the courts. The resulting alcohol abuse evaluation and referral service was extensively used even in the most rural areas. At the end of 6 months, a second staff member was added, and the Alcohol Abuse Service was made permanent. While funding was still problematic, the new service had become an integral part of the county network of services.

Other types of substance abuse have also been studied. The research of Sarvela, Takeshita, and McClendon (1986) in rural northern Michigan suggests that the use of marijuana increases with age and, in certain age groups, is higher than national averages. In that area, male involvement with the drug was greater than female involvement. Peer usage was a major factor in the drug's consumption by early adolescents. This finding about peers is noteworthy when considering the Mookherjee (1984) study of teenage drinking in rural Tennessee. He concluded that "well-trained peer counselors may be the most effective single group in influencing prevention of alcohol abuse among teenagers" (Mookherjee, 1984, p. 56). If there is similarity between adolescent consumption of marijuana and alcohol, and if peer influences are a major factor in this consumption and peer counselors play major roles in its possible control, then social service planning and provision in rural communities must include peer counseling in this context.

## Working in the Rural Climate

Four probation and parole officers (Rath et al., 1991) have written about their work in rural Minnesota counties with both juvenile and adult offenders and with both probationers and parolees. The variety of tasks they perform requires that they be true generalists. At least some of these workers are involved in the following diverse activities: case investigation and supervision, alcohol and drug assessments, custody studies, divorce mediation, guardian programming, restitution, community service supervision, juvenile diversion, and home detention. A resource is thought of as local "if it is within 100 miles" (Rath et al., p. 230) of these areas where community resources are scarce. Working in such nonurban places demands "tolerance, flexibility, creativity, and practicality" (Rath et al., p. 228).

In these rural communities, the clients encountered professionally are often personal acquaintances and friends. One worker had high school students whom he had hired as babysitters turn up in his caseload as a result of a school lark gone astray. Adult friends whom he had seen socially at home later became clients whom he saw professionally in his office. Handling his own unruly children in church brought attention from others who wished to see how the "child guidance" professional handled misbehavior (Rath et al., p. 228).

Intolerance, fear, and stigma have been cited as problems in rural areas with regard to crime, delinquency, or substance abuse. The degree of fear, for example, varies according to the nature of the offense and other factors. In urban locations, some of these attitudes exist, but they may be less intense and more diffuse and therefore impinge less directly on the offender, the family, the victim, and persons working with the criminal justice clientele.

Similar intolerance and fear face persons with AIDS in rural communities. Rounds (1988) suggests organizing a local AIDS task force to assist with such activities as educating the community, developing a service network, and influencing state policy. Some of the strategies proposed by Rounds for working in the rural AIDS context are also applicable to corrections. Having a local group of citizens who can provide leadership on matters pertaining to the community's response to crime and delinquency is invaluable. The time and energy expended by a social worker in bringing together such a group can be an important investment.

One of the greatest needs in the criminal justice context is for an enlightened, rational public that knows and understands that the vast majority of crimes are not violent personal crimes but property offenses. This awareness would help the public to be less influenced by sensationalized, lurid media headlines about bizarre murders and other less typical crimes. Progress will have been made when the public realizes the tremendous costs and futility of locking up property offenders for long periods of time.

Using a task force to institute a service network can be especially critical at a time of austerity and budget cutbacks in such fields as corrections. Andrews and Linden (1984), writing about rural child abuse programming, noted that services can actually be expanded at times of public fund retrenchment by creative planning and staffing. In one small city in a rural state, a local service club initiated a program through which some of its members act as unpaid "probation officers" with first-time offenders who were previously unsupervised and unserved (Mozer, 1992). This is an example of volunteerism that can be workable in rural areas. Critics may deplore programs of this nature because they represent deprofessionalization, but it should be noted that, in the absence of these volunteers, no attention was given to this group of clients. In such situations, "probation" would seem to be meaningless without the volunteers.

Influencing state policy is Rounds' (1988) last strategy. Perhaps in no field is this more important than in criminal justice. Whether the issue is juvenile/criminal code legislation or funding of programs, it is essential that the views and experiences of local citizens in communities impact decision making at the state and federal levels. There is a need for decriminalization of some acts, especially those having to do with alcohol and drugs, so that law better reflects contemporary practices and standards. Deinstitutionalization is needed in many states with regard to certain offenses, particularly some property crimes. Funding to encourage initiation or expansion of promising programs on the local level is essential. Whatever the issue, citizens organized locally can be a valuable resource in corrections.

Rural spouse abuse is a topic relevant to crime, in part because of recent changes in state laws that require law enforcement officers to make arrests when there is probable cause to conclude that an assault has occurred. Rural communities often deny the existence of domestic violence and other problems, such as rape. Part of the social worker's job in this situation is to sensitize the community to its problems and needs. Providing visibility to the problem is an important first step in developing resources.

Three obstacles to the reporting of wife abuse in small communities are isolation, lack of assistance networks, and a traditional rural mindset (Schorer, 1990). One abused farm woman indicated that she did not report her injuries to law enforcement because she knew the police dispatcher. When "everyone knows everyone," as is often the case in rural areas, it is especially difficult to reveal family problems. Part of rural tradition is male authoritarianism, including the view of some men of their right to inflict abuse. Another part of the tradition is that personal problems are kept within the family; the idea of seeking help from social services is foreign.

Domestic violence shelters for abused spouses and children have recently been developed. The location of these facilities is often kept confidential in order to protect the residents, something that would be difficult to do in a rural community. Most of these shelters, however, are in cities, which means that a rural person needing such a resource might have to travel to another community. On the other hand, 24-hour domestic abuse telephone hot lines have become quite common. In one rural Midwestern state, these hot lines operate in 31 locations in most regions of the state (Schorer, 1990). With the expansion of this resource, support groups, preventive education, and other services will become increasingly available in widespread locations.

A rural social work practitioner who assists in developing programs for the victims of family violence makes a major contribution to human well-being. Although technically termed a "caseworker," the practitioner is actually a generalist who must be able to develop programs, recruit and train volunteers, work with self-help groups, provide information and education, participate in fund raising, and engage in the dozens of other activities necessitated by environments with many social problems but with limited services and resources. Such is the way of life for a rural social worker in criminal justice, substance abuse, and related fields.

## Conclusion

In spite of the image of rural America as free of social problems, crime is present and growing. The three subsystems of the criminal justice system operate in rural communities, and social work's role in the corrections field is most extensive. In spite of limited rural resources and extended distance factors, innovative and effective programs for substance abusers and for crime victims and offenders flourish in small communities. What the future holds for problems of crime and delinquency and for this field of social service depends heavily on our society's ability to provide social justice. For the greater the social justice, the less is the need for criminal justice measures.

## References

Alston, L. T. (1986). *Crime and older Americans*. Springfield, IL: Thomas.

Andrews, D. D., & Linden, R. R. (1984). Preventing rural child abuse: Progress in spite of cutbacks. *Child Welfare, LXIII*(5), 443-452.

Barton, W. H., & Butts, J. A. (1990). Viable options: Intensive supervision programs for juvenile delinquents. *Crime & Delinquency 36*(2), 238-256,

Brown, B. (1989). *Lone tree*. New York: Crown.

City crime rates higher than on farms. (1992, June 8). *Des Moines Register,* p. 3A.

Farley, O. W., Griffiths, K. A., Skidmore, R. A., & Thackeray, M. G. (1982). *Rural social work practice*. New York: Free Press.

Federal Bureau of Investigation. (1991). *Crime in the United States*. Washington, DC: U.S. Government Printing Office.

General Accounting Office. (1990). *Rural drug abuse: Prevalence, relation to crime, and programs* (GAO/PEMD-90-24). Washington, DC: Author.

Hagan, F. E. (1986). *Introduction to criminology*. Chicago: Nelson-Hall.

Iowa State Training School. (1992). *Annual Report*. Eldora, IA: Author.

Johnson, H. W. (1983). Rural and urban criminal justice. In A. R. Roberts (Ed.), *Social work in juvenile and criminal justice settings* (pp. 67-86). Springfield, IL: Charles C. Thomas.

Johnson, H. W. (1987). Crime, delinquency and corrections: Rural perspectives. In A. Summers, J. M. Schriver, P. Sundet, & R. Meinert (Eds.), *Proceedings of the 10th National Institute on Social Work in Rural Areas* (pp. 97-105).

Johnson, J. M., & DeBerry, M. M. (1990). *Criminal victimization 1989* (U.S. Department of Justice No. NCJ-125615). Washington, DC: U.S. Government Printing Office.

MacDonald, D. C. (1986). *Restitution and community service.* (U.S. Department of Justice No. NCJ-104456). Washington, DC: U.S. Government Printing Office.

MacKenzie, D. L., & Ballow, D. B. (1989). *Shock incarceration programs in state correction jurisdictions—An update* (U.S. Department of Justice No. NCJ-120287). Washington, DC: U.S. Government Printing Office.

Maguire, K., & Flanagan, T. J. (Eds.). (1991). *Sourcebook of criminal justice statistics— 1990* (U.S. Department of Justice No. NCJ-130580). Washington, DC: U.S. Government Printing Office.

Maypole, D. E. (1981). Alcoholism detoxification services in a rural community: A formal development approach. *Alcohol Health and Research World, 5*(4), 42-47.

Maypole, D. E., & Wright, W. E. (1979). The integration of services of a medical clinic and a community mental health center in a rural area. *Social Work in Health Care, 4*(3), 299-308.

McGarrell, E. F. (1991). Differential effects of juvenile justice reform on incarceration rates of the states. *Crime and Delinquency, 37*(2), 262-280.

McKinney, C. M. (1992). Why do we remain silent? *Social Work, 37*(3), 261-262.

Mookherjee, H. A. (1984). Teenage drinking in rural middle Tennessee. *Journal of Alcohol and Drug Education, 29*(2), 49-57.

Mozer, M. (1992, June 4). Area Rotarians step up to help courts handle probation caseload. *Iowa City Press Citizen,* p. 1A.

Mulford, H. A., & Fitzgerald, J. L. (1983). Changes in the climate of attitudes toward drinking in Iowa 1961-1979. *Journal of Studies on Alcohol, 44*(4), 675-687.

Petersilia, J. (1988). *House arrest.* (U.S. Department of Justice No. NCJ-104559). Washington, DC: U.S. Government Printing Office.

Poole, J. E. (1987). Reducing repeat alcohol related offenses and other treatment management problems: A pilot project conducted in a rural Southeastern county. *Journal of Alcohol and Drug Education, 32*(2), 32-44.

Rand, M. R. (1990). *Crime and the nation's households, 1989.* (U.S. Department of Justice No. NCJ-124544). Washington, DC: U.S. Government Printing Office.

Rath, Q. C., Arola, T., Richter, B., & Zahnow, S. (1991). Small town corrections— A rural perspective. *Corrections Today, 53*(2), 228-230.

Reid, S. T. (1987). *Criminal justice.* St. Paul, MN: West.

Rounds, K. A. (1988). Responding to AIDS: Rural community strategies. *Social Casework, 69*(6), 360-364.

Sagarin, E., Donnermeyer, J. F., & Carter, T. J. (1982). Crime in the countryside— A prologue. In T. J. Carter, G. H. Phillips, J. F. Donnermeyer, & T. N. Wurschmidt (Eds.), *Rural crime* (pp. 10-19). Totowa, NJ: Allanheld, Osmun.

Santiago, F. (1992, April 25). Two centers to hold juveniles now open. *Des Moines Register*, p. 2A.

Sarvela, P. D., Takeshita, Y. J., & McClendon, E. J. (1986). The influence of peers on rural Northern Michigan adolescent marijuana use. *Journal of Alcohol and Drug Education, 32*(1), 29-39.

Schmidt, A. K. (1991). Electronic monitors–Realistically, what can be expected? *Federal Probation, LV*(2), 47-53.

Schorer, F. (1990, November 30). Rural wife abuse. *Des Moines Register,* pp. 1T-3T.

Senna, J. J., & Siegel, L. J. (1987). *Introduction to criminal justice* (4th ed.). St. Paul, MN: West.

Stephan, J. J., & Jankowski, L. W. (1991). *Jail Inmates 1990.* (U.S. Department of Justice No. NCJ-129756). Washington, DC: U.S. Government Printing Office.

Treger, H. (1975). *The police-social work team.* Springfield, IL: Thomas.

University of Iowa. (1992). *The 1992 heartland survey report.* Iowa City: Iowa Social Sciences Institute.

Wilson, G. R. (1982). Rural law enforcement and crime prevention: A role in transition. In T. J. Carter, G. H. Phillips, J. F. Donnermeyer, & T. N. Wurschmidt (Eds.), *Rural Crime* (pp. 244-256). Totowa, NJ: Allanheld, Osmun.

# 18

# AIDS in Rural Areas: Challenges to Providing Care

by Kathleen A. Rounds

This study was conducted to examine the development and provision of services to persons with acquired immune deficiency syndrome (AIDS) and their families in rural areas and barriers to the delivery of care. The 15 respondents in this study coordinated or provided services to persons with AIDS and their families, and most of the persons with AIDS were gay men; thus, the focus of this article is rural gays with AIDS. However, all persons with AIDS in rural areas experience many of the same barriers to care, particularly barriers related to the stigma of having AIDS.

## Rural Characteristics that Affect Care of Persons with AIDS

Some authors base their definition of "rural" on demographics, others on a way of life or value system.[1] For the purposes of this article, *rural* refers to

> the environmental surroundings, the social systems, and the people who reside in areas that have relatively low population density, usually either in the country or in small towns or villages.[2]

To understand the experience of AIDS and the challenges to providing AIDS care in rural communities, one first must examine characteristics unique to rural areas that influence social and health care.

Rural America is not homogeneous; however, rural areas have certain characteristics in common. Compared with their urban counterparts, rural residents consider religion and the role of the church to be very important

---

[1] O. W. Farley et al., *Rural Social Work Practice* (New York: The Free Press, 1982).

[2] G. K. Weber, "Preparing Social Workers for Practice in Rural Social Systems," in H. W. Johnson, ed., *Rural Human Services* (Itasca, IL: F. E. Peacock Publishers, 1980), p. 204.

---

Reprinted from *Social Work* (May–June 1988) with permission from the National Association of Social Workers.

in community life, hold more traditional moral values, expect greater conformity to community norms, and are less tolerant of diversity.[3] Rural residents also believe that the community should take care of its own and provide care through primary relationships and informal networks, rather than through formal bureaucratic systems, in part because access to social and health services is greatly limited.[4] These characteristics influence the delivery of health and social care to persons with AIDS and their families living in rural areas.

Geographic isolation, one characteristic of rural areas that affects care of persons with AIDS, limits access to social and health services for most rural residents. Particularly in the rural South, poverty, the maldistribution of health care providers, and lack of transportation and services make obtaining health care difficult for residents.[5] In addition, rural areas contain more than half of the nation's substandard housing units.[6] The delivery of in-home health services to persons living in such housing can be a complicated task.

Another characteristic of rural areas is that residents rely heavily on social networks to provide social support and other services that more formal agencies often provide in urban areas.[7] Although changes in rural areas, such as out-migration associated with lack of employment opportunities, have begun to erode these support systems, they still are powerful providers of social and health care because formal services are so limited.[8] Strong social networks usually are perceived as a positive aspect of rural communities, but they are not value-free and can stigmatize as well as protect members. Wodarski notes, "because of the closeness of social net-

---

[3] L. H. Ginsberg, ed., *Social Work in Rural Communities: A Book of Readings* (New York: Council on Social Work Education, 1976); and E. E. Martinez-Brawley, "The New Small Town and Locally Based Social Care," in S. C. Matison, ed., *The Future of Rural Communities: Preservation and Change.* Proceedings of the Eighth Annual National Institute on Social Work in Rural Areas, Cheney, Washington, July 1983, pp. 137-143.

[4] P. A. Keller and J. D. Murray, "Rural Mental Health: An Overview of the Issues," in P. A. Keller and J. D. Murray, eds., *Handbook of Rural Community Mental Health* (New York: Human Services Press, 1982), pp. 3-7.

[5] B. C. Bedics and R. E. Doelker, "Health Services for Undeserved Areas in the Rural South," *Health and Social Work* 11 (Winter 1986), pp. 42-51; and Keller and Murray, *Handbook of Rural Community Mental Health.*

[6] Keller and Murray, *Handbook of Rural Community Mental Health.*

[7] J. Davenport and J. Davenport III. "Utilizing the Social Network in Rural Communities," *Social Casework,* 63 (February 1982), pp. 106-115; and M. B. Kenkel, "Stress-Coping Support in Rural Communities: A Model for Primary Prevention," *American Journal of Community Psychology,* 14 (October 1986), pp. 457-478.

[8] J. S. Wodarski, *Rural Community Mental Health Practice* (Baltimore, MD: University Park Press, 1983), p. 25.

works in rural areas, individuals who exhibit deviant behaviors are labeled more readily."[9] Waltman describes the helping among members of natural networks as helping those who are "deserving," defined as "compliant with unwritten community moral codes in areas of money management, sexual conduct, alcohol or drug abuse, and the work ethic."[10] Thus, persons with AIDS and their family members may receive much less support from networks than if they were coping with another disease such as cancer, particularly if AIDS was contracted through intravenous drug use or "unacceptable" sexual behavior.

Religion is another important characteristic of rural communities.[11] In rural communities, religious values and groups affect other aspects of community functioning such as the delivery of community health and social services.[12] Congregations act as support networks for people in need and help people to define their problems, discuss their fears, get assistance, and build support systems and coalitions. The church also could prevent disease by educating and advising members about health risks and available services and by promoting healthy community environments and life-styles.[13] However, because the incidence of AIDS still is low in rural areas, the capacity of churches to provide care to persons with AIDS and their families and to educate the community about AIDS has yet to be tested.

Lack of tolerance for diversity is a final characteristic that affects care of persons with AIDS in rural communities. A noted author concluded,

> If otherness became okay in rural America, it is possible we could face the pain of the world better than we do.[14]

---

[9] J. D. Murray and S. Kupinsky, "The Influence of Powerlessness and Natural Support Systems on Mental Health in the Rural Community," in Keller and Murray, *Handbook of Rural Community Mental Health*, pp. 62-73.

[10] G. H. Waltman, "Mainstreet Revisited: Social Work Practice in Rural Areas," *Social Casework*, 67 (October 1986), p. 469.

[11] O. F. Larson, "Values and Beliefs of Rural People," in T. Ford, ed., *Rural U.S.A.: Persistence and Change* (Ames, IA: Iowa State University Press, 1978), pp. 91-112. As cited in D. M. Meystedt, "Religion and the Rural Population: Implications for Social Work," *Social Casework*, 65 (April 1984), pp. 219-226; and R. W. Hood, " Social Psychology and Religious Fundamentalism," in A. W. Childs and G. B. Melton, eds., *Rural Psychology* (New York: Plenum Press, 1983), pp. 169-192.

[12] Meystedt, "Religion and the Rural Population"; and B. E. Swanson, R. A. Cohen, and E. P. Swanson, *Small Towns and Small Towners: A Framework for Survival and Growth* (Beverly Hills, CA: Sage Publications, 1979).

[13] J. W. Hatch et al., "Rediscovering Traditional Community Health Resources: The Experience of Black Churches in the USA/The General Baptist State Convention Health and Human Services Project," *Contact*, 77 (1984), pp. 1-7.

[14] C. Bly, "Soft-Hearted Hard Thinking on Rurality," in Matison, ed., *The Future of Rural Communities*, p. 8.

In most rural communities otherness includes being gay. To avoid stigma, rural gays must assume low visibility, avoid publicly declaring their sexual orientation, and fit into "routine family and community life."[15] This difficult task takes a psychological toll that is particularly great when gay individuals internalize the negative attitudes toward homosexuality that exist in most rural environments.[16] Some gay individuals choose another option—to leave rural communities to live in a more accepting, usually urban, environment—and thus the family and community maintain their denial of the existence of homosexual individuals among them.[17] Unfortunately, staying and assuming low visibility or leaving and becoming invisible never force the community to deal with differences and so reinforce the distance between the gay person and the rural community.[18] Because these two mechanisms of denial are upset when a gay person who left a rural community is diagnosed with AIDS and returns home to be with his family, the community and family must confront their feelings about homosexuality as they deal with their fears about AIDS.

Among the problems of being gay in rural America is limited access to support systems, which contributes to a deep sense of isolation among rural gays.[19] Support is difficult to access for several reasons: Because without a large, visible, and diverse gay community, gays must depend upon nongays for support; because professionals in the formal support system may not understand or be responsive to the needs of gay clients; and because major informal community support systems, such as family or church, may exclude gays if their sexual orientation is known.[20] Also, in rural environments, where conforming to traditional institutions is expected and where the church plays a major social role, many gays find themselves in conflict with religious norms and unwelcome in the church community.[21] Thus, lack of tolerance for diversity greatly reduces the positive supportive functions of rural social networks and churches, and

---

[15] A. R. D'Augelli and M. M. Hart, "Gay Women, Men, and Families in Rural Settings: Toward the Development of Helping Communities," *American Journal of Community Psychology,* 15 (February 1987), pp. 79-93.

[16] L. Crew, "Just as I Am," *Southern Exposure,* 5 (1977), pp. 59-63; and A. E. Moses and J. A. Buckner, "The Special Problems of Rural Gay Clients," *Human Services in the Rural Environment,* 5 (September-October 1980), pp. 22-27.

[17] D'Augelli and Hart, "Gay Women, Men, and Families in Rural Settings."

[18] Ibid.

[19] Ibid.; Moses and Buckner, "The Special Problems of Rural Gay Clients"; and B. Charde and D. Viets, "Rural Mental Health Practice: A Gay/Lesbian Therapeutic Support Group," in A. Summers et al., eds., *Social Work in Rural Areas.* Proceedings of the Tenth National Institute on Social Work in Rural Areas, Columbia, Missouri, July 1985, pp. 126-142.

[20] D. D. Dulaney and J. Kelly, "Improving Services to Gays and Lesbians," *Social Work,* 27 (March 1982), pp. 178-183.

[21] Charde and Viets, "Rural Mental Health Practice."

persons with AIDS (particularly if they are gay) and their families may encounter hostility and neglect rather than support.

## Study Methodology

This study was designed to examine challenges to care for persons with AIDS and their families. During a four-month period in 1987, in a Southeastern state in which 48 percent of the population is rural, 15 persons who were coordinating or delivering services to persons with AIDS and their families were interviewed.[22] The sample was derived using the "snowball" method.[23] That is, a contact in an AIDS service organization recommended several individuals who were knowledgeable about support services for persons with AIDS in rural areas, who in turn nominated other potential respondents. The total sample included social workers, nurses, health educators, administrators, and lay volunteers from a variety of organizations such as hospitals, AIDS support organizations, hospice and home health care agencies, members of local and state AIDS task forces, and public health and social service departments. Although the sample did not necessarily represent all providers working with persons with AIDS, the sample did represent a wide range of organizations, professionals, and geographic areas. Information and minutes from meetings of the state AIDS task force, a statewide AIDS conference attended by the author, and discussions with individuals familiar with rural human services also inform the findings.

The response rate was 100 percent, as all persons asked to be interviewed agreed to participate. The structured interviews lasted from one-half hour to two hours. Interview questions were developed based on the literature discussed earlier in this article. The interviews focused on barriers to services for rural persons with AIDS and their families and also covered the following general areas: the respondent's role and experience in working with rural persons with AIDS, problems experienced by persons with AIDS living in rural areas, issues in providing care to persons with AIDS in rural areas, and strategies to improve the delivery of services.

The data were coded and analyzed using techniques for working with qualitative data described by Chesler.[24] Pattern coding also was used to

---

[22] U.S. Bureau of the Census, *1980 Census of Population and Housing,* Part 35 (Washington, D.C., 1983). *The sample was limited to 15 respondents, when "theoretical saturation" was achieved as discussed in* B. D. Glaser and A. L. Strauss, *The Discovery of Grounded Theory* (Hawthorne, N.Y.: Aldine Publishing Co., 1967), pp. 61-62.

[23] E. Babbie, *The Practice of Social Research,* 4th ed. (Belmont, CA: Wadsworth Publishing Co., 1986), p. 246.

[24] M. Chesler, "Professionals' View of the Dangers of Self-Help Groups." Working Paper #345, Center for Research on Social Organization, University of Michigan, 1987.

analyze the data.[25] This technique involved first coding the data and then grouping segments of the data into clusters. These clusters then were contrasted and compared to discover themes related to challenges to providing care. Several themes emerged as challenges to providing care to persons with AIDS and their families living in rural areas.

## Challenges to Providing Care

### Structural Factors

First, structural factors such as lack of services and geographic distance to services affect the provision of health and social care to persons with AIDS in rural areas. A major structural problem for most rural persons with AIDS is the distance to health care facilities that treat AIDS patients. Transportation to a secondary or tertiary care hospital or to a medical clinic in an urban area, lodging, and missed work time for the caregivers are expensive and time-consuming as well as extremely difficult for persons with AIDS who are experiencing pain and discomfort. These factors, coupled with a hesitancy to use medical care or limited knowledge of the disease process associated with AIDS, prevent people with AIDS and their families from seeking the care that they need.

One respondent-provider described the structural problem of providing *buddy support* (a volunteer from an AIDS service organization) as a "geographic nightmare. . . it's hard to send out a buddy when the person lives almost a hundred miles away on two-lane roads." In many cases, contact with a buddy must be by phone because of geographic distances; agencies with AIDS hotlines overcome some of the geographic barriers to support.

Distance also makes discharge planning particularly difficult, because it compounds the difficulties for hospital staff in dealing with the community agencies' problems or inexperience in providing care to persons with AIDS. In these interviews, hospital staff expressed concern about quality of home care and confidentiality once the persons with AIDS were discharged to communities, and respondents from community agencies reported that hospital staff were unaware of the limitations in some rural communities and had unrealistic expectations of what services could be arranged with short notice. For example, poverty and poor housing in some rural areas make the delivery of home health services very difficult; with no refrigeration and running water in some homes, administration of intravenous antibiotics that require refrigeration becomes a complex procedure.

---

[25] M. B. Miles and A. M. Huberman, *Qualitative Data Analysis* (Beverly Hills, CA: Sage Publications, 1984).

## Confidentiality

As a second theme that emerged from the interviews, every respondent identified confidentiality and the fear of disclosure as affecting the delivery of services to persons with AIDS. Respondents consistently stated that "in rural communities everyone knows everyone, and everyone knows your business." Several respondents described incidents that involved breaches of confidentiality; for example, the consequences of such a breach by workers in a local lab was that the caregiver of a person with AIDS was asked to leave her church. Several respondents stressed asking each person with AIDS or family to specify what information could be disclosed and from whom in the community the service provider could obtain needed support and still protect confidentiality.

Respondents reported that persons with AIDS dealt with their concerns about confidentiality in various ways. Some relied heavily on AIDS hotlines for information and support rather than depend on people in their own small communities. Other persons with AIDS chose to receive all medical care in a tertiary hospital even if it required traveling long distances. Others prolonged seeking help as long as possible. Unfortunately, fear and anxiety about disclosure prevent people from receiving critical services and isolate them at a time of tremendous need. The fear that confidentiality might be broken also reduced the willingness of persons with AIDS and their families to share their experiences with others in similar circumstances, thus cutting off an important avenue of support:

> We had two patients in the unit from the same town. Neither family would tell the other that their family member had AIDS; they told each other that it was something else.

> Family members have told us that they are willing to talk with other families who are dealing with AIDS, but not in a group, only on a one-to-one basis, and they want us to arrange the contact.

Concern that "others in the community will find out" prevents families from grieving openly about the death of a loved one from AIDS. Efforts to maintain secrecy about the cause of death interfere with family members' attempts to explore their own pain, give meaning to their experience, and ultimately resolve a range of confusing feelings that may surround a death from AIDS. Respondents reported:

> It's not uncommon for families to tell their neighbors, their minister, and even other relatives that their son is dying of cancer, not AIDS.

> I went to the funeral of a patient that I took care of, and there were all these people from this small town there, and his mother came up to me in tears and said "I'm so glad you're here, you're one of the few people who really knows that he died of it.". . . How's this mother ever going to work through her grief over her son's death, if she can't talk about what he died of?

Closely related to the issue of confidentiality are the two other themes that emerged as challenges to providing care to people with AIDS: (1) fear of AIDS contagion and (2) homophobia. If these two attitudes did not exist, confidentiality might be of less concern than it is.

## Fear of AIDS Contagion

Most respondents stated that it was difficult to arrange for services in certain communities because of the fear of AIDS contagion. Some hospices and home health agencies would not accept referrals because they had not yet developed staff policies and training for working with persons with AIDS or they did not have volunteers who were willing to make home visits. Respondents could not determine if this hesitancy to care for persons with AIDS reflected lack of awareness about the need for services, agency denial that AIDS had spread to their community, or fear of contagion. Arranging for county social services department chore workers or homemakers to work in homes of persons with AIDS also presented problems.

Respondents reported that some community residents believed that their risk of infection was increased by receiving care from individuals or agencies that provided care to persons with AIDS. Thus, those who work with persons with AIDS in rural areas also experience the stigma of AIDS, and this high-visibility stigma affects service delivery in various ways:

> None of the doctors here want to take care of AIDS patients, they either don't have the expertise or don't want it known that they treat AIDS patients in their practice for fear that other patients will not use them.

> We don't openly advertise that we treat AIDS patients, because then there will be a lot of publicity about it, which may affect other referrals or volunteers. . . . The community prefers to deal with this issue with denial. . . . They won't openly support you nor will they try to stop you as long as you don't broadcast what you're doing.

## Homophobia

Because AIDS was associated with the gay male community so early, separating homophobic reactions from reactions associated with fear of AIDS often is difficult. However, respondents identified incidents in which homophobia clearly interfered with persons with AIDS' receiving support, especially among the many gay persons with AIDS who had lived in urban areas and returned to their families after they were diagnosed with AIDS. Respondents stated that in some families the person with AIDS was allowed to move home only if he agreed to cease contact with gay friends and lovers, thus increasing the person's sense of isolation. One respondent said that the most difficult task in working with gay persons with AIDS was to prevent them from internalizing the homophobia prevalent in rural communities. Gay persons with AIDS who return to rural communities at a time of particular vulnerability to self-blame often confront the belief of many in the community that "AIDS is God's punishment for your sins."

Homophobia also has forced AIDS service organizations to struggle with how they identify themselves—as a gay organization providing services to all persons with AIDS or as an AIDS organization. Such organizations are aware that their identity influences funding, community support, and referrals. One respondent, who was a volunteer for an AIDS service organization, noted that even though the organization worked very hard to be identified as an AIDS organization, it often was perceived as a gay organization that served persons with AIDS, which reduced the number of referrals of nongays:

> We don't get the referrals that we should, because if the person isn't gay, they (the referring agency) think that the referral isn't appropriate. Just recently a wife of a [person with AIDS] contacted us for information on home precautions safe sex. She said that she wished that she had known about us earlier, because the information was very helpful. We were aware that the primary agency providing care had not told the wife about our organization because her husband wasn't gay.

In contrast, some AIDS service organizations have chosen to remain clearly gay-identified; they believe that providing a needed community service is one way to project a positive image and to bridge the gap between the gay and nongay communities. Several respondents stated that when health care providers deal with gay-identified men and women in professional roles and gay-identified human service organizations, the providers are forced to reexamine their stereotypes. Several of these organizations have been asked to present in-service training on homophobia to medical center staffs.

## Enhancing Service Provision

The social work interventions proposed in this article focus on coordinating, strengthening, and expanding existing community resources and networks rather than creating new delivery systems. Structural barriers to health and social services in rural areas are longstanding and likely will not be overcome without major economic changes and new directions in health care policy and delivery. Furthermore, because the number of AIDS cases in rural areas will remain low relative to the number in urban areas, developing separate agencies that provide services to persons with AIDS is not practical in small towns. Therefore, existing community agencies such as county public health and social service departments, and local home health and hospice agencies will need to work closely with informal community networks to provide AIDS care.

One way to reduce the effects of the geographic, cultural, and educational distance between the urban hospital and the rural community is to develop mechanisms to promote continuity of care. Coordination between hospital social workers who perform discharge planning and community agency social workers who function as case managers can be increased through education and the development of follow-up systems. Rural social workers can educate hospital social workers about the strengths, limitations, and indigenous care systems of rural communities; hospital social workers can share their expertise about the psychosocial dimensions of AIDS and the care needs of specific patients and families and explain the organizational pressures they experience to arrange for timely discharge. Follow-up systems should provide feedback to the hospital social workers about the outcome of discharge planning and to the community social worker about the hospital treatment plan when the patient eventually is readmitted.

Concerns about confidentiality need to be dealt within the context of improving continuity of care and as a critical component of discharge planning. Through collaborative efforts between the hospital and community social workers, the importance of confidentiality should be reinforced with community agencies. Breaches of confidentiality in the community can be dealt with quickly by the community social workers. Because community workers are knowledgeable about rural norms and social networks, they can work closely with the person with AIDS and the family to decide who in the community should be told about the AIDS diagnosis and how the information can be shared to mobilize support and protect confidentiality.[26]

Through support and education, social workers in the hospital and in the community can strengthen existing informal and formal networks that provide care to persons with AIDS and their families. Social workers need to explore with families ways that they can enlist help from their network. One strategy is for the social worker to bring together members of the network selected by the person with AIDS and the family to explain the person's diagnosis, prognosis, and care needs and to suggest ways that extended family, friends, and neighbors can provide support. Newmark and Taylor suggest another social work task in assisting families in obtaining support is to teach families how to get services from community agency staff who may have no previous experience with persons with AIDS and may feel uncomfortable and hostile.[27]

---

[26] J. Moore-Kirkland and K. V. Irey, "A Reappraisal of Confidentiality," *Social Work, 26* (July 1981), pp. 319-322.

[27] D. A. Newmark and E. H. Taylor, "The Family and AIDS," in C. G. Leukefeld and M. Fimbres, eds., *Responding to AIDS: Psychosocial Initiatives* (Silver Spring, MD: National Association of Social Workers, Inc., 1987), pp. 39-50.

Social workers also should prepare agencies to provide humane and compassionate care to persons with AIDS and their families. An important preliminary step in this process is to respond to the stigma attached to persons with AIDS and to agencies working with them.[28] One of the roles of rural social workers is to reduce stigma that interferes with clients receiving services.[29]

First, however, social workers need to educate themselves about AIDS and deal with their own fears and homophobia. When asked about AIDS education for health care professionals, a health care worker interviewed for the study discussed in this article stated, "to begin with, they need the same education as lay people; they're not immune to prejudice and fear."

Recognizing and working with the fears and homophobia of staff in social service and health care agencies is the next step in this educational process. Also, acknowledging the effects that caring for AIDS patients will have on staff, particularly in hospice and home health agencies, is crucial.[30] Hospice workers who traditionally have cared for older people dying of cancer will need considerable preparation and ongoing support to deal with the stress of caring for young people who are deteriorating mentally and physically. Social workers, nurses, physicians, and health educators from larger communities who have dealt with staff concerns about providing humane care to persons with AIDS and about AIDS transmissibility can be consulted by local home health and hospice staffs who are developing agency policies and procedures and in-service education. However, providing information will not be enough; ongoing sessions that encourage staff who work with persons with AIDS to openly express their homophobic attitudes and fears about AIDS contagion will be necessary. For people to confront and overcome their fears, they need a forum to discuss them in an atmosphere that promotes honesty and openness.[31]

When existing networks are unable or unwilling to provide care, social workers will need to build a network of people in the community who will provide support to persons with AIDS and their families. According to several respondents in the study, a one-on-one approach works better than community forums in smaller towns and with some cultural groups,

---

[28] A. L. Furstenberg and M. M. Olson, "Social Work and AIDS," *Social Work in Health Care,* 9 (Summer 1984), pp. 45-62; and C. Ryan and L. Caputo, "AIDS at the Interface: Policy, Practice, and Social Change." Paper presented at the National Association of Social Work Professional Symposium, Chicago, Illinois, November 1985.

[29] Wodarski, *Rural Community Mental Health Practice.*

[30] S. Geis and R. L. Fuller, "The Impact of the First Gay AIDS Patient on Hospice Staff," *The Hospice Journal,* 1 (Fall 1985), pp. 17-36.

[31] Ibid.; and J. Gramick, "Homophobia: A New Challenge," *Social Work,* 28 (March-April 1983), pp. 137-144.

because the approach does not call attention to the problem or "create a stir" and fits in with the "way people do things around here." By cautiously identifying individuals in the community and in health and social service agencies who might be interested in working with AIDS patients, social workers can develop networks to provide support and assistance to families caring for persons with AIDS. Social workers also might involve potentially supportive ministers and church communities, especially if the person with AIDS or the family belongs to the local church.

Another approach to network building is to invite selected community members to an AIDS educational session. Sheehan describes how a rural hospice successfully used this approach.[32] The hospital presented an educational program before persons with AIDS were in the community so that people could express concerns and have their fears and questions addressed. This hospice not only provided leadership but also confronted the stigma attached to an agency that works with persons with AIDS. By asking people to reframe their definition of community—not as "us and them" but instead as "they are part of us; we are all in this together"—the hospice challenged assumptions that difference deserves a different level of care. Residents who are asked to confront their fears as a community and to reexamine their value system in light of change in their community will be less likely to use denial of the problem to keep AIDS out of the community. When a respected agency brings a community together to address AIDS concerns and publicly states a commitment to provide care to AIDS patients, community fear and stigma are confronted, and thus health care providers can help rural communities to provide sensitive social and health care to persons with AIDS and their families.

---

[32] C. J. Sheehan, "Hospice, AIDS and the Community," *Caring*, 5 (June 1986), pp. 35-37.

# 19

# Limited Access:
# Health Care for the Rural Poor,
# Executive Summary, March 1991

by Laura Summer

M any rural residents face difficulty in obtaining health care. Access to health care for these residents may be limited by economic as well as geographic barriers and by a shortage of medical providers in rural areas.

These problems are most acute for those rural inhabitants who have low incomes. A substantial fraction of the rural population is poor, with the poverty rate for rural areas exceeding that for urban areas. In addition, when compared with the urban population, a larger proportion of rural residents in general–and of the rural poor in particular–lack health insurance coverage.

## Health Status of Rural Residents

In general, rural residents are not as healthy as residents of urban areas. While the differences between the metro and nonmetro populations are not great for most measures of health status, the nonmetro population consistently fares worse on these measures than the metro population does. Within the rural population, the health status of low income residents is inferior to that of residents with higher incomes. Poor rural residents are also more likely to be in poor health than are their poor urban counterparts.

One indication that health problems are somewhat greater in rural areas comes from the National Health Interview Survey, conducted annu-

---

In this report, the terms "urban," "metropolitan," and "metro" are used interchangeably to describe those areas designated by the Census Bureau as metropolitan statistical areas. The terms "rural," "nonmetropolitan," and "nonmetro" are used interchangeably to describe areas the Census Bureau designates as outside metropolitan statistical areas.

This Executive Summary is reprinted with permission from the Center on Budget and Policy Priorities, Washington, DC.

ally by the National Center for Health Statistics at the U.S. Department of Health and Human Services. In this survey, people are asked to assess their health status as excellent, very good, good, fair, or poor. The survey results show that a larger proportion of the nonmetro population than of the metro population reports itself to be in fair or poor health.

- For the years 1985 through 1987, fair or poor health was reported by 12.6 percent of nonmetro residents, but by 9.3 percent of metro residents.

- This difference holds across race and age lines with higher proportions of blacks, whites, and elderly people reporting themselves to be in fair or poor health in nonmetro than in metro areas.

- This disparity shows up among low income people, as well. Some 18.8 percent of nonmetro respondents with incomes below $20,000 rated their health as fair or poor, compared with 16.2 percent of metro residents in this income bracket.

- These differences in health assessments between metro and nonmetro residents are accompanied by a second, sharper set of differences: those between low income nonmetro residents and the rest of the nonmetro population. While 18.8 percent of nonmetro residents with incomes below $20,000 rated their health as fair or poor, just 5.7 percent of nonmetro residents at income levels above $20,000 did.

Data on the incidence of medical conditions provide a more objective measure of the health status of rural and urban residents. The incidence of acute conditions–short-term illnesses–is similar in metro and nonmetro areas. But the rate of "restricted activity days" associated with acute conditions–days on which a person must restrict ordinary activities–is greater among nonmetro residents. In addition, nonmetro residents are more likely than metro residents to be affected by chronic conditions–long-term illnesses–and also are more likely to incur injuries.

## Use of Health Care Services in Rural and Urban Areas

Although their health appears to be poorer, rural residents–and particularly poor people in rural areas–generally use health care services to a lesser extent than do their urban counterparts.

When health status is taken into account, nonmetro residents are less likely than metro residents to receive routine care from physicians. In the years 1985 through 1987, nonmetro residents in fair or poor health had fewer annual contacts with physicians than did metro residents in fair or poor health.

Similarly, while pregnant women in nonmetro and metro areas are equally likely to have medical conditions that could affect their pregnancies adversely, a larger proportion of women in nonmetro areas receive inadequate prenatal care. Pregnant women who live in rural areas are more likely than those in urban areas to begin prenatal care late in pregnancy and to make fewer than the recommended number of prenatal visits. Rural residents are also less apt than urban residents to receive adequate pediatric care. Children in fair or poor health see physicians less frequently in rural than in urban areas.

Rural residents in need of primary care services are less likely to receive them than are residents of urban areas. On the other hand, hospitalization rates among individuals in fair or poor health are similar in metro and nonmetro areas, and hospitalization rates among *all* individuals are actually higher in nonmetro areas. It may be that in the absence of primary care providers, rural residents must depend on hospitals to a greater extent than urban residents do.

## Barriers to Health Care Services for Rural Residents

For rural residents, particularly those who live in sparsely populated areas, geographic barriers to receiving health care services are significant. Often the population base in rural areas is simply not large enough to support the type of medical facilities and practitioners available to residents of more densely populated areas. In an emergency, the lack of proximity to care can be life threatening. For routine services, the need to travel great distances can be a deterrent to seeking care.

Rural residents with limited resources have more difficulty contending with the limited supply of health care providers. They are more likely to be discouraged by the amount of time required to travel for care, particularly if it results in a loss of income from hours lost at work. Also, transportation may be difficult to arrange. Public transportation is generally not available, and private transportation is often not affordable for low income households.

### Scarcity of Physicians

One factor limiting access to health care services is the scarcity of physicians in rural areas.

- In 1988, some 111 nonmetro counties in the United States had no physician at all. No metro county lacked a physician.
- That same year there were 97 practicing physicians per 100,000 people in nonmetro counties, compared with 225 per 100,000 people in metro counties.

Primary care physicians—those in general practice, family practice, general internal medicine, general pediatrics and obstetrics and gynecology—provide the majority of care in rural areas. Nevertheless, the supply of physicians participating in each of the primary care specialties is much more limited in rural than urban areas.

The shortage of obstetrical care providers is a particular problem. In 1988, there were 1,473 counties—all of them nonmetropolitan—that lacked even a single obstetrician. This represents almost two-thirds of all nonmetro counties. In addition, 22 states, including all of the 10 most rural states, had large regions with no practicing obstetrician in 1988. This shortage of obstetricians is eased to some extent by the availability of other physicians, such as family practitioners, who provide obstetrical care. Even when other providers are taken into account, however, obstetrical care is less available to women in rural than in urban areas. This problem is likely to worsen in the future, since the number of physicians providing obstetrical care is declining. Escalating malpractice insurance rates, low reimbursement rates from public and private insurers, and an increasing proportion of patients who cannot pay for maternity care are contributing to a continuing drop in the number of maternity care providers.

In 1988, there were also 1,488 nonmetro counties with no pediatrician. The number of pediatricians for every 100,000 women of childbearing age was more than three times higher in metro than in nonmetro areas.

### Vulnerability of Rural Hospitals

For most rural residents, access to hospital care is not as limited as access to ambulatory health care. There are indications, however, the financial viability of some rural hospitals is being threatened. Hospital closings can have a significant impact not only on access to hospital care in rural areas, but also on the availability of primary care services. Communities without hospitals have a harder time attracting and retaining health care professionals.

From 1981 through 1988, some 398 community hospitals closed. About half—48 percent—were located in rural areas. The percentage decline in the number of nonmetro hospitals during that period—7.8 percent—far exceeded the 2.1 percent decline in the number of metro hospitals.

### Financial Barriers

Many rural residents face significant financial barriers to receiving health care. Poverty rates are higher in rural than urban areas. Some 15.7 percent of the nonmetro population had incomes below the poverty level in 1989, compared with 12 percent of the population in metro areas.

Also, a substantial proportion of the rural population has no health insurance. Some 16.9 percent of all nonelderly nonmetro residents had no health insurance coverage in 1988, compared with 15.4 percent of nonelderly metro residents. In addition, during a 28-month period ending in May 1987, some 32 percent of nonmetro residents—nearly one in every three—lacked insurance for at least one month.

Insurance coverage rates are particularly low for the poor, women of childbearing age, and single-parent families. For all these groups, nonmetro residents have lower coverage rates than do metro residents. For example, 37.1 percent of the nonelderly poor in nonmetro areas lacked coverage in 1988, compared with 34.3 percent of those in metro areas.

A number of factors are associated with low health insurance coverage rates in rural areas. The poor are more likely to be uninsured than those with higher incomes, and a higher proportion of the nonmetro than of the metro population is poor. Also, health insurance coverage is closely related to employment, but a smaller proportion of nonmetro than of metro employees receive coverage through their jobs.

The differences are especially large among small businesses. A 1989 survey found that 46 percent of small businesses in rural areas do not sponsor health insurance for their employees, a figure far above the 28 percent of small businesses in urban areas that decline to provide coverage. In addition, 40 percent of all rural agricultural workers and their families had no coverage in 1988.

Another factor accounting for lower health insurance coverage rates in rural areas is the variability in Medicaid eligibility rules from state to state. Medicaid eligibility rules tend to be more restrictive in rural than in urban states. As a result, low income residents in rural areas are not as well served by Medicaid as their urban counterparts.

- In 1988, 38.7 percent of the nonmetro poor had Medicaid coverage.

- Some 44.8 percent of poor residents in metro areas had such coverage.

## Role of Federal Programs

### National Health Service Corps

The National Health Service Corps (NHSC) was established in 1972 to address problems stemming from the uneven geographic distribution of health care providers in the United States and the resulting inadequate access to health care services for many population groups. The Corps recruits physicians and other health professionals to serve in areas with a shortage of health professionals. These areas are known as health professional shortage areas, or HPSAs. The NHSC is particularly important to rural areas. Of 1,956 HPSAs in 1990, some 70 percent were in rural areas.

Over the years, the NHSC has placed thousands of health care practitioners in needy communities. These practitioners agree to serve in HPSAs in exchange for financial assistance with their educational expenses. Unfortunately, however, the effectiveness of the Corps has diminished sharply over the past decade, as funding for the program has been reduced. Funding peaked in fiscal year 1980 with an NHSC appropriation of $153.6 million. By contrast, the appropriation for fiscal year 1990 was only $50.7 million. This represented a decline of 77 percent, after adjusting for inflation.

As a result of these reductions, the field strength of the Corps has declined. At its peak, the Corps had 3,300 health care professionals in service. By 1989, only 1,944 professionals remained–fewer than half what the Department of Health and Human Services estimated was needed to provide service in health professional shortage areas. Many HPSAs now lack health care providers.

In October 1990, legislation was enacted to reauthorize the NHSC through the year 2000 and to begin rebuilding the Corps. The legislation includes provisions designed to increase the number of health care providers in HPSAs. A scholarship program that had attracted medical students to the Corps, but was terminated in 1987, is reinstated, and a student loan program is made more attractive. Other provisions are aimed at increasing the proportion of providers who will remain in HPSAs after their term in the Corps ends.

This legislation should help revitalize the NHSC–*if* funds are available to implement the initiatives and to recruit a sufficient number of health care providers. The fiscal year 1991 appropriation of $91.7 million for the Corps represents an increase of $41 million over the fiscal year 1990 appropriation. However, after inflation is taken into account, the appropriation for fiscal year 1991 is still 64 percent lower than funding was a decade earlier. In addition, the Bush Administration's funding request for fiscal year 1992–$96.1 million–does little more than maintain the fiscal year 1991 level, after adjustment for inflation.

The number of providers delivering health care services will eventually increase, as students now entering the scholarship program graduate and enter in the Corps. The Corps, however, will be able, in the immediate future, to supply only a modest fraction of the health care providers needed in underserved areas. The current scarce supply of NHSC providers continues to leave many rural communities without health care professionals.

### Community and Migrant Health Centers

Community health centers provide primary health care services in areas designated as "medically underserved" by the Department of Health and Human Services. The Migrant Health Centers program funds facilities much like community health centers that serve migrant and seasonal agricultural workers and their families. Many health centers receive funding from both the Community and Migrant Health Centers programs.

While the health services provided by community and migrant health centers are available to anyone in the area a center covers, the centers primarily serve patients with limited resources. In 1989, almost half of community and migrant health center patients–49 percent in rural centers and 48 percent in urban centers–were uninsured. Most other patients had insurance through a government program.

Community and migrant health centers are a particularly important source of health care services for low income rural residents. In 1989, some 60 percent of the community health centers were located in rural areas. Almost all funding for the migrant health center program supports centers located in rural areas. Nevertheless, due to funding constraints, many rural areas lack access to a community or migrant health center. Three of the ten most rural states–Montana, North Dakota, and Wyoming–have just one or two centers in the entire state.

In addition, in areas that have a center, the need for health care services often outstrips the ability of the center to provide them. A survey of community health centers in 1987 found long waiting lists of individuals seeking care. The waiting lists averaged between 15 percent and 28 percent of patient enrollment.

Adding to the centers' problems are rapidly rising health care costs. Many centers must devote increasing portions of their budgets to recruiting physicians, offering more competitive salaries, and paying the escalating cost of medical malpractice insurance premiums. Some centers must also pay for needed capital improvements. Other centers have been affected by the reductions in the ranks of the NHSC; in 1990, more than two-fifths of all physicians at community health centers were members of the Corps. In addition, the centers face an increased patient load. Between 1984 and 1988, the number of patient visits at rural community health centers rose from 9.3 million to 11 million. Finally, the centers are burdened financially by a patient population increasingly unable to pay for health care.

Despite these financial burdens, federal funding for community health centers has remained virtually unchanged since 1981, after adjusting for inflation. If the adjustment is made using inflation in medical care costs, rather than inflation in the economy as a whole, funding is found to have declined significantly. During the same period, funds for migrant health centers have fallen 21 percent, after adjusting for inflation. The Bush administration's fiscal year 1992 budget request includes no additional funding for Community and Migrant Health Center programs. With inflation, program funding will actually decline about four percent in fiscal year 1992.

Community and migrant health centers should benefit financially from federal legislative changes. These changes will increase the level of reimbursement the centers receive for providing services to Medicaid and Medicare beneficiaries. These increased reimbursements should enable some centers to reduce waiting lists and to provide care for a larger number of individuals who lack health insurance coverage. Some centers may also be in a position to expand the range of health care services they offer. Nevertheless, if new health centers are to be established in a substantial number of medically underserved areas, the Medicaid and Medicare changes will be insufficient. Significant increases in appropriations for the Community and Migrant Health Center programs will also be needed.

## The Medicaid Program

Both federal and state funds finance Medicaid, a health insurance program that pays for medical services for low income families with children and low income people who are elderly or have disabilities. States administer the program, and within federal guidelines, they make many of the key decisions on where to set income eligibility limits, which groups to cover, and which services to pay for.

Medicaid eligibility rules are generally more stringent in rural than urban states. Consequently, the proportion of low income people eligible for Medicaid is lower in nonmetro than in metro areas.

### Variations in Eligibility for Families with Children

Federal law requires all states to provide Medicaid benefits to pregnant women, infants, and children under age six with family incomes below 133 percent of the federal poverty line. However, states have the option of going beyond these mandates and providing Medicaid benefits to pregnant women and infants with family incomes up to 185 percent of the poverty line.

- As of July 1990, four of the ten most rural states had income limits for pregnant women and infants greater than 133 percent of the poverty line. By contrast, eight of the ten most urban states did.

- None of the frontier states sets income eligibility limits for pregnant women and infants above 133 percent of the poverty line.

As of July 1, 1991, states will also be required to extend coverage to poor children age six and older who were born after September 30, 1983. This requirement will phase in Medicaid coverage over the next 12 years for poor children from the ages of 6 through 18. By October 1, 2002—when this requirement will be fully phased in—virtually all poor children less than 19 years of age will be eligible for Medicaid.

For many members of low income families—including women who are not pregnant and (until October 1, 2002) some poor children age six and over—Medicaid eligibility remains based either on eligibility for Aid to Families with Dependent Children (AFDC) or, in some states, on income limits for the Medically Needy component of the Medicaid program. This is an optional program that provides Medicaid coverage to some individuals who have high medical expenses.

- In eight of the ten most rural states, Medicaid income limits for families with children are below 50 percent of the poverty line. This is true in only one of the ten most urban states.

- The median Medicaid income limit for a family of three is $373 per month in the ten most rural states. It is $638 per month in the ten most urban states, a difference that far exceeds any variation in the cost-of-living.

### Variations in Eligibility for People Who Are Elderly or Have Disabilities

Medicaid eligibility rules for the elderly and for people with disabilities also tend to be more restrictive in rural than in urban states. The

**State Definitions**

In this report, states are ranked as urban or rural according to the proportion of the population in each state living in metro and nonmetro areas.

The ten most rural states are: Arkansas, Idaho, Maine, Mississippi, Montana, North Dakota, South Dakota, Vermont, West Virginia, and Wyoming.

The ten most urban states are: California, Connecticut, District of Columbia, Florida, Maryland, Massachusetts, New Jersey, New York, Pennsylvania, and Rhode Island.

States in which approximately half or more of the counties are very sparsely populated are termed "frontier states." The 10 frontier states are: Alaska, Colorado, Idaho, Montana, Nevada, New Mexico, North Dakota, South Dakota, Utah, and Wyoming.

Medicaid eligibility rules for these groups are tied closely to eligibility for the Supplemental Security Income program (SSI). In about half of the states, the federal SSI income limit effectively serves as the Medicaid income limit for people who are elderly or have disabilities. Most of the remaining states add a state supplemental SSI benefit to the federal SSI benefit. In these states, SSI income eligibility limits are raised when state supplemental benefits are provided. This usually leads to an increase in Medicaid income limits as well. Rural states are less likely than urban states to provide these SSI supplemental benefits. As a result, Medicaid income limits for SSI beneficiaries tend to be significantly lower in rural than in urban states.

States also have an option to extend Medicaid eligibility to elderly people and people with disabilities who are not on SSI but who still are poor. Essentially, states can cover elderly people and people with disabilities whose incomes fall between the state's SSI income limit and the poverty line. As of July 1989, some 13 states had adopted this option. Urban states make greater use of the option than rural states do.

Taking into account the various state options, the most urban states have considerably more generous Medicaid eligibility rules than the most rural states do. (Income eligibility limits for people with disabilities generally are the same or similar to those for the elderly.)

- In 1989, Medicaid income at eligibility limits for elderly individuals and couples was at the poverty line or higher in eight of the ten most urban states.

- By contrast, in eight of the ten most rural states, Medicaid income limits for elderly individuals and couples fell below the poverty line.

- In all nine frontier states, Medicaid income limits for elderly people were below the poverty line.

## Facilitating Application and Enrollment

Some of those eligible for Medicaid benefits may not receive them because of a cumbersome application process. States have a number of options available to streamline the application process. However, many rural states fail to use these options.

One such option is known as "presumptive eligibility." This enables publicly funded health clinics to make temporary determinations of Medicaid eligibility at sites where pregnant women receive health care. The women must then apply for benefits at the Medicaid agency before the end of the following month. In states adopting this option, pregnant women receive immediate Medicaid coverage for prenatal care. In states without presumptive eligibility, pregnant women must go to the local welfare office to apply for Medicaid and then may have to wait up to 45 days for their application to be processed.

- As of July 1990, three of the ten most rural states had elected the presumptive eligibility option. Six of the ten most urban states had.
- Four of the nine frontier states had a presumptive eligibility program.

In a majority of states, poor elderly people and people with disabilities who receive SSI benefits are automatically enrolled in Medicaid. No separate Medicaid application is required. In six states, a separate application must be filed with the state Medicaid agency, even though all SSI recipients who apply will be granted Medicaid coverage. Three of these states—Idaho, Nevada, and Utah—are frontier states. Filing a separate application is particularly burdensome for elderly applicants living in rural areas and frontier areas where the population is widely dispersed.

In all states, a new group of low income elderly people and people with disabilities is eligible for a limited form of Medicaid assistance. Known as Qualified Medicare Beneficiaries, these people have incomes below the poverty line but are not otherwise eligible for Medicaid coverage in their states. They now are eligible to have Medicaid pay all Medicare cost-sharing charges for them—but to receive this assistance, they must file an application with the Medicaid office. Preliminary data indicate that many eligible elderly and disabled poor are not aware of this and have not applied. Major outreach efforts in this area appear to be needed. Such efforts are particularly significant in rural areas; a disproportionate share of the people eligible for this new benefit are rural residents.

## Services Covered under Medicaid

In addition to having discretion over many Medicaid eligibility rules, states have considerable discretion over which medical services will be covered. While federal law requires coverage for 9 core services, whether to provide coverage for 33 additional services is left up to the state. In 1990, only 2 of the 10 most rural states covered more than 25 of the 33 optional services. By contrast, six of the ten most urban states did.

States are also allowed to provide additional services for specific groups of beneficiaries. For example, states may choose to cover a number of special "enhanced prenatal services" for pregnant women. Half of the highly rural states fail to provide coverage for enhanced prenatal services. Most of the highly urban states do cover these services.

## Provider Participation

For Medicaid beneficiaries, access to services is also determined by the willingness of health care providers to accept Medicaid patients. The scarcity of medical practitioners willing to accept Medicaid patients is a growing problem in many areas of the country. Participation among obstetricians is particularly low, and participation among pediatricians has declined in recent years. In rural areas, where there is a shortage of maternity care providers, concerns about the effect of low Medicaid participation by these providers is particularly acute. In a National Governors' Association survey, 35 states reported that lack of maternity care providers was a significant problem for low income women in rural areas. Only three states reported such a problem in urban areas.

One reason physicians commonly cite for low Medicaid participation is the low rates the program pays for medical services. A study by the American Academy of Pediatrics found that pediatricians were less likely to participate in Medicaid in 1989 than they had been in 1978. Those who did participate in 1989 were more likely to limit their participation. When pediatricians were asked to identify reasons for not participating in Medicaid or for limiting participation, 71 percent cited low Medicaid reimbursement rates. A survey by the American College of Obstetricians and Gynecologists finds considerable variation among states in Medicaid reimbursement rates with the rates for routine obstetrical care generally lower in rural states than in urban ones

## Recommendations

The recommendations in this report focus on several programs that could improve rural residents' access to health care–the National Health Service Corps, Community and Migrant Health Center programs, and Medicaid. This approach emphasizes changes that can have positive effects now. In the long term, both a restructuring of the health insurance system and a policy to insure that health care services are widely available are needed. But the lack of agreement about how to restructure the health care system and finance major changes in it makes it unlikely large-scale restructuring is imminent. Moreover, if major health care reform legislation is enacted and financing becomes available, such changes are likely to take some years to implement. In the interim, existing programs will need to be as strong as possible. In addition, these programs may also become part of a reformed health care system.

### The National Health Service Corps

Congressional action in 1990 reauthorizing the National Health Service Corps through the year 2000 represents a federal commitment to improve access to health care in areas with a shortage of primary health care providers. With adequate funding of the NHSC, the supply of health practitioners in rural areas should increase. The critical issue is funding. To build a strong NHSC, substantial increases are needed.

Unfortunately, the large federal budget deficit and the new spending ceilings on domestic nonentitlement programs make it probable the amounts appropriated will remain insufficient to achieve the program's goals in full. If primary health care services are to be available in all areas of the country, state efforts will need to complement the work of the Corps.

- Substantial increases are needed in the federal funds appropriated for the NHSC.

- States should establish programs that offer financial assistance in return for a commitment from recipients to practice medicine in designated areas of the state.

- Financial aid should be directed to the training of primary care practitioners.

### Community and Migrant Health Centers

The majority of community and migrant health centers are located in rural areas, and they improve access to health care for many rural residents. The centers provide health services to many low income rural people who might otherwise go without care. But Community and Migrant Health Center programs could have a greater impact if existing centers could serve more patients and if more centers could be established.

- Funding for community and migrant health centers should be increased significantly so that waiting lists can be sharply reduced or eliminated and necessary improvements made at these centers—and also so that centers can be established in more medically underserved areas.

- The Federal Tort Claims Act should be extended to cover all practitioners providing obstetrical care in community and migrant health centers so that the centers do not have to use large portions of their federal grants to pay for escalating malpractice insurance costs.

### The Medicaid Program

Efforts to expand Medicaid eligibility, to reach and enroll newly eligible people, and to ensure that those with Medicaid coverage are able to receive the health care services they need can significantly increase access to health care for the low income rural population.

While the federal government pays at least half of all Medicaid costs, any expansion requires state funds. With the current economic downturn, some states will have difficulty contemplating further Medicaid expansions in the near future. But economic problems are more severe in some states than in others. In addition, states may be able to consider these improvements when the economic downturn ends and the economy—and state revenues—begin to grow at a more normal pace.

In assessing the Medicaid recommendations discussed here, states should consider longer term effects as well as short-term costs. In particular, since the federal government pays a substantial share of Medicaid costs in all states, Medicaid brings federal funds into state economies.

This is particularly significant for rural states, because the percentage of Medicaid costs paid by the federal government is generally higher there than in urban states. In the ten most rural states, the federal government pays from 62.8 percent to 80.2 percent of Medicaid costs. In six of these states, the federal matching rate exceeds 70 percent.

Since Medicaid is administered and financed through a federal-state partnership, some changes are most appropriately made at the federal level, while other changes involve state decisions to take greater advantage of program options.

## Federal Action

- Income eligibility limits should be increased to provide Medicaid for all pregnant women and infants with family incomes below 185 percent of the federal poverty line.
- The assets test for pregnant women, infants, and young children should be eliminated.
- Congress should give states the option to increase income eligibility limits to provide Medicaid for children with family incomes below 185 percent of the federal poverty line.
- Elderly people and people with disabilities should be permitted to apply at Social Security offices to become Qualified Medicare Beneficiaries.
- Efforts should be made to better publicize the availability of Qualified Medicare Beneficiaries.

## State Action

- In the absence of federal mandates, states should expand Medicaid coverage for pregnant women and infants with family incomes up to 185 percent of the poverty line.
- Medicaid offices should work with community and migrant health centers to establish systems for the on-site acceptance and initial processing of applications for Medicaid from pregnant women and children.

- All Medicaid programs should offer "presumptive eligibility" for pregnant women.
- States with automatic Medicaid eligibility for SSI recipients should remove the requirement for elderly people and people with disabilities to file a separate application for Medicaid.
- States should publicize new Medicaid income eligibility limits and emphasize that Medicaid coverage is available apart from participation in the AFDC or SSI program.
- Outreach efforts should be targeted to reach families who do not ordinarily participate in public assistance programs.
- States should publicize the Medicaid EPSDT program so more families are aware that comprehensive coverage for preventive and curative services is available for children.
- Outreach efforts should be targeted to reach elderly people and people with disabilities who do not ordinarily participate in public assistance programs.
- Medicaid programs should provide coverage for a wide range of enhanced prenatal services.
- States should take steps to improve the likelihood that beneficiaries are able to find a provider who will deliver the services their Medicaid program offers.
- Medicaid programs should provide coverage for home and community-based services for the frail elderly.
- Medicaid programs should offer higher reimbursement rates for obstetricians and pediatricians who practice in areas with provider shortages.
- Medicaid programs should provide other incentives to encourage the participation of health care providers who practice in geographic areas or medical specialties with a shortage of Medicaid providers.

# 20

# Homelessness in Rural Areas: Causes, Patterns, and Trends

by Richard J. First, John C. Rife, and Beverly G. Toomey

Efforts to address the problem of homelessness with emergency responses during the 1980s have failed to stop the growth of this social condition. Although homelessness is not new to the United States (Hoch, 1987), the number of people without a home has risen dramatically during the 1980s (Burt & Cohen, 1989). Stereotypical portraits of homeless people as skid-row alcoholics and happy wanderers have been replaced by more accurate portrayals that show people who are homeless because of economic and social factors beyond their control (Hopper, 1986; U.S. Committee on Government Operations, 1985). Most prior studies on homelessness have focused on large urban areas (Hombs & Snyder, 1982; Rossi, Fisher, & Willis, 1985; U.S. Conference of Mayors, 1986, 1989); few studies have examined homelessness in rural communities (Redburn & Buss, 1986). Yet homelessness in rural areas appears to be growing (Frank & Streeter, 1987; Housing Assistance Council, 1987; Patton, 1987; Wilkerson, 1989). The lack of knowledge about the needs of people who are homeless in rural and other nonurban areas and about the causes of their homelessness has prevented social workers and policymakers from adequately addressing the problem.

This chapter presents the results from the first major statewide study of rural and nonurban homelessness. During a six-month period in 1990, 919 homeless adults were interviewed in 21 randomly selected rural counties in Ohio. The results document the characteristics, needs, and resources of people who are unable to locate and afford a place to live in rural America.

## Homelessness in Rural Areas

Rossi (1989) noted that about 40 studies of homelessness have been completed in large and mid-sized cities in the United States. Estimates of the number of homeless people in the United States varied in the early 1980s from 250,000 to 3,000,000 (Hombs & Snyder, 1982; U.S. Department of Housing and Urban Development, 1984). More recently, studies have estimated that between 500,000 and 735,000 individuals are homeless on any given

Reprinted from *Social Work* (January 1994), with permission of the National Association of Social Workers.

night (U.S. Department of Housing and Urban Development, 1989). In 1990 the U.S. Bureau of the Census attempted to count the number of people who were homeless throughout the country. Their results have been criticized as undercounting (Burt, 1992). Of 39,000 surveys sent by the U.S. Bureau of the Census to local officials across the country to identify shelter and street locations for data collection, only 10% were returned. Of those returned, nearly all were from urban centers with more than 50,000 people (Ohio Coalition for the Homeless, 1990). Although a definitive national count of homeless people is not available, there is widespread agreement that the number of homeless Americans has grown significantly since 1980 (Burt & Cohen, 1989; Reyes & Waxman, 1989; Wright, 1989).

Reports also have begun to note that rural homelessness appears to be growing (Patton, 1987; Segal, 1989). The rate of poverty in rural areas is increasing more rapidly than in urban areas, and unemployment rates are as high as 20% (McCormick, 1988). However, people who are homeless in rural areas are often less visible than their urban counterparts because of the scarcity of social services and shelter programs to assist them. Instead, they often must rely on relatives, friends, and self-help strategies (Patton, 1987). The increase in the number of people who are homeless in rural areas has placed a significant strain on these traditional support systems. The U.S. Commission on Cooperation and Security in Europe (1990) noted, "While the rural homeless do not face with equal intensity many of the problems associated with homeless conditions in urban areas, their need for shelter and other comprehensive services appears similarly pressing" (p. 22).

During the past decade many rural Americans have experienced an economic crisis unmatched since the Great Depression (Patton, 1987). Social and economic changes have severely affected the fortunes of many rural people. For example, from 1981 to 1987, 650,000 farm foreclosures occurred, and it is estimated that at least 500,000 jobs have been lost in low-wage, labor-intensive rural manufacturing industries (Sinclair, 1987). Murdock et al. (1988) estimated that by the middle of the 1990s, agriculturally dependent counties will experience substantial losses in local earnings and tax revenues. In addition, the foreclosure of farms results in negative secondary effects in the business sector: For every six to seven farms lost to foreclosure, one business fails (Lobao, 1990). These events have resulted in human suffering that has been amply documented (Beeson & Johnson, 1987; Joslin, Link, & Rosmann, 1986; Norem & Blundall, 1988).

These social and economic changes have seriously jeopardized the well-being of many people who live in rural areas. Inequality between rural and urban areas, once thought to be closing, is now widening. Median family income among rural residents declined more significantly than among urban residents during the 1980s, and one out of four rural children lived in poor households (O'Hare, 1988). Yet during the past decade, federal programs have been inadequately funded to address the growing problems of poverty and homelessness in both rural and urban areas (First, Toomey, Rife, & Greenlee, 1990). The U.S. Commission on Cooperation and Security in Europe (1990), in reviewing the country's compliance with the Helsinki Human Rights Accords, found that federal policy responses to the problem of homelessness in the United States were inadequate:

> Despite the demonstrated need for more federally subsidized housing, which dramatically and visibly increased each year, federal low-income housing assistance has diminished, programs aiding the poor have been severely cut, and the minimum wage remains insufficient to provide economic viability for adequate housing. America's poverty population has grown substantially, and consequently, so has homelessness. (pp. 2-3)

With the economic crisis facing many parts of rural America, it is surprising that so little attention in social work has been given to the problem of rural homelessness. To date the rural homeless population has not been adequately described or quantified (Burt, 1990; Rossi, 1989). In the largest descriptive study completed to date, the Ohio Department of Mental Health (Roth & Bean, 1986; Roth, Bean, Lust, & Saveanu, 1985) provided a picture of homelessness in 16 randomly selected rural Ohio counties. However, in the time since publication of these findings, service providers and advocacy groups have observed that the faces of homelessness are changing; increasing numbers of rural people, children and families, and minority people are becoming homeless (U.S. Conference of Mayors, 1989). Unfortunately, no large-scale systematic studies of rural homelessness have been published. The statewide study described here sought to address this deficiency by identifying the characteristics, needs, and resources of people who are homeless in rural areas.

## Method

### Study Setting

The study was conducted from February through July 1990. The sample was obtained by attempting to locate and interview all homeless adults in 21 randomly selected rural counties that represented 26% of the rural population of the midwestern state. The midwestern state's 88 counties were initially divided into five geographic regions. Thirteen urban counties were eliminated from the study. The sampling frame for the study was 75 rural counties. To be designated as rural, a county must have had less than 200,000 in total population and a designated area of at least the state mean (26.7%) of the total rural area per county. Four counties were randomly selected from each of the five regions, and one more was drawn from the region with the most counties.

The counties represent a variety of nonurban contexts ranging from very sparsely populated rural farm and mining areas to growing suburban communities adjacent to large cities. These counties range from one to nine on the Beale code defining rural and nonurban counties based largely on density of population (U.S. General Accounting Office, 1989). Counties in this sample ranged from 11,000 to 150,000 in population, with no city having a population of more than 50,000. The three counties with the largest populations (more than 100,000) reflect different patterns of population density and proximity to metropolitan areas. For example, the most populated county had an evenly distributed population with a county seat of about 3,000, whereas another county's population was more centrally located in the county seat.

The percentage of county land area classified as rural in the sample ranged from 32.7% to 100%, with a median amount of 73.2%. Eight of the 21 counties met the most rural classifications of the Beale codes with low density and distance from highly populated counties. Six counties had moderate-size populations and limited proximity to urban areas. Seven counties were more densely populated because they bordered on an urban county.

The poverty rates of the sample counties in 1990 ranged from 5.1% to 36.6%, with a median of 11.6% (Council for Economic Opportunities of Greater Cleveland, 1991). The distribution of nonfarming to farming jobs in the sample counties helps describe the types of economy that were represented at the time of data collection. The five with the most farming jobs had employment ratios from 8.6 to 13.7, and the four with the fewest farming jobs had ratios of 95.7 to 143.1 (Ohio Department of Agriculture, 1987; Ohio Department of Development, 1988).

### Definition of Homelessness

This study used the same operational definition of homelessness that was used in the previous study of homelessness in Ohio (Roth et al., 1985). Each potential respondent was screened using this definition. If potential respondents stated they did not have a permanent residence or home, they were defined as homeless if they

- slept in limited or no shelter for any length of time
- slept in shelters or missions operated by religious organizations or public agencies that serve homeless people and charge either no fee or a minimal fee
- slept in inexpensive hotels or motels where the actual length of stay or intent to stay was 45 days or fewer
- slept in other unique situations where the actual length of stay or intent to stay was 45 days or fewer, including staying with family or friends for short periods of time.

The inclusion of this last category was important because many rural counties do not have formal services such as shelter care for homeless people (Patton, 1987).

## Study Instrument

The authors used the Homeless Person Survey Instrument, which was adapted from Roth et al. (1985). The instrument consisted of three sections:

1. The Demographic and Life Experience Information section contained 101 questions about living arrangements, reasons for being homeless, patterns of homelessness, transience, use of human services including mental health services, employment history, medical concerns, drug and alcohol use, family structure, social support, and general well-being.

2. The Psychiatric Status Schedule used 10 selected scales of the Psychiatric Status Schedule developed by Spitzer, Endicott, and Cohen (1970).

3. The Interview Postmortem section contained items that were completed after the interview by the interviewers, including the setting where the interview occurred, respondent characteristics (gender, unusual behaviors based on observation), and an assessment of the accuracy of respondents' answers.

## Data Collection and Analysis

This study attempted to locate and interview all of the homeless people in the 21 sample counties over the six-month data collection period. To facilitate the identification of homeless people, the investigators and project staff built relationships with knowledgeable residents in each county. Using a snowball technique and telephone contacts, meetings with advocacy groups, and frequent field visits to the counties, a referral and interviewing network was established in each of the 21 counties. The network included county coordinators who supervised the data collection process in each county, interviewers, and key advisors who identified and referred homeless people for interviews. Of 1,100 adults who met the definition of homelessness in the study, all completed the eligibility screening process, and 919 (83.5%) were interviewed. There were no significant differences between the total number screened as eligible and those interviewed on race and gender, the only variables easily recorded on those people not interviewed. Those who were not interviewed either refused or were unable to be interviewed because of disability. Although the authors acknowledge that some homeless people may have been missed during the interview process, this is the most exhaustive and representative sample studied in nonurban areas to date.

Interviewers were carefully selected for their ability to use the instruments reliably, to engage homeless people for interviews, and to respect those who were interviewed. Most interviewers had at least a bachelor's degree and training or experience in the social sciences or human services. Ninety-five interviewers and five central office staff members conducted all the interviews. The interviewing staff included both men and women and people of all age groups from college students to senior citizens. Interviewers were predominantly white, but some were African American and Hispanic. The county coordinators and the interviewers were contract employees of the project. The county coordinators received a monthly retainer, and a fee of $30 was paid to the interviewers for each completed interview. To ensure standardized use of the instruments, training sessions were held for all interviewers.

Interviews took place in offices, service settings, diners, motel rooms, and cars as well as out-of-the-way spots such as state parks, barns, laundromats, bars, and under railroad trestles. Interviewers were trained to know community resources and make referrals for respondents who wanted services; however, they were cautioned to respect client wishes and not be coercive or break a respondent's confidentiality. Many interviewers were able to assist respondents with referrals or resources even though it was not inherent in the project. The average length of interviews was 45 minutes; some took only 30 minutes, and others lasted as long as two hours.

All completed interviews were reviewed by the research staff to ensure eligibility of the respondents. When sensitive questions were asked, respondents were given the option of refusing to answer. Interviewers were asked to rate respondents' level of honesty as part of the Interview Post-mortem section of the questionnaire. Overall, interviewers rated respondents as being fairly to completely accurate 95.4% of the time. Double counting of respondents was avoided through two safeguards. First, participants were asked during eligibility determination if they had been interviewed previously. Because there was no payment for the interview, there was little incentive to repeat it. Second, each interviewer established a code number comprising the respondent's birthdate and first three letters of their last name. Two duplicates were found and eliminated from the analysis.

This is a descriptive study using the sample obtained as a full population of homeless people in the sample counties. No inferential tests were performed. Generalization to the nonsample rural counties and other areas are suggested only when the environmental context appears similar.

## Findings

### Characteristics of Respondents

Of the 919 homeless people interviewed in this study, 48.5% were male and 51.5% were female (Table 1). Minorities accounted for 14.3% of the sample, and 10.1% were African Americans. By comparison, the percentage of African Americans in the sample counties, according to the 1990 census, was only 3.04%. Thus, minorities were overrepresented in the sample.

The age range of respondents was 18 to 85 years. The mean age was 31.5 years, and the median was 29 years. More than three-quarters (78.4%) of the respondents were between 18 and 39 years. Only 7.7% were 50 and older. More than half (56.7%) of the homeless respondents had graduated from high school. Thirty-five percent had completed grades nine through eleven, whereas only 7.4% had an education of eighth grade or less.

Nearly one-third (32.0%) of the respondents had never been married; 38.9% were separated, divorced, or widowed; and 28.0% were married or in a couple. More than one-eighth (13.7%) were military service veterans, including 4.6% who reported being Vietnam-era veterans. Most (85.8%) reported that they had not previously served in the military.

Differences in respondents based on gender were found (Table 2). Women in the sample tended to be younger than men and were more likely to have been married. Women were also more likely to be heading families with children and to be doubling up with family and friends. The men were more likely to have completed high school; were more mobile; had been homeless

*Table 1.* **Demographic Characteristics of Respondents (N = 919)**

| Characteristic | n | % |
|---|---|---|
| Gender | | |
| Male | 446 | 48.5 |
| Female | 473 | 51.5 |
| Ethnicity | | |
| White | 779 | 84.8 |
| African American | 93 | 10.1 |
| Hispanic | 23 | 2.5 |
| Other | 16 | 1.7 |
| No answer | 8 | 0.9 |
| Age | | |
| 18–29 years | 480 | 52.2 |
| 30–39 years | 241 | 26.2 |
| 40–49 years | 124 | 13.5 |
| 50–59 years | 46 | 5.0 |
| 60 years and older | 25 | 2.7 |
| No answer | 3 | 0.3 |
| Education | | |
| Completed grades 1–8 | 68 | 7.4 |
| Completed grades 9–11 | 322 | 35.0 |
| High school graduate | 521 | 56.7 |
| No answer | 8 | 0.9 |
| Marital status | | |
| Married or living together | 257 | 28.0 |
| Separated or divorced | 340 | 37.0 |
| Widowed | 18 | 1.9 |
| Never been married | 294 | 32.0 |
| No answer | 10 | 1.1 |
| Veteran status | | |
| Yes | 126 | 13.7 |
| Vietnam veteran | 42 | 4.6 |
| No | 788 | 85.8 |
| No answer | 5 | 0.5 |

longer; and were more likely to stay in shelters or in limited shelter, such as cars, abandoned buildings, and public facilities. Women were more likely to cite family conflict or dissolution as reasons for their homelessness than were men.

Few demographic differences based on race or ethnicity were identified. White respondents were more likely to be married and to identify family conflict as a primary reason for homelessness than were Hispanic or African American respondents.

## Patterns of Homelessness

At the time of interview, 14.5% of the respondents reported living in limited shelter or having no shelter; 39.1% reported living in missions,

*Table 2.* **Gender Differences of Respondents (N = 919)**

| Characteristic | Male (n = 446) | | Female (n = 473) | |
|---|---|---|---|---|
| | n | % | n | % |
| Ethnicity | | | | |
| White | 367 | 82.3 | 412 | 87.1 |
| African American | 51 | 11.4 | 42 | 8.9 |
| Hispanic | 16 | 3.6 | 7 | 1.5 |
| Other | 7 | 1.6 | 9 | 1.9 |
| No answer | 5 | 1.1 | 3 | 0.6 |
| Age | | | | |
| 18–29 years | 198 | 44.4 | 282 | 59.6 |
| 30–39 years | 127 | 28.5 | 114 | 24.1 |
| 40–49 years | 73 | 16.4 | 51 | 10.8 |
| 50–59 years | 26 | 5.8 | 20 | 4.2 |
| 60 years and older | 20 | 4.5 | 5 | 1.1 |
| No answer | 2 | 0.4 | 1 | 0.2 |
| Education | | | | |
| Completed grades 1–8 | 45 | 10.1 | 25 | 5.3 |
| Completed grades 9–11 | 135 | 30.3 | 186 | 39.3 |
| High school graduate | 260 | 58.3 | 260 | 55.0 |
| No answer | 6 | 1.3 | 2 | 0.4 |
| Marital status | | | | |
| Married or living together | 104 | 23.3 | 153 | 32.3 |
| Separated or divorced | 141 | 31.7 | 199 | 42.1 |
| Widowed | 12 | 2.7 | 6 | 1.3 |
| Never been married | 183 | 41.0 | 111 | 23.5 |
| No answer | 6 | 1.3 | 4 | 0.8 |
| Veteran status | | | | |
| Yes | 122 | 27.4 | 4 | 0.8 |
| Vietnam veteran | 42 | 9.4 | 0 | 0 |
| No | 320 | 71.8 | 468 | 98.9 |
| No answer | 4 | 0.8 | 1 | 0.2 |

shelters, or inexpensive hotels and motels (Table 3). Nearly one-half (46.1%) were doubling up with family members and friends.

For many respondents, homelessness was a relatively new experience. Nearly 89.2% had been homeless for one year or less, 50.1% for 49 days or fewer. Some respondents had been homeless for extended periods, including 56 people (6.1%) who had been homeless for more than two years. The mean length of time homeless for all respondents was 220.6 days, just over seven months.

In regard to mobility, 52.3% of the respondents were either permanent or long-term (more than one year) residents of the area where they were interviewed. Thirty percent were recent arrivals who had lived in the area four weeks or less. More than one-half of the nonpermanent residents (51.1%) had moved from another state, and 48.6% had moved from another in-state county.

Respondents were asked to identify the most important reason for their current homelessness. Up to three responses were recorded. The first answer is reported here as the most important. Economic factors (eviction,

*Table 3.* **Patterns of Homelessness (N = 919)**

| Measure | n | % |
|---|---|---|
| Most important reason for homelessness | | |
|     Family conflict or dissolution | 279 | 30.4 |
|     Eviction or problem paying rent | 241 | 26.2 |
|     Unemployed | 173 | 18.8 |
|     Other (such as government benefits stopping) | 98 | 10.7 |
|     Disaster victim | 58 | 6.3 |
|     Alcohol or drug abuse | 47 | 5.1 |
|     Just liked to move around | 22 | 2.4 |
|     Deinstitutionalization | 16 | 1.7 |
|     No answer | 7 | 0.8 |
| Where respondent stayed night prior to interview | | |
|     Doubling up | 424 | 46.1 |
|     With family | 250 | 27.2 |
|     With friends | 174 | 18.9 |
|     Mission or shelter | 276 | 30.0 |
|     Limited or no shelter | 133 | 14.5 |
|     Car | 73 | 7.9 |
|     Street | 39 | 4.2 |
|     Other | 21 | 2.4 |
|     Inexpensive hotels and motels | 84 | 9.1 |
|     No answer | 2 | 0.2 |
| Resident of county one year or more | 481 | 52.3 |
| Length of time homeless | | |
|     Mean | 220.6 days | |
|     Median | 49 days | |
|     Range | 1 day to 14 years | |

problems paying rent, and unemployment) were cited by 45.0% of the sample. Family problems were cited by 30.4% of the respondents. Only 5.1% indicated that they were homeless because of alcohol or drug problems, and only 2.4% stated that they were homeless because "they just liked to move around." Deinstitutionalization was reported by only 1.7% of the respondents. Of the 60 other reasons, the most frequent answers were poor health (1.3%) and lack of affordable housing (1.0%).

### Resources and Needs of Respondents

Most of the respondents (90.0%) had worked for pay previously in their lives, and nearly one-third (31.2%) had worked for pay in the month preceding their interview. Of the 287 respondents who had worked in the past month, 43.2% had worked in permanent full-time positions, and 20.2% had worked in permanent part-time positions (Table 4).

About two-thirds of the respondents (67.6%) had received income in the month preceding their interview. For those having income in the past month, the most frequently mentioned sources included earnings (38.8%), welfare (38.3%), Supplemental Security Income/Supplemental Security Disability Income (10.6%), and social security or pension (3.1%). Although many respondents stayed with relatives, income provided by family and friends was very limited (4.8%).

More than one-half of the respondents (52.1%) stated that they had relatives they could count on for help, and 53.0% indicated that they had friends they could count on for help. These same questions were previously asked of a random sample ($N = 2,157$) of the general rural adult population in the same state (Stefl, 1983); more than 90% of that study's respondents indicated they had family and friends they could count on for help. A smaller percentage of this sample believed they had relatives or friends they could count on.

More than one-eighth of the respondents (16.4%) had been hospitalized at least once for emotional or mental health problems. This percentage is much lower than the percentage of homeless people who have reported psychiatric hospitalizations in prior urban studies (Fischer, 1991; Rossi, 1989). Less than one-tenth (6.1%) had been hospitalized at least once in a state psychiatric facility, and 11.4% had been hospitalized at least once in a general hospital setting for psychiatric reasons.

Using the Psychiatric Status Schedule and criteria of seriousness developed by Spitzer, Endicott, Cohen, and Nee (1980), only 41 individuals (4.5%) were identified as having serious symptoms on the psychiatric severity scale. This scale included depression and anxiety, suicidal thoughts, grandiosity, and suspicion-hallucination elements. Disorders labeled behavioral disturbances such as memory deficits, agitation, and belligerence were measured on the behavioral disturbance severity scale. Fewer than one-tenth (6.4%) were found to have serious problems in this area. To support the validity of these scales, differences were tested between those who reported prior hospitalization for mental health reasons and those who did not. Formerly hospitalized respondents had significantly greater mean scores on both scales than did respondents with no history of psychiatric hospitalization ($p < .01$).

Most (91.2%) of the respondents reported their general health status to be either good or fair. Only 8.1% stated their health was poor. However, when asked if they had major health problems for which they should see a doctor, 25.2% indicated that they did. The most frequently mentioned health problems included heart and circulatory problems, respiratory problems, problems with pregnancy, musculoskeletal diseases, and injuries and poisoning. More than one-third (35.7%) of the respondents stated that they had seen a medical professional in the past three months, and 28.9% indicated that it had been one or more years since they had seen a medical professional.

*Table 4.* **Resources and Needs of Respondents ($N = 919$)**

| Resources and Needs | n | % |
|---|---|---|
| Employment history | | |
|    Have been employed | 827 | 90.0 |
|    Worked in past month | 287 | 31.2 |
|    Worked full-time | 124 | 13.5 |
| Had income during the past month | 621 | 67.6 |
| Primary source of income for those who had | | |
|    income during the past month | | |
|    Earnings | 241 | 38.8 |
|    Welfare | 238 | 38.3 |
|    Supplemental Security Income or | | |
|    Supplemental Security Disability Income | 66 | 10.6 |
|    Family or friends | 30 | 4.8 |
|    Other | 27 | 4.3 |
|    Social security or pension | 19 | 3.1 |
| Respondents with relatives they could count on | 479 | 52.1 |
| Respondents with friends they could count on | 487 | 53.0 |
| Mental health needs | | |
|    Prior hospitalization | 151 | 16.4 |
|    Serious behavior problems | 59 | 6.4 |
|    Serious psychiatric problems | 41 | 4.5 |
| Physical health needs | | |
|    No medical care for more than a year | 265 | 28.9 |
|    Have health problems | 232 | 25.2 |
|    Pregnant | 39 | 4.2 |
|    Not receiving prenatal care | 11 | 1.2 |
| Other indicators of need | | |
|    Sought help for alcohol problem | 154 | 16.8 |
|    Served time in prison | 96 | 10.4 |
|    Experienced out-of-home placement as a child | 268 | 29.2 |

## Discussion

Given the regional diversity of the rural counties and the large sample size in this study, the findings provide a current and in-depth picture of the problem of rural homelessness in one state. A major finding from this study is that differences exist in the demographic characteristics of the rural homeless population as compared to urban populations (Fischer, 1991; Interagency Council on the Homeless, 1991; Rossi, 1989). Data from this study indicate that homeless people in rural areas are younger, are more likely to be single women or mothers with children, are more highly educated, and are less likely to be disabled. They are also more likely to be homeless because of economic reasons than because of mental illness or drug and alcohol abuse. These rural-urban demographic differences are consistent with patterns established in the Roth et al. (1985) study.

Similar to homelessness in urban areas, patterns of homelessness in rural communities are varied. This research identified five major groups of homeless persons in rural areas:

1. young families (26.8% of the sample) who are no longer able to close the gap between housing costs and total household income

2. individuals who are currently employed full- or part-time (31.2%) but who have too little income to afford housing

3. women (median age 27) who are unable to work because of child care responsibilities or who have limited skills to meet the demands of a changing labor market

4. men, who are generally older (median age 31), homeless longer, and more likely to be disabled with fewer social supports when compared to women

5. disabled people who are without the social networks and social program support needed to live independently in the community.

This study reflects the fact that many individuals and families are unable to secure affordable housing in the heartland. Many respondents in this study were receiving income from employment or public assistance sources and were still unable to secure affordable housing. For social workers who practice in rural areas, meeting the needs of these people is a significant challenge because of high rates of unemployment, inequitable emergency relief funding, low levels of child care and transportation services, and a lack of low-income housing (First, Rife, & Greenlee, 1991). To address this growing problem, attention by social workers is needed in two related areas: emergency services and longer-term solutions.

### Emergency Services

Social workers who advocate for the homeless population had cause to hail the passage of the Stewart B. McKinney Homeless Assistance Act in

1987. However, when understood in the context of federal policy toward the poor population during the Reagan administration, this legislation provides only minimal first steps. In rural areas, additional funding is needed to provide shelter, food programs, and safe homes, particularly for women and children who are fleeing domestic violence. Case management services for those people most at risk of becoming homeless are needed (Rife, First, Greenlee, Miller, & Feichter, 1991). Social agencies must also work with families who are housing others to prevent an increase of literal homelessness in rural areas. Child care, transportation, and adult education services must reach out to those who are vulnerable.

Local city and county governments are attempting to develop temporary housing strategies appropriate for rural communities. Instead of building "shelters," existing motel and hotel rooms are rented on a nightly basis to provide temporary shelter, or people are transported to nearby urban centers for shelter. Vacant houses are restored for temporary use. Churches take in homeless people on a single-night basis.

However, efforts to address the problem of homelessness with emergency services alone have failed to stop the growth of this social condition. One opponent of increased services, Ellickson (1990) asserted that "greater governmental spending on shelter programs increases the reported number of homeless persons" (p. 46). His contention is that defining the problem and providing assistance only increases the numbers of needy people. Blaming those who provide the service and count the needy is like blaming the messenger who brings the bad news. Nevertheless, a part of Ellickson's message is valuable: Efforts fixated at the classic charity level are not contributing to long-term solutions.

### Longer-Term Solutions

The characteristics and patterns of rural homelessness presented in this study underline the need for further discussion of the relationship between homelessness, poverty, and a depressed rural economy. Rural homelessness is a symptom of the growth in rural poverty. In a recent study of rural poverty in New York, Fitchen (1991) documented how plant closings, layoffs, cutbacks, and other declines in the nonfarm economy have created a dependence on low-wage employment, resulting in higher numbers of working poor people. The data reported here support the thesis that low-wage jobs and unemployment are critical issues that face many of the women, younger families, and other homeless people in rural communities.

Depressed economies in rural areas during the 1980s have resulted in an increase in rural poverty. This economic squeeze has also created a greater demand for low-cost rental housing. The shortage of affordable housing, combined with persistent levels of high unemployment and underemployment, have resulted in homelessness. To date policies have not been developed to address either the symptoms of rural poverty or the underlying structural causes.

Burt (1992) suggested that the changing economy and government retrenchment of the 1980s have resulted in an increase in homelessness for many people with work histories and skills who would have been protected in previous decades. The findings of this study support the view that a coherent national strategy on homelessness is lacking (DiNitto, 1991). Longer-term and more systemic approaches to policy development on homelessness are needed. Levitan and Schillmoeller (1991) concluded that "Homelessness is not a top priority of either the Bush administration or Congress" (p. 32). Funding levels for programs to address homelessness have not changed significantly since the beginning of the Clinton administration. There must be a strong national policy that will protect the poor and near-poor populations in both rural and urban localities from the effects of a changing and depressed economy. Policy-making on homelessness needs to focus on three interrelated levels of efforts: (1) assisting people who are currently homeless through the provision of emergency assistance; (2) protecting poor people who are at risk of becoming homeless by providing housing assistance, job training, and supportive services; and (3) preventing others from becoming homeless because of depressed economic conditions by increasing both the supply of jobs paying a livable wage and the supply of affordable housing in rural areas.

Increasing the supply of affordable housing is an ongoing challenge. The most available resources in rural areas are frequently vacant, deserted, or abandoned properties. Advocates have obtained Section 8 government subsidies for these units following volunteer rehabilitation efforts. More community leadership and dollars could be spent to organize the use of existing vacant housing for temporary or permanent low-income housing in rural areas, which would prevent blighted properties and the unnecessary development of public shelters.

## Conclusion

An understanding of the relationships between homelessness, poverty, unemployment, and depressed rural economies is missing in the current view of homelessn6s and must be addressed more actively by social workers. Ultimately, success in preventing homelessness in rural areas will depend on eliminating poverty and increasing the amount of affordable housing stock. Social workers, through organized legislative and policy advocacy, must address these issues. The political retrenchment of the 1980s is having a severe impact on the lives of rural young adults and others unable to achieve self-sufficiency in the job market. Reversing this trend and preventing the growth of homelessness in the 1990s requires more concerned and coherent efforts by the social work profession.

## References

Beeson, P., & Johnson, D. (1987, May). *A panel of change (1981-1986) in rural mental health status: Effects of the rural crisis.* Paper presented at the National Institute of Mental Health National Conference on Mental Health Statistics, Denver.

Burt, M. (1990). *Developing the estimate of 500,000–600,000 homeless people in the United States in 1987.* Washington, D.C.: Urban Institute Press.

Burt, M. (1992). *Over the edge: The growth of homelessness in the 1980s.* New York: Russell Sage Foundation.

Burt, M., & Cohen, B. (1989). *America's Homeless: Numbers, characteristics, and programs that serve them* (Urban Institute Report 89-3). Washington, D.C.: Urban Institute Press.

Council for Economic Opportunities of Greater Cleveland. (1991). *Ohio poverty indicators: 1970–1991* (Vol. 6). Cleveland: Author.

DiNitto, D. (1991). *Social welfare politics and public policy.* Englewood Cliffs, NJ: Prentice Hall.

Ellickson, R. (1990). The homeless muddle. *Public Interest, 99,* 45-46.

First, R., Rife, J., & Greenlee, R. (1991, March). *Rural homelessness: Findings from a 1990 statewide replication study.* Paper presented at the Annual Program Meeting of the Council on Social Work Education, New Orleans.

First, R., Toomey, B., Rife, J., & Greenlee, R. (1990). Homelessness and federal grant-in-aid policy in the United States. *Social Development Issues, 13*(1), 55-64.

Fischer, P. (1991). *Executive summary of alcohol, drug abuse and mental health problems among homeless persons: A review of the literature, 1980–1990.* Rockville, MD: U.S. Department of Health and Human Services.

Fitchen, J. (1991). *Endangered spaces, enduring places: Change, identity, and survival in rural America.* Boulder, CO: Westview Press.

Frank, R., & Streeter, C. (1987). Bitter harvest: The question of homelessness in rural America. In A. Summers, J. Schriver, P. Sundet, & R. Meinert (Eds.), *Social work in rural areas: The past, charting the future, acclaiming a decade of achievement. Proceedings of the 10th National Institute of Rural Areas* (pp. 36-45). Columbia: University of Missouri at Columbia, School of Social Work.

Hoch, C. (1987). A brief history of the homeless problem in the United States. In R. D. Bingham, R. E. Green, & S. B. White (Eds.), *The homeless in contemporary society* (pp. 16-32). Beverly Hills, CA: Sage Publications.

Hombs, M., & Snyder, M. (1982). *Homelessness in America: A forced march to nowhere.* Washington, D.C.: Community for Creative Non-Violence.

Hopper, K. (1986). Homelessness. In W. H. McCarthy (Ed.), *Perspective on Poverty* (pp. 47-61). Washington, D.C.: National League of Cities.

Housing Assistance Council. (1987). *The homeless crisis from a rural perspective.* Washington, D.C.: U.S. Government Printing Office.

Interagency Council on the Homeless. (1991). *The 1990 annual report of the Interagency Council on the Homeless.* Washington, D.C.: Author.

Joslin, F., Link, E., & Rossmann, M. (1986). Mental health response to farm crisis victims. In S. Andrews, J. Egan, & E. Kohn (Eds.), *Rural mental health conference proceedings* (pp. 171-184). Omaha: University of Nebraska.

Levitan, S., & Schillmoeller, S. (1991). *The paradox of homelessness in America.* Washington, D.C.: George Washington University.

Lobao, L. (1990). *Locality and inequality: Farm structure, industry structure, and socioeconomic conditions.* Albany: State University of New York Press.

McCormick, J. (1988, August 8). America's third world. *Newsweek,* p. 21.

Murdock, S., Potter, L., Ham, R., Backman, K., Albrecht, D., & Leistritz, F. (1988). The implications of the current farm crisis for rural America. In S. Murdock & F. Leistritz (Eds.), *The farm financial crisis: Socioeconomic dimensions and implications for producers and rural areas* (pp. 141-168). Boulder, CO: Westview.

Norem, R., & Blundall J. (1988). Farm families and marital disruption during a time of crisis. In R. Marotz-Baden, D. Hennon, & H. Brubaker (Eds.), *Families in rural America* (pp. 21-31). St. Paul, MN: National Council on Family Relations.

O'Hare, W. (1988). *The rise of poverty in rural America* (Occasional Paper No. 15). Washington, D.C.: Population Reference Bureau.

Ohio Coalition for the Homeless. (1990, March). *Census review opinions.* Columbus: Author.

Ohio Department of Agriculture. (1987). County summary highlights: 1987. In *Ohio census for agriculture* (pp. 142-153). Columbus: Author.

Ohio Department of Development. (1988). *Ohio county profiles.* Columbus: Author.

Patton, L. (1987). *The rural homeless.* Washington, D.C.: Health Resources and Services Administration.

Redburn, F., & Buss, T. (1986). *Responding to America's homeless.* New York: Praeger.

Reyes, L., & Waxman, L. (1989). *A status report on hunger and homelessness in America's cities: 1989.* Washington, D.C.: U.S. Conference of Mayors.

Rife, J., First, R., Greenlee, R., Miller, L., & Feichter, M. (1991). Case management with homeless mentally ill people. *Health & Social Work, 16,* 58-67.

Rossi, P. (1989). *Down and out in America.* Chicago: University of Chicago Press.

Rossi, P., Fisher, G., & Willis, G. (1985). *The condition of the homeless of Chicago.* Chicago: National Opinion Research Center.

Roth, D., & Bean, G. (1986). New perspectives on homelessness: Findings from a statewide epidemiological study. *Hospital and Community Psychiatry, 37,* 712-719.

Roth, D., Bean, G., Lust N., & Saveanu, T. (1985). *Homelessness in Ohio: A study of people in need.* Columbus: Ohio Department of Mental Health.

Segal, E. (1989). Homelessness in a small community: A demographic profile. *Social Work Research & Abstracts, 25*(4), 27-30.

Sinclair, W. (1987, May 24). Grief is growing on farm land. *Washington Post,* p. A3.

Spitzer, R., Endicott, J., & Cohen, J. (1970). The Psychiatric Status Schedule: A technique for evaluating psychopathology and impairment in role functioning. *Archives of General Psychiatry, 23,* 41-55.

Spitzer, R., Endicott, J., Cohen, J., & Nee, J. (1980). The psychiatric status schedule for epidemiological research. *Archives of General Psychiatry, 37,* 1193-1197.

Stefl, M. (1983). *The impact of rapid social change on the mental health of a rural population.* Cincinnati: University of Cincinnati.

Stewart B. McKinney Homeless Assistance Act, P.L. 100-77, 101 Stat. 482 (1987).

U.S. Commission on Cooperation and Security in Europe. (1990, August). *Homelessness in the United States.* Washington, D.C.: U.S. Government Printing Office.

U.S. Committee on Government Operations. (1985). *The federal response to the homeless crisis* (H.R. 99-47). Washington, D.C.: U.S. Government Printing Office.

U.S. Conference of Mayors. (1986). *The growth of hunger, homelessness and poverty in America's cities in 1985.* Washington, D.C.: Author.

U.S. Conference of Mayors. (1989). *A status report on hunger and homelessness in America's cities: 1988.* Washington, D.C.: Author.

U.S. Department of Housing and Urban Development. (1984). *A report to the secretary on the homeless and emergency shelters.* Washington, D.C.: U.S. Government Printing Office.

U.S. Department of Housing and Urban Development, Interagency Council on the Homeless. (1989). *The 1989 annual report of the Interagency Council on the Homeless.* Washington, D.C.: U.S. Government Printing Office.

U.S. General Accounting Office. (1989). *Rural development: Federal programs that focus on rural America and its economic development* (Publication No. RCED-89-56BR). Washington, D.C.: U.S. Government Printing Office.

Wilkerson, I. (1989, May 2). As farms falter, rural homelessness grows. *New York Times,* pp. Al, A14.

Wright, J. (1989). *Address unknown: The homeless in America.* New York: Aldine de Gruyter.

# 21

## No Home, No Family: Homeless Children in Rural Ohio

by Ronald K. Green, Alice K. Johnson,
Michael D. Bremseth, and Elizabeth Tracy

T he mid-1990s have sparked a major public policy debate on the nature of public support to meet the needs of families with income and housing needs. Although value issues have emerged in this debate, the primary driver of "welfare reform" appears to be fiscal and clearly related to how to move toward balancing the federal budget. This paper examines the relationship between rural homelessness and what happens to children in the child protection system. Based on this examination the authors identify how the failure to meet the housing needs of non-urban poor families results in long-term costs for the child welfare system. This includes both the social costs related to family break-up and the fiscal costs of maintaining children in long-term out-of-home care. The implications for changes in child welfare practice with homeless families and in the shape of welfare reform are identified.

### Review of the Literature

Only a few studies have examined the scope and nature of rural homelessness (First, Rife, & Toomey, 1994; Nooe & Cunningham, 1992; Roth & Bean, 1986; Segal, 1989). Although no national data is available, two of these studies on rural homelessness in the state of Ohio (First et al., 1994; Roth & Bean, 1986) provide an emerging picture of rural homelessness. Compared to urban homeless persons, rural homeless persons have more extensive work histories and a higher level of education. Rural homeless persons are younger and more likely to be single women or mothers with children. They are less likely to be disabled and less likely to have been hospitalized for psychiatric problems.

According to Patton (1988), rural homelessness is a symptom of increasing rural poverty and the invisibility of homeless people in rural areas. This is partially due to the lack of social services that prevent home-

Reprinted from *Human Services in the Rural Environment* (Fall/Winter 1995–96), with permission of the Eastern Washington University School of Social Work and Human Services.

less people from congregating in certain locations. In addition, most rural communities are generally unprepared to deal with the problem of homelessness and homeless people are often left to rely on family, friends, and self-help strategies. Although no research has focused on the implications of homelessness for children who are involved in the child welfare system, these dimensions of rural homelessness suggests that homeless adults in rural areas may turn to family or friends for substitute care for their children.

In urban areas, there are some exploratory studies that suggest that homeless children have been placed in foster care. Johnson's (1995) qualitative research on formerly homeless families in New Haven, Connecticut reports that foster care placement is a precipitating factor to homelessness for substance abusing women because of the resultant loss of income from Aid to Families with Dependent Children (AFDC). Brown and Ziefert (1990) report that many women in a Michigan shelter have either lost a child or are on the brink of losing a child to foster care because of their homeless situation. In addition, some children of these homeless mothers are in the temporary care of family or friends. Williams (1991) argues that while homelessness—in and of itself—does not constitute child abuse, neglect triggered by the condition of being homeless is a possible cause for child neglect. In Pennsylvania, case workers report that as many as one-third of the children in foster care have mothers who are homeless (Quinlan, 1995).

Out-of-home placement for children may put them at risk of becoming homeless as adults. According to Mangine, Royse, Wiehi, & Nietzel (1990), homeless adults are 4 times more likely to have experienced out-of-home placement as children than adults in the general population. Children who are in out-of-home placement are also at higher risk for sexual abuse than children who always live with their biological parents (Finkelhor, 1980) and at higher risk for all types of maltreatment than children in the population at-large (Bolton, Laner, & Gai, 1980). Maltreatment in foster care settings is one factor contributing to the problems of "runaways" or homeless youth (Robertson, Koegel, & Ferguson, 1989). Consequently, researchers have called for research on women who have lost their children after they became homeless (D'Ercole & Struening, 1990; Milburn & D'Ercole, 1991). This paper begins to address this gap in the literature by looking at the situation of homeless children in out-of-home placement in the non-urban counties of Ohio.

## Research Methods

### Sample

The data reported here were gathered as part of a statewide study in Ohio (c.f., Tracy, Green, & Bremseth, 1993). The purpose of the study was to determine supportive services needs and gaps in services for children and families served by Ohio's child welfare system. The study population consisted of all children in Ohio who received state department of human services placement prevention or reunification services and who were listed as active cases on July 1, 1989. In the original study, probability samples were drawn using simple random sampling. Cases were first stratified by metropolitan (containing large cities) versus non-metropolitan counties. A listing of all cases was generated and a computer program was used to select individual case numbers. Counties were then instructed to make the selected case records available for review. Simple random sampling procedures produced sufficient reunification cases so it was not necessary to stratify the sample on case goal (placement prevention versus family reunification).

## Data Collection

The organizing principle underlying data collection and coding was the casework sequence followed in the assessment and delivery of protective services. Child protective services typically include a wide range of social services coordinated and delivered on behalf of children who are at risk for or have experienced abuse or neglect (Child Welfare League of America, 1989). In this study, casework decisions were examined at various points in the casework process in order to determine one of two possible permanent plans: (1) family preservation for children not yet removed from their homes and (2) family reunification for children who had experienced out-of-home placement.

Data were collected by in-depth case reviews of 455 cases and several levels of information were collected. These included demographic information, presenting problems, service history, family service needs (assessment), services planned, services actually delivered, level of service effort, and case status at point of case closing or the last case review prior to the examination.

Since the selected child was the unit of analysis, demographic information included information about the child, other children in the family, the caretakers, and the family situation as a whole at the time of case plan development. Variables in the presenting problems category captured the nature and number of problems precipitating the need for intervention by the child protection system. These included the maltreatment type (type of abuse or neglect), the child's mental or physical disabilities, and family stress factors such as substance abuse, economic difficulties, or problems with their physical living conditions. Data on service history noted the sequence and outcome of case work activities such as source of referral, date of case transfer to ongoing services, number of case transfers, and reason for case closing.

Ten categories of child–family service needs were included. Only service needs that would place a child at risk for placement or prevent or pose obstacles to reunification efforts were included, such as housing needs, material resource needs, social support needs (c.f., Magura, Moses, & Jones, 1987). Definitions for each service need and subcategory were developed to facilitate accurate coding. Twenty categories of supportive services as defined by the Ohio Administrative Code (1988) were included as study variables. Where appropriate, subcategories were devised to collect more detailed information about the service. For example, the type of counseling service was described as individual, group, family, or marital and the intended recipient of the service was specified.

Service characteristics referred to a number of service delivery factors that may affect the family's receptivity to supportive services and, ultimately, service effectiveness. Therefore, data on planned intensity or frequency and duration of service were collected, along with information on the steps taken by the worker to ensure that supportive services would be provided. Finally, in addition to collecting information on the status and outcome of each service planned, measures of the degree to which the stated case work goal (placement prevention or family reunification) was achieved were included.

Case record data were gathered by trained case reviewers using a 14-page precoded data collection instrument. Case monitors visited six sites during the data collection period to determine interrater reliability. The monitor's responses to six selected variables were compared to the coders' responses. The number of agreements and disagreements on each review case was recorded. In addition, each coder was asked to review an additional sample test case which had been precoded by the investigators. The number of agreements and disagreements for this test case was also recorded. Percentages of agreements between 39 data collectors and seven monitors were calculated both for test cases (72 percent) and review cases (84 percent). In reported findings, valid percentages were reported, which takes into account any missing data on selected variables.

To generate the subset of the sample for this analysis, several non-metropolitan (but still primarily urban) counties were excluded along with the metropolitan counties (total of ten urban counties) to produce a non-urban set of cases. This resulted in producing 163 (35.8%) non-urban cases and 292 (64.2%) urban cases

## Analysis

Data were analyzed using SPSS for Windows. The analysis included constructing a family service need variable called "homeless" which included situations of literal homelessness (living in an emergency shelter, car, etc.), at-risk of homelessness (about to lose their housing through eviction, condemnation, etc.), or "hidden homelessness" (temporarily living with friends or relatives and lacking the privacy and/or space to provide adequate child care in an independent living situation). Thus, in this study, homelessness is defined as the lack of any *permanent* residence. This constructed variable was then cross-tabulated with all other variables and analyzed using parametric and non-parametric statistical procedures as appropriate. Correlations were run between major variables including service outcomes, demographics, service needs and homeless/non-homeless. After excluding variables which were correlated at greater than .04, a stepwise multiple regression procedure was run to examine the independent contributions of selected variables in terms of what the placement status of the child was at case closing or date of last review.

The major thrust of the analysis is focused on trying to gain an understanding of what difference being homeless made to the child and family coming into the child protection system. Although the total statewide sample was sufficient to produce a 95% confidence level of +/- 4.5%, the subset of non-urban cases is of a size (n=163) that some caution is called for in the interpretation of the data. What is presented should be considered suggestive of the realities in the non-urban areas.

## Findings

### Characteristics of Non-Urban Homeless/Non-Homeless Children

As compared to non-homeless children in the child protection system, homeless children are younger and more likely children of color. Approximately 45% of homeless children are 6 years old or younger as compared with 31.5% of non-homeless children. Only 10% of homeless children are teenagers as compared to 38.6% of non-homeless children. Although gender is not a distinguishing characteristic, race is. Children of color were 2.3 times more likely to be homeless at the point of case plan development than white children. Moreover, while children of color represented only 12.6% of the non-urban caseload, 31.6% of those were homeless. This is in sharp distinction to the finding that of the 87.4% of the caseload who were white children, only 13.6% were homeless ($\chi^2$=4.00, $p$=.046).

Homeless children were also less likely to have behavior problems. Only 4.2% of the homeless children had a presenting problem of behavior or being completely out of control (i.e., stays out all night) compared to 35.3% of the non-homeless sample ($\chi^2$=9.30, $p$=.002). This suggests that many children are being forced into the child welfare system when there is no other problems except the lack of housing.

Homeless children are almost four times more likely to have a problem maintaining a bond with their parents than non-homeless children. This finding may be explained by the fact that homeless children are much more likely to have been living with relatives or other out of home placements.

### Characteristics of Non-Urban Homeless and Non-Homeless Families

As compared with the non-homeless families of children in the system, homeless families tend to be younger. Almost 29% of the primary caretakers in homeless families are under the age of 26 and 86% are under the age of 36 compared to only 16% of non-homeless caretakers under 26 and 65% under the age of 35. Homeless families are also more likely to be working part-time or, at least, employable. At the same time, they tend to lack the kind of job skills that lead to economic self-sufficiency. In 61% of the homeless families, the primary caregiver either was working part-time (11.1%) or unemployed but looking for work (50.0%). This was considerably higher than the 39% of the non-homeless families. In about 25% of the homeless cases the primary caregiver lacked the job skills to become financially self-sufficient. This was 3 times higher than in non-homeless families, suggesting that these younger families often have the industry to work but not the skills necessary to generate sufficient income to maintain an independent housing status.

Homeless families showed about a 10% higher incidence of serious substance abuse problems than non-homeless families. However, this difference was not statistically significant ($\chi^2=2.02$, $p=.155$). In both homeless and non-homeless cases, the majority of families did not have a serious substance abuse problem. In about 8% of the homeless situations, however, the presenting problem related to an inability to plan ahead to meet the needs of a newborn. In these cases, the homeless situation may have been precipitated by the impending birth of a child that resulted in a boyfriend or parent throwing an unwed about-to-be mother out of the house. In about 30% of the cases of homeless families, the birth parent(s) were having problems relating to a substitute caregiver, but in only 8% of the cases was it indicated that the homeless parent felt guilt or shame about having to have their child in placement.

### Situation at Point of Agency Intervention

There is a high level of extended family involvement in the cases where the family is homeless. The homeless child is 7 times more likely to be in the home of a relative at the point of initial case plan development than the non-homeless child. In 37.5% of all homeless cases the child was in a relative's home, as opposed to only 5.3% of non-homeless children ($\chi^2=29.96$, $p=.000$). This perhaps explains why 30.4% of the referrals to the agency came from relatives of homeless children whereas only 11% came from relatives on non-homeless children. In 37.5% of the cases involving homeless children, the lack of shelter was the primary element of maltreatment cited in the case plan ($\chi^2=29.96$, $p=.000$). Although this suggests that in many cases there are multiple elements of maltreatment, it is important to note that some 5% of all the cases coming to the child protection agency in non-urban counties are only there because no shelter has been made available to the family.

### Factors Impacting Case Outcomes

The stated goal for all children in the child protection/child welfare system is that they have a permanent, lifelong relationship with the same caregivers. Preferably this is with the birth parents, but if this is not possible, then someone who can provide a permanent, lifelong relationship with the child. The case goals for the children in this study were either placement prevention (remain with birth parents) or, in cases where placement had been necessary, reunification (be placed back with birth parents). Therefore, a case was considered to have a successful outcome if at the point of case closure or the date of the last case review the child was back home with the birth parent. For each child in the sample, it was determined if they were home, with relatives, or in some other type of out of home placement (foster home, group care, etc.).

There was a significant difference in outcome between those children who were homeless at the point they entered the system and those who had homes. A child who was homeless at the point of case plan development was 2.5 times more likely to be in out-of-home placement at the point of case closing or last review. While 77% of the non-homeless children had successful outcomes, only 41.7% of the homeless children did. Only 14.4% of the non-homeless were in foster homes or group care compared to 25% of the homeless children in such placements. Relatives played a major role in the life of the homeless children. One third of all homeless children were placed with relatives at the point of last review or case closing compared to only 8.6% of the non-homeless children ($\chi^2$=15.18, $p$=.00051).

Based on this strong correlation between being homeless and having poor service outcomes, a regression was run holding outcome as the dependent variable and demographic and service need variables (including homelessness) into the equation. The result produced four variables that impact service outcomes. The following variables explain 22% of the variance and have a positive influence on producing the outcome of the child being home at case closure or date of last review. These are: having a larger number of people in the household, being a younger child, being white, and not being homeless at the point of initial case review. The obverse of this—that which will influence the likelihood that a child will still be in out-of-home placement— is coming from a smaller household, being older, being a child of color, and being homeless at point of first case plan development.

## Implications for the Child Welfare System

### Failure of the Formal and Informal Support Systems

These findings suggest that neither formal nor informal support systems in non-urban counties in Ohio are serving homeless families well. Although it appears that there is considerable involvement by the relatives of homeless families (informal system) and that they are extending help in terms of caring for the children of the homeless, this is not proving to be a long-term solution. In almost 40% of the homeless cases, the child is in the home of a relative at the time the case is opened and 30% of the referrals to the child protection agency come from relatives. While this does indicate how many homeless children/families are being successfully supported by relatives, it does suggest that there are many situations where kinship care simply does not work and the relative or some other person calls the child protection agency for help.

The evidence also suggests that many rural homeless families are industrious and willing to work but lack the training to earn a living wage. If so, the number of homeless children in protective care could be a symptom of increasing rural poverty. One hypothesis is that a primary care giver loses a job which results in the loss of residence. The homeless parent turns to relatives for temporary help, but eventually the child ends up in out-of-home placement in the child protection system and gets stuck there.

Longitudinal studies of rural homeless children are needed to affirm this.

The data also suggest that the public child protection system is failing to adequately provide an effective service for homeless children and their families. If, indeed, in almost 40% of the cases when a homeless child comes into the system the only problem is lack of adequate shelter, it is a sad statement that the public solution is to place the child away from his family. This is particularly disturbing in light of the finding that once a homeless child is placed there is over twice the likelihood that the child will remain in placement compared to children who are not in out-of-home placement. It suggests that the formal child protection system is putting children at tremendous risk when the "abuse and neglect" issue is that the family is unable to secure liveable shelter.

## Lessons for the Child Protection Agency

The primary lesson for child protection agencies is that in cases where the only risk to the child is the fact that the family is homeless, there is a responsibility to find shelter for the family instead of placing the child away from the family and exposing the child to a whole new set of risks. At a minimum, it is the responsibility of child protection agencies in this scenario to collaborate with homeless shelters and develop cooperative arrangements with low-income housing services. Federal child protection law requires that agencies must demonstrate they have made a "reasonable effort" to keep the family intact and prevent placement of the child (Adoption Assistance and Child Welfare Act of 1980). It is hard to see how agencies are in keeping with either the letter or the spirit of federal law by placing homeless children in protective services.

The data also suggest that more attention needs to be paid to kinship care. In many states placements with relatives are not given the same kind of attention or support by the agency which it gives to foster home placements (Dubowitz et al., 1994). This study suggests that there are numerous situations in which homeless children staying with relatives are not working. It may be possible to stabilize some of these situations by providing basic care payments to relatives for family foster care or providing other types of formal and informal supports.

Since often the issue is not with the willingness of primary caregivers to work but their skill level that prevents them from the economic independence they need to sufficiently care for their children, child protection agencies need to see its job as helping families connect with skill training resources in the community. This suggests that the role of the child protection worker needs to be perceived in more "holistic" family-focused, community-based terms. In a sense, what is needed is a return to a concept of a community-based child welfare worker—a concept currently found in programs providing intensive in-home services using a family-based service model (c.f., Pecora, Whittaker, & Maluccio, 1992). Unfortunately, in the overall statewide study from which this data was drawn, the services most often provided by the county agencies were "counseling and therapeutic" interventions (Tracy et al., 1993). It appears, however, that what many of these homeless families need is a case worker who can help them find shelter, develop job skills, and find a job that pays a liveable wage so that they can secure housing and resume parenting.

## Lessons for Public Policy and Further Research

Given the nature of much of the public debate related to welfare reform the findings from this study can be used to inform that ongoing debate. In the mid-nineties we have seen an emerging policy consensus among leaders at both the federal and state levels that would result in limiting basic financial assistance, job training and housing programs for poor families while leaving in place federal entitlement support for caring for children in out-of-home placements. The data that emerged from this study strongly suggest that this is a flawed public policy. Poor families need support for low-cost shelter, job training and basic financial assistance for transitioning into economic self-sufficiency. They do not need a child protection system which takes their children from them, places them in the care of other people, and leaves them there.

In this case there is a convergence of interest between these families and the taxpayer. With the major focus at the federal level on reducing the growth of federal budget expenditures one would think that the least cost-effective way to meet the needs of homeless families is to place their children in the care of others when it assures the likelihood that they will remain there over the long term. It is neither good child welfare practice nor good economics to continue a system that has failed to adequately serve these families in this way.

It is also clear that we do not fully understand the relationship between children being placed in out-of-home care due to homelessness and why they tend to remain in care over the long term. Additional research is needed that will help lead to a fuller understanding of what happens to homeless families after the child is placed. Could it be that homeless, "childless" families find it more difficult to locate permanent housing? Do these families tend to move elsewhere in search of work and leave their children behind? Do they develop "long term" multi-family living arrangements that do not provide for space which would enable them to take their children back? The answers to these and similar questions could help shape more effective positive interventions to help resolve the "no home, no family" problem in the non-urban United States.

## References

Adoption Assistance and Child Welfare Act of 1980, Pub. L. No. 96-272, 42 U.S.C. §627 et. seq. (1980).

Bolton, F., Laner, R., Gai, D. (1980). For better or worse: Foster parents and foster children in an officially reported child maltreatment population. *Children and Youth Services Bulletin, 3*(1-2), 37-53.

Brown, K. S., & Ziefert, M. (1990). A feminist approach to working with homeless women. *Affilia: Journal of Women and Social Work,* 5, 6-20.

Child Welfare League of America. (1989). *Standards for services to strengthen and preserve families with children.* Washington, DC: Author.

D'Ercole, A., & Struening, E. (1990). Victimization among homeless women: Implications for service delivery. *Journal of Community Psychology, 18*(2), 141-152.

Dubowitz, H., Feigelman, S., Harrington, D., Starr, R, Zuravin, S., & Sawyer, R. (1994). Children in kinship care: How do they fare? *Children and Youth Services Review, 16*(1/2), 85-106.

Finkelhor, D. (1980). Risk factors in the sexual victimization of children. *Child Abuse and Neglect, 4*(4), 265-273.

First, R.J., Rife, J.C., & Toomey, B.G. (1994). Homeless in rural areas: Causes, patterns, and trend. *Social Work, 39*(1), 97-107.

Johnson, A.K. (1995). [Interviews with former homeless families in New Haven, Connecticut]. Unpublished raw data.

Magura, S., Moses. B., & Jones, M. (1987). *Assessing risk and measuring change in families: The family risk scales.* Washington, DC: Child Welfare League of America.

Mangine, S.J., Royse, D., Wiehi, V. R., & Nietzel, W. (1990). Homelessness among adults raised as foster children: A survey of drop-in center users. *Psychological Reports, 67,* 739-745.

Milburn, N., & D'Ercole, A. (1991). Homeless women. Moving toward a comprehensive model. *American Psychologist, 46*(11), 1161-1169.

Nooe, R.M., & Cunningham, M.L. (1992). Rural dimensions of homelessness: A rural-urban comparison. *Human Services in the Rural Environment, 15*(4), 1-5.

Ohio Administrative Code, Chapter 5101:2-39 (1980).

Patton, L. (1988). The rural homeless. In: Committee on Health Care for Homeless People (Ed.), *Homelessness, health, and human needs,* (pp. 183-217). Washington, DC: National Academy Press.

Pecora, P.J., Whittaker, J.K., & Maluccio, A.N. (1992) The child welfare challenge: Policy, practice, and research. New York: Aldine de Gruyter, 269-312.

Quinlan, I. (1995). Personal interview with foster care worker. Cleveland, OH.

Roth, D., & Bean, G. (1986). New perspectives on homelessness: Findings from a statewide epidemiological study. *Hospital and Community Psychiatry, 37,* 712-719.

Robertson, M.J., Koegel, P., & Ferguson, L. (1989). Alcohol use and abuse among homeless adolescents in Hollywood. *Contemporary Drug Problems, 16,* 415-452.

Segal, E. (1989). Homelessness in a small community: A demographic profile. *Social Work Research & Abstracts, 25*(4), 27-30.

Tracy, E.M., Green, R.K., & Bremseth, M.D. (1993). Meeting the environmental needs of abused and neglected children: Implications from a statewide survey of supportive services. *Social Work Research and Abstracts, 29,* 21-27.

Williams, C. W. (1991). Child welfare services and homelessness: Issues in policy, philosophy, and programs. In J. H. Kryder-Coe, L. M. Salamon, & J. M. Molnar (Eds.), *Homeless Children and Youth: A New American Dilemma,* (pp. 285-299). New Brunswick: Transaction Publishers.

Wolf, L. A. (1991). The welfare system's response to homelessness. In J. H. Kryder-Coe, L. M. Salamon, & J. M. Molnar (Eds.), *Homeless Children and Youth: A New American Dilemma,* (pp. 271-283). New Brunswick, NJ: Transaction.

# Contributing Authors

**Michael D. Bremseth**
Computerized Research
  Technologies
Knoxville, TN

**Iris Carlton-LaNey**
School of Social Work
University of North Carolina
  at Chapel Hill

**Joseph P. Chandy**
School of Social Work
University of Missouri
Columbia, MO

**Raymond T. Coward**
Dean, College of Health and
  Human Services
University of New Hampshire
Durham, NH

**Joseph Davenport III**
Private practice
Columbia, MO

**Judith A. Davenport**
School of Social Work
University of Missouri
Columbia, MO

**Martha J. Denton**
Private Practice
Radford, VA

**Roy T. Denton**
School of Social Work
Radford University
Radford, VA

**Jeffrey W. Dwyer**
Institute of Gerontology
Wayne State University
Detroit, MI

**Richard J. First**
College of Social Work
Ohio State University
Columbus, OH

**Janet M. Fitchen** (deceased)
Department of Anthropology
Ithaca College
Ithaca, NY

**Leola D. Furman**
Department of Social Work
University of North Dakota
Grand Forks, ND

**Carel B. Germain** (deceased)
School of Social Work
University of Connecticut
West Hartford, CT

**Leon H. Ginsberg**
College of Social Work
University of South Carolina
Columbia, SC

**Ronald K. Green**
Department of Social Work
Winthrop University
Rock Hill, SC

**Wilburn Hayden, Jr.**
School of Social Work
State University of New York
  at Buffalo

**Alice K. Johnson**
Mandel School of Applied
  Social Sciences
Case Western Reserve University
Cleveland, OH

**H. Wayne Johnson**
School of Social Work
University of Iowa
Iowa City, IA

**Emilia E. Martinez-Brawley**
School of Social Work
Arizona State University
Tempe, AZ

**Jay L. Memmott**
School of Social Service
Saint Louis University
St. Louis, MO

**Joanne Mermelstein**
School of Social Work
University of Missouri
Columbia, MO

**Pam Miller**
Department of Social Work
Ball State University
Muncie, IN

**James R. Moran**
Graduate School of Social Work
University of Denver
Denver, CO

**Shirley L. Patterson**
School of Social Work
Arizona State University
Tempe, AZ

**John C. Rife**
Department of Social Work
University of North Carolina
  at Greensboro

**Kathleen A. Rounds**
School of Social Work
University of North Carolina
  at Chapel Hill

**Laura Summer**
Center for Budget and Policy
  Priorities
Washington, DC
(position at time of original
  publication)

**Gene F. Summers**
Department of Rural Sociology
University of Wisconsin
Madison, WI

**Paul Sundet**
School of Social Work
University of Missouri
Columbia, MO

**Beverly G. Toomey**
College of Social Work
Ohio State University
Columbus, OH

**Elizabeth Tracy**
Mandel School of Applied
  Social Sciences
Case Western Reserve University
Cleveland, OH

**Reginald O. York**
School of Social Work
East Carolina University
Greenville, NC

**Michael Kim Zapf**
University of Calgary
Calgary, Alberta, Canada

# Index